Rhetorical Democracy

Discursive Practices of Civic Engagement

Selected Papers From the 2002 Conference of the Rhetoric Society of America

Rhetorical Democracy

Discursive Practices of Civic Engagement

Selected Papers From the 2002 Conference of the Rhetoric Society of America

Edited by

Gerard A. Hauser
Amy Grim
University of Colorado

2004

LAWRENCE ERLBAUM ASSOCIATES, PUBLISHERS
Mahwah, New Jersey London

Lawrence Erlbaum Associates, Inc., Publishers
10 Industrial Avenue
Mahwah, NJ 07430

Cover photo by Jean Hauser

Cover design by Sean Trane Sciarrone

Library of Congress Cataloging-in-Publication Data

Rhetorical democracy : discursive practices of civic engagement / Gerard A. Hauser & Amy Grim, editors.
p. cm.
Includes bibliographical references and index.
ISBN 0-8058-4264-0 (cloth : alk. paper)
ISBN 0-8058-4265-9 (pbk. : alk. paper)
1. Rhetoric—Political aspects. I. Hauser, Gerard A. II. Grim, Amy.

P301.5.P67R49 2003
808—dc21

2003044362
CIP

Books published by Lawrence Erlbaum Associates are printed on acid-free paper, and their bindings are chosen for strength and durability.

Camera ready copy for this book was produced by the editors.

Printed in the United States of America
10 9 8 7 6 5 4 3 2 1

Table of Contents

II President's Panel: The Rhetoric of 9/11 and Its Aftermath

III Selected Papers

Preface

This volume takes as its point of departure the idea that democracy remains an unfinished project. Even as the United States attempts to export its brand of democracy to the rest of the world, scholars and citizens wonder aloud about the health of our own democracy and question whether our practices indeed live up to our democratic principles. The forces of globalization, technology, capitalism, multiculturalism, and other social changes compel us to continually reinvent democratic practices well before we can begin to judge their viability. As we approach an uncertain future, we look with nostalgia to the past. We seek wisdom from the idealized democracies of ancient Athens and Rome only to realize that we cannot simply resurrect democratic practices developed for times and cultures vastly different from our own. One lesson from our ancient forbearers endures, however: the idea that democracy and rhetoric are inextricably linked. Tending to the business of democracy means tending to its rhetorical practices.

The Tenth Biennial Conference of the Rhetoric Society of America specifically invited participants to reflect on this theme. In May of 2002, over four hundred scholars from eight nations convened in Las Vegas, Nevada to discuss the range of concerns associated with democracy's promise and its pitfalls. Amidst the hyperreality of the Las Vegas strip, rhetoricians of all stripes gathered to create a discursive space in which rhetorical democracy was more than a dream—it was made present in the formal and informal conversations that took place that weekend. The 2002 conference was by far the largest RSA conference to date, and it brought together rhetorical scholars housed in Communication, English, and Writing departments as well as colleagues from allied disciplines in the humanities and social sciences. The broad interpretation of and enthusiastic response to the conference theme suggests a deep concern with what it means to practice democracy at the beginning of the twenty-first century. It also suggests that although rhetorical scholarship is too often marked by institutional divisions and diverse interests, our common aspirations to foster democratic practice can bring us together.

This volume represents only a fraction of the papers presented in Las Vegas. Even so, it is difficult to categorize in any simple way the thirty-nine papers appearing in this collection. Their range suggests that tending to rhetorical democracy means attending to political oratory, sermons, and courtroom rhetoric, as well as to art, history, literature, and poetry. It means listening to the voices of leaders, activists, and authors, as well as to marginalized and vernacular voices of the citizenry. It means critically examining rhetorics of gender, race, religion, science, economics, and foreign policy. It means surveying cultural landscapes as diverse as sixteenth-century Mexico, Old English literature, American Reform Judaism, global civil society, and cyberspace. From the tiniest letter of the Hebrew alphabet to the broadest conceptions of literacy and orality, this collection of papers demonstrates the tremendous range of the rhetorical practices of civic engagement. The collection summons us to reflect upon and retool our pedagogy to meet the enduring promise—but ever-changing practices of—democracy.

We could not have produced this volume without the help of a great many people. First, we thank all of the people who planned and managed the conference in Las Vegas, especially Tom Burkholder, Mike Halloran, Danette Paul, David Palmer, and the Rhetoric Society of America Board of Directors. We're also grateful to our colleagues who generously devoted their time and expertise to review over 600 conference proposals, as well as those who volunteered to chair sessions and handle registration. We thank the participants for their interdisciplinary spirit and their vital contributions to the rhetorical conversation. All of you made the conference robust and memorable.

We hope we have captured the spirit of the conference in the proceedings, and for the volume itself we have many more people to thank. This book would not have been possible without the invaluable assistance of our editors at Erlbaum, Linda Bathgate, Karin Wittig Bates, and Sarah Wahlert. Our reviewers deserve special recognition for lending their knowledge and wisdom to the selection of papers in Part III. They include: Fred Antczak, Greg Clark, Rosa Eberly, Mary Kahl, William Keith, Andrea Lunsford, James McDaniel, Edward Schiappa, Robert Scott, Herb Simons, and Susan Wells. We thank the authors not only for their contributions, but also for keeping the process running smoothly despite the limitations of space and time. An additional word of thanks is due to our colleagues and friends in the Department of Communication at the University of Colorado who supported us through every phase of this two-year effort, especially Christy Standerfer and Robert Agne for their encouragement as well as their eleventh-hour labor. Finally, we wish to thank our friends and our families, who remind us why we have faith in the voice of the people in the first place.

1

Rhetorical Democracy and Civic Engagement

Gerard A. Hauser
University of Colorado

The expression "rhetorical democracy" seems both obvious and problematic. The Western tradition looks with reverence, if not longing, to democracy's Athenian roots. It is a rhetorical form of governance in which all citizens are equal, everyone has a say, everyone has a vote, and decisions are based on the most compelling arguments. This is a utopian ideal of a state governed by deliberation in which citizens are guided by reason and the better angels of the human spirit. On the other hand, rhetoric is not entirely rational and humans do not always heed their better angels. Viewed in this light, a rhetorical democracy opens the Pandora's box of persuasion, which may lead to manipulation for personal gain under the guise of the common good.

If this seems to describe the condition of democracy at the dawn of the twenty-first century, we would do well to acknowledge that the fault lies not entirely in the human spirit. Democracy is, at best, a reflection of the culture in which it is situated, and it carries the price of permitting the wise and the foolish their say. The Athenian democracy, as we know, was a hotbed of equality only if you were not a woman, slave, or barbarian, and its decision-making process was not remarkable for the commitment of Athenians to be guided by the strength of the better argument, as Plato and Aristotle lamented ad nauseam. Nor were the philosophers alone in their concern for a political system open to the pitch and sway of citizens susceptible to the swells of emotional displays. In the *Hellenika*, for example, Xenophon recounts how, in 406 BCE, members of the ekklesia considered whether to convey a laurel wreath on the generals whose fleet was victorious in the naval battle at Arginoussai, or execute them for deserting a contingent of men who were lost in the confusion of battle and subsequently perished when a stormy sea prevented their rescue. The argument went back and forth, but displays of bereavement by relatives and friends took their toll. Convulsed with emotions of shared grief over the lost sailors and lust to avenge their loss, the citizens voted to execute the generals. After further reflection, however, they changed their minds, but it was too late to undo their verdict. Burdened with guilt for ordering an execution they now regretted, the citizens redirected their emotion toward those who had prosecuted the case against the generals by lodging a complaint against them for having "deceived the People."

The problematic aspects of Athenian democracy, in fact, are reflected through its association with rhetoric. The principle of majority rule rests on an assumption that your neighbor can be trusted to participate in a reasonable fashion to resolve public problems. However, the educated have always been wary of the mob's susceptibility to the demagoguery of unscrupulous rhetorical practices. The observation that the people reign while the elite rules is borne out in ancient Athens and since, as the educated few have engaged in political practices that sought to capitalize on the advantages of organization and publicity afforded by wealth, status, and power. On the other side, the politics of *philoi* or friendship bonds that gave the elite the considerable rhetorical advantage of speaking with one voice was overcome when the *phouloi* or common men, who were prone to act as separate and often disorganized individuals, gained the advantage of their superior numbers by acting in concert. Democracy's possibility of direct appeal to the *demos* provided the window for political opportunists, such as Kleon and Alcibiades, who recognized the equalizing power of oratory to so organize the *phouloi* (Connor 91-98). From its beginning, democracy has been in tension between the elite, who invoke their privilege to decide based on superior training to engage in rational deliberation (education), and the common citizens, who point to their numbers as the expression of public will. The ideals of the Athenian *polis* may be far removed from the realities of modern Western democracies, but the ideals of deliberative decision making by competent citizens and of popular sovereignty through the authorizing agencies of the people's voice and vote remain alive at least at the level of aspiration. We find this expressed most commonly today in the wave of scholarship devoted to advancing the idea of deliberative democracy[1] and the renewed concern and debate about civic engagement (see Barber, *Strong Democracy;* Cohen and Arato; Hall; Hauser, *Vernacular Voices;* Putnam, *Making Democracy Work*). These literatures idealize a process that is projected as a manifestation of reasonableness, if not reason, and that carries a commitment to the principle that the voice of the people should carry force.

Even if democratic leaders do not actually rely on public discussion of the people's business to guide their political conduct, they treasure the political cachet of appeals to "the people," which reflects acknowledgment that their acts in some way require authorization (Bitzer 73-75). Hence, their rhetorical efforts to solicit and solidify public support are at pains to project the image that they do listen and heed. The idealization of the people shaping the course of governance may never have been completely realized, but the resilience of the Athenian linkage of the people's voice to rhetorical discourse is more than a vestige of democracy's origin. Western politics sustains the connection between discourse on civic issues and setting public policy because democratic governance—which regards the people's interests as its rhetorical, if not theoretical, foundation—has narrated advancing their interests as a primary virtue of good governance. This is a democratic leader's public trust, and democracies have taken a dim view of leaders who have betrayed it.

On the other hand, invoking popular will to legitimize state action has not been the sole preserve of democrats. Acknowledging the legitimating force of the people's voice expresses the fundamental principle of a democracy; it also signals what lies at the heart of political power. Consequently, monarchs and democrats alike have exploited the rhetorical capital of "*vox populi, vox dei*," even though their definitions of "the people" and their interests have fluctuated to suit radically different ends and tastes (Boas; McGee). We need look back no farther than the 1980s to find an apt and relevant illustration in the "people's democracies" that emphasized giving form to the sovereignty of the people. The former Soviet states were lacking in liberal content and, under a rubric that treated the people and the state as inseparable, subjected the masses to the will of the state (Touraine 117). This recent example of a most "undemocratic" political system by Western standards reminds us that the concept of governance responsive to the will of the people has a variety of meanings, each in some way requiring some means for representing official acts as a reflection of public opinion.

The diversity of constitutional forms in which the people's voice has been used as the authorizing agency for state action has particular salience today. During the last fifteen years, democracy's wave has broken across the planet and washed across the lives of peoples with no prior history of liberal democratic political participation. Popular participation in governance that seems normal to citizens of Western representative democracies took centuries to evolve. The United States, for example, which heralds its victory in the Cold War as a mandate for exporting democracy to the former Soviet states, the Arab world, and beyond, took 150 years to learn how to govern itself as a democracy. It was only after the English colonials had gone through a learning period of differentiation from living as subjects to the British monarchy that they were ready to separate from English rule. For those living in newly democratized parts of the world, the development of a new political consciousness and commitment to egalitarian traditions can hardly require less adjustment. The rise in these countries of *the public* as a voice to be taken seriously represents a sea change in political relations that requires political learning by leaders as well as the people.

These changes in world politics are just one example of the dynamic context in which democracy is experienced and lived—in the rhetoric of a people and in the consequences that follow. Times change, conditions of political involvement evolve, who gets to speak and how voices might best be heard are not graven in stone. We no longer live in a direct democracy, and the problems of representation in a democratic republic are shaped as profoundly by the realities of communication as by political structures. Within this context, the challenge of making a democracy work requires that we form an understanding commensurate with how it is lived. That challenge can only be met if our understanding of the communication practices and possibilities are themselves not idealized or, to put it positively, if our conception is sensitive to communication practices shaping understanding and choice. In short, we must tend to the messy business of a democracy's rhetoric. That project requires reconsidering democratic life in light of a number of factors that are not part of the Athenian legacy on which so much of our theory and criticism of rhetoric rests.

RHETORICAL DEMOCRACY OF CIVIL SOCIETY

The waning years of the Cold War were marked by Western societies heeding the call of Central and Eastern European dissidents for civil society. The concept of civil society—which had emerged in the moral, political, and economic writings of the Enlightenment—had been moribund for at least the preceding half-century. Struggles such as the Solidarity movement in Poland and the Charter 77 movement in Czechoslovakia signaled an aspiration not merely for democracy but for a society responsive to the diversity of the contemporary world. The drama of 1989, in which mostly bloodless revolutions toppled the USSR's client regimes in Central and Eastern Europe and which witnessed political dissent in China, provided a climax to the yearnings of subjugated peoples for an authentic cultural, social, and economic life. Not everyone was consumed by politics, but people were responsive to an image of society in which they could practice their religion, speak their minds, educate their children, or share in the fruits of their labor without the heavy hand of the state regulating their activity and threatening their freedom.

Dissident rhetoric throughout the last half of the twentieth century advanced a persistent vision of a society whose members would have freedom to assemble and exchange ideas on matters of mutual concern in order to negotiate relations of interdependence. Whether in the dissident writings of Adam Michnik or of Nelson Mandela, arguments for political inclusion began from a vision of social inclusion resting on a distinction between the state (which engages in unifying action through exercise of power) and political society (which is concerned with a political and juridical order that reflects a vision of equity). Civil society stood between them as the network of associations in which conflicts of diversity could be mediated by the realities of mutual dependence that encouraged the self-regulating activities of compromise, alliance, and cooperation. Michnik and Mandela understood that their societies were more complex than being merely an exclusively Roman Catholic Poland or a South Africa only for indigenous Africans.

Social inclusion requires shared activity based on social relations and cultural values that are often in conflict; it aims at self-regulation for reconciling differences. This activity is manifested in discursive practices of disagreement, negotiation, and cooperation; it is as dependent on its rhetorical practices of engagement as on its balancing of economic interests. Civil society is guided by recognition of mutual dependency and, therefore, of differences that must be valued at least to the extent that they are treated as relevant to political relations that are to emerge.

This is not an easy state to achieve or maintain, as the sad history of the years immediately following the end of the Cold War have proven. Aspirations for a free society were accompanied in many cases by an equally strong desire for an authentic national life. National identity marked a sharp divide between the state and the people in most Central and Eastern European countries, not only during the Cold War period but also in many instances historically. As national identity was fused with ethnicity, independence fueled a nationalism based on a narrow understanding of who were rightfully joined as a social-political-economic-cultural entity. In some cases, such as the former Czechoslovakia, a peaceful separation occurred. In others, such as the former Yugoslavia, the intermingling of ethnicities made separation into parts a ghastly spectacle. Fueled by a rhetoric that preyed on ancient ethnic fears and grievances, wars in Bosnia and Kosovo, and to a lesser extent in Croatia, unloosed the genocidal fury of ethnic cleansing. Even in Germany, the sense among some that a nation should be exclusively for its native people led to a wave of violence targeting foreign guest workers and expressions of anti-Semitism in the years immediately after the fall of the Berlin Wall. These challenges and catastrophies underscore both the difficulty and significance of civil society to postmodern democratic life.

The rhetorical democracy of the twenty-first century rests on the hurly-burly of civil society. Citizens still adhere to the ancient tenet that democratic politics must be a public activity open to all and distinct from the private preferences reflected in commercial transactions. Even though citizens in a modern liberal democracy do not have a direct say in the decisions of the state, a liberal democracy's reliance on the voice of the people is no less real than in the ancient city-state. However, conditions of mass society and the rise of civil society have changed the manner in which this voice is expressed and the role that it plays in the lived realities of a democracy (Taylor). The modern state is concerned, in large measure, with international relations that bear on the security and economic well-being of the country. In matters of foreign affairs, the *vox populi* may serve as a rhetorical justification for public consumption if it supports the leader's position, but no leader makes decisions of national defense by plebiscite. These are decisions formulated in response to the international situation vis-à-vis national security. The political public is addressed in such cases to explain and justify already-determined or even executed action, to generate widespread support for the state's policy, but not to get a sense of what the majority thinks the state should do. Indeed, national welfare is regarded as a bipartisan concern above the political fray, so that the *topos* of "playing politics" with national interest is invoked whenever a leader is perceived to be placing partisan interests ahead of national security. On the other hand, even in this extreme case where citizen voices do not play a role in formulating policy, they remain significant, as the U.S. experience of citizen voices in opposition to the Vietnam War proves. Expressions of public opinion via opinion polls, by leaders of political parties and movements, or by vernacular rhetoric are very different measures of public sentiment, each with its own implications for how decisions are reached in a rhetorical democracy (Hauser, *Vernacular Voices*).

These are expressions of public opinion. Public opinion as a rhetorical formulation and as a rhetorical expression lies at the core of civil society's role in contemporary democracy. If, as Alain Touraine observes, civil society is a precondition for the modern democracy (41), then the rhetoricity of public opinion is central to our understanding of democracy as we live and experience it today.

THE RHETORICAL IDEAL OF PUBLIC OPINION

A liberal democracy is predicated on the principle that representatives are aware of the views of the represented. It relies on interested members of society forming reasoned judgments that influence the course and direction of the state. It understands public opinion to be more than a nose count. A genuinely *public* opinion entails a prior process by which citizens arrive at an understanding of how public problems intersect with their lives, what their interests are, and a reasoned judgment on how best to protect them. For now I wish to set aside the debatable characterization of public opinion reflecting a reasoned judgment to concentrate on the process by which it is to be reached.

This prior process can be summarized in terms of two fundamental principles: the principle of publicity and the principle of free speech. The publicity principle holds that a society has the right to access all relevant information and viewpoints on public problems. As a corollary, it holds that a member of society has the right to call society's attention to matters that he or she regards as public concerns. The principle of free speech holds that a person has the right to express his or her opinion without being subjected to legal penalties. From these two principles we can elaborate a more complete statement of basic rights protected by law and the necessary structures of public policy that guarantee a well-functioning liberal democratic state. Publicity and free speech are the *sine qua non* for these necessary guarantees to have effect and on which they ultimately rest.

Publicity and free speech disclose the centrality of rhetoric to a democracy by implying that public opinion is a tendency of common understanding and judgment emerging from citizen conversations—that it is more than an aggregate of raw, blind opinion (Hauser, "Vernacular Dialogue"). They imply that public opinion is found in the discursive practices of interested citizens—a public. A public conveys a tendency of common understanding and judgment—a public opinion—that certifies the validity and legitimacy of conduct by bodies empowered to act and that can offer them instruction on how to act. Insofar as public opinion claims to reflect, in some significant respect, public reasoning, publicity and free speech advance rhetorical communication—communication that urges a point of view—as the necessary condition for redeeming that claim. More specifically, the *character* of an antecedent rhetoric underwrites public opinion's claim to represent, in some significant respect, emergent tendencies of understanding among those who are aware of the issues entailed by a public problem and have reached a conclusion on them. Conversely, the discursive requirements of publicity and free speech call into question assertions about public opinion that lack an empirical foundation in citizen discourse. As Pierre Bourdieu has argued, without a tether to the actual discursive practices of social actors, we lack *prima facie* evidence for membership in a public: that the opinion givers are even remotely engaged by the matters in question.

The type of political discourse implicit in the principles of publicity and free speech are often portrayed as the ideals of public deliberation that are assumed to hold in a representative democracy. C. Wright Mills summarizes these assumptions as including:

> that the individual conscience was the ultimate seat of judgment and hence the final court of appeal [...] that among the individuals who composed [the public] there was a natural and peaceful harmony of interests, [...] that before public action would be taken, there would be rational discussion between individuals which would determine action, and that, accordingly the public opinion that

> resulted would be the infallible voice of reason, [... and] that after determining what was true and right and just, the public would act accordingly or see that its representatives did so. (300-01)

Even if Mills's idealized public of politically capable citizens is entirely theoretical, the position accorded public *deliberation* and public *opinion* by his summary remains a central tenet of representative democracies that, at least superficially, seems to endorse the participatory spirit. However, the migration of conscience from the *polis* into the individual can produce consensus-building rational discussion only if we assume that autonomous individuals share "a natural and peaceful harmony of interests." Without that assumption, the inviolate primacy of the individual opinion italicizes the curious absence of a corporate voice from this account and reduces public opinion to an aggregate of single voices speaking their separate consciences. Mills's account raises questions about the ways that participation is manifested, how opinion is expressed, how we may come to know it, and the status that public participation and opinion should be accorded.

PROBLEMS OF DEMOCRACY AND THE REHABILITATION OF PUBLIC OPINION

These are not questions that rest gently on the minds of citizens or scholars of democratic processes. To begin with, public opinion has come to mean the results of opinion polls. Opinion polls, if well conducted, may provide invaluable information, but they also are flawed measures of opinion susceptible to the problems of survey research well known among the scholarly community (Dryzek; Yankelovich). Unfortunately, these problems are not publicized or well known among the general populace. By appearing to offer an objective account of where matters stand and a reliable measure for situating one's personal views with respect to what the majority thinks, polls seem to provide citizens with information that satisfies their quest for the range, intensity, and collective weight of citizen thought. They become a rhetorical form in their own right by offering citizens an authoritative account of what their neighbors think. They displace citizen discourse as a means for forming an opinion with the objectivist discourse of the percentage array of responses to survey questions (Hauser, *Vernacular Voices* 190-98).

The problem with this deflection from discourse is not its epistemological assumption that inferences about public opinion can be drawn on the basis of numerical count. The idea of public opinion inherently involves a sensed assessment of the common mind. Historically, this sensed assessment has been viewed as a question of an idea's relative strength among community members, which in some way has always required gauging the comparative size and strength of commitment among those who held this or that view (Boas; Herbst; Noelle-Neumann; Speier). The basic problem lies in a confusion between a sociology of science (as reflected in the prevailing practice by media and political parties to regard public opinion as what opinion polls report) and a philosophy of science (in which the status of a claim is determined by its ontological fidelity to the phenomenon it purports to describe).

This relationship of claim to ontological fidelity has been a problem for opinion polling as an applied methodology almost from its outset. The contest between the social determinism of Lazersfeld's Columbia group and the social psychologism of Miller's Michigan group resulted in a general consensus in Miller's favor. However, as Miller himself acknowledged, "we did not have any theory which argued that political behavior was any different from social or economic behavior" (qtd in Dryzek 162). The absence of such a distinction remains today, according to Dryzek, and is significant because a democratic society makes important assumptions about the role of discourse in establishing political relations.

The pollsters' assumptions about individual behavior—based on individual attributes of attitude, belief, and opinion—neither take into account nor account for the discursive character of political behavior. Consequently, of the many possible political worlds that can be and are brought about through the discursive nature of political relations, survey research projects only one: a political world in which the individual must choose sides among contesting forces. Dryzek concludes that, in this world, the only rational choice is to choose the side that best advances one's interests, thereby making rationality consist exclusively of instrumental action. This view leads to a rhetoric of instrumental reasoning in which the rhetorical democracy is overrun by "public relations" in order to produce, in Habermas's felicitous phrase, "manufactured public opinion."

Second, the idealized portrayal of participation and opinion is problematic in terms of its adherence to a procedural model for ensuring the rationality of public judgment. This model, perhaps most associated with although not exclusively advanced by Jürgen Habermas, holds that no a priori position should be held above the test of warranted assent, and therefore testing the adequacy of a point of view requires a procedure designed to give every interested party the same opportunity to participate in democratic processes. Procedural democracy is difficult to object to in principle because its tenets seem to rest on a commitment to a reasonable equity principle: The legitimacy of a decision is a function of the fairness of the process by which it was reached. The ideal conditions of the public sphere advanced by Habermas offer a clear summary of what these conditions are: equal opportunities to present and have views considered, to respond, to access information and media of dissemination, and to forge consensus on the basis of warranted assent (Cohen).

Although this has the appeal of apparent justice, pluralistic politics makes this standard of deliberative democracy suspect. Diversity and interdependence among members of civil society pose the challenge of reaching a decision in which partners are able to assemble, participate, speak, and publicize freely. Equal rights often are compromised by inequity of resources. Procedural rationality inadvertently favors those with maximum resources to participate in the process over those at the edges.

Moreover, if the precondition for modern democracy is civil society, then its associated networks of diverse individuals and groups in relationships of mutual dependence will at least occasionally preclude shared standards of rationality. The fairness of procedural norms we have inherited from antiquity and have thematized as the basis of democracy are not particularly accommodating of such pluralism. Liberties such as religious liberty, liberty of conscience, liberty of thought and expression, and rights of person and personal property can constrain democratic procedures by what political scientist Joshua Cohen calls "'the fact of reasonable pluralism'—the fact that there are distinct, incompatible understandings of value, each reasonable, to which people are drawn under favorable conditions for the exercise of their practical reason" (408). The fact that reasonable citizens holding irreconcilable views may make good-faith efforts to live with one another on mutually acceptable terms does not mean that there will be convergence on a single philosophy of life, as the criterion of warranted assent implies.

A rhetorical democracy is not merely a collection of whatever is said under the banner of free speech, nor is it synonymous with deliberative democracy if that formulation implies a normative standard of rational discourse. Relations that involve conflicts, negotiation, and compromise seldom adhere to philosophers' standards for reaching rationally warranted assent. The motivation to engage in deliberation arises from the impact of communal conditions on attachments and a perceived need to protect or advance them. Political issues and decisions are, as Aristotle observed, in the realm of the contingent and contingencies are resolved through the *dynamis* of rhetoric not entirely explicable in rationalistic terms. For rhetoric to be democratic, it must go beyond procedural norms to embrace practices of *deliberative inclusion*. Inclusion means more than giving voice to a point of view. Rhetorical democracy at its best does not expect contestants to find one another's reasons acceptable as their own, but it does respond to them as legitimate contributions to the deliberative process. Otherwise, these views and those who hold them are not being treated as equal, which violates the horizontal relations among citizens participating in a deliberative process that is more than nominally democratic.

Third, idealized participation and the force of public opinion assume that we have trustworthy neighbors, but it does not address the problem of trust inherent in civil society. A liberal democracy is always vulnerable to the influence of lobby politics, which emphasizes a rhetoric of self-interest. Aside from the excessively costly option of forming one's own lobby, the idealized model of deliberation leaves no effective counter to the organization of vested interests. It results, by default, in a weak sense of democracy caught in a Hobbsean nightmare of each against all. This is at cross-purposes to the discursive dimension of democracy on which rationalizing the relationship of state action to the will of the people depends.

The democratic end of a public good requires processes and structures that can foster building trust among partners whose different interests may, at times, conflict. That antiquity's model of civic virtue is no longer the norm for political action (Hauser, "Civil Society") does not mean that rhetoric is dead. Civil society's character is inherently rhetorical. Its web of associations are rhetorical arenas in which "strangers encounter difference, learn of the other's interests, develop understanding of where there are common goals, and where they may develop the levels of trust necessary for them to function in a world of mutual dependency" (Hauser and Benoit-Barné 271). Its relations are collaborative as well as contestive.

Civic community does not depend on citizens thinking alike, or even having consensus on underlying values. It does require citizenly competence to participate in civic conversation and trust that it will be consequential on how we address public problems. Moreover, it requires citizens to trust that their partners will participate honestly and honor their commitments. In situations of uncertainty, in which we must choose between alternatives in the face of the unknown about how our partners will behave, we rely on past experiences to form expectations. However, trust goes beyond past experience to define the future in the face of risk. It always involves risk and raises the question of how trust is built.

Certainly, trust is not entirely a rhetorical accomplishment; deeds corresponding to words matter. However, civil society's characteristic negotiation over how we shall act and interact in relationships of mutual dependence provides the rhetorical experience of mutuality on which trust relies. Civic conversations of this sort are a form of political learning both necessary to a democracy and redemptive of public life's epistemological relevance. Before we can have a productive civic conversation with difference, we first must overcome the menace of difference that provokes distrust and the antidemocratic rhetorics of intolerance, cynicism, or withdrawal from the political process. For democracy to be a functional form of governance in a society of strangers, citizens must learn how to engage difference in a way that recognizes the individual and the group as a subject.

Engaging difference in this way is not easily accomplished. The ideals of participation and opinion do not account for the politics of the subject. The subject is the actor for whom democracy holds the hope of freedom from domination. It is self-centered, not community centered, in its integration of identity with techniques whereby it experiences liberty. As such, the subject is always an incomplete project. It is not reducible to roles it plays, is not accounted for by duty or the general will, and instead seeks, in MacIntyre's words, "the narrative of unity."

The concept of individual subjects whose primary identification is not with the community and whose primary motivation does not grow from a sense of duty to country before quest for self-integration is a recent social phenomenon. Certainly, it is contrary to the understanding of democracy we inherit from the Athenian polis. Athenians did not see the subject seeking escape from domination but, like Antigone, as torn between a sense of duty to community and loyalty to family. The politics of the subject, by contrast, seeks independence from the community's power to impose a sense of worth. At the same time, the migration of moral judgment from the community to the self—a migration charted by Enlightenment thinkers such as Adam Smith—cannot be sustained without accounting for the social relations in which the individual is enmeshed, because plurality and interdependence are material realities. Subjectivity is not entirely a function of the self-contained individual. It also involves identity, which is inseparable from the social groups with which the individual identifies and their bearing on the quest for self.

Group identification, coupled with iterative relations of cooperation and dependence, are not exclusively rhetorical constructions. Differences have material as well as symbolic antecedents. Nevertheless, self-esteem is a condition of happiness requiring liberty, which, under conditions of cooperation and dependence, requires recognition of the other's subjectivity and structures that permit the individual to organize experience without constraints. To be a subject is to have freedom to use reason in concert with cultural identity; to perform the ongoing construction of a "narrative of unity" while being part of a larger family that provides historicity. The politics of the subject points toward democracy as the form of social and political being, and doing that permits the individual subject to emerge as an integrated whole.

This involves a political learning process that is more than dialogical exchange of face-to-face interaction. In a complex mass society, it involves the multilogue of civic conversations across a variety of settings and through a variety of media from which we experience the dialogizing of difference (Bakhtin) and learn about the adequacy of our paradigms for democratic action. These dialogues are conducted in a montage of settings and with a variety of partners who, in some way, are linked in civil society. As we find our expectations defied by worldly responses to our choices for conduct, the rhetorical democracy exposes us to a world of individuals and groups with history, memory, customs, and values projected through the exemplars, tropes, narratives, and political styles that have currency in vernacular and formal rhetoric. These rhetorical modes of reasoning invite us to reimagine and restructure our relationships, to learn new understandings of the world that will foster survival, and to arrive at an opinion that seems to comport with the gestaltlike experience of rhetorical assessment that transpires in a multilogue on an indeterminate but, in important ways, recalcitrant world. They refigure the rhetorical democracy from a series of procedures to a free space (Evans and Boyte) in which we may critique what is and in which the subject may emerge.

An opinion poll model of citizen participation in a democracy, finally, is not commensurate with this political learning process because it does not account for civil society as the locus of public spheres. The approach of social scientists seeking to account for why citizens engage in civic community and the activities that mark a vibrant civic community have focused on features of social structure to explain the development and acquisition of social capital (Barber, *A Place;* Coleman; Putnam, *Bowling Alone;* Fullinwider). The evidence they put forward, however, suggests the *sine qua non* of a well-functioning civic community is engagement in the formal and vernacular rhetoric of civil society.

We no longer live in a rhetorical culture that fosters, much less encourages, the eloquence of antiquity. That the podium has receded as the dominant locus of political learning and deliberation does not mean that modern mass societies are bereft of a rhetorical culture. Its culture is found in the secondary associations that constitute the web of civil society. The rhetorical culture of these associations produces social capital by exposing their members to alternative rhetorics—to the range of difference and the mediating grounds of similarity that make a civic community based on relations of collaboration a possibility. Their internal and emergent public spheres are the arenas in which members enact horizontal relations of equality and develop deliberative competencies through consideration of issues that have internal and external significance for their association and the networks in which they are involved. These arenas are rhetorical constructions; they emerge from member practices by which they develop not only the voice necessary to participate in deliberative democracy, but also the social capital (Coleman; Putnam, *Bowling Alone*) necessary to participate in such deliberations with a trustworthy voice. Their work of creating the salient meanings by which we understand our world and form a judgment on the desirable future are beyond the radar sweep of an opinion poll.

RHETORICAL DEMOCRACY AND CIVIC ENGAGEMENT

The idea of a rhetorical democracy, as I have attempted to argue, is not identical with that of a deliberative democracy. As the chapters in this volume show, it is historical formation stretching from antiquity to the present, cutting across cultures, and manifesting itself in different modes. It recognizes that the partisan impulse is present and not easily curbed by criteria of rationality. It accommodates the differences among citizens that prompted Madison to warn a newly emerging nation about the threat of factions and the tyranny of the majority. It expands the frame for democratic participation from the negotiating table to the myriad forms by which free people express their social, political, and personal aspirations and identities. It values the tumult of differences being contested and the search for solutions to common problems with strangers who share them and who are our partners in relationships of mutual dependence. These relationships found in civil society are the defining characteristic of a modern democracy and pose a significant problem for it: the creation of a discursive practice in which citizens may pursue the possibilities of civic engagement.

The challenge of creating such a discursive practice ties scholars and teachers of rhetoric to their forbearers, who in each age have had to confront the consequences of changing conditions for the viability of rhetorical practices. Today's conditions may be remarkably dissimilar from those of past ages, however it bears recalling that instruction in rhetoric rose to prominence in antiquity from its understanding that oratorical competence was inherent to participation in the Athenian democracy and the Roman republic. It was the practice whereby democratic political structures became more than nominal. Skillful expression resulted in public decisions based on public deliberation rather than private arrangement. As such, rhetoric lay at the heart of citizenship and of the citizen's public identity. This position of centrality is rhetoric's birthright.

As the Enlightenment project has moved Western societies steadily toward logics of knowledge and decision-making structured on the objectivism of science and the privileged voices of epistemic elites, the transparency of political processes has been obscured by the decisiveness of technical discourse. The art of effective expression known as rhetoric, in turn, has been reduced from a method of public deliberation to the "mereness" of gambits and ploys detached from material content and designed to secure the uninformed assent of the governed. By not contesting its steady marginalization, Rhetoric Studies squanders its birthright and reneges on its promise to democracy.

Scholars and teachers of rhetoric can, indeed must, reclaim their birthright by reasserting the centrality of rhetoric to democratic life in the twenty-first century. Of the number of ways by which we may meet this challenge, the most ready at hand is our classrooms, in which we profess to instruct our students in the arts of effective argument, adapting appeals to their audience, expressing ideas in language that engages others and, on occasion, even inspires, and the relationship between the discourse they craft and the world they inhabit. Our instruction often is framed as teaching a skill. Perhaps as a first step toward reclaiming our birthright, we might think of it instead as enabling our students to live as free human beings who have it within their power to influence the communities in which they will work, make their homes, form friendships, raise families, educate their children, enjoy public arts, and pursue their private pleasures.

The quality of communities is not given; the reality of democratic life is one of tenuous relationships at best. The commonness that binds us usually is greater than the differences that divide, but without a sense of how to productively encounter others in a community of strangers, this may be difficult to grasp. Communicating across the divide is perhaps the central issue confronting the current discussion about civic engagement, and Rhetoric Studies has a great deal to contribute to it. In the 1960s, the United States addressed itself to the challenges of the Cold War by initiating a series of curricular reforms that placed greater emphasis on science and math and encouraged students to gain the knowledge necessary to advance a national agenda of discovery and innovation. We may hope for a similar federal initiative to foster the engaged citizen. Regardless of whether one develops, we can play a part in educating such a change through the way we envision our courses and our curricula. The problems I have outlined are within our reach to address by focusing our instruction in rhetoric as the place to develop the links of understanding and common cause among differences. These are the relations on which democratic culture depends.

NOTE

1. As of November 3, 2002, Barnes & Noble listed 33 titles on its best-seller list with "deliberative democracy" in the title. See <http://www.barnesandnoble.com>.

WORKS CITED

Bakhtin, M. M. *The Dialogical Imagination*. Ed. Michael Holquist. Trans. Carly Emerson and Michael Holquist. Austin: U of Texas P, 1981.

Barber, Benjamin. *Strong Democracy: Participatory Politics for a New Age*. Berkeley: U of California P, 1984.

---. *A Place for Us: How to Make Society Civil and Democracy Strong*. New York: Hill, 1998.

Bitzer, Lloyd. "Rhetoric and Public Knowledge." *Rhetoric, Philosophy and Literature: An Exploration*. Ed. Don M. Burks. West Lafayette, IN: Purdue UP, 1978. 67-95.

Boas, George. *Vox Populi: Essays in the History of an Idea*. Baltimore: Johns Hopkins UP, 1969.

Bourdieu, Pierre. "Public Opinion Does Not Exist." *Communication and Class Struggle*. Ed. Armand Mattelart and Seth Siegelaub. New York: Bagnolet, 1979. 124-30.

Cohen, Jean L., and Andrew Arato. *Civil Society and Political Theory*. Cambridge, MA: MIT P, 1992.

Cohen, Joshua. "Procedure and Substance in Deliberative Democracy." *Deliberative Democracy*. Ed. James Bohman and William Rehg. Cambridge, MA: MIT P, 1997. 407-37.
Coleman, James. "Social Capital in the Creation of Human Capital." *American Journal of Sociology* 94 (1988): S95-S120.
Connor, W. Robert. *The New Politics of Fifth-Century Athens*. Princeton, NJ: Princeton UP, 1971.
Dryzek, John S. *Discursive Democracy: Politics, Policy, and Political Science*. New York: Cambridge UP, 1990.
Evans, Sara M., and Harry C. Boyte. *Free Spaces: The Sources of Democratic Change in America*. Chicago: U of Chicago P, 1992.
Fullinwider, Robert K., ed. *Civil Society and Democracy, and Civic Renewal*. New York: Rowman, 1999.
Habermas, Jürgen. *The Structural Transformation of the Public Sphere*. Trans. Thomas Burger with Frederick Lawrence. Cambridge, MA: MIT P, 1989.
Hall, John A., ed. *Civil Society: Theory, History, Comparison*. Cambridge, MA: Polity, 1995.
Hauser, Gerard A. "Civil Society and the Principle of the Public Sphere." *Philosophy and Rhetoric* 31 (1998): 19-40
---. "Vernacular Dialogue and the Rhetoricality of Public Opinion." *Communication Monographs* 65 (1998): 83-107.
---. *Vernacular Voices: The Rhetoric of Publics and Public Spheres*. Columbia: U of South Carolina P, 1999.
---, and Benoit-Barné, Chantal. "Reflections on Rhetoric, Deliberative Democracy, Civil Society, and Trust." *Rhetoric & Public Affairs* 5 (2002): 261-75.
Herbst, Susan. *Numbered Voices: How Opinion Polling Has Shaped American Politics*. Chicago: U of Chicago P, 1993.
MacIntyre, Alasdair. *After Virtue*. 2nd ed. Notre Dame, IN: U of Notre Dame P, 1984.
Madison, James. "Federalist No. 10." 23 Nov. 1787. *Federalist Papers*. 15 May 2003 <http://memory.loc.gov/const/fed/fedpapers.html>.
Mandela, Nelson. *Long Walk to Freedom*. New York: Little, 1994.
McGee, Michael Calvin. "In Search of 'The People': A Rhetorical Alternative." *Quarterly Journal of Speech* 65 (1975): 235-49.
Michnik, Adam. *Letters form Prison*. Trans. Maya Latynski. Berkeley: U of California P, 1985.
Mills, C. Wright. *The Power Elite*. New York: Oxford UP, 1957.
Noelle-Neumann, Elisabeth. *The Spiral of Silence: Public Opinion—Or Social Skin*. 2nd ed. Chicago: U of Chicago P, 1993.
Putnam, Robert D. *Bowling Alone: The Collapse and Revival of American Community*. New York: Simon, 2000.
---. *Making Democracy Work*. Princeton, NJ: Princeton UP, 1993.
Smith, Adam. *The Theory of Moral Sentiments*. 1790. 6th ed. Ed. D.D. Raphael and A.L. Macfie. Oxford, UK: Clarendon, 1976.
Speier, Hans. "Historical Development of Public Opinion." *American Journal of Sociology* 55 (1950): 376-88.
Taylor, Charles. *Philosophical Arguments*. Cambridge, MA: Harvard UP, 1995.
Touraine, Alain. *What Is Democracy?* Trans. David Macey. Boulder, CO: Westview, 1997.
Xenophon. *Hellenika* I-II 3.10. Ed. and trans. Peter Krentz. Warminster, UK: Aris, 1989.
Yankelovich, Daniel. *Coming to Public Judgment: Making Democracy Work in a Complex World*. Syracuse, NY: Syracuse UP, 1991.

I

Plenary Papers

2

Citizen Voices in Cyberpolitical Culture

Bruce E. Gronbeck
University of Iowa

> We cannot cram the world of tomorrow into yesterday's conventional cubbyholes.
>
> —Alvin Toffler (*Masters of the Wired World* 22)

I take as the text for this chapter's sermon Alvin Toffler's sententious articulation of where we are in time and space, which is to say, where we are not at present. We live neither in yesterday nor in tomorrow, but in a liminal today. The culture of today, to most futurists, stands between a fluid, inventible tomorrow and an ossified, conventional yesterday. For those of us from rhetorical and communication disciplines, the yesterday that was the twentieth century was the era of modernist politics running on mechanically reproduced images—political posters, photography and photojournalism, first silent and then sound film. It then evolved into the era of electronically reproduced sounds and images, as we adapted personal and public political life (especially in the West) to the telegraph, telephone, radio, television, and the early years of the computer. Politically, it was the culture of whistle-stop campaigning and governing from afar giving way to the newsreel in local theatres; the radio and television broadcasts into our homes; and telegraphic, telephonic, and 9-digit Zip-code-sorted mail access to centers of power and political process.

But now? What of now? "The dominant change taking place in the advanced economies," Toffler intones, "is a shift from mass societies based on brute force technologies to de-massified societies that, like the new economy, are much more granular, internally differentiated, more complex and fast moving" (23). The so-called de-massified societies, to both Toffler and Gronbeck, are on the edge of a political revolution. It is a revolution more significant than the bottom-up rebellions of the second half of the twentieth century. The *uhuru* movement that decolonized Africa; the civil rights movements that struck at America's racism, sexism, and classism; the Solidarity movement that spread from Poland to most of the rest of the Western hemisphere; even the democracy movement that made Tiananmen Square a metaphor for political resistance—all of these movements, although dear to my heart, comprise less significant changes in citizen-oriented political activity than what we will be experiencing in the cyberpolitical world of tomorrow.

I may be a child of the '60s, my ears still may ring with "Hey, hey, LBJ, how many kids have you killed today," and I may long for the teach-ins and public interest research groups that were a part of the University of Michigan culture when I took my first job there. However, I believe that I ain't seen nothin' yet, and neither have you.

I want to tackle this volume's theme—*Rhetorical Democracy: Discursive Practices of Civic Engagement*—by viewing it from a cyberpolitical perspective. I am a rhetorician by training. More than that, I am a rhetorician who clings to the axiom that governing is a quintessentially symbolic activity. Yes, politics involves institutionalized redistribution of resources via what some political scientists label rational choices. But those resources are valued or not thanks to discursive meaning making, the debates leading to rational choices are vigorously argumentative exercises, and both talk among political players and interactions between the political elite and their constituents depend rhetorically on what Kenneth Burke called "dancing an attitude" (9). Rhetoricians make their livings on what this volume's theme calls "discursive practices within governmental systems"—systems viewed not as structures, but as communication channels.

And yes, I am interested in civic engagement, more precisely, in citizen-based political activity, and still more precisely in what counts as political activity in our time. A dozen years ago, I published my first essay on what I termed "electric rhetoric" (Gronbeck, "Electric"), which I took to be rhetorical-political practice as conditioned by radio, film, television, and the computer. At that time, I focused primarily on characteristics of political messages and our experience of them based on how they were adapted to America's culturally conditioned systems of mass media. Then five years later, I did another essay (Gronbeck, "Rhetoric") that focused more broadly on various dimensions of what I called "telespectacle": the multimediated, electronically mediated, narrativized connections between politicians and their constituents in a fractured political world where coalition or constituency-building is the heart of the process of gaining power through citizen assent.

However, what I have not attempted to do before is to muse conceptually about civic engagement per se in a digital world—that is, about citizen activity that can and even must be termed political as it is exercised via the World Wide Web. I want to try that here, working at a hopelessly airy level, seeking only to provide a framework within which to build arguments about citizen voices in our time. First, I sketch in narrative form a vision of the traditional political world in the West, a world beholden to the Greek, the Roman, and especially the British experience with the *polis* and the *demos*. Second, against that backdrop I examine recent citizen activities on the Internet that I urge you to call "political," so that I can, in the third place, reconceptualize the idea of "political activity" and, more particularly, the notion of citizen voices in political spheres. That should allow me to conclude with a sermonette on where the World Wide Web might take studies of citizen engagement in an digitized rhetorical democracy.

EVOLVING CONCEPTIONS OF POLITICS

It is tempting, of course, to begin a story of the idea of citizenship with Plato who, in dialogues such as *Statesman*, depicts human beings as animals interested only in bodily needs and pleasures and as deficient in the knowledge needed to run an orderly world (Jowett 349-59). Alternatively, I could review *The Republic* and its discussions of excessive liberty or of the economic destruction of the political that can happen in a loosely run democracy (*ibid.*, 328-37). Actually, I come back to those views later. But, more constructively, I prefer to begin with Aristotle, particularly his *Politics*. I would frame the *telos* of Western politics with the famous passage at the end of his discussion of citizenship in Book 3, where he articulates a relationship between the governor and the governed. He says: "But prudence is the only virtue peculiar to the ruler. The others, it would seem, must necessarily be common to both rulers and ruled, but prudence is not a virtue of one ruled, but rather true opinion; for the one ruled is like a flute maker, while the ruler is like a flute player, the user (of what the other makes)" (92). Here, the word for prudence, of course, is *phronêsis*, and for true opinion, *doxa aletheia*. Grounded in the flute metaphor is, I would argue, the premodern foundation of Western political ideals. The *êthea* or folkways of a people are depicted here as containing *doxa* or opinion powerful enough to demand of their leader *phronêsis* or prudence. The governor can play a little music, but only within the tonalities approved by the citizenry.

Set deeply into Western political thought, especially within the treatise or handbook tradition, therefore, is an understanding of a collective sociomoral space within which political acts are executed. And, as we move from Aristotle's *Politics* to Cicero's work on moral duties, *De officiis*, that space becomes more sharply defined. To Cicero, the general virtues undergirding politics are wisdom, justice, fortitude, and temperance, which in turn can be broken into a full alphabet of subsidiary virtues—from affability, ambition, beneficence, and brotherhood to sociality, steadfastness, stoicism, and utility. In *The Prince* (ch. 15), Machiavelli noted that virtues could be the ruin of and vices, the source of security and prosperity for, the state. But, conceptually, Machiavelli did not prevail.

Thus, for hundreds of years, politics in the West was understood as the study of moral rule by governors steeped in the *doxa aletheia* of their people. Politics, which dealt with the affairs of *status civitatis*, were to operate within a moral space paralleling that of the *status ecclesiae*. The realm temporal was understood as homologous to the realm spiritual. I don't have to tell you, of course, that few governors lived their civic lives in accordance with wisdom, justice, fortitude, and temperance. However, the West certainly was committed to such ideals even in the eras in which something near to absolute rule was the order of the day. A citizen could only hope that the *status civitatis* would be governed by devout and not wrathful lieutenants of the Lord.

Then came the modernist state. Both in understanding it as a complex organism, as did Thomas Hobbes in *The Leviathan* (1660), and in arguing that political power was reciprocally shared by rulers and the ruled, as did John Locke in his *Second Treatise on Civil Government* (1690), Western principalities were reconceived in highly significant ways. Slowly but surely, the focus on governing the state morally metamorphosized into the idea of managing the state politically (pace Palonen).

Government came to be understood as an organismic institution operating in time and space. The nation-state was conceived of as a rationalized space, subdivided into major units, each of which was further subdivided again and again, until one could access the smallest unit—say, a borough in England or a precinct in the American system. Citizens, in turn, had varied political rights and responsibilities in regard to each of those spaces, spelled out in constituting documents at the national, state or county, and local levels. Furthermore, political time was stabilized with equal rationality. Parliaments sat for specified periods, both during the year and through a series of years that constituted a sitting. Elections regularly were held—at least in most Western countries by the eighteenth century—as leaders reached down to the led for electoral legitimation. Even when the elections offered little in the way of choice, they gave material form to the idea of governing as established on the consent of the governed.

Political processes in parliaments and legislatures likewise were rationalized and stabilized. Parliamentary procedure created symbolic space between antagonists and complex rituals for controlling legislative activity (Gronbeck, "Symbolic"). The rule of law took form as legal historians such as Coke and Blackstone in the British tradition codified judicial procedure. And so, the branches of western governments—the executive, the legislative, and the judicial—were cultured; that is, symbolically constructed within a web of substantive and procedural rules that controlled their public activity. Never mind the regular violations of those procedures—again, it is their presence, not their universal observation, that is important to our understanding of Western conceptions of politics.

In contemplating these conceptions of popular sovereignty, consider, for example, the case of Edmund Burke. Most of his political life he held a safe seat, a so-called pocket borough, Malton in Yorkshire. But in 1774, he was put forward as a candidate for Bristol, a city where electors actually voted. Flattered, Burke ran for the seat. As he talked to the electors of Bristol in November of 1774, he obviously sensed pressures to represent their commercial interests in the House of Commons. That pressure he expressed in this way:

> Your representative owes you, not his industry only, but his judgement; and he betrays instead of serving you if he sacrifices it to your opinion. Parliament is not a congress of ambassadors from different and hostile interests; which interests each must maintain, as an agent and advocate, against other agents and advocates; but parliament is a deliberative assembly of one nation, with one interest, that of the whole; where, not local purposes, not local prejudices ought to guide, but the general good, resulting from the general reason of the whole. You choose a member indeed; but when you have chosen him, he is not a member of Bristol, but he is a member of parliament.

This segment of the 1774 speech articulated what we have come to know as a *theory of virtual representation*. What I find more interesting, however, is the fact that Edmund Burke felt constrained to have to articulate it at all. In so-called popular boroughs, even before the American and French revolutions, a sense of citizen rights was in the air.

But how strong was it? What of the citizen? As the modernist state took shape, what happened to the citizen—the source of moral guidance that Aristotle and Cicero hoped would contain the agents of power and that Burke feared might presume to influence his votes?

My answer to these questions cannot be developed fully, but I hope that I can outline it with enough clarity to pique your interest. My answer is this: Although Locke's compact theory of government seemingly ensconced popular legitimation processes in the heart of democratic theory, in fact it was the citizen, not the ruler, who was constrained and disciplined by Western political operations. The mechanisms for such containment and discipline were numerous. Consider four:

1. *Material requirements for the franchise.* In 1647, Oliver Cromwell's Army officers held a two-day debate in the church at Putney about voting in England. What is interesting to contemporary eyes reading that debate is that not even the most radical Leveller, those requesting something close to universal suffrage,[1] could conceive of voting and hence citizenship as a right attached simply to the person. Rather, the debate actually revolved around material questions about how much freehold property one would have to own or how much tax a person would have to pay before being given voting rights (Emery). Rights and those holding them could be conceptualized only in terms of real assets.

2. *Requirement for the presence of the body.* By the eighteenth century in England, the franchise was exercised through public, physical presence. The 1784 election in Westminster, for example, went on forty-five days, and citizens voted by publicly signing their names. Now they could change their vote—and therein lay the corruptibility of the system—but only by reappearing and publicly signing the voting record again. Similarly, dividing the House of Commons in those days was a matter of moving one's body to one side or the other of St. Stephen's Chapel. People voted with their feet.

3. *Demands for the absence of the body.* The galleries of the House of Commons could be cleared whenever a Member of Parliament cried, "I spy a stranger." Such strangers, of course, often were scribes surreptitiously taking notes on the proceedings—an act that was illegal until late in the nineteenth century. As well, citizens who engaged in political activities "out of doors" (i.e., not in buildings legitimized as houses for national, county, or local politics) could be fined or jailed. The fears of citizen activity in public places ran through centuries of British commentaries on politics.

4. *The civic disciplining of the body.* In Great Britain and elsewhere, the citizens' bodies were subjected to corporeal governmental control, to be flogged for misdemeanors, garreted when declared insane or debts were unpaid, jailed when associated with more serious crimes, and hanged on festive public occasions when adjudged guilty of capital offenses (Lofland).

My point is, in the parliamentary-democratic governments that developed in the modernist era, the *vox populi* was muted and the body politic was strapped down. Modernist politics has regularly enacted Alexander Hamilton's judgment in *Federalist No. 7* that "men are ambitious, vindictive, and rapacious," and the sentiments of William Livingston from the same period that "the people have been and ever will be unfit to retain the exercise of power in their own hands" (qtd in Rimmerman 14). These views bring us full circle—back to Plato's *Statesman* and *The Republic*.

In sum, the modern political state was regularized via statute and precedent, ordered in time and space, and put in charge of citizens, who legitimated its existence, yes, yet also were subject to its discipline. Aristotle may have recognized that the household existed before the state and Locke may have argued that society's needs are prior to those of government's (see, e.g., Hauser 20-21), yet the modernist European and North American state, often in the name of social order, was strongly regulatory. Habermas (esp. *Structural*) as well certainly was correct in identifying the eighteenth-century citizens' search for noninstitutionalized political spaces as places to create publicity, that is, publicness, and even to constitute citizens as a "public," something that could generate and urge "public opinions" (see Hauser 34). The efficacy of those opinions, however, as mechanisms for making policy and creating a polity with a sense of its own well-being, is moot.

The story of the modern political state in its nineteenth- and twentieth-century operations is interesting, but I cannot pause to tell it. If I had time, I would talk about the mobilization, especially in the United States, of the electorate, primarily in three ways: by tribe (i.e., on the basis of ethnic identification as in the Italian and the Irish votes); by client (i.e., on the basis of the patronage and services big-city bosses could deliver to their precincts); and by issue (as in the fight over greenbacks and the gold standard producing fractionated parties by 1896) (Piven and Cloward).

And if I had even more time, I would move to what I see happening to politics with the coming of mechanically and electrically reproduced sounds and images—the politics of posters, photography, radio, film, television, and the early days of the computer. The electoral and the governing processes now could be brought into the community and even the home in the forms of radio news and actualities; the radiocasts of Franklin Roosevelt, Huey Long, and Father Coughlin; larger-than-life newsreels and film documentaries; live television reports, white papers, and other forms of reality TV; and all of the other trappings of specular politics (Gronbeck, "Presidency," "Rhetoric," "Electric").

And then, with even more time, I would talk about the development of one more electronic marvel within the political system: the public opinion poll. Developing from the salons of Paris in the eighteenth century and growing into a multibillion-dollar industry in our time, public opinion polling has produced what Susan Herbst calls "numbered voices"—scaled, quantified, rationalized, and publicized political requests and judgments sculpted by statisticians and then probed by political staffers for their mandates. Philip Davies and I were part of a team examining the numbered voices featured in the *New York Times* and the *Washington Post* during the last two weeks of Campaign 2000 (Alsina, Davies, and

Gronbeck). We found a staggering total of 270 stories built around polls over those fourteen days of campaign news, with only about forty percent of them dealing with particular issues. The rest dealt with the horserace (who's ahead and who's behind), the militarylike strategies of the candidates, and the theatrical performances crafted by candidates in the *denouement* of the campaign drama.

Were I, then, to have talked about nineteenth-century citizen mobilization, twentieth-century politics in the age of mechanical and electrical reproduction of images, and citizen voices that spout not ideas but percentages, I would have had perhaps a fitting end to my story of modernist politics. In the final pages of that story, the political actors become disembodied, producing what Parry-Giles and Parry-Giles recently analyzed as hyperreal, imagaic, postmodern politics. As Sidney Blumenthal depicts "the permanent campaign," the scramble for voter allegiance heightens the need to publicly exhibit governors in pictures and postures attractive to their constituents.

As well, those final pages would have to have talked about nineteenth-century tribalism, clientism, and issue-centered loyalties, all of which forced the literal mobilization of the body politic—a body giving way, however, to a blended sense of publicness. Yes, throughout the twentieth century, we continued to organize citizens into ideological parties, as with the Roosevelt Democrats and the Reagan Democrats, and into the sprawling issue-oriented movements and political action committees that we came to love and loathe in the 1960s and 1970s. Yet, even as some beat the drum to organize peoples' marches, actual political activity in the executive and legislative halls seemed more influenced by the numbered voices of the printout than the bull-horned voices of the streets. On many days, it seems as though a favorable poll would produce more response than a sit-in would. On many days, the voice and the body politic mattered only in quantified form.

In our time, the last page of the story would announce that the modernist political machine is videocasting governors who are in dialogue with statistically sampled and segmented citizens. The voices of both governors and the governed are electronically modulated. But then, that perhaps is at it should be in the last days of the late-modernist model of democracy, when the economic sphere has become so much a part of the political sphere that the stakes are too high for the system to care much for the social sphere. And thus public relations-driven political communicators, even the great ones such as Ronald Reagan or Bill Clinton, meet a stratified sample of the citizenry, with its ±3.5 percent of error. They do lunch, then the governors return to dinner with Fortune 500 CEOs, and the governed return home Wednesday nights to watch NBC's liberal romance, *The West Wing*.

CYBORG CITIZEN

Chris Hables Gray's recent book, *Cyborg Citizen*, devotes a chapter to "Cybocracy, Mobocracy, and Democracy." In that chapter, Gray notes that the printing press is credited with jumpstarting not only the Reformation but movements toward democratic, grassroots politics. Similarly, both Marshall McLuhan and, more recently, Robert Logan have argued that political awareness and rejuvenation were among the activities characteristic of the life created in the Global Village. And, wonders Gray, is it true "that computer technology might have the same cascade effects on politics" (41)?

To open that question, consider first the penetration of the Internet into American homes:

- As of September 2001, 143 million Americans—about fifty-four percent of the population—were using the Internet, with new users being added at a rate of more than 2 million per month (US DOC).
- Even among disadvantaged populations, Internet use has been increasing recently: twenty-five percent annual growth in the lowest-income households, thirty-three percent and thirty percent annual growth rates among African Americans and Hispanics, respectively, and twenty-four percent annual growth rate for rural citizens, fifty-three percent of whom now are wired, equaling the population in general (*ibid.*).
- Forty-five percent of the population uses e-mail, and a third of the American populace searches for product and service information (*ibid.*). The other primary uses of the Web include general browsing, finding entertainment information, and reading news (Cole).
- More intriguingly, 72.3 percent of Americans—almost three-quarters—went online somewhere in 2001, averaging 9.8 hours per week. Further, 44.4 percent of those who were not connected to the Internet before expect to go online in 2002 (Cole).

And, to take this search for quantified citizenry one step farther, such surveys tell us even more about political uses of the Internet, power, and the potentials for political persuasion:

- Almost half (45.1%) of the Americans using the Internet agree that "by using the Internet people like you can better understand politics" (Cole 82).
- A quarter (25.6%) believe that "by using the Internet people like you can have more political power," whereas a fifth (20.9%) assume that "by using the Internet people like you will have more say about what the government does" (*ibid.*).
- In March 2000—during the primary and caucus period of Campaign 2000—over a third (35%) of Internet users surveyed had used the Net to find information about politics, and that percentage rose about almost half (46%) for so-called "veteran enthusiast" users (Horrigan).
- In late 2000—and remember the post-Campaign 2000 debacle—seventeen percent of Internet users got political news online, about doubling the usual percentage, which supports the conclusion that heightened political interest can exert pressure on citizens to use their computers for political information gathering (More Online).2

- Yet, from focus group research, many believe that there is a significant gap between the information that Web audiences want and what is being supplied by congressional office, committee, and leadership sites (Congress Online), which suggests that citizens are driven elsewhere for political information.

That last point, of course, is the intriguing one. More and more people are spending more and more time on the World Wide Web—so much so, as a matter of fact, that for the first time ever the amount of time the television set is on in the average American home per week is actually dropping. Maybe that is because moms with kids under eighteen are averaging almost seventeen hours per week online—which is about five hours a week more than teenagers average ("Moms"). Yet, the focus group research suggests citizens are not gaining the information they want from the representatives of the state. They're going elsewhere, but where are those elsewheres?

That is something we don't know for sure. As I said, the search for political news in particular picked up sharply near the end of Campaign 2000, but why? A survey done during that election (*Youth Vote* 1) suggested that politically interested Web users were looking for convenient information, more information than they found in other media, information not available in other media, and news sources that "reflect personal interests." The next question, of course, is where are they going for more and convenient political information—especially information that reflects so-called "personal interests"? We don't know.

In my studies of political Web sites during the last two presidential elections (Gronbeck, *Politicking 1997*, *Politicking 2000*), I noted that Yahoo! found about 1,000 political Web sites during Campaign 1996, but some 25,000 during Campaign 2000. I sorted them into such categories as those mounted by political parties and campaigners, political activist groups that fall into both major and fringe categories, political news services, professionals selling their campaign services, e-democracy or what sometimes are called "good government" groups, and sites featuring political humor, especially satire. The point I want to make here is that this array of Web sites presents a variegated spectrum of political information and commitments.

The array allows one to get political news from CNN.com, the Republican or Democratic spin on CNN's stories, not only the NRA or ACLU view on gun control but also that of the White Supremists and the Christian Action Network. And if the National Gay and Lesbian Task Force has an opinion on that issue, you can bet it is on their Web site—and, of course, given the handgun-related violence against non-straights, you can bet that they do. Thus, we have increasing numbers and more varied groups of citizens spending more time each election looking for political information—and I suspect frames for assessing political issues—on the Internet.

Now, given that we live in Putnam's era of *Bowling Alone* and his concern about the near-complete disintegration of social structures in the United States, the vision of a public finding connections with each other via e-mail, listservs, chat rooms and bulletin boards, MOOs, and ever-more sophisticated computer-mediated interfaces might provide comfort on two grounds. For one thing, the citizens online are, as a matter of fact, seeking affiliation, perhaps personal and social identity, and, probably useful—what consultants call *actionable*—information. If the citizenry is electronically looking especially for politically relevant data and frames for those data, then it is engaged in a patently political activity in collectivist ways. This is important. For too long, we have taken a prototypically modernist-scientistic position that political activity should be defined in strictly behavioral terms, and hence have focused almost exclusively on the number of bodies voting and showing up at public forums or protests. Surfing the Net with politics and politicalization on one's mind assuredly must be counted as a kind of political activity—and it is sharply on the rise.

Second, not only is political information seeking a sign of health in the American *polis,* but it's also a sign of citizen independence. The Internet is an essentially unregulated discursive space—a place for free speech—and it's chaotic enough to make an effort at control it almost impossible. That is why futurists argue that "this new electronic communication will shift power from elites to the common people" (Davis 37). In this view, not only is the Web freeing, liberal in a political sense, but it also provides new avenues through which a citizenry can identify and call attention to its self-interested political agenda.

The Internet's very strengths as a political medium and as a site for politics itself, however, also could to be its greatest weaknesses:

- *It allows for ultratargeting* (Selnow 191). If you're interested in abortion as a political issue, there are numerous sites where you can gather information about abortion-related legislative and bureaucratic activity, platforms of political candidates, news on fundraisers and other rallies, and e-mail lists of politicians you should be contacting. With no trouble at all, you can make abortion your issue, your political litmus test, especially if you use the computer service called NewsTracker to scan Web periodicals devoted to your interests. The kind of ultratargeting possible on the Internet may even diminish a citizen's political capacity. Why?

- *Ultratargeting can drive other issues out of the electoral decision-making process.* If abortion becomes a litmus test, then as a voter I'm not likely to care much about candidates' stands on the environment or Social Security or foreign aid to Israel.

- *And then, the electorate is fragmented in a potentially damaging way.* Now, of course, there's nothing wrong inside a two-party country such as the United States with breaking the ideological hold on issues by those parties. But once the parties' backs are broken—and every presidential election since 1988 has seen less than half of the actual voters registered as party members—then the question of political vision and coherence is raised more urgently. As David Broncoccio of Public Radio International's Marketplace program has noted, "the Web's capacity to winnow down exposure to a limited range of stories can be dangerous to a population that needs common references" (paraphrased in Selnow 194). The potentially most serious damage of Internet politics is what a decade ago Arthur Schlesinger, Jr. called "the disuniting of America." Can you run a country of some 300 million souls with a radically fragmented citizenry—people who can use the computer's hyperlinking capabilities to run away from centers of power, action, and coherent policy to more and more esoteric locations?

The digital revolution, therefore, is for now to be neither celebrated nor feared by the student of rhetorical democracy—only watched very, very carefully. With a view to civic engagement, the World Wide Web can amplify the *vox populi* even literally, thanks to all of the dot-gov sites to which you can address e-mail and to all of the political action sites that will speak to the hubs of power for you. It also breaks the straps of time and place that restrain the body politic. Political institutions check their e-mails, more or less, on a daily basis, no matter whether it's electing time or time for hearings, and of course citizens are no longer geographically limited in their contacts with like-minded others. New spaces for both political action and political identity are created, spaces with beautiful electronic landscapes, without the fences of cultural boundaries and the shackles of repressive governments (pace Morley and Robins).

SO WHAT'S A RHETORICIAN TO DO?

Before I conclude, I really should engage in direct address to this audience. What are we to make of a rhetorical democracy that's powered by Intel and shepherded by Microsoft, Inc.?

Now, of course, it's obvious that we should be looking at more than single speeches. Don't get me wrong: I love to analyze speeches, I still teach speeches from Kennedy to Bush in my contemporary political rhetoric class, and I even publish books and book chapters analyzing political speeches. My official University of Iowa title includes the phrase "Professor of Public Address," and in fact I profess "public address" in quite a traditional way.

But I also do more. I analyze filmed and video political materials, teach a seminar on twentieth-century visual politics in the United States, and try to write rhetorically about the multimediated discourses—that is, discourses whose messages tend to develop not within but across the verbal, the visual, and the acoustic codes of film and television. Most of us were trained to shred a literate-verbal work. To be maximally useful to our students, to outfit them for the communication environment of our time, we'd better be training them to shred multimediated work with equal expertise, because nobody else is.

This brings me to what I find as special challenges of computer-mediated, especially hypertextual, communication. What ought we to be doing to Internet-based communication, especially political communication? We face some very special challenges here:

- First, many Web messages are both oral and literate in tone and form, sometimes chatty, at other times formal, and they can—but need not—rely on visual technologies for controlling meaning-making by the way they're laid out. A political group such as the Women for Aryan Unity offers a series of straightforward position papers on relevant topics; such a Web site is amenable to traditional rhetorical analysis. But an attack website from Campaign 2000 such as "Skeleton Closet—Al Gore, the Dark Side" needs an Adobe Acrobat Reader to access, and is complicated enough to let you select your preferred issues for skewering him: his wife, his stand on tobacco, his contributors, his votes on environmental issues, and of course everyone's favorite—the claim that he invented the Internet. Varied sites require varied analytical schemata and semiotic interests.

- Weblogs—also called just plain blogs—are excellent sites of rhetorical-political research. Blogs have been around since 1997 (Weblogs). They're individuals' personalized collections of Web sites on a topic of interest to those people, often updated daily in diary form. By now, there are e-journals that enumerate them, and one can even subscribe to them. There are journalists with weblog beats ("News"). Blogs allow people to keep up with the latest Web-based developments in areas of their interests, led by a favorite blogger. They are ripe for rhetorical analysis for the kinds of information winnowed in and winnowed out, the rhetorical persona of the blogger, and their ideological framing.
- Similarly, we must find ways as rhetoricians to study the political search processes in which individuals engage. Only then will we be able to understand the heart of the political messages coming to citizens.

That last point is particularly important for students of rhetoric, I think. Consider this: The hyperlinking function of computers allows its users—you and me and those mothers with kids under eighteen—to build their own messages. Herein lies a rhetorical enigma: the authors of those messages and the audiences of those messages are the same people. The rhetors and the auditors are one. How, then, are we to understand rhetorical process? Who is building what for whom? Who is persuading whom and why? Are there processes of identity formation and confirmation at work when people go trolling on the Internet, looking for political information that tells them they're okay in how they think and act in the world? In other words, not only are the rhetoricians' critical objects in the political arena changing, but so are the questions we should be asking. Civic engagement, I would argue, is as much a matter of understanding the building and maintenance of political identity (i.e., questions about polity) as it is about getting legislation passed (i.e., questions about policy). Nowhere is that more clear than in politically interested listservs and chat rooms, where citizens peddle their politics and form both individual and collective political identities.

BETWEEN YESTERDAY AND TOMORROW

Toffler was right. We are living between yesterday and tomorrow, in the case of Americans, between what during yesterday was the world's most expensive political machine—and I fear it will be that way even in 2003, when campaign reforms go into effect—and what tomorrow will be the world's most advanced political communication system that people will continue to use more often and with more effect. The next, some call it postmodernist, political revolution is here. Yesterday's pundits are racing to see if they can manage working in tomorrow's inventible political environment. And you are standing here, watching the show and trying to figure out whether it's worth rethinking some of your scholarly skills and apparatuses in order to capture that environment in interpretively and theoretically significant ways.

Civic engagement in a rhetorical democracy ultimately depends on an empowered public comprised of flute makers, legitmatizers of political forms and policies, and rhetors willing to demand of their leaders all of the virtues that Cicero catalogued and all of the wise policy that Edmund Burke assumed legislators could formulate. How a public does those things is what we as rhetoricians ought to be studying. To do that, Gerard Hauser asserts, "To learn what a public thinks, we first must monitor the social conversation within a reticulate public sphere to ascertain who is speaking to whom about what. [...] Their rhetorical exchanges provide more than data; their narratives of common meaning, web of associations, and historicity each reveal the reference world of meaning they are coconstructing and provide the context for understanding their specific judgments" (279).

I could not better set your charge for tomorrow myself. I wish you exciting and productive conversations about rhetorical democracy and civic engagement.

NOTES

1. The Levellers in the debate wanted the franchise distributed in all cities, counties, and boroughs according to the number of inhabitants in each, although not everyone living in an area would be defined as "inhabitant." Almost everyone in the debate started from the supposition that having an "interest"—in terms of an estate consisting of taxable property—was a demand of citizenship. The few who would deny that supposition were ignored.
2. Another Pew Institute survey (Youth Vote) points to a serious jump in political use of the Internet during presidential elections. Four percent of the public said it went online for political news during the 1996 campaign, with that percentage jumping to eighteen percent in 2000. (Among regular online users, those numbers were twenty-two percent and thirty-three percent, respectively.) For those going online for election news, fifty-six percent said the information is more convenient; twenty-nine percent, too little news on other media; twelve percent, information not available elsewhere can be found on the Net; and six percent, they could find news reflecting their "personal interests."

WORKS CITED

Alsina, Cristina, Philip H. Davies, and Bruce E. Gronbeck. "Preference Poll Stories in the Last 2 Weeks of Campaign 2000." *American Behavioral Scientist* 44 (2001): 2288-2305.

Aristotle. *The Politics*. Trans. Carnes Lord. Chicago: U of Chicago P, 1984.

Blumenthal, Sidney. *The Permanent Campaign: Inside the World of Elite Political Operatives.* Boston: Beacon, 1980.

Burke, Edmund. *From the Speech to the Sheriffs of Bristol, 3 November 1774*. 22 May 2002 <http://www.conservativeforum.org/quotelist.asp>.

Burke, Kenneth. *The Philosophy of Literary Form: Studies in Symbolic Action*. 1941. Berkeley: U of California P, 1973.

Cicero (1938). *De officiis*. Trans. Walter Miller. Cambridge, MA: Harvard UP, 1938.

Cole, Jeffrey I. *Surveying the Digital Future: Year Two.* The UCLA Internet Report. Los Angeles: UCLA, 2001.

Congress Online: Assessing and Improving Capitol Hill Web Sites. Washington, DC: Congress Online Project of the Congressional Management Foundation, 2002. 22 May 2002 <http://www.congressonline.org/publications.html>.

Davis, Richard. *The Web of Politics: The Internet's Impact on the American Political System.* New York: Oxford UP, 1999.

Emery, Jack, ed. *The Putney Debates.* Cambridge, UK: Rampart Lions, 1983.

Gray, Chris Hables. *Cyborg Citizen: Politics in the Posthuman Age.* New York: Routledge, 2002.

Gronbeck, Bruce E. "Electric Rhetoric: The Changing Forms of American Political Discourse." *Vichiana,* 3rd series, vol. 1. Napoli: Loffredo Editore, 1990. 141-61.

---. *Politicking on the Information Superhighway* [sample websites from Campaign 1996 w/ accompanying paper]. 15 April 1997 <http://www.uiowa.edu/~commstud/faculty/Gronbeck>.

---. *Politicking on the Information Superhighway* [sample websites from Campaign 2000]. 20 October 2000 <http://www.uiowa.edu/~commstud/faculty/Gronbeck>.

---. "The Presidency in the Age of Secondary Orality." *Beyond the Rhetorical Presidency.* Ed. Martin J. Medhurst. College Station: Texas A&M UP, 1996. 30-49.

---. "Rhetoric, Ethics, and Telespectacle in the Post-Everything Age." *Postmodern Representations: Truth, Power, and Mimesis in the Human Sciences and Public Culture.* Ed. Richard Harvey Brown. Chicago: U of Chicago P, 1995. 216-38.

---. "Symbolic Dimensions of Parliamentary Procedure in the Late 18th Century English Commons." *Parliamentary Journal* 23 (1982): 42-55.

Habermas, Jürgen. *The Structural Transformation of the Public Sphere.* Trans. Thomas McCarthy. Cambridge: MIT P, 1989.

Hauser, Gerard A. *Vernacular Voices: The Rhetoric of Publics and Public Spheres.* Columbia: U of South Carolina P, 1999.

Herbst, Susan. *Numbered Voices: How Opinion Polling Has Shaped American Politics.* Chicago: U of Chicago P, 1993.

Hobbes, Thomas. *Leviathan.* 1610. Ed. J. A. C. Gaskin. New York: Oxford UP, 1996.

Horrigan, John B. *New Internet Users: What They Do Online, What They Don't, and Implications for the Net's Future.* Washington, DC: Pew Internet and American Life Project, 2000. 22 May 2002 <http://www.pewinternet.org>.

Jowett, Benjamin, ed. *The Works of Plato.* New York: Tudor Publishing, n.d.

Locke, John. *The Second Treatise on Civil Government and A Letter Concerning Toleration.* 1690. Ed. J. W. Gaugh. Oxford, UK: Blackwell, 1948.

Lofland, John. *State Executions, Viewed Historically and Sociologically.* Montclair, NJ: Patterson Smith, 1977.

Logan, Robert K. *The Sixth Language: Learning a Living in the Internet Age.* Toronto: Stoddart, 2000.

McLuhan, Marshall. *Understanding Media: The Extensions of Man.* New York: McGraw, 1964.

"Moms Spend More Time Online Than Their Kids." *Iowa City Press-Citizen* 14 May 2002: 7A.

More Online, Doing More. Washington, DC: Pew Internet & American Life Project, 2001. 22 May 2002 <http://www.pewinternet.org>.

Morley, David, and Kevin Robins. *Spaces of Identity: Global Media, Electronic Landscapes, and Cultural Boundaries.* New York: Routledge, 1995.

"News by the People, for the People." *USC Annenberg Online Journalism Review.* 20 May 2002 <http://www.ojr.org/ojr/future/1021586109.php>.

Palonen, Kari. "Introduction: From Policy to Polity to Politicking and Politicalization." *Reading the Political: Exploring the Margins of Politics.* Ed. Kari Palonen and Tuija Parvikko. Tampere, Finland: Tammer-Paino Oy, 1993. 6-16.

Parry-Giles, Shawn. J., and Trevor Parry-Giles. *Constructing Clinton: Hyperreality & Presidential Image-Making in Postmodern Politics.* New York: Lang, 2002.

Piven, F. F., and R. A. Cloward. *Why Americans Still Don't Vote: And Why Politicians Want It That Way.* Rev. ed. Boston: Beacon, 2000.

Machiavelli, Niccolo. *The Prince.* 1505/1515. The Constitution Society [website]. 22 May 2002 <http://www.constitution.org/mac/prince00.htm>.

Putnam, Robert D. *Bowling Alone: The Collapse and Revival of American Community.* New York: Simon, 2000.

Rimmerman, Craig A. *The New Citizenship: Unconventional Politics, Activism, and Service.* 2nd ed. Boulder, CO: Westview, 2001.

Schlesinger, Arthur M., Jr. *The Disuniting of America: Reflections on a Multicultural Society.* 1991. rpt. New York: Norton, 1993.

Selnow, Gary W. *Electronic Whistle-Stops: The Impact of the Internet on American Politics.* Westport, CT: Praeger, 1998.

Toffler, Alvin. "Shocks, Waves and Power in the Digital Age." *Masters of the Wired World.* Ed. Anne Leer. San Francisco: Financial Times Management, 1999. 22-30.

US DOC [United States Department of Commerce]. *A Nation Online: How Americans are Expanding Their Use of the Internet* [census data report]. Feb. 2001 <http://www.esa.doc.gov/508/esa/USEconomy.htm>.

Weblogs [a website defining weblogs or "blogs"]. 22 May 2002 <http://www.rebeccablood.net/essays/weblog_history.html>.

Youth Vote Influenced by Online Information. Washington, DC: Pew Internet & American Life Project. 3 Dec. 2000 <http://www.people-press.org>.

3

Identification and Resistance: Women's Civic Discourse Across the Color Line

Shirley Wilson Logan
University of Maryland

At the first RSA Conference organized by Charles Kneupper, Lloyd Bitzer concluded in his keynote address, "George Orwell's Rejection of Tyrannical Rhetoric," that Orwell conceived a rhetoric of resistance to tyranny. This rhetoric would work against oppressive forces arising from control, power, and will, in the absence of true wisdom (Bitzer 6). I consider here some of the discursive responses of African American women to their own racist and sexist oppression as they spoke across the color line. The title of this chapter, "Women's Civic Discourse across the Color Line," was meant to signal an exchange. I did not mark the category "black" women, since my goal was to consider primarily nineteenth- and early twentieth-century bidirectional discursive practices—white women addressing black audiences, black women addressing white audiences—with the hope of uncovering instructive differences and commonalities. It turns out that I have had no trouble finding texts to fit the latter category but few to fit the former. This absence makes sense for any number of reasons, but primarily because the exigence of needing to resist the tyranny of power with respect to race and the burden of proof lay heavily with black women. Furthermore, black women, attempting to reach various publics, placed themselves in what Frances Beale called in 1970 a "double jeopardy" in their representations of racial and sexual oppression. Marsha Houston, who credits Beale with this expression, adds that if one includes other forms of class oppression, this can even be refigured as a multiple jeopardy (Houston 48). Thus, this chapter focuses instead on unidirectional discourse across the color line—black women speaking and writing to predominantly white audiences. Analyzing the tactics they employ, I offer here some features of a resistive rhetoric appropriate for the twenty-first century.

> The problem of the twentieth century is the problem of the color-line,—the relation of the darker to the lighter races of men in Asia and Africa, in America and the islands of the sea. It was a phase of this problem that caused the Civil War; and

> however much they who marched South and North in 1861 may have fixed on the technical points of union and local autonomy as a shibboleth, all nevertheless knew, as we know, that the question of Negro slavery was the real cause of the conflict. (Du Bois 54-55)

This, of course, is from W.E.B Du Bois's *Souls of Black Folk*, published almost 100 years ago, in 1903. I chose this passage because it seems to characterize the tenor of much contemporary discourse based on difference. The color-line problem, as an element of difference, is one about which we hear or say too little. I invoke Du Bois in an essay about black women's public discourse, realizing, at the same time, that he did not consistently support or recognize their participation in public spaces. Joy James has labeled him a "profeminist," in that although he was antisexist he also presented a paradigm of male dominance. James notes that much of his work projects a "selective memory of the agency of his contemporaries" (142). For example, he was on occasion dismissive of the public discourse of Anna Cooper and Ida Wells Barnett, failing to acknowledge their turn-of-the-century political contributions. Thus, one could say that Du Bois supported the emancipation of women—by men. Traces of this perspective linger even in his well-known 1920 profeminist essay "The Damnation of Women."[1] Still, Du Bois was a major voice for women's equality.

Kenneth Burke's theory that we constitute ourselves through various ways of being in the world and that we share those ways or substances with different people in different ways, consubstantially, provides a way to frame the rhetorical tactics of these women. He claims that we cannot understand the act of identification without division, alienation, or dissociation, deriving from our separate physical bodies, our individual loci of motives, and, I would add, our unique experiences of being. We use rhetoric, he asserts, to bridge those divisions.

Delindus Brown and Wanda Anderson interpreted black women's rhetorical strategies of identification and resistance historically under the rubric of a "sequential theory of persuasion" (234). In their 1978 *Journal of Black Studies* article "A Survey of the Black Woman and the Persuasion Process: The Study of Strategies of Identification and Resistance," they argue that, for black women, resistance and identification were equal components of this sequential persuasion. Brown and Anderson distinguish two kinds identification, conscious and unconscious. With unconscious identification, the individual communicates acceptance in unintentional behavior; with conscious identification, the individual makes an intentional effort to relate to a set of physical or verbal conditions, "to identify her ways with the ways of her public audience" (239). Brown and Anderson define resistance as a subsequent conscious rejection of the "persuasive appeals of the perceived enemy" (243). Starting with Phillis Wheatley and enslaved plantation women of the eighteenth century and ending with the words and acts of politicians Barbara Jordan and Cordiss Collins, the authors focus as much on these women's physical acts of resistance and identification as on the women's discursive claims. They call attention to various conscious and unconscious manifestations of identification and resistance, both discursive and physical, on the part of the women themselves, rather than an identification invoked in the audience solely though language. Nonetheless, this article suggested an organizing principle for my own chapter.

My central claim is that effective discourse across the color line or the line of difference must always engage in both identification and resistance. There must be an acknowledgment of difference concurrent with identification—an embracing and a pulling back. Now, we often talk about the embrace, the need to recognize what we all share in common, those points of intersection that to some extent make communication possible. But I want to argue that just as important is the act of resistance, not so much a general resistance to the endeavor as a resistance to erasure or assimilation. We speak and write much about establishing communion with our various audiences as we reason about values. Chaim Perelman and Lucie Olbrechts-Tyteca, believing agreement to be the starting point of argumentation, list various figures of communion to include allusion, quotation, and the participatory figures apostrophe and oratorical questions. But they also write of dissociative acts of separation, of ways to disconnect, decouple, divide, and break associations between elements that, in the rhetor's view, have been inappropriately linked. These are forms of rhetorical resistance, ways of asserting difference.

In her 1977 MLA talk, from which I'll quote more later, Audre Lorde speaks eloquently about the importance of accepting of this kind of resistance to erasure and about accepting difference, when she asserts that "it is not difference which immobilizes us, but silence" (305). We must also not be afraid to embrace individual difference, recognizing the need for freedom from intragroup essentializing, freedom for individuals to enact their uniqueness, their separateness, from any category into which they have been placed or into which they choose to place themselves. We need to speak our differences, all of our differences without fear of chastisement or group regulation. Thus, as relates to this essay, identification and resistance should take place intraracially and interracially. Even Cicero, in 63 BCE, said that "our character is not so much the product of race and heredity as of those circumstances by which nature forms our habits, by which we are nourished and live" (qtd in Southgate 54-55).

Furthermore, language is never neutral, and hence when we speak of categories of identity and categories of difference we should remember the extent to which such categories come to us always and already fixed. Judith Butler describes these "prediscursive structures" and the harm they do when we conceive of language as an "exterior medium or instrument" of categorization. This process of categorization "conceals its own workings" (173-76). Thus, even as we use these terms—*black, white, people of color*—we want to complicate them, for, in Burkean fashion, we share different substances with different people.

In what follows, I consider texts by nineteenth- and twentieth-century black women in which they make these two important moves, one toward identification and another toward resistance, and then suggest that this pattern over time offers up possibilities for effective discourse around and across the twenty-first-century color line. The women are Phillis Wheatley, Sojourner Truth, Frances Harper, Victoria Matthews, Mary Church Terrell, Esther Haith, Shirley Chisholm, Barbara Jordan, and Audre Lorde.

One can hear early refrains of identification and resistance in these lines from Phillis Wheatley's 1773 poem "On Being Brought from Africa to America":

> Twas mercy brought me from my Pagan land,
> Taught my benighted soul to understand
> That there's a God, that there's a Savior too:
> Once I redemption neither sought nor knew.
> Some view our sable race with scornful eye,
> "Their colour is a diabolic die."
> Remember, *Christians*, *Negroes*, black as *Cain*,
> May be refin'd, and join th'angelic train. (41, emphasis in original)

As Brown and Anderson point out and as these lines reveal, Wheatley engages in unconscious identification with her environment through acceptance of its religious teachings and adherence to its standards. But although her behavior implies identification, her words also imply resistance to a certain denied equality: Even as she embraces Christianity, she does so with the assertion that this conversion offers proof of black humanity and entitlement to redemption: "Remember, Christians, Negroes, black as Cain,/May be refin'd, and join th'angelic train."

Speaking at the first annual meeting of the American Equal Rights Association in 1867, Sojourner Truth pointed out that "There's a great stir about colored men getting their rights, but not a word about the colored women; and if colored men get their rights, and not colored women get theirs, you see the colored men will be masters over the women, and it will be just as bad as it was before" (28). Now, Sojourner Truth fairly consistently aligned herself with woman's rights. We can think of this tactic as her way of juggling a value hierarchy in which she ranked her rights as a woman as having more urgency than her rights as a black person. She engaged in a breaking of the connection that traditionally submerged black women under the category of black men, who in turn were supposed to represent the race. Truth resisted this association and reidentified herself primarily as a woman. Here, then, the move was from resistance to identification, creating a nontraditional alliance.

Over one hundred years later, Shirley Chisholm would employ this same tactic in her May 21, 1969 address to the United States House of Representatives, "Equal Rights for Women." Chisholm also proceeds in the opposite order, reminding her auditors first of her difference, then moving to identification:

> It has been observed before that society for a long time, discriminated against another minority, the blacks, on the same basis—that they were different and inferior. The happy little homemaker and the contented "old darkey" on the plantation were both produced by prejudice. As a black person, I am no stranger to race prejudice. But the truth is that in the political world I have been far oftener discriminated against because I am a woman than because I am black. (pars. 4 & 5)

Claiming common origins for the oppression of women and blacks ("the happy little homemaker and the contented 'old darkey'"), Chisholm works in this passage to improve political relationships among elected officials with diverging interests.

With Frances Harper, resistance and identification occur differently. Speaking at the Eleventh National Woman's Rights Convention, she first identifies with the interests of her audience, an audience that included Elizabeth Cady Stanton and Susan B. Anthony: "We are all bound up together in one great bundle of humanity, and society cannot trample on the weakest and feeblest of its members without receiving the curse in its own soul. You tried that in the case of the negro" (217).

Later, in the same speech, she asserts resistance:

> I do not believe that giving the woman the ballot is immediately going to cure all the ills of life. I do not believe that white women are dewdrops just exhaled from the skies. I think that like men they maybe divided into three classes, the good, the bad, and the indifferent. The good would vote according to their convictions and principles; the bad, as dictated by preju[d]ice or malice; and the indifferent will vote on the strongest side of the question, with the winning party. (218)

Throughout her life, Harper associated with various white women's organizations, including the Women's Christian Temperance Union, the American Woman's Suffrage Association, and the Universal Peace Union, but she rarely missed an opportunity to remind their members of the differences as well as the similarities between their interests and those of black women.

At the 1897 Annual Convention of the Society of Christian Endeavor, Victoria Matthews identified with the audience of white women on the common ground of social feminism in her address, "The Awakening of the Afro-American Woman." Karlyn Kohrs Campbell explains that by accepting traditional roles for women while arguing that their "distinctive influence should be extended to areas outside the home," social feminism provided a way for women to enter the public sphere without challenging masculine authority (121). Matthews also called on the women to identify with her through their common "Christian womanhood": "As I stand here to-day *clothed in the garments of Christian womanhood*, the horrible days of slavery, out of which I came, seem as a dream that is told, some horror incredible. Indeed, could they have been, and are not? They were; they are not; this is the sum and substance, the shame and the glory of the tale that I would tell, of the message that I would bring" (150; emphasis added).

This was a rhetorical situation often repeated in post-bellum America—black women speaking to white women about black women—and it elicited "distinctive and recurring patterns of rhetorical practice," a definition offered by Herbert Simons, to account for what happens when a speaker fills certain generic slots with his or her particular cause or special interest, while remaining within a predictable frame (50). Thus, "The Awakening" assumed features of previous responses designed to highlight what black women had accomplished since Emancipation. Matthews also invokes the common Christianity that Phillis Wheatley invoked, reminding her auditors, in the midst of this strong identification, of her difference, her need to resist.

In "The Progress of Colored Women," an 1898 address before the National American Woman's Suffrage Association, Mary Church Terrell invokes history as a source of identification and resistance, as did Barbara Jordan at the 1976 Democratic Convention almost eighty years later. Terrell reminds her auditors that:

> Fifty years ago a meeting such as this, planned, conducted and addressed by women would have been an impossibility. Less than forty years ago, few sane men would have predicted that either a slave or one of his descendants would in this

century at least address such an audience in the Nation's Capital at the invitation of women representing the highest broadest, best type of womanhood, that can be found anywhere in the world. Thus to me this semi-centennial of the National American Woman Suffrage Association is a double jubilee, rejoicing as I do, not only in the prospective enfranchisement of my sex but in the emancipation of my race. (pars. 1 & 2)

In Jordan's address "Who Then Will Speak for the Common Good?" *common* signals identification as the central claim, but there is a subtext of resistance as she too recalls history:

> But there is something different about tonight. There is something special about tonight. What is different? What is Special? I, Barbara Jordan, am a keynote speaker. A lot of years passed since 1832 [when the Democratic Party first met in convention to select a Presidential candidate], and during that time it would have been most unusual for any national political party to ask that a Barbara Jordan deliver a keynote address [...] but tonight here I am. (pars. 2 & 3)

As Linda Horowitz points out in her dissertation "Transforming Appearances into Rhetorical Arguments," Jordan engages in both explicit and implicit enactment, allowing the auditors to understand that although her speech did not explicitly discuss racial issues, her very presence there as keynote speaker reflected an unstated enactment of difference (44-46). Even as she speaks for the "common good," her body enacts difference.

To return to Terrell's address, she later asserts further resistance and division:

> For, not only are colored women with ambition and aspiration handicapped on account of their sex, but they are everywhere baffled and mocked on account of their race. Desperately and continuously they are forced to fight that opposition, born of a cruel, unreasonable prejudice which neither their merit nor their necessity seems able to subdue. Not only because they are women, but because they are colored women, are discouragement and disappointment meeting them at every turn. (par. 4)

Barbara Jordan, in her 1974 "Opening Statement to the House Judiciary Committee Proceedings on the Impeachment of Richard Nixon," blended identification with resistance by first pointing to the contradiction in the Constitution's own appeal to identification:

> Earlier today we heard the beginning of the Preamble to the Constitution of the United States, "We, the people." It is a very eloquent beginning. But when that document was completed, on the seventeenth of September in 1787, I was not included in that "We, the people." I felt somehow for many years that George Washington and Alexander Hamilton just left me out by mistake. But through the process of amendment, interpretations, and court decision I have finally been included in "We, the people."
>
> Today, I am an inquisitor. I believe hyperbole would not be fictional and would not overstate the solemness that I feel right now. My faith in the Constitution is whole, it is complete, it is total. I am not going to sit here and be an idle spectator to the diminution, the subversion, the destruction of the Constitution. (qtd in Rogers 214)

Sequence is another important aspect of these rhetorical performances. Jordan, in both speeches, chooses to end with identification because her goal was ultimately to create goodwill and to talk of a "common good" transcending individual difference. Terrell, however, projects ambivalence about this identification, reminding her auditors, even at the close of her speech, that still there remained the critical difference of race: "Seeking no favors because of our color, nor patronage because of our needs, we knock at the bar of justice, asking an equal chance" (par. 24). Whether the rhetor ends with resistance or identification depends on what she hoped the address would accomplish. Thus, Truth, Chisholm, and Jordan, in the texts considered here, end with the embrace of identification; Wheatley, Harper, Terrell, and Matthews end on a note of difference.

Esther A. Haith maintains a balance between embrace and rejection in a series of two handwritten letters to President Woodrow Wilson's Secretary of State Robert Lansing. They illustrate how one black woman's resistive discourse challenged those in power to act against the tyranny of mob violence. The first letter was written November 18, 1918, a week after the Armistice that ended World War I and during a period in this country of increased lynchings and heightened racial tension.[2] Unlike the more prominent racial uplift women or the 1890s, Esther Haith, a resident of Flint, Michigan, was apparently an ordinary woman, who took it upon herself to speak truth to power across the color line. Haith opens her letter with words of congratulations to Lansing:[3]

> [a]fter reading how readily you interceded with President Wilson at the special request of the German Chancellor for peace negatations. And through you he heard the voice of our enemy, the enemy of the world, an enemy to the rights of its weaker subjects, enemy of all humanity, enemy to young womanhood and you did intercede and through you he heard the voice of a conquered sufferer, regardless of former depredations.
>
> I as an American Citizen and loyal subject pray you will intercede with the President for me and my people for the love of God do not allow without protest from him such lynching as was done on the 11th Nov. last, the day that democracy and peace reigned supreme (the law breakers take his silence as consent) out of pity for suffering humanity pleas grant to my people the right to be happy there is a lasting peace to prove that democracy is a reality and peace is no mockery, by declaring war against the Hun in the hearts of the American whites, especially those of the south land. Oh! how I have prayed and praying as I write this that you will not humiliate us any farther. By forcing our soldiers to ride in Jim Crow cars when he comes back home. When he pays first class fair. I am sure if you knew how some of the white trash take advantage of our enforced segregation from decent people and humiliating remarks and filthy advances they try to make to our girls and women you would certainly do something to remedy it.

The letter continues in this vein with Haith expressing the hope in a postscript that she would receive in reply "a declaration by the President of his opion of the mater to the Associated press" (Haith 11/18/18).

Alvey Adee, Second Assistant Secretary, replied to Haith that "so far as the jurisdiction of the Federal Government extends no discrimination is shown in the protection of, and administration of justice to, American citizens of the African race." In other words, such actions were state matters. In response to Adee, Haith wrote a second letter, pointing out that the reply was not what she had requested. She added, "It is a miracle that you even, the fourth man down could find time to answer though that answer was not satisfactory," and went on to point out that "the federal court is the place to take all the cases that the states don't seem to have made any laws to handle." She closed this second letter with another move toward identification: "I am yours truly Christian citizen loyal american for a better understanding between races, justice and equal sufferage," and signed it E.A.H. (Haith 2/28/19). Haith's ironic tone, the juxtaposing of the administration's accomplishments on the international scene with its lack of accomplishments with respect to a serious domestic crisis, as well as her request of a announcement to the Associated Press, reveal her astute understanding of the way power operates. Haith also enclosed a newspaper clipping describing the lynching she referred to in her first letter. Spelling errors suggest a lack of formal education, but syntax and content reveal rhetorical savvy and a clear understanding of the issues. Haith even offers them an excuse, suggesting that her first letter may not have solicited the desired response because it had been ill-timed and too emotional:

> It is possible impassioned as I was at the time I wrote before I may not have applied at the right time or quarters. While our government was receiving the congratulations of the world and being declared the deliverer of humanity and President Willson being put upon a pedistal that made eveny the Kaiser green with envy then have some one dash ice water even such a small drop as to remind him of his private huns in his own country. (2/28/19)

We have here a sophisticated example of controlled rage of the kind also evident in Ida Wells's well-known antilynching speeches. Esther Haith engaged resistance and identification skillfully as she argued for greater attention to mob violence.

Perhaps the speaker who has most effectively articulated the point I hope to make here is Audre Lorde in her 1977 MLA speech, "The Transformation of Silence into Language and Action," as well as in others in which she asserts the centrality of difference. In the 1977 speech, Lorde argues in the realm of Marsha Houston's "triple jeopardy," speaking as a woman, a lesbian, and an African American. In the following excerpt, she observes the futility of ignoring difference with its inherent resistance:

> I have come to believe over and over again that what is most important to me must be spoken, made verbal and shared, even at the risk of having it bruised or misunderstood. That the speaking profits me, beyond any other effect. [... W]hat I most regretted were my silences. Of what had I even been afraid? To question or to speak as I believed could have meant pain, or death. But we all hurt in so many different ways, all the time, and pain will either change or end. (302)

Absent from Lorde's rejection of identification and embrace of difference is bitterness. Lester Olson discusses this rejection and embrace in his article "Liabilities of Language: Audre Lorde Reclaiming Difference," pointing out that "Lorde uses a rhetorical technique of first promoting identification among women in opposition to patriarchy as a means of bringing those insights about relational practices to bear on analogous relations of domination among women across class, age, race, and sexuality" (454). For Lorde, acknowledgement of difference is ultimately a stronger way to build alliances than is the false assumption of sameness: "My silences had not protected me. Your silence will not protect you. But for every real word spoken, for every attempt I had ever made to speak those truths for which I am still seeking, I had made contact with other women while we examined the words to fit a world in which we all believed, bridging our difference" (302).

Of particular salience to scholars of rhetoric is Lorde's recognition of the limitations and possibilities inherent in language in forming alliances across difference:

> Each of us is here now because in one way or another we share a commitment to language and to the power of language, and to the reclaiming of that language which has been made to work against us. In the transformation of silence into language and action, it is vitally necessary for each one of us to establish or examine her function in that transformation and to recognize her role as vital with that transformation. (304)

A contemporary example of failure to engage difference comes from a participant's experience at the 1999 Feminism(s) and Rhetoric(s) Conference in Minneapolis. During the question-and-answer period following a plenary session with four black women scholars of rhetoric, one attendee stood and asked, "I hear a challenge from these women. How are we going to respond to this challenge?" The participant observes: "I understood her to mean that, by racializing rhetorical history and remarking on the lack of African-American female role models in the profession, these women were challenging the social relations and the politics of race in composition studies." She continues:

> Yet, there is something troubling about the audience member's question. By posing race as a "challenge," racial difference unwittingly becomes an object of (non)recognition, a difference that does not unsettle disciplinary assumptions and priorities, prompting compositionists to think differently about the construction of rhetorical history, as much as it warrants a response to a challenge. In its aggressiveness, and no doubt despite the questioner's intentions, this question displaces the actual work these scholars are doing in order to focus on the largely white audience's "response" to the challenge of difference. The question posed by a white woman seemed to function as a shaming strategy that identified her as an enlightened brave voice in a vast sea of voiceless, unenlightened white faces. Her question elicited a number of predictable, disappointing responses: praise, celebration, and gratitude for the work being done by the African-American scholars. Absent from this conversation, however, were rigorous engaged responses like those posed to Judith Butler during her plenary talk the previous day. [...] In short, blackness became an exotic difference as audience members complimented the panelists' work, but did not demonstrate an ability or willingness to recognize and respond to it as intellectual work. (Micciche 8-9)

I was one of those panelists, but not until I read Micciche's analysis of what took place did I understand the emptiness I felt as the session ended. It was the result of what was not said rather than what was. This is an example of the silence about which Audre Lorde wrote.

Especially in academic settings, we must explore the possibilities for an engaged communication that emerges, not just from acceptance of or tolerance for difference, but from actually privileging difference. We must understand that difference is not a quality possessed by others. Otherness and difference must be mutually perceived. It is not only the case that others are different from us but also that we are different from others—a reciprocal otherness.

A December 23, 2001 *New York Times Magazine* interview of Dr. Sima Samar is telling in this regard. Dr. Samar had just been appointed Afghanistan minister for women's affairs. Closing the exchange, the interviewer asked, "Is your model of a liberated Afghanistan a Western one?" Dr. Samar answers, "Why should everything be Westernized? Liberation is not just a Western idea. Everyone wants it" (15). Samar's response reminds us that otherness is reciprocal and that such concepts as liberation do not originate in Western culture.

Jacqueline Jones Royster argues the importance of reciprocal difference in her 1999 CCCC Chair's address when she asks, "What might happen if we treated differences in subject positions as critical pieces of the whole, vital to thorough understanding, and central to both problem-finding and problem-solving?" (34).[4]

There's no remarkable discovery here after all. Instead, there is a reminder or let me say a call, that we engage our differences—that an effective civic discourse across the color line, one that resists the tyranny exerted through power and control, the tyranny that Orwell (through Bitzer) decries, must first and foremost engage in meaningful not just superficial exchanges among rhetors who are not afraid to broach the difficult subjects, to speak truthfully, to enter what Mary Louise Pratt calls "the contact zones," to identify, and to resist.

I think Audre Lorde should have the last words: "The fact that we are here and that I speak these words is an attempt to break that silence and bridge some of those differences between us, for it is not difference which immobilizes us, but silence. And there are so many silences to be broken" (305).

NOTES

1. See W. E. B. Du Bois, *Darkwater: Voices from Within the Veil.* New York: Schocken, 1969.
2. Official records indicate that over 370,000 black soldiers fought in WWI, yet they returned home to a series of racial incidents. Sixty blacks were reported lynched in 1918. During the previous twelve months, race riots occurred in East St. Louis, Illinois; Chester, Pennsylvania; and Philadelphia. A race riot in Houston between black soldiers and white citizens resulted in thirteen soldiers being hanged for alleged participation. The twenty-six riots during the summer following Haith's letters led it to be dubbed the "Red Summer" of 1919. See Lerone Bennett, Jr. *Before the Mayflower: A History of Black America.* New York: Penguin, 1984.
3. Texts of Haith's letters are reproduced as in the originals.
4. For a recent and timely discussion of methods of resisting students' own resistance in the classroom, see Elizabeth Flynn's *Feminism beyond Modernism.* Carbondale: Southern Illinois UP, 2002. In a chapter titled "Employing Resistance in Postmodern-Feminist Teaching," Flynn describes activities designed to counter resistance to discussions of homosexuality, gender, and race.

WORKS CITED

Adee, Alvey. Letter to Esther Haith. 22 Nov. 1918. U.S. Record Group 59, Records of the Department of State. RG 59, File 811.4106, No. 13. College Park, MD: National Archives II.

Bitzer, Lloyd. "George Orwell's Rejection of Tyrannical Rhetoric." *Oldspeak/Newspeak: Rhetorical Transformations*. Ed. Charles W. Kneupper. Arlington, TX: Rhetoric Society of America, 1985. 1-6.

Brown, Delindus, and Wanda F. Anderson. "A Survey of the Black Woman and the Persuasion Process: The Study of Strategies of Identification and Resistance." *Journal of Black Studies* 9.2 (1978): 233-48.

Burke, Kenneth. *A Rhetoric of Motives*. Berkeley: U of California P, 1969.

Butler, Judith. "From Parody to Politics. Gender Trouble: Feminism and the Subversion of Identity." *The Routledge Language and Cultural Theory Reader*. Ed. Lucy Burke, Tony Crowley, and Alan Girvin. London: Routledge, 2000. 174-79.

Campbell, Karlyn Kohrs. *A Critical Study of Early Feminist Rhetoric: Man Cannot Speak for Her*. Vol. 1. Westport, CT: Greenwood, 1989.

Chisholm, Shirley. "Equal Rights For Women." 1969. *The Gifts of Speech: Women's Speeches from Around the World*. Sweet Briar College. 25 February 2002 <http://gos.sbc.edu/c/chisholm.html>.

Du Bois, W. E. B. *The Souls of Black Folk*. New York: Penguin, 1969.

Haith, Esther A. Letters to Robert Lansing. 18 November 1918 & 28 February 1919. U.S. Record Group 59, Records of the Department of State, RG 59, File 811.4016, No. 13 National Archives II, College Park, MD.

Harper, Frances. "We Are All Bound up Together." *A Brighter Coming Day: A Frances Ellen Watkins Harper Reader*. Ed. Frances Smith Foster. New York: Feminist, 1990. 217-19.

Horowitz, Linda Diane. "Transforming Appearance into Rhetorical Argument: Rhetorical Criticism of Public Speech of Barbara Jordan, Lucy Parson, and Angela Y. Davis." Diss. Northwestern U, 1998.

Houston, Marsha. "The Politics of Difference: Race, Class, and Women's Communication." *Women Making Meaning: New Feminist Directions in Communication*. New York: Routledge, 1992. 45-59.

James, Joy. "The Profeminist Politics of W. E. B. Du Bois with Respects to Anna Julia Cooper and Ida B. Wells Barnett." *W. E. B. Du Bois on Race and Culture: Philosophy, Politics, and Poetics*. Ed. Bernard Bell, Emily Grosholz, and James Stewart. New York: Routledge, 1996. 141-60.

Jordan, Barbara. "Who Then Will Speak for the Common Good?" 1976. *The Gifts of Speech: Women's Speeches from Around the World*. Sweet Briar College. 25 February 2002 <http://gos.sbc.edu/j/jordan1.html>.

Lorde, Audre. "The Transformation of Silence into Language and Action." *Available Means: An Anthology of Women's Rhetoric(s)*. Ed. Joy Ritchie and Kate Ronald. Pittsburgh: U of Pittsburgh P, 2001. 302-305.

Matthews, Victoria. "The Awakening of the Afro-American Woman." *With Pen and Voice: A Critical Anthology of Nineteenth-Century African-American Women*. Ed. Shirley Wilson Logan. Carbondale: Southern Illinois UP, 1995. 149-55.

Micciche, Laura. "Postcolonial Principles and Composition Studies: Toward Ethical Recognition and Response." Unpublished essay, 2002.

Olson, Lester C. "Liabilities of Language: Audre Lorde Reclaiming Difference." *Quarterly Journal of Speech 84* (1998): 448-70.

Perelman, Chaim, and Lucie Olbrechts-Tyteca. *The New Rhetoric: A Treatise on Argumentation*. Notre Dame: U of Notre Dame P, 1969.

Rogers, Mary Beth. *Barbara Jordan: American Hero.* New York, Bantam Books, 1998.

Royster, Jacqueline Jones. "When the First Voice You Hear Is Not Your Own," *College Composition and Communication* 47.1 (February 1996): 29-40.

Samar, Sima. Interview. *New York Times Magazine.* 23 December 2001: 15.

Simons, Herbert W. "'Genre-alizing' about Rhetoric: A Scientific Approach." *Form and Genre: Shaping Rhetorical Action.* Ed. Karlyn Kohrs Campbell and Kathleen Hall Jamieson. Falls, Church, VA: Speech Communication Assn., 1978. 33-50.

Southgate, Martha. *The Fall of Rome.* New York: Scribner's, 2002.

Terrell, Mary Church. "The Progress of Colored Women." 1898. *The Gifts of Speech: Women's Speeches from Around the World.* Sweet Briar College. 26 February 2002 <http://gos.sbc.edu/t/terrellmary.html>.

Truth, Sojourner. "Speech Delivered to the First Annual Meeting of the American Equal Rights Association." *With Pen and Voice: A Critical Anthology of Nineteenth-Century African-American Women.* Ed. Shirley Wilson Logan. Carbondale: Southern Illinois UP, 1995. 27-28.

Wheatley, Phillis. "On Being Brought from Africa to America." *Black Writers of America: A Comprehensive Anthology.* Ed. Richard Barksdale and Keneth Kinnamon. New York: Macmillan, 1972. 41.

4

Plato's Shibboleth Delineations; or, the Complete Idiot's Guide to Rhetoric

Rosa A. Eberly
Pennsylvania State University

I

a reply to Greek and Latin with the bare hands...
To make a start,
out of particulars
and make them general, rolling
up the sum, by defective means—

In ignorance
a certain knowledge and knowledge,
undispersed, its own undoing.

—William Carlos Williams ("Preface," *Paterson* 2, 3, 4)

I've been wanting, somehow, to call Bill Clinton. I've been wanting to ask him about information he released in mid-September (2001), information I first noticed when it flowed like a pithy stock quote across the bottom of the increasingly busy screen of what passes for journalism in the corporate media. This was the headline: "PRESIDENT CLINTON SAYS 25 TERRORIST ATTEMPTS THWARTED DURING HIS SECOND TERM." I want to ask Clinton this: What made you decide to release that information? What made you decide to release it *when you did*? Did you *have* to declassify it? What precedents exist for releasing it, or statutes exist for declassifying it? Do you think the current administration is using appropriate, prudent, democratic definitions of what is and what is not classified information? Do you think your administration did?

Perhaps the headline caught my attention because, just the day before, President Bush had thrown a tantrum about the release of what he referred to as classified information about U.S. military operations in Afghanistan. Bush, in what is now among my favorite executive oxymorons, said: "The release of classified information is *not* in the public interest."

Is the President an idiot?

After last fall's [2001] news turned from the events of September 11 to U.S. bombing of Afghanistan to one Anthrax story after another, this free-range rhetorician was wondering out loud—and, now, wondering along with you; thank you for the company—about rhetorics of "classified information." For me, some of the very best places to wonder out loud in good company about such questions are rhetoric classrooms understood as protopublic spaces, spaces where students can try on types of rhetorical agency by acting as participants in several and overlapping publics. As I have written elsewhere, despite its many theoretical flaws, *stasis* theory, to cite just one example of rhetoric's powerful lexicons for language-in-use, provides citizens and others who want to engage in study and practice of public discourse the best means of analyzing, responding to, and inventing public rhetoric (Eberly). The *stasis* questions allow publics not only to keep track of the contours of public discourse (e.g., what definition of classified information pertains in a particular case); the *stasis* questions and rhetoric's other powers also provide individuals means of becoming agents through words and deeds in those publics. In other words, rhetoric is a *productive* and *practical* as well as a theoretical or hermeneutic art; the habituated, collaborative practice of rhetoric is the best chance democracy has. I know this kind of hope is theoretically incorrect, but in the wake of Foucault, Lyotard, and the fragments of liberal humanism—here we are, still, together. What now?

Because most citizens in the United States have little hope of affecting political outcomes at any level, I have come to understand that I need faith in rhetoric. Oligarchic control by a handful of corporations of what used to be the public airwaves and a political system in which dollars are allowed to stand in as equivalent for speech combine to keep most citizens from having the information and agency they need to make collaborative judgments on public issues, that is, issues of concern to all in a particular public—following Isocrates, *koine* issues. Furthermore, a political culture that suggests through its practices that citizenship is a matter of buying flags or trading stocks or sending a dollar to the children in Afghanistan robs citizens of any potential to habituate the processes of active, critical civic engagement—and, yes, I know, that "civic engagement" is also a theoretically flawed term. I need faith in rhetoric because the evidence of robust democracy—evidence of the existence of public processes of deliberation and judgment wherein the people might rule—is mighty slim.

When our students know they have little if any voice—other than, of course, their commodified demographic, their brand preferences, and their ability to use credit cards—what hope do we have of encouraging students to be ethical, politically involved citizens, to use rhetoric for public deliberation and judgment? Ultimately, I've been thinking for a few years now about "faith in rhetoric" because, given that rhetoric and democracy developed at roughly the same time in ancient Greece, perhaps faithful practice of one might help revitalize the other.

II

A history that has, by its den in the
rocks, bole and fangs, its own cane-break
whence, half hid, canes and stripes
blending, it grins (beauty defied)
not for the sake of the encyclopedia.

Were we near enough its stinking breath
would fell us.

—Williams ("The Delineaments of the Giants," *Paterson* 22)

My willingness to talk about faith in rhetoric is inspired in part by the work of such scholars as Andrea Lunsford, Susan Jarratt, Patricia Bizzell, Cheryl Glenn, and Jan Swearingen, who have worked historiograph-ically and methodologically to tell fuller tales of the histories of ancient rhetorics. Secondly, my philological warrants come from Father Grimaldi and Brother Leo (the latter being James Kinneavy's name when he served as a Christian brother). Grimaldi turned Aristotle's *pisteis* on their heads, thereby exposing their hearts—arguing that, contrary to earlier interpretations, ethos and pathos as well as logos have their rationalities and that all three work by example and enthymeme. And Kinneavy made a careful case for a soulful relationship between ancient and New Testament or *koine* understandings of the *pisteis*, as well as the place of faith in each. *Pistis*, the ancient Greek word for "means of persuasion" in its singular sense, is the word translated as "faith" in the New Testament.

Faith in *rhetorike*? That *-ike* ending: the suffix that in English puts the *-ic* in rhetoric. Made famous by the John Poulakos-Edward Schiappa interchange in the journal *Philosophy and Rhetoric*, the question of Plato's probable coining of *rhetorike*—the art of rhetoric with maybe, maybe not, a subject matter of its own—haunts me now, nearly every time I use the word. And I use it a lot. I wish I could just call it "rhet," as in Phil and Rhet, two dogs sniffing each others' butts through the so-called history of ideas.

In this chapter, I'd like to put before you a few of the hard choices rhetoricians have to make for the purpose of suggesting some common—that is, *koine* or *koinos*, a word to which I will return, along with its inevitable antithesis, *idia* or *idios*—concerns that rhetoricians from various intellectual traditions might share. First, I'll discuss choices we're faced with about what we call ourselves and the work we do. This will involve brief discussions of Plato and Isocrates and, as you might have guessed, the use of some smelly old Greek words. Second, I'll address the choices we're faced with in dividing our time among teaching, research, and service. My fervor comes not only from my passion for rhetoric as an object of study but also from my experiences of teaching rhetoric and from my attempts—not stunningly successful—through writing, speech, and action, to practice rhetoric in public as well as academic forums. When it is focused on instances of contested public memory in classrooms exercised as protopublic spaces, when it is used to form as well as to study social movements, the accrued vocabularies and powers of rhetoric can help students who become so inclined to develop and practice rhetorical agency as a possible antidote to political powerlessness. My aim is to give renewed energy and focus to teaching and service, as well as research, as means of understanding and enacting rhetoric as transdisciplinary.

III

> Twice a month Paterson receives
> communications from the Pope and Jacques
> Barzun
> (Isocrates). His works have been done into French
> and Portuguese. And clerks in the post-
> office ungum rare stamps from
> his packages and steal them for their
> children's albums.
>
> —Williams ("The Delineaments of the Giants," *Paterson* 9)

Rhetoricians—or "rhetori*ti*cians," as I've heard more than a few deans pronounce us—have hard choices to make, insofar as we still believe in the idea of choice. I know we're not alone in facing hard choices—and I say "we" because whether you self-identify primarily as "rhetorician" or not, you are reading this, and thus I think it's fair to claim that you and I have some common, some *koine* interest in rhetoric. Forgive me if that turns out not to be true.

As rhetoricians in twenty-first century higher education, our choices of what we call ourselves, how we affiliate, and how we talk about what we study, teach, and practice are heavy. No theoretical perspective or vocabulary or history or canon is satisfactory; our colleagues and institutions often see our work as remedial or hopelessly arcane—or, somehow, both; most within and beyond the academy understand rhetoric pejoratively; and, maddeningly, the very word we most often use to talk about what we do—*rhetoric*—has that pesky, Platonic *-ike* ending. Plato's shibboleth delineations; or is it sibboleth?

If you haven't thought about who put the *-ic* in rhetoric, well, you're *still* not the idiot I was thinking of when I titled this paper. The idiot I was thinking of is the idiot—*idiotas*—in the Isocratean sense (see, e.g., *Areopagiticus* 72-73): private person or layperson, one who cannot imagine what might be in the common or public interest, one who cannot practice with common purpose. The idiots I'm thinking about are the idiots of Enron; the idiots of the second Bush administration who have only contempt for the importance of *parrhesia* or free speech in a democracy. I have argued before that rhetoric is an amateur, vulgar, and trivial art; here, I want to argue that it can and should be a common, *koine*, art and practice, too—one that can, even as we are interpolated as consumers and demographics rather than citizens and publics, help us and others invent common processes and common purposes.

Plato's *-ike* ending—which scholars the likes of Schiappa, John and Takis Poulakos, Susan Wells, Sharon Crowley, Jeff Walker, and Janet Atwill have written about extensively—is bad for rhetoric, by nature and by consequences. By nature, the *-ike* ending brings epistemological baggage to rhetoric that it should not need to deal with; by consequences, the *-ike* ending has across the centuries robbed rhetoric of much of its transdisciplinary power—the power that Walker writes about in his *Rhetoric and Poetics in Antiquity*, and that Atwill writes about in *Rhetoric Reclaimed*. Walker puts *rhetoric* in quotes nearly consistently throughout the introduction to his second book, and that's a choice I admire—although it's hard to pull off in certain discursive interactions, and it suits academic writing better than public discourse. Plato's *-ike* ending splits rhetorical power into disciplinary shards; the *-ike* long succeeded in separating rhetoric from ethics, poetics, politics. Plato's *-ike* ending, whatever good intentions a reconstructed and rhetoric-friendly Plato might have had, has often left rhetoric pinned and wriggling on the wall, allowing rhetoric to describe only those discursive practices of which Plato seems not to have approved; for in Plato's usage, *koine* is more often pejorative than not. Thanks at least in part to the *-ic* in rhetoric, we have, as Sharon Crowley writes in her essay called "Let Me Get This Straight," "a discipline and its related practices that are hoary with age but now in serious disrepute" (8).

There's another word that makes for hard choices: *discipline*. Read and reread Isocrates in translation, and put the Greek alongside. You'll see the English word *discipline* stand in for several very different Greek words. I can live with *discipline* a bit more easily if I think of Isocrates' word *diatribē*—way of life, choice of how one wears away time. If we want to *teach and practice rhetoric explicitly*, in addition to studying it, we need to talk beyond field or discipline in ways our uncommon tongues rarely allow. For, given rhetoric's material and spiritual parts in the conditions of the possibility of democracy, our hard choices also involve whether and how to engage praxiswise with Plato's disciplining of *rheō* and *rhētor* and *rhetoreuō*—did you know rhetoric used to be a verb?—with the *-ike* ending. Plato's *-ike* ending removed from rhetoric's reach politics, ethics, teaching, and discursive studies and practices more generally, as well as rhetorical questions about how discursive practices not only affect but shape our shared world.

Of all the many great gigs I had during my time at the University of Texas at Austin, my annual three hours with Plan II Honors faculty was my favorite—and by far my most challenging. Once a year, Paul Woodruff, venerable professor of philosophy and translator of Plato, venerable head of UT's most venerable honors program, summoned me to talk to professors of Plan II courses about how to teach writing. The first year, I started by sticking to the script I'd used when I'd had discussions with other faculty across the university, telling about various ways of intervening in students' writing processes rather than merely obsessing about—line editing in most cases—the final drafts of student writing. Before I knew it, however, I had uttered and then jotted on one side of the Plan II dry erase board the recursive stages of the writing process (under the heading "composition") and the five canons of rhetoric on the other side (under the heading "rhetoric"). I included also the *stasis* questions, suggesting that introducing the language of conjecture, definition, value, and procedure is a helpful way of habituating students into making collaborative judgments about what they are discoursing about, why, and for whom.

When the word *invention* went on the board—along with *heuriskein*, the ancient Greek infinitive meaning "to make or to find"—Woodruff's venerable face lit up. "Do you mean to suggest," he asked me, "that you can teach invention? Soon you'll be claiming to teach virtue, too." Because I'd already handled a colleague from Germanic studies who'd jumped all over me for talking about Habermas and an astrophysicist who refused to entertain the idea that the "fact" of gravity was arguable, I was ready for Woodruff. "I don't think rhetoric needs Plato's *-ike* ending," I said. "If rhetoric must be understood as a discipline, it is a discipline in the sense of a way of life. Call that 'teaching virtue' if you must. But I don't call it that."

IV

certainly NOT the university,
a green bud fallen upon the pavement its
sweet breath suppressed; Divorce (the
language stutters)
unfledged. . . .

Everybody has roots.
We go on living, we permit ourselves
to continue—but certainly
not for the university, what they publish
severally or as a group: clerks
got out of hand forgetting for the most part
to whom they are beholden.
spitted on fixed concepts like
roasting hogs, sputtering, their drip sizzling
in the fire
Something else, something else the same.

—Williams ("The Delineaments of the Giants," *Paterson* 21, 31-32)

Given what seems to be an increasing interest in civics education, I submit that a *koine* issue for rhetoricians is to get better at explaining to colleagues across our campuses and to wider publics how rhetoric—its study and practice—is the material means of being citizens together... "citizens," of course, asterisked, with qualifications that citizenship concerns discourse and action as well as legal status, although legal status can certainly limit the kinds of actions one is able to take. And given the growing sense that our democracy is composed of deliberating bodies that no longer know how to deliberate, of publics that can imagine themselves as nothing other than consumers, and of leaders who hold in contempt the idea that democracy requires information to be held in common, I'd like to talk about one more smelly old Greek word: *politeuesthai*. In Isocrates, the middle-voice infinitive *politeuesthai* means "to be citizens together" or "to engage in politics together." The middle voice—which English doesn't quite have—denotes that the subject is both an agent of an action and also somehow affected by an action. In Plato, *politeuesthai* means "to meddle in politics." It sounds like a definition Dick Cheney would love. Politics is not, I guess, in the public interest.

Consider middle-voice democracy. Public opinion polls won't get us there. Demographic-based niche-marketed media products won't get us there. Only the discursive practices of a robust public rhetoric, taught in schools and colleges, habituated, openly and faithfully practiced, will enable us to begin to live up to the idea of democracy—rule by the people: governing together.

Reflecting on the chasm between rhetorical theory and practice, Sharon Crowley wrote words that I read regularly as a check against my faith in rhetoric: "Many [...] people," Crowley says, "want their scholarship to reach beyond the people to whom they seem always to be talking. Some even want to participate in bringing about an end to, or changes in, various oppressive cultural practices. They are, however, more or less mystified as to how this might work" (8).

You all may decide that I am still mystified, too. But in my scholarship, teaching, and service, my focus has come to rest on the production of student speech and writing in response to campus and other local issues and as a means of habituating rhetorical agency in students—particularly lower-division undergraduates. In my undergraduate teaching, in classrooms that I conceive of as protopublic spaces, I set out to examine public processes—or their lack—and to create the possibility for students to practice their rhetorical agency and to create sustainable publics. These are *koine* questions for those who teach, study, and practice rhetoric across and beyond the "disciplines." Additionally, they are questions that require the common engagement of all of us, *despite* our differences and precisely *because of* our differences.

When's the last time you've been on an embassy for rhetoric? Lester Faigley once called the gigs I did across campus at the University of Texas at Austin "being a cheerleader for writing." I prefer to think of them as embassies; I am an ambassador for rhetoric across and beyond the university. During my time at UT, several colleagues across the U started assigning public writing to their students, asking students to end a semester-long substantial writing component class by revising a research paper into an op-ed or a call to a local radio talk show. I travel across campus, talking with colleagues from every imaginable field about their students' needs, abilities, powers, habits. In the process, I've shared with colleagues across the university, and fellow citizens beyond it, the amateur, trivial, and common powers of rhetoric.

WORKS CITED

Atwill, Janet. *Rhetoric Reclaimed: Aristotle and the Liberal Arts Tradition.* Ithaca: Cornell UP, 1998.

Bizzell, Patricia. "Feminist Methods of Research in the History of Rhetoric: What Differences Do They Make?" *Rhetoric Society Quarterly* 30 (2000): 5-17.

---, guest editor. Preface. Special Issue on Feminist Historiography in Rhetoric. *Rhetoric Society Quarterly* 32 (2002): 7-10.

Crowley, Sharon. "Let Me Get This Straight." *Writing Histories of Rhetoric.* Victor Vitanza, ed. Carbondale: Southern Illinois UP, 1994. 1-19.

Eberly, Rosa A. "From Readers, Audiences, and Communities to Publics: Classrooms as Proto-public Spaces." *Rhetoric Review* 18 (1999): 165-78.

Glenn, Cheryl. "Truth, Lies, and Method: Revisiting Feminist Historiography." *College English* 62 (2000): 387-89.

Grimaldi, William M. A. *Aristotle, Rhetoric I: A Commentary.* New York: Fordham UP, 1980.

Isocrates. *On the Peace. Areopagiticus. Against the Sophists. Antidosis. Panathenaicus. Loeb Classical Library.* Trans. George Norlin. Cambridge: Harvard UP, 1929.

Jarratt, Susan. "Rhetoric and Feminism: Together Again." *College English* 62 (2000): 390-93.

---. "Toward a Sophistic Historiography." *Pre/Text* 8 (1987): 9-26.

Kinneavy, James. *Greek Rhetorical Origins of the Christian Faith.* New York: Oxford UP, 1987.

Lunsford, Andrea, ed. *Reclaiming Rhetorica: Women in the Rhetorical Tradition.* Pittsburgh: U Pittsburgh P, 1995.

Poulakos, John. "Interpreting Sophistical Rhetoric: A Response to Schiappa." *Philosophy and Rhetoric* 23 (1990): 218-28.

Poulakos, Takis. *Speaking for the Polis: Isocrates' Rhetorical Education.* Columbia: U South Carolina P, 1997.

Schiappa, Edward. "History and Neo-Sophistic Criticism: A Reply to Poulakos." *Philosophy and Rhetoric* 23 (1990): 307-15.

---. *Protagoras and Logos: A Study in Greek Philosophy and Rhetoric.* Columbia: U South Carolina P, 1991.

Swearingen, C. Jan. "A Lover's Discourse: Diotima, Logos, and Desire." *Reclaiming Rhetorica: Women in the Rhetorical Tradition.* Ed. Andrea Lunsford. Pittsburgh: U Pittsburgh P, 1995. 25-51.

Walker, Jeffrey. *Rhetoric and Poetics in Antiquity.* New York: Oxford UP, 2000.

Wells, Susan. *Sweet Reason: Rhetoric and the Discourses of Modernity.* Chicago: U Chicago P, 1996.

Williams, William Carlos. *Paterson.* Ed. Christopher MacGowan. New York: New Directions, 1995.

5

The Temple Issues Forum: Innovations in Pedagogy for Civic Engagement

Herbert W. Simons
Temple University

In a crowded auditorium at Temple University, a Temple economist and a Swarthmore psychologist square off on the question: "Is capitalism good for the poor?" The debate proves provocative, so much so that a local public affairs radio station invites the academics to air their differences on *Radio Times*, its award-winning talk show. Tapes of that talk show are later dissected by students training to assume the roles of discussion moderators and panelists. "What would your first question to the economist have been?" they are asked. Then, "What did you think of the moderator's question?" Next, "How would you have answered it if you were the economist?" And so on, for round after round of Q & A.

Welcome to the Temple Issues Forum (TIF) and to its student arm, the TIF Debate and Discussion Club (TIF D&D). Launched as a faculty initiative in 1998, TIF is mainly in the business of public affairs programming. The TIF Debate and Discussion Club is a registered student activity with two distinct branches. The Public Debate and Discussion Group (PDD), gets training in public debate and discussion, and stages forum events of its own. The Temple Debate Team (TDT) represents a return of competitive debate to Temple after a twenty-year hiatus. A listing of TIF events is provided in Appendix A. Records of TIF video productions as well as PDD events are provided in Appendix B. Details about most TIF and PDD events can be found on the TIF Web site: <www.temple.edu/tif>.

TIF originated as a campuswide activity but then became known to a regional audience by way of coproductions with WHYY (91 FM) of *Radio Times Live at Temple*. With recent conference presentations featuring video highlights of TIF's all-day forum on the 9/11 terrorist attacks, news of TIF has spread, and some universities—among them Colorado, Illinois-Chicago, and Drake—are considering ways to adopt the TIF model while adapting it to their own special needs. TIF and TIF D&D seem to me to be both exportable and expandable. That is a claim I defend in the final section of this chapter. Characterizing the TIF model is the task of the first section of this chapter. The middle section is about the TIF Debate and Discussion Club, particularly its PDD branch.

TEMPLE ISSUES FORUM

The basic components of the TIF model are as follows: (1) Two or more competent advocates for opposing positions, (2) are engaged in a public discussion or debate, (3) superintended by an experienced moderator, (4) on a current events or campus issue, (5) which is expected to be of widespread interest to the university community. (6) The forum is presented live (7) in a discussion-friendly auditorium, (8) before an audience consisting largely of undergraduates, (9) and in a manner calculated to stimulate audience involvement and participation. TIF has done several such events per academic year, recently with WHYY, and often in cooperation with other institutional entities at Temple, such as academic departments or research centers. An executive committee makes policy, approves topics, and oversees the work of the coordinator. A much smaller advisory committee works closely with the coordinator to organize, publicize, and stage TIF events.

Mission

From its inception, Temple Issues Forum was committed to Robert Putnam's vision of the engaged—or reengaged—university. Lamenting the turn toward careerism at many universities, TIF's faculty planners saw TIF as a way of reasserting traditional academic commitments to preparation for citizenship and for the life of the mind. TIF was also inspired by Gerald Graff's pioneering efforts at redesigning university curricula so as to air differences among faculty over educational goals, methods, and perspectives, rather than keeping them hidden from students. Graff called it "teaching the conflicts." And TIF was inclined toward widening the conversation, rather than restricting it to elites. In Gerard Hauser's words, it was committed to "rhetorical democracy."

Temple, then, was to become a place at which faculty and students tested ideas in John Stuart Mill's "free marketplace of ideas." Issues that faculty normally took up behind closed doors, or in the single-teacher classroom, were now to be addressed publicly and collectively. Expertise was to be given its due, but everyone present was to be afforded the opportunity to speak.

Issue Selection and Treatment

Moreover, the issues had to engage the audience; they needed to matter or be made to matter by the manner in which they were presented. These values found expression at TIF's very first public event: "Should Faculty Take and Defend Controversial Positions in the 'Studies in Race' Classroom?"

Faculty advocacy in the classroom had been a topic of widespread concern at least since the 1960s (see Gleiss and Smith). It had been on the academic front burner during the period of the culture wars (see Graff; Sparks). Its power to arouse was brought home to me personally at an election debriefing back in 1984, after the conferees had been shown a scathing critique of the religious right in a documentary put out by the liberal "People for the American Way." I was much moved by the documentary and contemplated showing it to students in my class on persuasion, but I wasn't at all sure how to teach it. Should I stand behind it? Critique it? Affect neutrality? Counter it with a video more sympathetic to the religious right? I decided to ask the conferees what they would do and wound up triggering intense debate. "A professor's job is to profess," said one professor. "A professor's job is to educate, not advocate," said another. "Your job is to teach students how to think, not what to think," said a third. "That's an untenable distinction," said a fourth. "Where I come from," said a fifth, "they'd hang the people who made that video" (Simons). Recalling the discussion of faculty advocacy at the election debriefing, I knew that the topic was ripe for a Temple Issues Foum.

Indeed, issues of faculty advocacy versus academic neutrality have circulated through a number of TIF events, particularly as regards race. Temple benefits from being a racially diverse public university. It also has a "Studies in Race" requirement, put in place a decade ago after an ugly, racially tinged incident outside one of the dormitories. Studies in Race was born in controversy, and the politics of getting it approved required that it have many course variants, with multiple and perhaps conflicting objectives. Students and faculty continue to be divided over the requirement, some complaining that it does not go far enough in exposing white racism, others alleging that some course variants combine propagandistic intent with the power of the grade. Launching the Temple Issues Forum with the question of whether faculty should take and defend controversial positions in the Studies in Race classroom was a way of signaling TIF's intention to address tough issues, including highly sensitive campus controversies. It also guaranteed that panelists and audience members could speak from experience, and it bid fair to advance consideration of a real problem. Three faculty members who had taught Studies in Race courses and three students who had taken them comprised the panel, and they were encouraged by the faculty moderator (a highly regarded journalism professor) to limit their opening comments to five minutes each. So too were audience members encouraged to restrict their remarks, and panelists were discouraged from responding to every audience comment or question. The idea was to keep things moving and to involve as many people as possible.

Building Attendance

How does one get commuting undergraduates at a public, urban university to come on their own in large numbers to hear three faculty members and three students discourse on the topic of faculty advocacy in the Studies in Race course?

The answer is that you can't—or at least that we couldn't, not back in 1998 when TIF began. Students had to be coerced to come by their instructors, and this is how we built attendance. Early on, the TIF executive committee (initially composed of "friends of Herb's," but since diversified to include representation from a wide array of schools and colleges serving undergraduates) decided to stage forum events so as to coincide with classes, and to select topics and times with foreknowledge of which faculty teaching at which hours would be most likely to bring their classes. Events were advertised by way of flyers and posters and some people came because they wanted to come, but faculty-mediated coercion was TIF's trick. Still, students' ratings were consistently high. They enjoyed not just the controversy but the break from routines, and especially the sense of community—of classes coming together for deliberations on an issue. Thus, at that fateful first panel discussion back in spring 1998, I recall a Journalism class, a Composition class, a class in Social Administration, and a couple of Studies in Race classes. Only years later were we able to pull in purely voluntary audiences of fifty or more.

WHYY and Community Outreach

On October 7, 1999, TIF's audience increased exponentially from less than 200 to 20,000 or more. The occasion was a conference and mayoral forum on "Higher Education and the City," cosponsored by various civic organizations in the city and featuring three hours of *Radio Times* as well as television rebroadcast by WHYY of the mayoral forum. The topic had been suggested by Temple's Vice President for Administration and supported by area civic and business leaders. They knew that the economic future of the city, and indeed of the Greater Philadelphia area, depended on its 70+ colleges and universities

In May 2000, WHYY approached TIF with a proposal to coproduce four events at Temple in the next academic year, each involving two hours of *Radio Times*. In the meantime I had been following up on the Higher Education and the City initiative along with the former dean of Temple's College of Arts and Sciences, Carolyn T. Adams. Together we plotted creation of an umbrella organization for area college students and recent graduates, designed to enrich their lives during their time in Philadelphia while also encouraging them to take up roots in the area. Toward that end we organized a conference at WHYY in October 2000, on "Philadelphia as College Town," again featuring *Radio Times* and attended by leading representatives of town and gown. Out of the conference came our much-sought organization, the Greater Philadelphia Collegetown Project (GPCP). Staffed by recent graduates, it has brought area Student Life administrators together, as well as representatives of student government, while also managing a very active Web site (www.campusphilly.org). Once having helped create GPCP, TIF returned to its main business of public affairs programming. Meanwhile, the TIF/WHYY connection continued into the next academic year.

Event Planning and Execution

On October 3, 2000, TIF/WHYY held the first of their coproduced events, *Radio Times Live at Temple*. The question for discussion was whether there should be a moratorium on capital punishment in Pennsylvania. Hour One, on state and national issues, featured Pennsylvania Attorney General Mike Fisher (later a 2002 gubernatorial candidate) and Ray Brown, host of an Emmy award-winning legal affairs shown on New Jersey public television. Hour Two, on capital punishment in Philadelphia, featured the chief of homicides in the Philadelphia District Attorney's office, and David Rudovsky, a prominent civil rights attorney and Penn professor. Presiding both hours was the venerable Marty Moss-Coane, whose talk show on public radio commanded a loyal listenership. Hour Three was given over to lunch and informal discussion. A team from Computer Media Services was on hand, as usual, to videotape the proceedings and interview selected audience members.

By all accounts, the event went exceedingly well. The auditorium was filled to capacity. The topic was engaging, the sound was good, the panelists responded well to Moss-Coane's probings, audience questions and comments were insightful, and everyone remembered to turn off their cell phones. How did it happen?

Preparation for public affairs productions requires adherence to the rule that whatever can go wrong will go wrong unless anticipated in advance. Even then, there are no guarantees. Thus, provisions must be set in place for responding quickly to emergencies: a late arrival by a panelist, a faulty sound system, a crowd in excess of a room's capacity. Experience helps, but so too does dumb luck.

Planning for the October 3 event began the previous spring and required seemingly endless meetings, e-mail exchanges, and telephone conversations with the scores of people who make such events work. Particularly vexing was the task of panel selection. One learns early on in arranging such events that there is no such thing as perfect balance, and that the varieties of expertise relevant to a topic exceed the number of slots available, or considered manageable, on a panel. Complicating matters is the need to combine balance with expertise during each hour. Thus, our event advisory committee went through lists of people in proximity to Philadelphia who had received media attention on the subject of capital punishment in the aftermath of the recently announced Illinois moratorium. They included victims' rights activists and DNA specialists, legislators and religious leaders. Many seemingly competent advocates were considered but none invited, not until we had found a formula for combining desired varieties of expertise with desired varieties of balance. Fortunately, one member of our advisory committee was well connected to major proponents of a moratorium, the other to major opponents, and the people we contacted were eager to appear on *Radio Times.*

TIF Post-9/11

Immediately following the terrorist attacks, TIF sprung into action. By 9/13, it was ready with an all-day forum on "The Bombings and Beyond," with faculty panels on topics such as "Roots of U.S.-Middle East Conflict," "The Changing Nature of National Security," "How Have the Bombings Changed America's View of Itself?" and "Media's Responsibility." The Counseling Center was on hand with a scroll at the entrance to the auditorium on which students could register their feelings, and the Center also presided at a final session, "Coping with Stress."

As these issues were addressed, others emerged. Temple's new President, David Adamany, stood up from the rear of the auditorium to denounce assaults on Muslim students, and to declare Temple's four-square commitment to the right of dissent. A student asked why Temple had remained open when other universities had shut down. Her comments were met with enthusiastic applause. But when a faculty member responded that class attendance had been made optional, and that many students were grateful for the opportunity to process 9/11 in class, she too received enthusiastic applause. Between sessions, informal meetings took place, some of them recorded on video. At one such meeting, a student expressed his ambivalence toward the remarks made by Joseph Schwartz, a democratic socialist who was chair of the Political Science department. They were disturbing, said the student, because they ran counter to what he usually heard on CNN. He even thought some comments were unpatriotic, an assault on the American Way. But, at the same time, he was intrigued by the comments, found them highly informative, and wanted to share them with his union buddies, whose immediate thought after the bombings had been to "go out and kill some Arabians." Still, he found Schwartz intimidating, not easy to relate to, and he told the interviewer so, in Schwartz's presence. The conversation shifted to the topic of intimidation, and concluded with consensus on ways to reduce the barriers to open discussion between students and faculty. All this is captured on TIF's professionally produced video, *Bombings and Beyond*. And these opportunities were made possible just two days after the terrorist attacks because TIF had been in business for three years and was able to mobilize for the event in a hurry.

Subsequent to that forum, TIF and WHYY combined for a *Radio Times* special on "U.S. Response to the Bombings," then an hour on "Ethnic and Racial Profiling of Arabs and Muslims." Then, as the Israelis occupied cities on the West Bank and the Palestinians continued their suicide bombings, TIF asked a panel (which included a senior Israeli political strategist) how President Bush should be dealing with the Israeli-Palestinian crisis. All the while, TIF D&D's Public Debate and Discussion Group was staging post-9/11 events of its own.

Administration and Budgeting

As stated earlier, TIF policies and program selections are made by its Executive Committee (formerly the Planning Committee). Program proposals are evaluated and honed in committee, and those selected are assigned to an event advisory committee. The reward/punishment for a good proposal is often hours spent helping organize an event, and perhaps moderating it. Disputes in committee most frequently arise over whether a proposal fits TIF's mission of presenting controversies rather than promoting positions. This distinction may in itself become a matter of controversy. For example, a committee member upset by what he perceives to be insufficient ideological diversity on campus, and in TIF programming, proposes that this very problem become the occasion for a TIF forum. I find the proposal attractive, but a dispute arises over what, in Temple's curriculum, ought to be considered controversial rather than indisputably true—hence, in need of being addressed from different perspectives. Thus are there tiffs about TIF within the TIF Executive Committee.

TIF is extraordinarily inexpensive for the value it produces. Government officials, civic and business leaders, academics, journalists, social activists, a Pulitzer Prize-winning writer, a Muslim theologian, and an antiterrorism expert are among those who have given generously of their time. Admittedly there are facilities costs, production costs, administrative costs, and other expenses that do not show up on the Cost Center reports. Still, on balance, TIF is a bargain for

Temple, and TIF-like activities at other institutions are likely to be cost efficient.

TIF's budgetary needs have been met by cobbling together funding and in-kind support from various vice presidents, deans, programs, departments, research centers, and faculty gifts. The situation is not ideal. Although nearly everyone in administrative authority at Temple heaps praises on TIF, each has good reason to expect some other office to carry a greater share of the financial load. This "structural" problem, as Carolyn Adams has defined it, is aptly described by the former Dean of Temple University Japan, Richard Joslyn. He worries, he says, that an enterprise like TIF, which is like a "public good," from which many benefit but no one unit benefits especially or particularly, will always be vulnerable to a lack of "interested" advocacy and free rider behavior. Still, he observes, many colleges and universities manage to overcome problems such as these.

TIF DEBATE AND DISCUSSION CLUB

In spring 1999, Temple Issues Forum created its student extracurricular offshoot, the TIF Debate and Discussion Club. Of TIF D&D's two components, TDT (the Temple Debate Team) is by far the larger, but PDD (the Public Debate and Discussion group) may have greater campus impact as a consequence of its forum events and public hearings. Students in TIF D&D often try out one, then the other, and a very few do both at once. They can earn up to two credit hours per semester for the former, one credit for the latter, for up to three semesters. Between them these activities offer what one TIF D&Der described as an "escape from escapism." Particularly as Temple increases its residential undergraduate population, TIF D&D fills an after-class need. Like the Temple Issues Forum, it also provides a counterforce to careerist preoccupations. Says Business School Professor Terry Halbert,

> In my college, there is a strong focus on *relevance*—not to the larger social and political questions, but to personal and more mundane questions, like: "What can I learn that will enhance my chances for getting a good job?" As we prepare business students to take their places in the world, we give them too few chances to consider what and how to think about the bigger context. And while there are many courses outside my college that address the bigger context, within them student inquiry is overwhelmingly controlled by us instructors, one way or another. *We* determine what questions will be under investigation; we determine the pace and scope of inquiry. TIF and its stunningly successful student Debate and Discussion Club constitutes the only sustained effort to address this problem that I've witnessed in 20 years teaching here.

Temple Debate Team

TDT prepares students for parliamentary debate in a league consisting largely of "Ivies" and "Little Ivies." The team is unusual in many respects, not least that its 25+ members rarely enter debate tournaments, although they spend hours each week ostensibly preparing for them. For many of these students, the practice sessions are satisfaction enough. Allocated only limited university resources and constrained in many cases by the need to earn money on weekends, they typically volunteer for no more than two or three tournaments per year. Moreover, as of this writing, their de facto coach is their captain, a most exceptional undergraduate, but nevertheless bereft of formal training as a coach. Hence, they improvise.

In keeping with the larger purposes of this chapter, I want to comment briefly on innovations in the training that TDT members receive, then move on to PDD, a group whose activities more closely parallel those of TIF itself.

Preparation for parliamentary debate usually begins with presentation to the group of one argument in support of one proposition. This is the assignment that "Goddess" Ndidi Anyaegbunam, the team's current captain, gives to each initiate. By the conclusion of the semester, the novices will have learned how to construct more elaborate cases and how to respond as the "Loyal Opposition" to arguments from the "Government" that they had never heard before, on topics they had not anticipated. (This is the particularly daunting challenge of parliamentary debate: propositions are not preannounced.) Hopefully, too, they will have been convinced of the need to keep abreast of the news on a daily basis. Their initial cases tend to betray ignorance of foreign and domestic policy issues, except those related to their generation's preoccupation with entertainment and lifestyles—whether the latest music should be free to Internet browsers, for example, or whether white rap artists should be aired on Black Entertainment Television.

Initial presentations and reactions to them frequently turn on feelings and personal anecdotes, but under the tutelage of the coach, arguments and counterarguments tend over time to become more sophisticated. On practice days devoted to case building, the debate team often functions more like a discussion society. As those hearing a case get caught up in a topic, it "takes over"—the original arguments are subsumed or displaced by others, and less thought is given to what will win over a judge than to an argument's intrinsic merits. At other times, debate practice resembles oral argument before the Supreme Court. As arguments are put forward they are immediately questioned, the captain/coach serving in effect as Chief Justice. At the conclusion of the semester, debate team members enrolled for course credit are expected to turn in a "pro-con brief," complete with arguments on each side of a controversy as well as rebuttals and responses to those rebuttals. This, together with their participation in training sessions, becomes the basis for their grades.

PDD in Process

The Public Debate and Discussion group, or PDD, has been in process of self-definition since its inception several years ago. After one year it gained prominence when it held "hearings" on Temple University's required Studies in Race course. Faculty and administrators were invited to testify; then the students deliberated and presented their conclusions to a faculty committee. This was a reversal of who got to ask questions at the university and who had to answer them. Even liberals among my colleagues were taken aback and some reacted defensively. This itself was instructive.

A semester later, PDD was at it again, this time with hearings on Grade Inflation. Faculty and administrators were once more invited to testify, and again PDD deliberated. Their investigation culminated in two hours of public discussion and debate following a faculty senate meeting, the first hour featuring three faculty members and an administrator in a panel discussion, the second hour presenting a student debate among members of the Temple Debate Team. Attending the grade inflation hearings, and sometimes contributing to them, were students in a newly created Discussion Methods class that I taught with a colleague, Diane Carlin.

This was not all PDD did in its first years. Interspersed between public events were private discussions among PDD members, other public discussions, as well as workshops led by David Hoffman (now at CUNY-Baruch) or myself. Sometimes in workshops we would microanalyze tapes of public discussions and debates: for example, *Nightline*'s Town Meeting on the Elian Gonzales case proved instructive, as did the TIF/WHYY forum on capital punishment. Tapes such as these have proven useful in teaching students how to participate in panel discussions, how to lead them, and also how to critique them.

John Dewey Lives

Often at TDT and PDD meetings I hear the voice of philosopher/educator John Dewey ringing in my ears. Dewey, a champion of learning by doing and a theorist of group problem solving, would have been pleased to overhear PDD members at their first meeting in fall 2001.

The plan for fall 2001—or so I thought—was for PDD to begin with several weeks of hearings on Student Activism. But when I voiced this assumption to the group, several new members demurred. A split developed among those who wanted hearings, others who wanted to stage public discussions, and those who wanted PDD discussions to be confined to the membership.

I stayed out of this meeting as much as a control freak can. What emerged was a creative compromise. The group as a whole would hold public discussions one week, and discussions among themselves the following week; during the latter they would reflect on the substance and process of the preceding meeting. Everyone would participate in the process of scheduling and topic selection, but then responsibility for staging individual events would be divided among three-person committees. Their tasks included panel and moderator selection, briefing of panelists, publicity, and room arrangements.

The events proved highly successful, but staging them was fraught with problems. Fortunately, the problems themselves were of a sort conducive to Dewey-style learning by doing and group problem solving. Running across several of the events were issues of bias. Who among the PDDers should moderate the first student-run session, on "Roots of Islamic Discontent With U.S. Foreign Policy"? The group's decision was to split the moderating task between Brendan, an ardent supporter of U.S. foreign policy, and Omer, a Pakistani critic of that policy. But Brendan felt that Omer had gotten carried away, and he was not alone. Brendan also voiced concern about possible bias in an upcoming panel discussion of "Reparations for Slavery." He thought having a non-black moderator would ameliorate the problem, but got no support from the group. I thought that panel selection for the "Reparations" discussion was lopsided, and I said as much afterward to the all-black planning committee, but I nevertheless supported their right to stage the event as they did. Likewise, I thought that inclusion of a left-oriented faculty historian on the topic of globalization would tip a delicate balance created by prior invitations to an activist critical of globalization and a faculty economist who supported it. This time I voiced my objection in advance of the panel discussion, and was politely rebuffed by its student moderator—fortunately so, because the historian added dimensions to the panel discussions that would have been sorely missed. I later congratulated the event planners for insisting on the decisions they had made after hearing my advice. It had been just that—advice.

The Importance of "Getting Real"

The term is John Angus Campbell's and he intended it for the public speaking context (Campbell, 1996), but it applies as well to discussion and debate. PDD has succeeded in large measure because the topics have been real to the students and the tasks they took on in preparing for them were real as well.

By spring 2002, PDD was well ensconced, with several returning members able to provide the necessary leadership. By February 7, an ambitious plan was in place for six topics, most of them to run for two weeks, as was the pattern the previous semester. But the first two topics would run for one week each. The extraordinary quality of these two meetings—fresh in my memory as I write—deserve some commentary.

Appropriately enough, the first of the events, held on Valentine's Day, was on "Love." As publicized over various Temple listservs, the question was: "Is true love here to stay or has it already been commodified away?" A decision was made to hold this discussion without panelists, on the assumption that we were all experts on the topic—and fools. Here is what one of the participants had to say about the experience:

> [A]bout the V-day discussion; I agree, I thought it went very nicely. [A]nd I think we got to discuss a number of related or peripheral issues as well, and that people were really able to bring up certain concerns and verbalize their own perspectives pretty well. And there seemed to definitely be a high level of maturity/mutual respect among the whole group, which was also nice. If only 202 Tuttleman were the rest of the world.

The second event was instigated by a former colleague of mine, Mark Sacharoff. He had called me a month earlier out of concern that the peace movement, and indeed the left generally, had nothing significant to say about how the U.S. government should be responding to the 9/11 attacks. Long retired, Sacharoff had been a peace activist himself, with impeccable credentials, but he believed that al Qaeda posed a far greater threat than even Saddam Hussein had a decade earlier. Why hadn't his left-oriented colleagues come to the same realization?

Sacharoff proposed a TIF-sponsored debate. I urged him to find a worthy opponent, select with the opponent a resolution for debate, and then present the debate at a PDD meeting. He and Peter Lems, a Quaker peace activist with the American Friends Services Committee, traded extremely good arguments and in a manner so civil that the term *opponent* came to seem inappropriate. By the conclusion of the debate, it was apparent to at least one listener that Sacharoff was right about the peace movement. But just as the peace movement is essentially silent on how in the immediate future the United States can hope to prevent another terrorist attack, Lems was equally convincing in questioning whether the measures being taken to thwart near-term dangers might not pose even greater dangers in the long term. As in many a good discussion or debate, this one didn't so much resolve an issue as advance its consideration.

Nearly fifty years ago, I took a course in Group Discussion. It was standard fare in Speech departments at the time, but, as I recall, rather boring. One reason was that the topics didn't typically grab at people. In Dewey's terms, they didn't address a "felt need."

Contrast that with the topic suggested by Sacharoff, or with the topics chosen by the students, or with the problems faced by the PDDers when differences arose within their ranks about how to stage a scheduled event, or about the quality of a previously conducted discussion. Terry Halbert was right: Learning is best when students are engaged. Dewey was also right: Group interactions work best when they engage a felt need.

EXPORTING TIF, EXTENDING TIF

At the outset of this chapter, I suggested that the TIF model was exportable to other colleges and universities; indeed, that several "higher eds" were already in the process of adopting it. I also suggested that TIF was expandable, by which I mean that it has interesting implications for curricular and extracurricular education, as well as for scholarship. In this concluding section of "provocations," I take up these claims.

Exporting the Basic TIF Model

Recall the basic elements of the TIF model. Broadcast transmission is not one of them, although the WHYY *Radio Times* connection has been a most welcome add-on. Neither are TIF's video documentaries an essential element, although I am delighted that we have been able to show "highlights" videos of two of TIF's most important events.

Perhaps the simplest way to run a TIF-like event is for two instructors, teaching at the same time, to bring their classes together as the nucleus for a public discussion or debate on a controversy of common interest to both. Journalism professor Pat Bradley and I did that before TIF was officially launched. At issue was the quality of media coverage in the first week of the Clinton/Lewinsky scandal. In private conversation it had become clear that a couple of Bradley's students and I had different takes on the matter. Bradley moderated, whereas I joined a student/faculty panel on the topic. Both classes profited, and so did the few people who came of their own accord. No executive committee was needed, no event advisory committee, no funding. Think of TIF as an extension of that pre-TIF experience.

Exporting TIF D&D

Many universities have parliamentary debate teams, but few have anything resembling the Public Debate and Discussion group, and still fewer tie a two-branched student extracurricular club to a faculty-initiated organization. The tripartite arrangement works reasonably well at Temple because the two branches of TIF D&D complement each other, and TIF and TIF D&D feed off each other. TIF's big events provide publicity for TIF D&D, and a measure of faculty protection, whereas some TIF D&Ders help with TIF events and are occasionally invited to appear on TIF/WHYY panels, or to interview audience members on video, or to moderate TIF's lunchtime discussions. TIF events also provide instructional models for TIF D&D, or fodder for criticism.

Sooner or later I expect the Temple Debate Team to become a stand-alone entity, leaving TIF and PDD in a symbiotic relationship. Whether other colleges and universities should adopt this or some other organizational arrangement must surely depend on local considerations, but here I want to make a brief for importation of something like the PDD model, with its hearings on campus issues, its forum events, and its workshops on public debate and discussion. Admittedly, this is faculty-intensive labor. Still, PDD is sheer joy for me, and it accomplishes many goals at once for those who participate: first, mastery of the skills of discussion, debate, and critical assessment; second, learning how to plan and organize public debates and discussions; third, assuming responsibility, and having done so, feeling empowered; and fourth, having a social, emotional and intellectual blast. *I would recommend importation by colleges and universities of something like the PDD model, whether or not they adopt the TIF model.*

Making Broadcast, Internet, and Video Connections

TIF has been extremely fortunate in having had the benefits of the WHYY *Radio Times* connection. *Radio Times* has meant higher-quality programming; added campus excitement; a large and uncommonly influential and well-educated listenership; and, not least, added stature for TIF and Temple. Still, arrangements such as the *Radio Times* connection are in some ways fortuitous and do not always last. Other colleges and universities might well find it expedient to market TIF-like wares to their campus radio station, or to public access television, or to an educational video network. Videotaped coverage can also be streamed via the Internet. It helps at the very least to have an organizational Web site such as the TIF site. TIF is also extremely fortunate in having had the digital video services of professional videographers. Universities considering adoption of the TIF model might well consider incorporation of these accoutrements into their business plans.

Reaching Other Student Populations

TIF was created to serve undergraduates at one university, but there is no reason in principle why the model cannot be adopted by graduate and professional schools, or by high schools, or by consortia of colleges and universities. Imagine, for example, a forum series explicitly designed for graduate students and faculty on the idea of objectivity in the human sciences, offered at a time when several different classes might converge in one auditorium to wrestle with this highly controversial issue. Imagine another forum series for the high schools on issues specifically tailored to teenagers and featuring, perhaps for the first time, some of their teachers in public but civil disagreement. And picture as well the possibilities of colleges and universities in a given locale, banding together to produce TIF-like events of common interest to them all at rotating sites, but with opportunities for call-ins from each. Here is a way to weld local higher eds together for something other than competitive sports.

Teaching Public Discussion, Studying Public Discussion

My experiences with TIF and TIF D&D have convinced me that our field is not doing enough with public discussion, both as an object of study and as requiring a set of skills or competencies every bit as useful as those developed in an introductory public speaking class. Much of communication today is interactive, whether in organizations, classrooms, or public settings. This is especially true of mediated public communications, as in talk shows, hearings, and press conferences. Students need to learn how to perform in interactive settings, and they also need to learn how to analyze and assess various types of interaction. From coaching PDD and coteaching the Discussion Methods class, I have found the rapid give and take of the talk show format to be particularly useful for honing speaking, reception and critical thinking skills. Students also tend to like it better than panel discussion because its rapidity comports with their experience growing up in the fast-paced world of television.

Moreover, at its best, public discussion is an art form, deserving of as much scrutiny as rhetorical critics bestow on oratory and campaign debate. Among its most innovative television moderators have been Fred Friendly, Bill Moyers, and Ted Koppel. Some televised discussions, such as the *Nightline* Town Meetings from Jerusalem, are historically significant as well. Just as there are courses examining the best in public address, so too should rhetoricians create courses around treasures of public discussion.

CONCLUDING COMMENTS

This chapter has brought news of the Temple Issues Forum and its student arm, the TIF Debate and Discussion Club. The discussion has moved between the philosophical and the practical, between the dialectics of pedagogy for civic engagement and the mundane logistics of organization. The burden of this chapter has been that TIF, along with its student arm, provides a model worth emulating, in whole or in part, at other colleges and universities. As founder and coordinator of TIF, I stand ready to assist other higher eds in adopting the TIF model while adapting it to their special needs.

On its Web site, TIF quotes that old curmudgeon, George Bernard Shaw: "The way to get at the merits of a case is not to listen to the fool who imagines himself impartial, but to get it argued with reckless bias for and against." My reckless bias is for TIF itself, and particularly for its commitment to a certain vision of the university as a site of public controversy, where preparation for citizenship and for the life of the mind counts every bit as much as career preparation. TIF utilizes today's talk show formats and communication technologies, but its core values are old, very old, dating back to the ancient Greeks and Romans. Academics have a special obligation to help preserve them.

WORKS CITED

Campbell, J.A. "Oratory, Democracy, and the Classroom." *Democracy, Education, and the School*. Ed. R. Soder. San Francisco: Jossey-Bass, 1996.
Gleiss, D.J., and B.H. Smith, eds. *The Politics of Liberal Education*. Durham: Duke UP, 1992.
Graff, G. *Beyond the Culture Wars*. New York: Norton, 1992.
Halbert, Terry. E-mail to the author. 21 Oct. 2001.
Hauser, Gerard. *Introduction to Rhetorical Theory*. 2nd ed. Prospect Heights, IL: Waveland, 2002.
Joslyn, Richard. E-mail to the author. 29 Apr. 2002.
Mill, John Stuart. *On Liberty*. 1859. Arlington Heights, IL: AHM, 1947.
Putnam, Robert D. *Bowling Alone: The Collapse and Revival of American Community*. New York: Simon, 2000
Simons, Herbert. W. "Teaching the Pedagogies: A Dialectical Approach to an Ideological Dilemma." *After Postmodernism: Reconstructing Ideology Critique*. Ed. H. W. Simons and M. Billig. London: Sage, 1995.
Sparks, P.M., ed. *Advocacy in the Classroom*. New York: St. Martin's, 1996.

APPENDIX A: TIF FORUM EVENTS

Teaching Race and Racism Courses at Temple: Should Faculty Take and Defend Controversial Positions in the Classroom—April 14, 1998

Bill Clinton's Starr-Crossed Future: Exploring the Options—October 1, 1998

Is Capitalism Good for the Poor?—November 2, 1998

The Emerging Welfare Crisis in Philadelphia—March 4, 1999

After Graduation: Then What?—March 26, 1999

Higher Education and the City—October 7, 1999 (TIF/WHYY event)
- What Can Mayors Do?
- Mayoral Forum
- Higher Education as an Engine of the City's Economic Growth
- Higher Education and the City's Public Schools

Race: What's Discussable? What's Not? Why Not? —November 9, 1999

Character Issues in Campaign 2000—February 22, 2000

Welfare Reform in Philadelphia: Getting Off the Roles, Staying Off the Roles—March 2 2000

Talkin' 'bout Race: Questions of Identity—September 25, 2000

A Moratorium on Capital Punishment in Pennsylvania?—October 3, 2000 (TIF/WHYY event)
- Issues of State and Nation
- Capital Punishment in Philadelphia

Greater Philadelphia College Town Idea—October 20, 2000 (at WHYY)
- Is Philadelphia a College Town? If It's Not, How Can We Make It One?
- Collegetown Philadelphia as an Engine of Economic Growth

Whatever Happened to Student Activism? —November 14, 2000 (TIF/WHYY event)
- Mainstream Political Activism
- Outside the Electoral Mainstream

Suburban Sprawl—April 11, 2001 (TIF/WHYY/CSC event)
- Dealing with Sprawl
- The Coming Water Shortage in the Philadelphia Suburbs

The Bombings and Beyond—September 13, 2001 (TIF/Provost's event)
- Roots of U.S. Middle East Conflict
- Changing Nature of National Security
- How Have the Bombings Changed America's View of Itself
- Media's Responsibility
- Coping with Stress

U.S. Response to the Bombings—October 30, 2001 (TIF-WHYY event)
- Expert Panel
- Student Panel

Issues of Identification and Identity—January 31, 2002 (TIF-WHYY event)
- Profiling of Arabs and Muslims in America
- When Is It OK to Use the "N" Word?

If You Had George W's Ear: What Advice Would You Give the President on How the U.S. Should Respond to the Current Arab-Israeli Conflict?—April 18, 2002

The Lives of Suburban Teenagers—April 25, 2002 (TIF/WHYY/CSC event)
- What Is It Like Growing Up in the Suburbs?
- Creating Teen-Friendly Suburban Environments

APPENDIX B

TIF VIDEO PRODUCTIONS

Higher Education and the City: Highlights of the TIF Mayoral Forum and Conference—October 7, 1999 (4½ minutes)

Blame the Professor? An examination of the causes of students' political alienation, drawing on student responses to the TIF Mayoral Forum as a case study (12 minutes)

Bombings and Beyond. Highlights of TIF's all-day forum, held just two days after the terrorist attacks (22 minutes); features discussions of media coverage, treatment of Arabs and Muslims in the United States, response options, role of the university, permissible dissent, and student-faculty dialogue.

TIF D&D FORUM EVENTS AND HEARINGS, 1999-2002

TIF D&D's Public Debate and Discussion Group has staged forum events and hearings on campus issues at which faculty and administrators are invited to testify. (Not listed here are TIF D&D events cosponsored with Temple Issues Forum.)

Should Hate Speech Be Free Speech at Temple University?

Affirmative Action at Temple University

Physician-Assisted Suicide

A Service Learning Requirement at Temple?

Where Should the New Stadiums Go?

Hearings on the "Studies in Race" Requirement

Whatever Happened to Student Activism? A Follow-Up

Hearings on Grade Inflation at Temple

Public Forum on Grade Inflation: A Discussion and a Debate

Roots of Islamic Discontent with U.S. Foreign Policy

Globalization

Reparations for Slavery

True Love: A Valentine's Day Special

Resolved: That the Peace Movement Has Had Nothing Significant to Say about How to Respond to 9/11

What's Fair Game for Dissent by Faculty Post-9/11, and What Should be Considered Out of Bounds?

Is Suburban Youth Culture Good for Suburban Youth? Is it Good for the Rest of Us? Why Is It So Often Maligned by the Media?

Racial and Ethnic Profiling Beyond Black and White

Hearings on a Possible Gender Studies Requirement at Temple

II

President's Panel: The Rhetoric of 9/11 and Its Aftermath

Introduction to the President's Panel

Gerard A. Hauser
University of Colorado

The September 11, 2001 attack on the World Trade Center and the Pentagon created a fissure in the American political conscience. For the first time since the War of 1812, its shores had been breeched by a foreign attack. Moreover, the attacker was not a nation but a terrorist network, perhaps as large as 40,000, and who did not fight in a conventional manner but engaged in guerilla warfare. For a nation that lived in security from foreign attack, the message was unmistakable and disorienting—you are not safe anywhere. The use of domestic passenger planes as bombs stated emphatically: We can attack at any moment, in any place, and are prepared to sacrifice our own bodies by using them as the lethal instruments of war. The response of the American President was equally swift and clear: This is an act of war. We will find you and, if necessary, kill you. We will regard those who harbor you as our enemy and use military force to depose them from power.

If these initial responses were swift and clear, what was to follow was anything but. How do you fight a war against terror? What are the terms of engagement? How do you know who is the enemy? How do we make sense of the act, the attacker, the waging of war against an enemy who is elusive, of uncertain identity, and appears to live among us, the demonizing of dissenters, the media coverage that seems eager to report without questioning? And where do you draw the line on the government's proposals to suspend certain of its citizens' civil liberties? These are complicated questions that arose fairly close to the al Qaeda attack and have remained at the fore of equally complicated disciplinary considerations ranging from the rhetorical construction of public understanding and commitment to the challenges of educating aware and active citizens and the role of rhetoric studies in that process.

The President's Panel was assembled during the week following the September 11, 2001 attack. A group of scholars was asked to focus on different aspects of the discourse that was likely to grow from the event and its aftermath, track it for the next nine months, and discuss their findings at the RSA meeting the following May. Their formal presentations follow.

6

Terrorist Rhetorics, Rhetorics of Democracies, and Worlds of Meaning

Francis A. Beer
University of Colorado

We all watched our televisions in horror as hijackings, building implosions, and anthrax incidents intruded into our comfortable world. These events involved countless individual tragedies, including the victims, their families, friends, and associates.

The visual rhetorics of these events have been so powerful that it was almost impossible not to fall into their reality. We were there. It happened before our very eyes. We saw planes crash into buildings and people jump out of them. And yet... were we there? Or were we watching television? Enhanced, concentrated television. Reality television.

We fell into terrorist rhetoric. The suicide bombers created their own ethos. They had the courage of their convictions; they were willing to make the ultimate sacrifice and die for their beliefs. There was plenty of pathos to go around. Children and adults alike were terrified and will carry the memories for their entire lives. We could not always see it, but the attack was an argument in the war for the liberation of Saudi Arabia and the Middle East from enemy infidel political, military, economic, and cultural occupation. The logos of the act included striking a blow at the heart of America, on iconic targets—the World Trade Center and the Pentagon. It included the irony, delicious to terrorists and their supporters, of using the enemy's own planes against it.

We also fell into our own rhetoric of terrorism. We had been attacked by "terrorists," not "soldiers of Islam." We saw our heroes—firefighters and police, Todd Beamer and Rudi Giuliani. We heard the speeches. The President called us to action. Recalling the words of Winston Churchill during the dark days of World War II, he told us that we would not tire, we would not falter, and that we would not fail in our war against evil. Dan Rather offered to sign up. There was biography, individual stories printed serially in the *New York Times* for each of the victims. There was metaphor. Osama bin Laden became one with Genghis Khan,

Bakunin, Hitler, Tojo, and Satan. September 11, 2001 was equated with December 7, 1941. Terrorism became part of a larger allegory—a tale of good versus evil, order against chaos, as the characters wrestled at the edge of the abyss at the end of the world.

Terrorist rhetorics feed into the rhetorics of democracy, as we and other democratic societies engage in a great debate, asking what we should do now. One body of opinion suggests that World War III is upon us. According to this narrative, Western civilization itself is under attack. It is faced with radical evil and needs to use whatever force is required to eradicate it. The many people who die—innocent as well as guilty, civilians as well as soldiers—are the necessary cost of maintaining American freedom and Western civilization. The United States, to recall the words of earlier times, will pay any price, bear any burden, to make the world safe for democracy.

The story is clear, but the path in the real world is uncertain. As U.S. military forces deploy for action across the globe, critics wonder if vast military actions are likely to achieve their aims. Can all of the guilty be so easily located in the distant mountains and deserts of the world? Is bombing completely innocent civilians consistent with our values? Do not these people also have individual biographies, collective metaphors and allegories? Will we encourage our allies or repel them? Will we persuade the billions of people in other cultures that they want to be our partners? Do we wish to follow policies that risk escalating the already terrible losses toward the very much higher casualty levels of World War I, World War II, Korea, and Vietnam? Alhough one could ask the same questions of those who undertook the attacks, we can, for the moment, only try to answer them for ourselves.

There are other stories, other questions. How will our actions produce a world in which terrorism is less likely to grow, a terrorist antiworld? We still focus narrowly on our immediate response to the terrorist attack. How do we remain true to ourselves and our long-term vision for our own open society? How do we work to create a more democratic, just, and peaceful future for ourselves and for all the other people on this planet? Do we do this alone or in a discourse with our democratic allies? Do we widen the violence against our enemies or restrict it?

The standard story of international relations suggests that world politics is a struggle for power in an amoral field of forces. A new postrealist understanding tells a more rhetorical story, seeing international relations as part of a global interpretive struggle for meaning. It is not yet clear how terrorist rhetorics and rhetorics of democracies play through each other. It is, however, obvious that the rhetorics of terrorism and democracy are major parts of emerging twenty-first century worlds of meaning.

7

The Triumph of Consolatory Ritual Over Deliberation Since 9/11

Dana L. Cloud
University of Texas–Austin

In the 1990s I wrote about the character of American public life during the Persian Gulf War:

> The American nation was figured as a unitary body—the body anti-politic—in need of comfort and reassurance. The framing of responses to the war in terms of emotional support represented a therapeutic displacement of political energy, effectively cordoning off and muting the voices of opposition to the war, thereby protecting the fragile social space from the anger of protesters. (*Control* 86)

If I was worried then, I am even more so now in the context of American foreign policy and the crisis of public deliberation since 9/11.

In this chapter, I only sketch the barest outlines of that crisis, its causes, and its consequences. Most of all, I want to exhort rhetoricians to adopt a more public role in enabling critical deliberation of foreign policy and war. Rhetoricians have long been aware of the power of epideictic discourse—the rhetoric of consolation, identification, and social unity around shared values. Recently, Gerard Hauser has explored the didactic function of epideictic in laying the ground for political action. Hauser argues against critical scholars who bemoan the inherently conservative tendencies in ceremonial discourse. Instead, he notes epideictic's democratic potential: Discourses of praise and blame instruct publics in moral rectitude and establish common ground for action; and sometimes epideictic can be a vehicle for controversy and insight.

I do not mean to write off emotion, desire, and identification as key components of rhetorical action. But unlike Hauser, I tend to regard epideictic discourse, as least as it happens in late capitalist society, as inimical to or containing of *krisis,* the moment of judgment and action that depends on its cognate, criticism. Especially when collectives are mobilized for war, epideictic warrants a more skeptical approach. Without condemning all epideictic discourse, I would suggest that in such situations, it can be profoundly undemocratic because it rules inappropriate and unwelcome anyone offering questions, criticism, or a plea for rational thought.

At the University of Texas, where I teach, the voices of progressive faculty were smothered in the thick consolatory space of mourning that followed the attacks of September 11. Several days after the attacks, journalism professor Bob Jensen published an op-ed in the *Houston Chronicle.* Jensen argued that if we found the indiscriminate targeting of civilians to be beyond justification on U.S. soil, we should also find it to be so in Afghanistan, where, if history were any guide, U.S. bombs would kill many innocent civilians. The President of the University of Texas, Larry Faulkner, published a scathing response in the *Chronicle.* Faulkner's letter, apparently provoked by a great deal of negative mail regarding Jensen's piece, attacked Jensen as a "disgusting" "undiluted fountain of foolishness" whom no-one takes seriously anyway.

Many of us among the progressive faculty found this public denunciation of a member of Faulkner's own faculty to be quite chilling (Cloud, "Jensen vs. UT"). Faulkner's letter was an emotional diatribe that did not respond meaningfully to the arguments and evidence that Jensen's writing presented. Rather, Faulkner cast Jensen out of the university community, designating his own employee as outside the fold. Interestingly, other faculty and alumni shared Faulkner's view on the basis of defining community in emotional and epideictic terms after September 11. The Chair of the Faculty Council, for example, told me that he thought Jensen was right to raise questions, but he should have waited a respectable number of days or weeks before violating the bubble of mourning. It was unclear in his remarks how long one should wait, as a nation prepares for and executes a war, to raise questions of life and death.

Today, it is impossible to watch television, go to a movie, drive down the street, or listen to politicians talk without being sucked into the imagined unity of American nationalism. Recently, I purchased postage stamps at my credit union. The teller gave me a sheet of American flag stamps, each of which bore the motto "UNITED WE STAND." Politely, I asked her whether there were any other choices for stamps. In a huff, she said no. When I began to inquire about something else, she directed me to a different window for assistance. Perhaps we ought to explore the postage stamp as epideictic discourse.

At my daughter's school musical, we were invited to sing along with the finale number, "God Bless America," which invokes not only national unity but a theistic one as well. Risking my daughter's playdates and any future I might have on the PTA, I stood, silent and uncomfortable as everyone around me belted out their sense of belonging. Images of the American flag accompany appeals to grief and fear from the West Wing (both real and fictive) to Spiderman. Despite a growing and vocal antiwar movement (most visible in Washington, D.C. on April 20, 2002 and February 15, 2003), there is not much cultural space for critical thinking or dissent about the war on terrorism. Meanwhile, the United States is gearing up for another war on Iraq, when the last one (and the subsequent sanctions) have left more than 2 million civilians dead and the entire nation bombed to rubble (Pollack). Certainly, epideictic discourse will play a role in mobilizing publics in support of this new war, too.

However, it is not the genre of epideictic that is to blame for uncritical nationalism. The impulse to national unity is a product, in part, of the tight-fisted corporate control over the media. Ninety percent of United States media outlets are owned and controlled by just four corporate media conglomerates. Media scholar Robert McChesney writes, "The corporate media system, in conjunction with the broader trappings of a modern capitalist society, necessarily generate a depoliticized society, one where the vast majority of people logically put little time or interest into social or political affairs" (xxxi).

The influence of corporate media in cultivating depoliticized citizens is backed up, as Gramsci suggested long ago, by the power of the state in its crackdown on civil liberties at home and abroad. "You are with us or you are with the terrorists," George W. Bush said, effectively criminalizing dissent and questioning. The war on terrorism has required not only media propaganda but massive witchhunts, secret detentions, roundups of thousands of Arab and Arab American immigrants and citizens; military tribunals, proposals for legalized torture, retinal ID cards, and internal passports; harassment and discipline of students, professors, and media reporters who speak out; a new racial profiling that has led to attacks and deaths; delay in visa processing for thousands of innocent immigrants; and many other repressive acts. The USA Patriot Act allows sweeping antidemocratic actions, including searches of citizens and noncitizens without probable cause, detention of immigrants without a hearing, e-mail and Internet spying, and tremendous expansion of government powers to spy on and prosecute political protesters, dissenters, and organizations (Cohn 19-20).

Thus, the American culture of consolation—antagonistic to controversy, history, and evidence-based reasoning—is cultivated even more strongly during wartime. I do not mean to blame ordinary people themselves, whose grief, shock, and horror on and since September 11 are real and honorable. Of course, some consolation is appropriate under such circumstances. However, I am targeting for critique the cultivation in politics, the news media, and popular culture of an addiction to epideictic. Identification feels good, whereas arguing with people in mourning while feeling devastated oneself does not. When the members of Congress sang "God Bless America" on the Capitol steps, it sent a clear message to the American public: Put aside your partisan disputes. Feel better. We're going to war!

In this context, rhetoricians need to prompt the asking of some key questions for deliberation: *What are the actual U.S. motives and goals in this war?* There is some evidence that the United States had been pressuring the Taliban in Afghanistan long before September 11 to cooperate with plans for a new oil pipeline from the Caspian Sea through the country. The world, its people, and its resources are fair game for transnational corporations. But these corporations still have national home bases to which their profits inexorably flow. When movements or rival states threaten a nation-state's transnational corporations' or geopolitical interests, that nation-state may respond with domestic policing or foreign military intervention. War is the face of globalization that reveals it to be little different than the imperialisms of any other capitalist period. But now, just as during the Persian Gulf War, the U.S. public is not encouraged to think beyond the stated motives of vengeance and elimination of terrorism.

What are the actual and likely consequences for ordinary people of this war? It is not likely that the war on terrorism will end terrorism. More likely, it will exacerbate the anger and despair of Arabs and others in countries affected by the austerity required of ordinary people by globalizers, the rain of bombs, the cruelty of sanctions, and the support of the United States in the Middle East for something that should be specified for what it is: colonialism and apartheid. In the process of achieving its economic and geopolitical aims, the United States has already caused the deaths of thousands of innocents, including as many as 3,800 people in Afghanistan, according to University of New Hampshire economics professor Marc Herold. As the London *Guardian* reported:

> Based on corroborated reports from aid agencies, the UN, eyewitnesses, TV stations, newspapers and news agencies around the world, Herold estimates that at least 3,767 civilians were killed by US bombs between October 7 and December 10. That is an average of 62 innocent deaths a day—and an even higher figure than the 3,234 now thought to have been killed in New York and Washington on September 11. (Milne 16)

University of Texas professor Jim Fishkin found, in a widely publicized experiment in deliberative polling, that when ordinary people are provided with enough information to deliberate and form well-reasoned opinions, they do so (Wolf). My colleague Jim Aune thinks political economists of the media are naive to believe that ordinary people, provided with more and better information, would automatically be more critical deliberators. I, on the other hand, see some cause for optimism: Rhetoricians have the resources to foster the dissemination of information from multiple points of view in public. In addition, we have the skills of criticism to expose propaganda and consolation as inadequate forms of discourse in a democracy. For this work, we need the tools of modernist ideology critique, including depth hermeneutics. *Depth hermeneutics* refers to the idea that there are some knowable realities underneath ideological discourses and that critics ought to be in the business of digging through the dirt to find them. Alternatively, given that we cannot know those hidden realities without understanding them in systems of signification either, the idea of depth hermeneutics is to expose and analyze contradictions in the answers we can find to the important questions. Especially during a war, hegemonic rhetorics exhibit the characteristics of propaganda, an old-fashioned but useful word describing opposition-silencing, agenda-obscuring texts.

We also need a guiding normative ideal of critical rationality if we are to challenge the nation's consolation addiction. Poststructuralist discourse theory takes what is in the true—in other words, what is accepted as true—as what must be accepted as true in a relativized world. On this view there are no truths "behind" the discourses that constitute truth in themselves. Thus, there can be no finding out about Conoco's interest, backed by the U.S. government, in an oil pipeline route through Afghanistan from the Caspian Sea. There is no point in discovering that the United States was planning an intervention in Afghanistan months before September 11, 2001. We cannot count the bodies of dead people if they are less than human in the reigning imaginary. We cannot name the war, constructed as a war for freedom, as a series of futile atrocities in the interests of oil companies. If Hussein and bin Laden are the dictators *du jour*, it is pointless to point out that the Taliban and Saddam Hussein were once friends and beneficiaries of the United States, or that there are countless other equally oppressive dictators who have been installed and buttressed by U.S. forces. Indeed, in a widely discussed article, conservative Sebastian Mallaby suggests that the U.S. need for a stable international scene and the failure of aid and development programs such as those overseen by the IMF and World Bank warrant a new imperialism in which the United States should impose its aims by force in every troubled nation. Mallaby argues that the United States might benefit by engaging in neo-colonial nation building.

Poststructuralist theorists, like wartime propagandists in a therapeutic culture, substitute identification for reasoning, image events for dialogue, and dissemination for deliberation as the key terms to describe how persuasion happens in late capitalism, replicating the dominance of epideictic over deliberation in American public life (DeLuca and Peeples; Greene). These theorists suggest that we resign ourselves to charting a hypermediated and irrational reality that is not, in any deep sense of the word, democratic. This work may accurately describe existing communicative practices in late capitalism. Yet, without a normative ideal of deliberation we cannot have a democracy. Deliberation includes the capacity to seek out and entertain multiple positions on a given event, the capacity to historicize events, the capacity to weigh competing evidence and reasoning and discard the less credible, the capacity to probe the motivation of discourses and adhere to those with the fewest privately motivated sponsors, and the capacity to take action based on this deliberative process. When pieces of what is "in the true" contradict one another, we must enable students and other citizens to decide who's most probably lying.

We can and must teach these skills to our students. Beyond that task, we have to find venues and media to encourage critical thinking among publics at large. We must disrupt the equations of war with justice and dissent with terror. We need to pay attention to instances in which exhortations to strong identification make for an ever-weaker democracy-cum-pep rally in which we have little relevance or influence. In a society without a deliberative public, we may as well all become therapists.

WORKS CITED

Cloud, Dana L. *Control and Consolation in American Culture and Politics: Rhetorics of Therapy*. Thousand Oaks, CA: Sage, 1998.

---. "Jensen vs. U.T.: Ideas Unwelcome?" *Houston Chronicle* 22 Sept. 2001: A39.

Cohn, Candace. "The Assault on Civil Liberties." *International Socialist Review* 22 (2002): 18-31.

DeLuca, Kevin Michael, and Jennifer Peeples. "From Public Sphere to Public Screen: Democracy, Activism, and the 'Violence' of Seattle." *Critical Studies in Media Communication* 19 (2002): 125-151.

Faulkner, Larry. "Jensen's Words His Own." *Houston Chronicle* 19 Sept. 2001: A39.

Gramsci, Antonio. *Selections from the Prison Notebooks*. 1936. New York: International, 1971.

Greene, Ronald Walter. *Malthusian Worlds: U.S. Leadership and the Governing of the Population Crisis*. Boulder, CO: Westview, 1999.

Jensen, Robert. "U.S. as Guilty of Committing Own Violent Acts." *Houston Chronicle* 14 Sept. 2001. 26 Sept. 2001 <http://www.chron.com/cs/CDA/printstory.hts/editorial/1047072>.

Hauser, Gerard A. "Aristotle on Epideictic: The Formation of Public Morality." *Rhetoric Society Quarterly* 29 (1999): 5-24.

Herold, Marc W. "A Dossier on Civilian Victims of United States' Aeriel Bombing of Afghanistan: A Comprehensive Accounting [revised]." *Cursor* March 2002. 11 May 2003 <http://www.cursor.org/stories/civilian_deaths.htm>.

Mallaby, Sebastian. "The Reluctant Imperialist: Terrorism, Failed States, and the Case for American Empire." *Foreign Affairs* (2002). 10 Sept. 2002 <http://www.foreignaffairs.org>.

McChesney, Robert W. *Rich Media, Poor Democracy*. New York: New Press, 1999.

Milne, Seumas. "The Innocent Dead in a Coward's War." *Guardian* (London), 20 Dec. 2001: 16.

Pollack, Kenneth M. "Next Stop Baghdad?" *Foreign Affairs* (March/April 2002). 10 Sept. 2002 <http://www.foreignaffairs.org>.

Wolf, Richard. "Poll Shows Voters' Flexibility: Immersion in Issues Can Change Minds." *USA Today*, 26 Jan. 1996: 9A.

8

Citizen Rhetorics After 9/11: Back to Bidness as Usual

Rosa A. Eberly
Pennsylvania State University

Frank Beer's comment that rhetoricians should stick to studying rhetoric rather than focusing on the issues of other disciplines—journalism, political economies of media, political science, to name a few—is likely well intentioned. It is also strangely flattering: Rhetoricians are not frequently encouraged to do more of whatever it is we do, if "rhetoric" as a "discipline" is even conceivable to whomever—dean, department head, colleague, neighbor, editor, donor—is doing the encouraging... or the disciplining. Still, Professor Beer offers yet another means of contextualizing my comments on this panel, wherein I am charged with saying something about Citizen Rhetorics in general and, perhaps more specifically, about Radio Rhetorics or citizen discourses on the radio in particular in the wake of "the events of September 11."

I'll say by way of departure, then, that rhetoric is often most powerful when it is juxtaposed with other disciplines and practices. In addition to the commonplace—or, arguably, counterfactual-yet-normative ideal—of something called "public deliberation," rhetoricians need to address political economies of media when they make claims about "encouraging citizens to participate in democratic practices." Too often, even when citizens might want to "engage"—when they have something they want individually or jointly to say—they do not have the means of getting what they want to say or share or ask or wonder or do before the eyes or ears (i.e., into the attention economies) of others. So part of my message here is that the nefarious consequences for public discourse of the Communication Act of 1996 (see McChesney and others for what is now a standard critique) further complicate any vehement but perhaps facile celebration of or call for increasing citizen voices after 9/11. This leaves many students and other citizens, in the language of Sharan Daniel, "all dressed up with nowhere to go"—if they have had the experience or education to make them want to engage in communities of action. Indeed, without the very combination of rhetoric with other critical tools—in this case, political economies of media—we could risk adding to our students' disillusionment with public affairs by asking them to invent and revise public discourses—to read widely, to work hard, to be rigorous, to give it their best—when the fruits of their labors have little chance of being read or heard by people who need to know what these students have to say. Rhetoric *and,* rhetoric *across,* rhetoric *beyond,* rhetoric *with*: Collaboration unleashes the transformative *dunamai* of rhetoric's productive and practical powers.

RADIO RHETORICS: "CALLERS ARE PROPS"

I'll start, then, with an observation that major market radio veteran Chuck Meyer made when he visited my undergraduate Radio Rhetorics class in January 2002. The class had been talking about and working on projects focused on talk radio's potential for growing public discourse. Chuck told us that we should not deceive ourselves: According to radio broadcasters, "personalities," producers, station managers, and consultants, "Callers are props." This infuriated nearly all of the students in the class, most of whom were listening closely to talk radio for the first time in their lives (undergraduate students are among those least likely to listen to talk radio or to read newspapers). In the context of an undergraduate rhetoric class that used radio as its architectonic *topos,* students took seriously my challenge not just *to study* but *to produce* radio discourses. Thus, the idea that what they were doing at the time outside of class—engaging in low-level culture jamming by calling local radio talk shows and attempting to make discourse do more than merely entertain—was merely to serve as props really angered them. It did not, however, surprise them.

Among the several media, radio remains the least studied yet arguably the most potent for moving people and shaping quotidian, vernacular public opinion. Although talk radio has played a central role in the changing political topology of the United States in recent years, it is not widely regarded as a central locus for public interaction. Whereas other communication media have been studied exhaustively—although perhaps not sufficiently—in terms of their effects on public discourse, few scholars of communication, rhetoric, or technology studies have looked at the relationship between the quantity and quality of discourse on local radio and the quality of local civic life and public discourse more generally.

On 9/11 and during the next few days, many radio stations deviated from their usual dross of syndicated fare and mind-numbing commercials: Instead of Rush and Dr. Laura and Opie and Anthony, many stations ran news and public affairs programming 24 hours a day for most of that week, and many opened lines to callers. Radio became a medium of public communication that week, much as it was initially and much as it should be—given that, by law, the airways—at least theoretically—belong to "the people," and given that corporations like ClearChannel (the people who brought us the list of songs banned after 9/11) and Infinity Broadcasting vow to operate "in the public interest" in return for the privilege of using the people's airways.

If you go to Lexis/Nexis and try to find transcripts of the radio talk during the week after 9/11, you'll see only one-line reports (e.g., "Discussion of Attack on

World Trade Center and Pentagon"). The archive of spontaneous human speech, the archive of voices attempting to make sense of what happened that day and what has happened since, is largely gone. So if you want to study radio, start taping. I recorded a lot of radio in Austin that week, mainly open lines on KUT (the local public radio station and NPR affiliate). Stations generally do not share tapes with listeners or scholars, if the stations even record what little local talk they might still broadcast.

One last word for now, on the power of the human voice and the perils of allowing corporations to use radio stations as short-term commodities to be bought and sold to maximize profits: When I was in New York State in late September 2001, I heard on WCBS that Verizon Wireless saved all voice mail from September 11 and offered recordings of lost loved ones' voices to families who might have missed their calls.

What is it about the human voice—*ethos, vox,* unique to every human—that compels us? What is it that spontaneous human speech, even when recorded and replayed, can do to us that no automated voice software or Ananova newscast can do? Finally, what is it, despite that power, that keeps us from reclaiming the airways that are rightfully ours? As Robert McChesney argued in *Rich Media, Poor Democracy*:

> The commercial broadcasters have become de facto owners of the public airwaves, and challenges to broadcast licenses on the grounds that a commercial broadcaster has failed to provide a public service are virtually impossible to win [...]. If there is no viable threat that a station-owner might lose its license if it fails to provide a public service, or if such failure is not otherwise severely punished, there can be no meaningful enforcement standards for public service on commercial broadcasters. (69)

Did you know the airwaves used to be *public,* in the sense that by law they *belong to the people*?

I'm eager to hear what you make of what you heard on the radio after 9/11. Did any of you call in to a station after 9/11? Tell us why and how it went. I'm also eager to hear what kind of radio you think it would take to operate "in the public interest" after 9/11. Obviously, radio provided a space for information and grieving in the first few days after 9/11. Since then, except for National Public Radio (whose audience grew significantly in the days after 9/11 and who is now using focus groups to try to maintain that larger audience by offering more entertainment-related stories to capture the elusive 18-to-24 demographic) it's pretty much back to bidness as usual.

WORKS CITED

Daniel, Sharan Leigh. "Rhetoric and Journalism as Interrelated Arts of Public Discourse: A Theoretical, Historical, and Critical Perspective." Diss. U of Texas at Austin, 2002.

McChesney, Robert W. *Rich Media, Poor Democracy.* New York: New Press, 1999.

9

The Rehabilitation of Propaganda: Post 9/11 Media Coverage in the United States

Mark Andrejevic
University of Iowa

The mainstream media responded to the challenges of what they call the "post-9/11 era" with an intriguing double gesture combining a renewed sense of purpose with a rediscovery of the strategic importance of propaganda in the ongoing battle against terrorism. On the one hand, pundits and news anchors publicly promised to wean themselves from a confessed addition to junk food news, whereas on the other hand they expressed a new-found and self-consciously patriotic interest in the role the media might play in the so-called "war of words." The notion that the media institutions in a free and open democratic society have an important role to play in a global propaganda campaign might seem anathema to journalists newly committed to a sense of professional purpose, but there is a precedent for this juxtaposition that harkens back to the era of the "great generation" for which aging news anchors seem to harbor a particular nostalgia. Indeed, it is hard not to discern in the media's reaction an attempt to resuscitate their own public image by drawing on their glory days of World War II (and consigning to the dustbin of history the aberrantly critical countercultural era of Vietnam and Watergate). This attempt was not merely successful, but also fit quite neatly with the desire of conservatives to overcome public reservations regarding U.S. military action abroad in the post-Vietnam era. The sense of moral outrage over an unquestionably heinous act of terror could be neatly channeled into a sense of the inherent justice of the U.S. response, effectively foreclosing/eclipsing a more general discussion of its global position and policies.

In the end, the emphasis on the "war of words" focused attention away from this more general discussion—which was treated at best as a separate issue from the immediate exigencies of the war in Afghanistan. As Richard Holbrooke put it on *Nightline*, "We need a better message, we need better messengers. And whether or not you want to change our policy, that's for some other time." At worst, the notion that U.S. foreign policy might help breed anger and resentment abroad was ruled out as a misguided and treasonous attempt to justify an unjustifiable crime.

The conservative line rules out a discussion of U.S. foreign policy with the assertion that, as William Bennett put it, "We are a target not because of anything we have done, but because of who we are, what we stand for, what we believe, and what our nation was founded upon: the twin principles of liberty and equality." The notion that our policies may not have always lived up to those stated principles is taken as an attack on the principles themselves.

The disturbing result is the prospect of an escalation of a war on terrorism in which the cannon fodder, at least on the U.S. side, is the very same populace that remains woefully uninformed regarding the agenda and consequences of the policies pursued in its name. It is this fact—that the majority of the lives sacrificed in any escalation of war will very likely be civilian rather than military—that is the least publicly acknowledged distinction between the war on terrorism and more "conventional" forms of warfare. Taken at face value, the conservative assertion that escalation is inevitable highlights the disingenuousness of the propaganda campaign itself: If our foes are driven by implacable evil, good PR isn't going to help. If, on the other hand, the pursuit of foreign policy that more closely adheres to a stated commitment to principles of freedom and justice in the region could promote goodwill that would help deescalate the war and save the lives of soldiers and civilians, the attempt to divert attention away from the material impact of U.S. policy past and present in the Middle East (and elsewhere) is the real act of treason. All of which is not to deny the appropriateness of taking action against those who have attacked the United States, but rather to suggest that the goal should be deescalation and a sincere commitment to the principles that we preach in our policies both at home and abroad.

SCARED STRAIGHT: THE RETURN OF REAL NEWS

In the wake of 9/11, I found myself approached by two journalists from reputable newspapers in my capacity as someone who writes about reality TV. The premise of the questions was the same in both cases: Why wasn't the reality TV trend fading away in the wake of the all-too-real situation that the nation was facing? It was a question that highlights the fundamental failure of the news media in the *pre*-9/11 era: The reporters seemed to assume that the only reason reality TV was popular was that there just wasn't enough real reality to go around. This premise was compounded by the reporters' willingness to believe their own self-congratulatory stories about the sudden return of real news and serious journalism in the wake of 9/11. A year-end headline in the *Buffalo News*, for example, summed up a spate of coverage about the media's rediscovered priorities: "A Year Divided; Remember when we cared about ab rockers, ruffled blouses and Eminem? Boy, did our priorities change on Sept. 11" (Violanti E01).

Reporters and anchors reveled in their newfound commitment to real news—a commitment promptly rewarded by a boost in the press's public opinion ratings, according to The Pew Research Center for the People and the Press, which found record increases in press popularity along all thirteen measures that it tracks ("Serious Agenda"). From a marketing perspective—and polls like this are good for little else—this is great news for media corporations, but we shouldn't confuse it with the assertion that news outlets are belatedly providing readers and viewers with the information they need. On this point, I disagree with Robert Hariman's assertion during the panel discussion that the media's reaction to the 9/11 attack proved that democratic debate was alive and well in the news media. This subject has been explored at length by media critics, and I limit myself here to suggesting that even if one accepts Hariman's qualification that the public debate was alive and well in the *New York Times* and on the Internet, the majority of Americans still receive their news from television. The question that needs to be asked is whether we believe members of the U.S. public have an adequate—not comprehensive, just adequate—grasp of the global consequences of the policies pursued in their name, of the interests that shape these policies, and of how and why the United States is viewed as it is by other nations—both friends and foes; at stake is more than a commitment to seemingly abstract principles of freedom and democracy, more than the suffering and strife of distant peoples. At stake is the way in which that strife remains directly linked to our own—the flipside of globalization.

In the end, journalism's newfound seriousness was hard to distinguish from the sensationalism ostensibly left behind. The topic seemed much less frivolous, perhaps, but the approach remained the same: the presentation of carefully engineered spectacles for consumption. The spectacle that remained conspicuously *absent* was that of the war in Afghanistan itself, once it got underway. Tight government/military control combined with media self-censorship meant that the images consumed on the homefront tended to be distant shots of impressive military equipment and coverage of generals in the command center in Florida pointing to maps. Interestingly, Al-Jazeera TV was the primary source of graphic images of the actual bombing for media around the world (except the United States, which relied on the tightly controlled images released to its media organizations), at least until the November 2001 bombing of its station in Kabul, just ahead of the arrival of the Northern Alliance troops in the city. One thing the return to serious journalism apparently did not entail was any attempt to hold the administration and its policies—past or present—up to critical scrutiny. Indeed, the media consensus seemed to be in strong accord with the Bush administration's apparent assumption that during an important and justified war, it would be inappropriate to subject them to criticism.

REHABILITATING PROPAGANDA

Alongside the media's renewed sense of purpose emerged a fascination with the role that the media itself had to play in the war effort. In particular, a focus on what was frequently called the "propaganda war" became a recurring theme in both the print and television coverage, which, in keeping with the reflexivity that has come to characterize "savvy" coverage (Gitlin), held up propaganda as an object for public consideration. Perhaps the most significant aspect of this coverage was the way in which it sought to recuperate the term *propaganda* itself by countering a perceived tendency to equate propaganda with totalitarian manipulation. As Ted Koppel put it in the introduction to his special report on the "The Battle Over the Message":

> Propaganda's gotten a bad name over the years. It has been used so often and so skillfully to distract our attention from monumental acts of wickedness that we are reluctant sometimes to even admit that the U.S. government uses it or needs it. [... W]hy do we need to shape or tweak or spin that reality into something more comfortable or palatable, something that people around the world will find easier to digest? Well[,] it will come as no surprise to you to learn that not everyone perceives reality the same way.

Because some people don't see it their way, even the good guys need to "spin" their policies.

This view of propaganda is explicitly associated in the post-9/11 media coverage with the World War II era and the need to muster public support at home and abroad for the pursuit of a just war. During the Cold War, however, the attempt to use the term *propaganda* as a way of distinguishing between the U.S. and Eastern-bloc media backfired by helping to fuel concern over so-called news management techniques pursued by the U.S. government during the Cuban Missile Crisis and the Bay of Pigs Invasion and eventually during the Vietnam War. Thus, the rehabilitation of propaganda neatly corresponds to the "great generation" era nostalgia associated with the rediscovered sense of journalistic purpose described previously: Both harken back to a version of U.S. policy freed from the taint of the Vietnam era.

The rehabilitation of propaganda, then, turns away from an inspection of U.S. policy to the way in which it is portrayed. Consequently, a number of politicians and pundits have suggested that the United States take advantage of the global hegemony of its media industries to improve its image. Former FCC chairman Newton Minow recently suggested that the United States devote one percent of its defense budget to so-called public diplomacy (as opposed, presumably, from the private kind, unfit for mass consumption). Minow, like many other would-be strategists in the "war of words," points to advertising and branding as his public diplomacy model of choice: "American marketing talent is successfully selling Madonna's music, Pepsi Cola and Coca-Cola, Michael Jordan's shoes and McDonald's hamburgers around the world [...]. Yet, the United States government has tried to get its message of freedom and democracy out to the 1 billion Muslims in the world and can't seem to do it" (Minow 17N). The answer, he somewhat illogically suggests, is *more* marketing. Oddly enough, the Bush administration seems to agree. Shortly after the 9/11 attack, it appointed Charlotte Beers, former head of two of the nation's most prestigious advertising firms, as Undersecretary of State for Public Diplomacy. Her appointment was greeted by Secretary of State Colin Powell as a welcome addition to U.S. diplomacy that would focus on "branding foreign policy, branding the [State] department, marketing the department, marketing American values to the world and not just putting out pamphlets" (Carlson C01).

In addition to the branding campaign and in keeping with a refeudalized model of news provision, the administration is turning to reality TV to help manage the public spectacle of U.S. military action. The Pentagon recently gave its approval for the producers of the film *Black Hawk Down* and the TV series *Cops* to produce a reality show for the ABC network about U.S. troops in Afghanistan. The producers, of course, would have to submit their footage to the Pentagon for security clearance, but in return they would receive the kind of access to the front lines that has hitherto been denied U.S. media organizations, according to network sources (Dowd 13). The military has also been cooperating with reality TV producers for a show on fighter pilots. Programs like these have helped create a new genre of so-called "militainment." If, in other words, the war coverage on the news side has bordered on being a tightly orchestrated spectacle for public consumption, the entertainment industry is providing the closest approximation to real war coverage available to viewers.

It is hard not to see the Pentagon-facilitated militainment genre as an extension of the war on words and the attempt to sell foreign policy at home. Indeed, in response to claims that such reality shows were designed to provide uncritical coverage of the military, Admiral Craig Quigley told news reporters that "There's a lot of other ways to convey information to the American people than through news organizations" (Burkeman 17). Of course, not all of these ways provide the public with the information they need to assess the policies that are being pursued in their name and the direct impact that such policies may have on their own lives. The proliferation of militainment recalls Walter Benjamin's disturbing observation (with respect to the Italian Futurists, who may have been ahead of their time) that humankind's "self-alienation has reached such a degree that it can experience its own destruction as an aesthetic pleasure of the first order" (242).

MINING THE CONTRADICTIONS

The current attempt to separate the war of words from the impact of U.S. foreign policy in terms of bombs and bodies, both past and present, relegates the public to the passive role of infotainment consumer. The "serious" model of reportage that marches in virtual lockstep with administration policy complements the rehabilitation of propaganda insofar as both suggest there is nothing the U.S. public can *do*, precisely because the 9/11 attacks were unrelated to anything that has been done in their name. The implicit leap of logic suggests that because the attacks were unjustifiable, there cannot be any flaws in U.S. foreign policy (and to suggest otherwise would amount to an attempt to justify the attacks). This approach clearly oversimplifies: It is surely possible that the attacks can be morally unjustifiable *and* that U.S. foreign policy may still be flawed such that fixing those flaws may help reduce animosity toward the United States and thus deprive terrorists of supporters and sympathizers. Finally, there is little doubt that U.S. policy in the Middle East region has repeatedly failed to live up to our nation's stated commitment to freedom, democracy, and the rule of law. On the contrary, the United States has gained a reputation for supporting corrupt, undemocratic regimes in the name of democracy and for underwriting oppression in the name of freedom. The fact that it has failed to get its "message" across is thus not a communication failure that can be addressed by simply rebranding U.S. policy.

Interestingly, the assertion that there is a purely arbitrary relation between the U.S. "message" and the material impact of its policies demonstrates the dialectical reversal whereby staunch conservatives unite with their ostensible arch-enemies, the "postmodernists" they roundly accuse of relativism. Those who believe that any policy can be marketed as democratic if the PR department is good enough clearly don't believe that democratic principles have any determinate content or any nonarbitrary relation to material reality. They seek not to confront contradictions but to paper them over, and in so doing posit an incoherently one-sided relationship between discourse and material reality: Determination can flow from the former to the latter, but not the other way around. One of the disturbing results is that because of the hypocrisy with which the United States has wielded its message of democracy, freedom, and self-determination, these values themselves have come to be seen in many quarters as ruses of a callous and cavalier imperialism. The marketing approach adopted by the Bush administration runs the risk of exacerbating this perception in the name of countering it. The alternative that should be considered very carefully by those whose lives are on the line—including U.S. civilians—is the attempt to address the contradiction directly: to resuscitate U.S. values by attempting to make our policies live up to our stated principles rather than spinning the principles into an alibi for our policies. A politically responsible rhetorical approach would mine the contradictions rather than licensing the attempt to smooth them over. Admittedly, such an approach does not guarantee victory in the struggle to defuse and defeat terrorism, but such a struggle cannot hope to succeed without it.

WORKS CITED

"The Battle Over the Message." *Nightline*. ABC. 1 Nov. 2001.

Benjamin, Walter. "The Work of Art in the Age of Mechanical Reproduction." *Illuminations*. Ed. Hannah Arendt. New York: Schocken Books, 1968. 217-51.

Bennett, William J. "What is AVOT? An Open Letter from William J. Bennett." *AVOT Home Page*. 14 Apr. 2002 <http://www.avot.org/stories/storyReader$29>.

Burkeman, O. "TV Series on Afghan Offensive." *The Guardian* [London] 22 Feb. 2002: 17.

Carlson, P. "The U.S.A. Account; Ad Woman Charlotte Beers's New Campaign: Getting the World to Buy America." *Washington Post* 31 Dec. 2001: C01.

Dowd, Maureen. "Coyote Rummy." *New York Times* 24 Feb. 2002: 13.

Gitlin, T. "Blips, Bites and Savvy Talk: Television's Impact on American Politics." *State of the Art: Issues in Contemporary Mass Communication*. Ed. D. Shimkin, H. Stolerman, and H. O'Connor. New York: St. Martin's, 1988. 213-22.

Minow, N. "Why the World Isn't Listening to Us." *Chicago Tribune* 19 Mar. 2002: 17N.

"Serious Agenda; Serious Interest." *Baltimore Sun* 24 Dec. 2002: 2A.

Violanti, A. "A Year Divided; Remember When We Cared About Ab Rockers, Ruffled Blouses and Eminem? Boy Did Our Priorities Change on Sept. 11." *Buffalo News* 30 Dec. 2001: E01.

10

Remarks for 9/11 Panel

James Arnt Aune
Texas A&M University

Those of you who have known me for awhile know that I am not usually the most optimistic person in the room, but today that is not the case. As I compare my fears today with my fears immediately after 9/11, what I am struck by is the fact that Americans actually seemed to have learned something about civil liberties during wartime. The Patriot Act—which is actually not entirely new, because its worst provisions date back to the McCarran-Walter Act of 1952—has been roundly criticized not just by the left but also by courageous libertarians and conservatives such as Bob Barr, and it is beginning to be scrutinized by the federal courts. And although we in the humanities have for years, as Emerson put it, listened to the "courtly muses of Europe," I believe it is instructive that whereas France has Le Pen (and Austria has Haider, and Italy Berlusconi), we have a goofy president who actually invited Muslim schoolchildren to the White House to talk about Ramadan. All those union members in New York City who worked day and night in the ruins of the World Trade Center showed us a form of patriotism far different from that of Rush Limbaugh. We are not, pace Noam Chomsky, a fascist state.

I believe that we need to be careful as academics in taking stands on political issues. We often fall prey to what Pierre Bourdieu called the "scholastic fallacy"—that is, we overestimate the power of discourse in human affairs; we become overinvested in ideological purity, multiplying unresolvable debates (Bitzer v. Katz, Biesecker v. Campbell) in order to stake out positions of institutional power; we commit ourselves to abstract rather than concrete values (in Perelman's and Olbrechts-Tyteca's sense); but we wonder why those abstract values do not persuade ordinary people. Real politics, as opposed to academic politics, is a world of compromise, log rolling, ideological impurity, and violence—which is, finally, not a text.

But what can we do, specifically as rhetoricians? The following set of commitments follow from our commitment to the rhetorical tradition:

First, we need to defend free speech. I was struck recently by economist Amartya Sen's finding that no nation with a free press and free speech ever has experienced a famine. We can be active on our campuses in promoting free speech, against groups like American Council of Trustees and Alumni (ACTA, who began drawing up an enemies list of disloyal academics last fall), but also against ourselves, who in the name of sensitivity have stifled classroom debate for a decade.

Second, we need to renew our commitment to argument in *utramque partem.* The greatest piece of cultural software we rhetoricians contributed and still contribute to the world is arguing both sides of an issue. It not only contributed to the development of the rule of law; it also helped contribute to the development of religious liberty during the Renaissance. But we have not been as careful as we should to include libertarian, conservative, religious, and other voices in our academic dialogues and debates.

A third important value is the importance of historical thinking. For many of our students, our classes are their only contact with the cultures of ancient Greece and Rome, or even with American history. Last fall, as I was teaching the unit on medieval rhetoric in my large lecture class on the History of Rhetoric, I was discussing the dark side of the period with a close analysis of Uccello's painting about Jewish desecration of the host. I described the concept of the blood libel, and one of my students raised her hand and asked, "Did Jews really do that?" (i.e., slaughter Christian infants to make matzah out of their blood). The concept has resurfaced this year, in the official newspaper of Saudi Arabia, our supposed ally, and in pamphlets circulated at Berkeley and San Francisco State—not to mention the brisk sales of the *Protocols of the Elders of Zion* at the UN conference on racism in Durban. A year earlier, in my course on Church and State Conflict, I was describing George Washington's lack of religious piety, and one of my students interrupted me to claim that I was getting my information from a biased source. She insisted that Washington was a bible-believing Christian who had been saved at Valley Forge by the direct intervention of an angel. If we are serious about developing citizen-critics, we need to insist that students learn basic facts and principles of U.S. government and history, even though all the current trends in the university, from the worship of quantitative methods to the poststructuralist assault on reason, work against such learning.

I spent a good deal of time in the 1990s worrying about postmodernism. If you live in Texas for awhile, however, you begin to realize that the main problem is actually *pre*modernism. A final imperative is to promote the ideal of what Edward Said has called "secular criticism." I have personally found precious little to agree with Professor Said since the Oslo Accords, but in this case I believe he was dead-on right. In the Arab world, Israel, and the United Sates, the trend has been toward "an ultimate preference for the secure protection of systems of belief and not for critical activity or consciousness." Even in the university, as Said writes, we have seen an "increase in the number of fixed special languages, many of them impenetrable, deliberately obscure, willfully illogical. [...] Intellectual debate increasingly resembles high-pitched monologue in narrow corridors" (292). Secular criticism refuses to treat any vocabulary as sacrosanct. In contrast, Tom DeLay and Ralph Reed support Israel not because of any political principles (the fact that Israel is the only democracy in a sea of petty tyrannies) but because Israel has a specific role to play leading up to the Rapture. The secular critic dares ask how much misery just in the past year has been created by devotes of the Abrahamic religions. What 9/11 suggests above all is how fragile are the values of the Enlightenment: reason, the rule of law, science, free inquiry. That so many in the university arena are now inclined to scoff at these things as "bourgeois," "modernist," or "merely liberal," suggests the danger in which we find ourselves.

WORKS CITED

Said, Edward. *The World, The Text, and the Critic.* Cambridge, MA: Harvard UP, 1983.
Sen, Amartya. *Poverty and Famines.* Oxford, UK: Oxford UP, 1983.

11

Public Culture and Public Stupidity Post-9/11

Robert Hariman
Drake University

Much has been made of the need for reflection following the events of September 11, 2002. On the left, we claim that there is need to examine anew American foreign policy, economic dependency on oil, and cultural arrogance. On the right, there is criticism of the extent to which the United States is an open society, the U.S. government is encumbered by international agreements, and the American public is complacent in the face of a clash of civilizations. As these reactions demonstrate, everyone's first response was to interpret the conflict through their most familiar frame of reference.

I happen to think that the criticisms from the left are far more important—and far less dangerous—than those from the right, but that isn't saying much in the context of this forum. What is most needed, I believe, is not more reflection itself but reflection by more people. If ever there was an occasion for public debate, this is it, because the issues involve everything from the ordinary citizen's sense of personal security to the conduct of "the world's lone superpower." As we get closer to the first anniversary of 9/11, however, it becomes clear that debate on the important questions of foreign policy and national power is fitful at best. Thus, the terrorist attacks provide another occasion for reflection: this time, on the state of the public culture.

Let me make a few observations to that end. What should be remarked on? First, the quality of news coverage was superb, as long as you knew where to look. If you read the *New York Times* and followed the news on the World Wide Web, you couldn't have asked for more. This may have been one of the finest hours of American journalism. It also was a renaissance of photojournalism, in part through the added value that comes from the circulation of still photos through the Web. And if the Gulf War was the first cable news war, 9/11 demonstrated the great value added that comes from news coverage and discussion over the Web and the Internet. By contrast, television news was vastly inferior in scope and quality to print and digital coverage. I hope someone will ask why.

My second observation is that the American people did just fine, thank you. In general—most but not all of the time—we proved to be more tolerant, pluralistic, civic minded, and generous than many expected. (Nor did it hurt the collective self-image that the disaster happened amid the deeply multicultural society of New York City, and at the heart of the American media establishment.) Moreover, this is how the American people were at the time of the event, and not because of it. This is good news, of course, and a testament to the progressive social movements and decades of social change preceding 9/11. The question remains whether people will change for good or ill because of it, and that points again to the question of the amount and quality of public debate, and to the question of who will succeed in framing interpretation according to what interests and worldview.

There also was some bad news. The Bush administration started a new cold war, the nuclear clock moved forward, and worldwide militarism grew larger and more dangerous to minority populations and democracies everywhere. And the American public revealed itself to still be stupid regarding foreign policy—dumb as a stump, way short of a load, stupid.

Now let me be clear about this last point: I am not saying that people in general are stupid, or that ordinary people are stupid, or that the public typically is stupid. As it happens, I believe in democracy. We need to face facts, however: Americans are by any measure incredibly ignorant about the rest of the world, inattentive to foreign affairs, and childishly supportive of the president's rhetoric and actions in all matters of world politics. It took about a decade of constant coverage and 40,000 American deaths before there was strong opposition to the Vietnam War, which still claimed another 10,000 American dead before it was ended. Support of dictatorships of every stripe makes no dent in any president's approval ratings, and the many, often transparently cynical, military interventions of the past decades typically boost them. Citizens who insist on their right to bear arms to protect themselves against their own government think nothing of crushing peaceful democratic movements abroad. The American public's neoliberal marriage with government is most evident in the conduct of foreign policy: As long as each leaves the other alone to do as they wish, everyone is happy.

Let me also be clear that my remarks are not made to blame the public. How could they be otherwise? Even without consideration of the role of ideology in opinion formation, there are three major obstacles to their wising up: First, there is the geographic isolation of the United States and the cultural assumptions that has produced. This is old news, so I'll move on to the second factor, which is the political economy of American journalism. Whether it is the revenue-driven composition of local news coverage or the working relationship between the national news organizations and their government sources, the result is a continual stream of euphemisms amid coverage that generally supports administrative action. This, too, is known well enough, so let me mark one other factor: Foreign affairs is the area of news coverage that is most removed from the actual, everyday experience of the viewer. Stated otherwise, it is the most highly mediated area of politics, and, therefore, the one most dependent on media practices and most disposed to be ignored or accepted uncritically. On any other issue—crime, welfare, taxes, education, and so on—the government policy is likely to overlap with the ordinary citizen's experience. That experience might be as simple as leaving one's car unlocked without incident, standing in a checkout line as food stamps are cashed, balancing a checkbook, or paying a textbook fee. The point is that the official rhetoric can be tested against personal experience. This is much less likely to happen, however, when hearing about the deployment of troops to Indonesia, the president's "balanced" stance toward the Palestinian problem, or the use of international law to falsely accuse American troops. Without the test of practical experience—and without the comprehensive sense of self-interest that was produced by the draft—there is little opportunity or incentive for critical thinking.

One result is that progressive intellectuals need to settle in for the long haul. Events will not educate by themselves, and a few university forums in the immediate aftermath of an attack will not suffice either. It is vitally important to educate the public about American imperialism, but it is also very difficult. The public can be brought to oppose unjust and dangerous actions, and perhaps even to endorse a just foreign policy, but it takes a long time and a lot of work to get there. It may well be that a democratic public can handle most of its problems without intellectuals, but not this problem.

12

Love and Theft After 9/11: Magnification in the Rhetorical Aftermath

Thomas Farrell
Northwestern University

Originally, I looked forward to the date of 9/11 as the release date of Dylan's long-awaited album, to be called *Love and Theft*, so that is the reason for this odd title. Professor Hauser assigned me the topic of magnification, and I am grateful to him for the challenge. Magnification is, of course, the active voice of magnitude; and it has a rich conceptual legacy throughout our rhetorical tradition. In fact, it is within the paradoxes of magnification, understood rhetorically, that we may begin to appreciate the terror that lurks beneath our war on terrorism.

Let's begin with the two meanings of *magnification*, at least as I understand them. Deriving from the Latin, *magnificare, magnification* may refer either to the rhetorical practice of embellishment, the embroidery of hyperbole we encounter in our everyday conventions of excess. *Or* (and this is an important corollary), magnification may refer to the enlargement of something apparently minute through extremely close scrutiny. I am tempted to consider this latter tendency a form of technological myopia, but it has also been with us as long as the rhetorical tradition itself (perhaps as an aside; I am thinking here of the casuistic stretching that occurs when we debate the virtues of Helen, how many angels can dance on the head of a pin, Zeno's paradox—you get the picture, or at least a minute portion of it). Both senses of magnification were with us during the period I would describe as rhetorical shock and bereavement following 9/11.

This would normally be the time to attack the media, as a sort of ominous enemy, an entity of wretched spectacular excess. But in general, the media (perhaps stunned by reality's cruel force) tended this time to let the facts speak for themselves. Embellishment, of a sort, had to occur, as we were originally informed that over 6,000 persons had been killed in the bombings. This turned out to be unnecessary overkill. No need for "pictures at eleven." For once, the facts did "speak for themselves." I have to agree with *Time* magazine's choice of Rudy Guiliani as Person of the Year if only for his sobering and eloquent remark that regardless of the final tally, the loss would be "more than the human heart can bear." Rarely, if ever, has a rhetor stood up to a public moment with such an admission of stark inadequacy. If there remains such a thing as public virtue, its traces may be glimpsed here.

All of God's orphaned children know by now that modernity "occurs" when system and lifeworld part company. But here, in the wake of 9/11, there are lessons aplenty. For one thing, despite Burke, Habermas, and a legion of critical theory minions, it hardly seems the case that some version of modernity is inevitable. If you simply consider the fruit loop who engineered this assault on modernity, before he became the zealot he was essentially the playboy of the Western world. So erase the board. Fundamentalism, the foreclosure of options, can also be seen to be an *option.* And if you don't believe that, consider that in NYC, at this very moment, there are twelve- and thirteen-year-old kids who are being "taught" that the suicide bombers of 9/11 were martyrs and heroes.

Thus let us turn to the second sense of magnification, that of intense scrutiny, in evidence in the wake of 9/11. First, there is the terror of the colloquial. You all will remember, as do I, that those bosom flatulent buddies, Falwell and Robertson, were reminiscing away about how the World Trade Center bombings were just God's way of opening a window of vengeance against us for—oh what?—allowing gays into the military, allowing women to begin to compete with men, allowing Clinton to remain president. Well, guess what? In the glare of crisis, when system and lifeworld have already parted company, colloquial comments can themselves be held up to intense scrutiny. These fundamentalist evangelicals were essentially revealed to be what they were and are, which are fundamentalists. So, if I may intervene, one important sense of magnification, at least in current circumstances, is that the colloquial, pedestrian asininity we might normally dismiss becomes, as they say, fraught with significance. Oddly enough, the intense scrutiny of monologism, in a time of crisis, revealed a pluralist theme. I do not have the time to go into the intricacies of this little episode, other than to say that having your own television channel apparently means never having to say you're sorry.

Another aspect of the lifeworld—the arts—suffered a more severe blow when Karlheinz Stockhausen decided to declare that the World Trade Center attack was "the greatest work of art that is possible in the whole cosmos" (qtd in Rosenbaum 68). He added, as if to elaborate, that "this is something in one act that we couldn't even dream of in music. You have people who are so concentrated on one performance, and then 5000 people [there's that magnification again] are dispatched into eternity in a single moment. I couldn't do that. In comparison with that, we're nothing as composers" (*ibid.*). Now, if you've ever listened to anything composed by Stockhausen, you will perhaps understand his nadir point of comparison. But that is not my point; my point is that once his doomed-to-be-disastrous performances were cancelled, this dilettantish modernist of all modernists blamed nothing less than the devil for having distorted his extemporaneous remarks. I guess the point here would be intense scrutiny of the colloquial in crisis quickly reverts to the fundamental.

Modernity, as we know, even under attack, is a sort of contest between the system and the lifeworld: the institutions and the culture that supposedly civilize and sustain us in rhetorical culture. When the system controls the culture, by force or inducement, we have what might be called *hegemony*. This is, if you will, change by force, or—in modern terms—strategic initiative. Then the forces of the culture, whether in margin or center, begin to strain against the hegemony of the institution, and we have the beginning of a rhetorical change I call, for want of a better phrase, "populist imperative."

It is obviously too early to sort out just how "magnification" from system to lifeworld and back again sorted itself out. My beloved (indirect and unnamed) coauthor has reminded me how the *New York Times* managed to humanize the otherwise unfathomable enormity of the 9/11 episode. They did day-by-day obituaries of each individual victim. Each was a sort of caricature of magnification. Thus, a person could be captioned as "Lover of practical jokes," or "Avid gardener." I am not intending to poke fun here—each of these folks was a living, breathing creature fatally deprived of his or her humanity—but what I am stressing is that a form of magnification often consigned to cliché became necessary as a way to humanize enormity. Long ago, Roland Barthes wrote of this sort of discourse as "Fait Divers," essentially the trifling stuff that fills in the gaps between important news. But it may be worth noting that the *New York Times* won a Pulitzer Prize for what amounts to an epic docudrama of obituary columns. "The death of one man is a tragedy. The death of thousands is a statistic." You know who said that? Joseph Stalin.

To magnify is, in a sense, to encapsulate, to essentialize. And, in its less than infinite wisdom, so did the institutions of governance. Their earliest attempts were not without difficulties. First, there was "infinite justice." One does not have to be a Kantian to know that this is a contradiction in terms. Then there was the short-lived "Crusade" against evil. This worked until someone figured out that prior "Crusades" had not exactly worked to recruit Byzantine and middle-eastern populations. Then followed "enduring freedom." But this is not without peril. I am not making this up. I actually heard a playoff announcer in baseball last fall (2001) solemnly intone that we should all sing "God Bless America," so that we might better be able to "endure our freedom." I guess it does matter whether you consider the modifier to be a verb or an adjective.

Because I am a proponent and ardent acolyte of appreciative criticism, I think it is time to pay tribute to a magnification that, in effect, paid off. Looking back to the weird tango between system and lifeworld after 9/11, it seems that hegemony had a more than willing accomplice with the *nomos* of our world. After all, Bono paraded around the stage draped in the American flag, and Paul McCartney sang about freedom as if it was his personal IRA account. Preservationist accounts notwithstanding (especially in the wake of Enron), freedom—in its most vital sense—is only even possible with the modern awareness of a collectivity. It is not a thing to be hidden under a mattress, to be preserved, but rather is always in the episodic state of becoming. It is something to be achieved through practice. Somehow, in the midst of all the clamor and turmoil of 9/11, a familiar—if discordant—voice emerged to help define and magnify this event. Like all the failed attempts before, it takes the familiar and the colloquial to make its point; but like the best of eloquence, it manages to make the familiar heroic, and even—within an outstretched imagination—identifiable.

So, let's roll. But where to? Where from? What is our trajectory? What is our velocity? I close with the three reasons you cannot win a war against an intangible. You might also think of these thoughts as three reasons why the culture of magnification (i.e., surveillance) hasn't generated the sense of outrage that people of an earlier generation might have anticipated. Reason one: We no longer have a viable dialectic of reflection in our culture. Our dialectics are not really about repression and expression so much as about inhibition and exhibitionism. Without wishing to throw too much mud (or other stuff) on an entire generation, we have a succession of generations with "nothing to hide." I refuse to speculate as to exactly why this is. As a charter AARP member myself, I find this both amusing and disturbing. Why are folks my age so disturbed at the prospect of the invasion of privacy whereas people of my son's generation remain so (what is the opposite), unperturbed? Imagine, for instance, a reality TV show that highlighted the MTV theme: "Gertrude gets her varicose veins treated." Big audience, right? So this remains a mystery. But I sincerely believe that this "stuff" has managed to immunize many of us to the darker aspects of our war culture. At present count, there are scads of reality TV shows, in which allegedly ordinary people are willing to display virtually and realistically any performative physical or psychical function for the entertainment of anonymous, out-there audiences. I'm not about attacking these people; I'm just saying that ever since *Candid Camera* we have been systematically immunizing ourselves to the surveillance culture. Look at the pioneering films, *Sex, Lies, and Videotape*, *The Conversation*, and especially *American Beauty* (which actually manages to portray distant surveillance as more authentic and intimate than conventional definitions of intimacy), and this will help to illustrate the point I am trying to make.

Reason number two, and I wish to put this as delicately as a left-leaning Democrat may state the matter, is that there is a fairly widespread sense that the current (George W. Bush) regime is notably bereft of, shall we say, intelligence? So, when you have the genius of Tom Ridge in charge of homeland security, when you have an entire agency that publicly announces it is in charge of spreading lies and disinformation, what is there really to fear, at least from the institutional infrastructure (what Molly Ivins calls "Guvmint")? Of course, there are many things to fear. At the same time when Green Berets are pulling a pregnant woman with a stroller over to inspect her nosehairs for concealed weapons, our ever-prescient authorities systematically managed to neglect the fact that people were going to flight training school but skipping the lesson about how to land. Thus, and this is just a speculation, my sense is that the government is widely perceived to be either too stupid to be afraid of, or that we—the so-called *informed* populace—don't need to even *try* to speak truth to power—if power seems to be dumber than a box of rocks. Codicil, and I intend no implied conspiracy charges here, *never underestimate the damage that can come from the dominion of the dumb.*

Reason number three, and this both puzzles and troubles me, I think there is a really serious issue when magnification enters the realm of attempting to caption intangibles. The best way I can place this is to start with the proposition that rhetoric is ultimately referential and eventful. This is not the same thing as Bitzer's scientific realism. I don't wish to go there. My point is rather different: Rhetoric emerges in contexts that need to be thought out, scoped out, and given alternative pictures and possible products. This is not some brilliant new insight. It is as old as Protagorasm, and it is as new as Pope John XXIII (although some, like Michael McGee might dispute this association). Hence, if the reflection isn't new, what is the problem? As near as I can get to it, it involves the problem of myopia. The closer we look at some aspect of appearance, the more likely we are to miss the overall "complexion" of the case. Journalists flocked to the CNN reviewing stand to applaud the success of the "Patriot" missiles in 1991. The missiles looked terrific on television; they just never, or rarely ever, hit their targets. We have tons of footage of the infamous TWA flight going down—we just don't know who did it. We have multiple streams of interview footage that are simultaneous with the Olympic bombing in 1996. Although there may be suspects, and a notorious case of mistaken suspicion, there is no one in custody. And, of course, as this chapter is written, the fact that hundreds and hundreds of Middle Eastern peoples in the United States currently being deprived of what I can only hope some future Supreme Court membership will determine are their rights goes without saying.

Thus, recall my opening theme of "love and theft." What is loved? Love is magnified in crisis. It should be. Crisis reminds you of what is important. I've had my differences with Tod Gittlin over the years, but I fully understand his impulse to drape an American flag over his Central Park apartment. In fact, as some of you may know, a prime mover in the Weather Underground found it necessary to cancel his book tour during this same period. I know both him and his wife (who was, at one point, No. 2 on the FBI's most wanted list—this may explain, by the way, why it was so easy for her to get away). In my view, the left—including Bill Ayers (there, I said it) were Patriots, of the same order as John Brown at Harper's Ferry. The deal between Ayers and Gittlin is an internecine squabble. Neither would question whether the cold-blooded butchery of completely innocent civilians was anything other than as I just characterized it.

Now let's turn to "theft." This is a forensic claim, and I wish to be clear that I am not making the claim here. As I (somewhat indecorously) remarked at the National Communication Association, these guys (i.e., "W" and his bunker-bound ventriloquist) couldn't even find the World Trade Center with a map and a tour guide. They are too dumb to have staged the deal. But this does not mean that a certain theft has not occurred. I am not a theorist of civil liberties. Was this deliberate, or in rhetorically generic terms, "deliberative"? Highly unlikely. Is it consequential? You bet... My point? Be extremely careful what you magnify. It may come back to haunt you. If there is a corollary, a dialectical counterpoint to magnification, it would not be inhibition. It would not be exhibition. It would be vision.

WORK CITED

Rosenbaum, Ron. "Degrees of Evil: Some Thoughts on Hitler, bin Laden, and the Hierarchy of Wickedness." *Atlantic Monthly* (Feb. 2002): 68.

III

Selected Papers

13

Populist Poetry or Rantum-Scantum? The Civil Disobedients of Poetry Slams

Jerry Blitefield
University of Massachusetts–Dartmouth

Reading Jeffrey Walker's *Rhetoric and Poetics in Antiquity,* I am struck by the similarities between Walker's account of ancient lyric poetry and modern day slam poetry (the original poetry performed at poetry slams). Although notable differences exist between the two, my focus here is not on that discussion. Instead, I explore several significant likenesses that qualify slam poetry to share Walker's claim for ancient lyric poetry: that, fundamentally, slam poetry is not rooted in appreciative aesthetics but in rhetorical judgment. But before I get to that argument, some background.

Chicago's Green Mill Tavern hosted the first "poetry slam" in 1986. At the time, The Green Mill saw withering audiences for traditional spoken word poetry readings, and slam was conceived as a means of recovery. It succeeded phenomenally, and since then slams have spread to cities large and small around the United States and Canada (56 teams competed in the 2002 National Poetry Slam in Minneapolis). In pubs, coffee houses, and now college campuses, poets regularly steel themselves to perform original pieces before often rambunctious audiences of slam devotees and curiosity seekers. In turn, five audience judges, selected randomly (often without expertise for the job), score those poems/poets "Olympic style" (e.g. 8.8, 7.2). Hyped as "verbal boxing matches" and "bouts," poets compete in "rounds." Each round's top scorers then advance upward into an ever-narrowing field until, at night's end, a champ is crowned.

In actuality, the whole process is high camp, and intentionally so. "Slam masters"—those who run the "bouts"—routinely deride the very competitiveness they officiate, ensuring that the clutches of *true* competition don't smudge the poetry ("The best poems often lose" is a regular tag). Still, there are rules, few and simple, but strictly adhered to: original poems only, no props or musical instruments, and performed poems must not exceed three minutes. Poets exceeding their three minutes lose points. The longer the overrun, the greater the deduction.

Audience rules are also simple and few: Always applaud the poet. When you (an audience member) hear a poem that you like, show the poet: clap, cheer, stomp your feet, raise the roof. Similarly, upon hearing a *score* that you like, show the judges: repeat the above. But when you hear a score you *don't* like, let the judges have it: boo, hiss, moan, wail.

Not surprisingly, slams' raucousness provides much for purists to criticize. However, if those criticisms diminish slam poetry's standing in the world of letters, those same criticisms should only increase its standing in the world of rhetors. For despite rhetoric's various definitions, all embed characteristics for which slam critics slam slams. For one, purposive messages (and their messengers) *do* compete, not only for acceptance but often simply to be heard. Arguing from the "margins" or from the position of the "subaltern" *ipso facto* means that those outlying positions present inherent rhetorical hurdles. Although not necessarily contentious, discourse from reduced status is by default competitive. If nothing else, in the West discourse competes for attention against capitalism's clamor.

Additionally, audience appeal cuts across rhetorical and slam poetry concerns. Although not every rhetor identifies with a marginalized group, every rhetor begins from a discursively marginal position: Simply put, the rhetor commences from the outskirts of an audience's awareness, and charting a pathway to that audience's ear must be discovered through appeal. This is so for any public discourse, be it of the marginalized or not, of the poet or of the rhetor.

Finally, the notion of "judging" is innate to rhetoric. Indeed, rhetoric evolved as midwife to human judgment, bearing the best judgment toward a course of action, a litigant's guilt or innocence, the values a society should honor and why. Rhetoric assumes that an audience, having judged one argument most sound among others, would more likely accept that argument as their own and be suaded by the rhetor's prescriptions.

At this point, some might counter that even if what I have said about rhetorical discourse is so, the connection between rhetoric and slam poetry remains flimsy. The criteria mentioned earlier—the competitive atmosphere, appealing to an audience, judging and scoring—suggest that much else not immediately thought to be rhetorical actually is: wine competitions, dog shows, gymnastics meets, and so on. What, then, about poetry slams merits them more serious attention?

Setting poetry slams apart is the role the audience plays—or doesn't. In the earlier examples—wine competitions, dog shows, gymnastics—the "judging" audience splits from the "spectating" audience, in a way that often models a courtroom. Courtroom spectators consume the performance and results of the adjudicating processes, but are formally excluded from those processes. Technically, spectators sit "outside" the dynamic of judging body and body judged, and whether at a wine competition, dog show, or gymnastics meet, the spectating audience knows it is not the *primary* audience, and indeed, not even a necessary one. In theory, it could all go on without them.

Not so with slam poetry, however, owing to slam's irreverent process of selecting judges. Slams select judges at random *from* the spectating audience, without regard for "expertise" (judges are often prized for their *un*familiarity with poetry slams). Consequently, the performing poets lack fixed, objective, reliable aesthetic criteria with which to craft pieces. No predetermined rubric of evaluation exists that the poet could be sure a sharp-eyed/sharp-eared "expert" would share, and reward. As anyone in the audience can be asked to judge, the audience/judge novice/expert divide gets erased, thereby dissolving nascent urges toward appreciating and rarefying slammed poetry as a lofty, arcane art form. If potentially anyone can judge, theoretically all are judges, and thus the poems performed—if to succeed—must have broad popular appeal.

Hence, from a competitive standpoint, academically trained slam poets face obvious difficulties, because those in the audience with heightened poetic sophistication are least likely to be chosen as judges. Lacking "sophistication," the accidental judges have no choice but to score on their visceral reactions to the poems. With no way of knowing each judge's viscera, poets are forced to aim for floating targets. In other words, the poet cannot simply play to the judges, because the poet has no way of knowing what, if any, discernible criteria a judge will use. Surely, most of the poets who perform want to score well, to "win," but they also know that because the scoring is a crapshoot they must abandon, at least to a degree, faith in a reliable causal connection between poem and score.

Missing channel markers, poets must then tack between the two shoals of pure personal expression and pure audience appeal, navigating amid self and public. And here is where slam poetry becomes most rhetorical, because if the ultimate aim of rhetoric is judgment, from which will come action (in contrast to static, aesthetic appreciation), in my experience slam audiences respond most to poems that present them with three minutes of political or cultural exigence. Poems asking the audience to judge, to take a position because something is gravely amiss, rivet most. Sure, audiences sometimes get wowed by verbal pyrotechnics or wooed by poems of splendorous love; I've seen poems sweet and light as powdered sugar bring down the house. But having observed numerous slams, I'd say slam audiences are more appetitive for conviction than for confection. I suggest this is so because the more substantial poetry—the poetry of exigence—endows the audience with a sense of agency, a sense of empowerment. That is, a good slam poem helps us negotiate our world, suggests that we have the individual power to do so, *even as it offers us art*. If the poet is on the mark, the poem gives us, the audience, a place to stand and a chance to act, as it gives us craft to behold.

Here we return to Walker, and to my claim: Although not yet two decades old, the audience-centered rhetorical discourse of slam poetry has spirits reaching back to classical times. In *Rhetoric and Poetics in Antiquity*, Walker points out that, insofar as it was publicly performed, the earliest poetic discourse served a civic function (and not simply an aesthetic one). Speaking of the categories *pragmatikon* (pragmatic civic discourse) and *epideiktikon* (epideictic civic discourse), Walker suggests that histories of rhetoric wrongly credit the pragmatic discourse of ancient Greek courts and assemblies with first developing civic rhetorical discourse. Rather, it was the epideictic discourse (not yet "rhetoric," because the term hadn't been coined) expressed in seventh to fifth century BCE, which is the zygote of "traditional" rhetorical discourse. Walker contends that the *epideiktikon* expressed in early poetry shaped the cultural ideals of the just and right (*dikê*) in the hearts and minds of audiences, which later got carried into the assembly and courts of the fifth and fourth centuries BCE. It was the precedence of epideictic discourse that formed the basis for the practical democratic discourse:

> In this view "epideictic" appears as that which shapes and cultivates the basic codes of value and belief by which a society or culture lives; it shapes the ideologies and imageries with which, and by which, the individual members of a community identify themselves; and perhaps, most significantly, it shapes the fundamental grounds, the "deep" commitments and presuppositions, that will underlie and ultimately determine decision and debate in particular pragmatic forums [...]. Conceived in positive terms, then, the distinction between the *epideiktikon* and the *pragmatikon* comes down to this: the *epideiktikon* is the rhetoric of belief and desire; the *pragmatikon* the rhetoric of practical civic business, a rhetoric that necessarily depends on and appeals to the beliefs/desires that epideictic cultivates. (9)

From this position, Walker suggests that epideictic is "the primary form of 'rhetoric' in its 'preconceptual' state, before it emerges into history as a named and theorized discipline" (16); that epideictic is functionally and civically prior to the pragmatic; and "that epideictic or 'poetic' discourse is the 'primary' form of rhetoric on which pragmatic discourse, and especially formalized pragmatic, is dependent for the major sources of its power—the culturally authoritative paradigms of eloquence and wisdom on which it draws" (16). As such, epideictic becomes the cornerstone of pragmatic judgment.

The transmillenial relationship that I contend exists between *epideiktikon* and slam poetry gets strengthened by way of Walker's explication of ancient lyric poetry. In the chapter "Theognis Octopus: On Poetry as Rhetorical Transaction," Walker begins by claiming that lyric poetry, defined as "a relatively short poem that typically can be understood as a single 'speech,'" is "the most basic, most fundamental of all poetic genres" (140).

This lyric poetry first appears in a "culture not yet informed by the disciplinary or 'philosophic' efforts to systematically theorize its [the poetry's] nature and proper function, such as we find in Aristotle's *Poetics*, or to provide principles of critical judgment that may shape the expectations of cultured audiences" (140). In other words, lyric poetry had not yet been critically formalized and formally criticized as so much poetry has been since.

Although it is inaccurate to refer to slam audiences as a "culture" in the way that Walker refers to early Greek culture, the comparison holds in that both lyric poetry and slam poetry developed within a milieu of few articulated critical preconditions, and for an identifiable audience. A crucial distinction exists, however, between the lyric and the slammed: The informality of lyric poetry endured largely because systemetizers had not yet coded it (Aristotle wouldn't be born for centuries), whereas the informality of poetry slams directly resists coded poetic formality and its interpretive ways.

The slam process of selecting judges willy-nilly bars "systematically theorize[d]" principles of "critical judgment" from occupying a slam, and hence the hegemony of formal poetics is given no ground. The three-minute rule applied to slam poems similarly confounds traditional formalism: For slam poets, the formal constraints are not structural but temporal.

Much more clearly arcs the millennia between lyric with slam poetry. Here again is Walker:

> as a fundamentally *rhetorical* practice, archaic lyric embodies a paradigm in which "poetry" may function (and did function) as culturally and politically significant discourse, that is, as an epideictic argumentation that can effectively shape communal judgments about *dikê*, or what is "right" in various kinds of circumstances, and so can effectively intervene in, intensify, or modify prevailing ideological commitments or value-hierarchies. (140)

Based on my experience, slam poetry is overwhelmingly interventionist, exigent to its core. The majority of slam poets are not concerned simply with amusing their audience; they exhort their audience, they want to change their audience, to move their audience. In many instances, slam poets seize the stage to demonstrate a world gone wrong, and to entreat the audience to set it right. I furthermore suggest that slam audiences don't want simply to be amused; they want the poets/poetry to intervene in their thinking. They come to slams to be challenged.

Good slam poets, then, like good lyric poets, deliver intervening poetry. They give the crowd what they came for: the power to see, and perhaps, then, to do. In stride with Walker, I claim that although not exclusively so, slam poetry is, like lyric poetry was, "a fundamentally rhetorical practice." Even if only to strengthen an audience member's commitment toward X, slam is rhetorical in that it first asks the audience to listen, then to judge, and then to act on that judgment.

The role of audience needs elaboration here, because one can argue about slam competitions, as well as about classical lyric performances, that the audience selects the poetry as much as the poet does. If, as Walker claims for lyric poetry and as I claim for slam poetry, these poetries are rhetorical in part because they both are interventionist, then poets could only survive public expression as long as they attended to public concerns. In other words, the simple reason why slam poetry is generally (perhaps generically) not about the purely aesthetic is that the audience doesn't want the purely aesthetic (critics would likely say the audience isn't schooled enough for pure aesthetics). If slam audiences did want pure aesthetics, those audiences would attract poets to fill the bill. Similarly, if classical audiences didn't welcome lyric poetry as "civic discourse [... to] shape communal judgements about *dikê*, or what is 'right' in various kinds of circumstances," audiences would have rejected lyric poetry's civic nature in favor of something less or non-civically oriented.

Hence, no audience is ever truly passive: Underpinning the claim of poetry as rhetorical discourse is the contention that the audience is *always actively judging*, trying on the poet's arguments and values for themselves, as ways to refit and redress their own being in the world. As such, any evaluative process contravenes passivity: Even though it may not seek specific action, epideictic rhetoric—here in the guise of publicly performed slam/lyric poetries—is ultimately a call to action. Enthymematically, if these poetries show us *dikê* in a convincing way, presumably our behavior would gravitate toward what is "right." Can it be that (slam) audiences really do look to (slam) poets for more than just verbal sportiveness, but for direction, a linguistic congealing of values? I think so. Ergo, the effects of poet on audience and of audience on poet flow bilaterally, ultimately rendering slam poetry a collaborative poetry.

Here is further judging, further rhetorical instantiation: Not only does the individual assess the poet and poem, the individual also assesses the audience's response to that poet/poem. That is, slam audiences experience more than just the poetry; they experience what Halloran, Martin, and Moore have referred to as "spectacle": "an event, bounded in time as well as place, in which a multitude of participants are consciously present to each other as well as to some object of common interest—articulating sharable experience and offering the possibility of an identification through which individuals become a public" (1). Within the spectacle, and when in synch with the collective, an individual will likely feel validated in his or her appraisal of the poetic performance and the values it demonstrates, its epideixus; if at odds with the collective response, he or she will likely try to account for the difference, and perhaps work it out. One thing is certain: No audience member can react to the slam poem oblivious to the reactions of the assembled, and remain untouched by them. The cultural appeal of the epideixus gets put to referendum, and the individual audience member must locate his or her values within the context of "the whole."

Such public spectacles endanger the prospects of private "contemplation" in the poetic transaction, because typically (or stereotypically) one's relationship with poetry is thought to be contemplative, pensive, self-paced. The pace of a slam (a "bout"), however, is, by design, anything but contemplative. It is poem (punch) and counterpoem (counterpunch), with only short breathers between rounds to tally scores. Slam masters consciously try to keep the poetry pressing ahead, and keep the audience involved and enthused. Consequently, the audience has little time to contemplate one poem before another begins.

According to Liam Rector, poet and director of the prestigious Bennington Writing Seminars, this is a corruption. In a 1997 PBS interview, Rector criticized slams on this very point: "Slams encourage a kind of instantaneous response. And to an essentially meditative and dramatic art that you want to read a poem twice [*sic*]. You want to think about more than your instant gut reaction to it" (*Greater Boston Arts*, screen 1).

Although gut reactions may cause problems for Rector and critics of his cloth, such visceral responses were acknowledged as vital in the early poetry of Walker's study. According to Walker, lyric poets knew that the path toward "judgment" (of the kind we have been considering) enters through the "heart":

> The rhetorical *sophia* ["skillfulness"], and the principle of answerability it implies, also includes a recognition that the role of the poet's audience is to *judge*, not simply to have an aesthetic experience, and not simply to understand what the poet means [...]. The person addressed will be presented with a "telling," a *mythos* (a word that can mean and does mean in this context, a speech or a piece of exhortation or advice); and the telling is to be at once *charis*, "charming," and *peithê*, "persuasive" to the listener's heart [...]. The function of the poet's telling is to persuade the listener's heart; the role of the listener is to exercise judgment. (143-44)

Pace Rector's poetic dyspepsia, slam finds ancient precedence in aiming for the gut, or slightly north of it, as a precondition to listener judgment. As I read him, Rector's ideal—an ideal I suspect shared by many print-preferring poets and scholars—connects poetry directly to mind, "reflection," a poetry of *logos*. Lyric and slam poetry likewise want to connect with the mind, "judgment," but aim to do so indirectly through emotional appeal, persuading "the listener's heart." Slam, like ancient lyric, is first a poetry of *pathos* that the audience converts to *logos*.

According to Walker, in the seventh to fifth centuries BCE, poetry seeded the public heart with *epideiktikon*, and it was that maturing heart later borne into the courts and assembly that served as chief counsel to the pragmatic mind. Writ small and moved ahead 2,500 years, slam has the potential to parallel Walker's tale.

WORKS CITED

Halloran, S. Michael, Virginia Martin, and Victoria Moore. "Rhetorical Spectacle on the Erie Canal: The Third Annual Tugboat Roundup." Rhetoric Society of America 10th Biennial Conference, Las Vegas, Nevada. 25 May 2002.

Rector, Liam. *Greater Boston Arts*. Transcript. 27 Mar. 1997. 28 Sept. 2001 <http://www.wgbh.org/wgbh/pages/bostonarts/1997/ps-competition.html>.

Walker, Jeffrey. *Rhetoric and Poetics in Antiquity*. Oxford UK: Oxford UP, 2000.

14

Alternative Articulations of Citizenship: The Written Discourse of a Nineteenth-Century African American Woman

Jami Carlacio
Cornell University

> The idea of an informed citizenry has been so familiar since the late nineteenth century, and so interwoven with the rhetoric of democracy and education, that we have been tempted to take it for granted.
>
> —Richard D. Brown (*Strength of a People* xiii)

When the authors of the Declaration of Independence and the framers of the Constitution smoothed out the parchment and waited for the ink to dry, they likely felt they had done well to assert Americans' rights to liberty, equality, and the pursuit of happiness as well as determine what kind of citizen ought serve the republic. These early patriots—and patriarchs—such as Benjamin Rush, declared in 1786 that '"no man should be a voter or a juror' without knowledge of 'reading, writing, and arithmetic'" (qtd in Brown 94). Complementing this basic literacy of the three "Rs," citizenship included the two linked concepts of virtue and morality; according to an 1812 legislative report, the latter were of "primary importance" (qtd in Brown 104). And thus, whereas statesmen such as Noah Webster maintained that citizens should be politically informed, that they should "know and love the laws," others asserted that religious knowledge was also tantamount to children's—and everyone's—education.

During the eighteenth and nineteenth centuries, biblical instruction was a commonplace component of literacy instruction; the inclusion of Scriptural studies reinforced the idea that an informed citizenry must also be a virtuous (and moral) one. Yet, the schoolroom was not the sole place for such pedagogy, for ideally not only white males but also women and African Americans would benefit from religious training. By 1830, all those who could read began receiving both moral and "useful" instruction in the most easily disseminated way—the periodical press, which had sprung up everywhere. Tailored to the specific audiences of Christians, farmers, tradesmen, and free African Americans, among others, historian Richard Brown explains that periodicals made learning possible in ostensibly every person's home for the relatively small price of a subscription. The public began cultivating knowledge about "the natural world, history, politics, and culture" (110). To this "useful knowledge" was added moral improvement. Citing the Book of Isaiah that "the earth shall be full of the knowledge of the Lord," for example, the American Bible Society in Petersburg, Virginia, contended that every inhabitant of the *earth* should be furnished with a bible. Good Christians, after all, would be good citizens (Brown 112).

The free African American population clearly understood the importance of "useful" knowledge; moreover, they recognized the socially proscribed need to be "virtuous, prudent, and industrious," as the editors of *The Colored American* reminded readers (Cornish and Russworm 1). To achieve these aims, they followed the lead of their Anglo American counterparts: They spread their message as far and as wide as possible, inaugurating a series of weeklies dedicated to racial uplift, to providing "useful knowledge," and to encouraging their readers to remain temperate and practice moral behavior. In the rest of this chapter, I focus on how the first African American woman to speak in public, Maria Stewart, availed herself of the printed medium in order to promote racial uplift and to assert African Americans' rights to the same equality and liberty demanded by and for Anglo (white) Americans in the newly established Constitution.

Her activism, both on the podium and in print, was instrumental in paving the way toward a more activist-oriented use of the periodical press. Stewart was a "dissident citizen," a phrase I borrow from feminist theorist Holloway Sparks, and her approach was eventually taken up by others who also learned to shape their arguments to fit the changing circumstances. Stewart reflected Sparks's conception of citizenship in her "commitment to unconventional forms of democratic engagement and opposition that nonetheless preserve the possibility of ongoing debate and disagreement" (75). As Sparks explains, "dissident democratic citizenship" is practiced by those on the (political) margins contesting the "prevailing arrangements of power" (83). Such contestations may take several forms, including using violence; remaining separate from the dominant culture; using the institutionalized and "acceptable" forms of democratic resistance; or, closer to what I am talking about, using unconventional, noninstitutionally sanctioned ways of calling into question the way a marginalized group is treated by the dominant group (83-84).[1]

The rhetorical and cultural work performed on the pages of African American periodicals can also be understood as what feminist theorist Nancy Fraser calls "counterdiscourses" (qtd in Sparks 85). Such rhetorical moves have more force than ordinary discourses, because they incite in their auditors a desire for change or, at the very least, knowledge that change is possible. For example, Stewart—and those who wrote and spoke publicly for the remaining years of the nineteenth century—laid the important groundwork that gave performative force to calls for equality and liberty, as well as for the other freedoms attached to the Declaration and the Constitution. In her 1833 "Masonic Hall" address and elsewhere, she called on her auditors to "turn [their] attention to knowledge, for knowledge is power" ("An Address" Part One 68). She meant to rouse, in her view, a slumbering black population "to exertion" and social activism. To achieve this aim, she employed an illocutionary rhetorical style; that is, she used her rhetoric to intend a particular action. Such speech acts do not simply regulate behavior, as linguist John Searle explains; rather, they "create and define new forms of behavior" (40-41). Thus, Stewart's promotion of dissident behavior required movement—physically, mentally, or both. Just as her rhetoric is illocutionary in nature, its counterdiscursive style allows for the new conception of "identities, interests, and needs," in Fraser's words (qtd in Sparks 85).

The implications of this new discursive conception become clear when we investigate the ways in which African Americans appropriated the press for their own brand of abolitionist activism. That is, they discovered how to employ their own periodicals to establish a site for identity construction and to use these as forums for community building. As the presses reached more and more readers, their potential to galvanize the free black population, and perhaps indirectly affect those enslaved, was enhanced. More than this, however, the dissident activities as they were materially evidenced in the voices of *Freedom's Journal*, *The Liberator*, *The Weekly Advocate*, and others, revealed the power inherent in the active pursuit and claim for citizenship. Claiming it was, however, only the first step; it would not be the last.

What made Stewart's rhetorical pursuits on the pages of abolitionist presses possible were two pioneers in the free African American periodical tradition—Samuel Cornish and William Lloyd Garrison. In early spring 1827, editor and publisher Cornish introduced *Freedom's Journal* to a specifically African American audience in order to reach as many free people of color in America as possible and to correct the various unfair assumptions that caused the black population to suffer from "being incorrectly represented" (Cornish and Russworm 1). Garrison, who began publishing *The Liberator* in 1831 (a periodical whose readership consisted almost entirely of African Americans), introduced the young widow Maria Stewart to its readers when he advertised her pamphlet, *Religion and the Pure Principles of Morality, The Sure Foundation on Which We Must Build*, for sale. Cornish, Garrison, and publishers of subsequent African American weeklies availed themselves of the most recent developments in printing technology that allowed for the fairly inexpensive distribution of a large number of copies to readers in various locales, including Pennsylvania, where 38,000 free people of color lived; New York state, which housed about 60,000; New Jersey, where about 38,000 lived; and in New England, which boasted 18,000 (Cornish, "Proposals and Plan" 1). In the prospectus for *Freedom's Journal*, Cornish explains his rationale:

> We deem it expedient to establish a paper, and bring into operation all the means with which our benevolent CREATOR has endowed for us the moral, religious, civil and literacy improvement of our injured race. Experience teaches us that the Press is the most economical and convenient method by which this object is to be obtained. ("Proposals for Publishing" 12)

Cornish's editorials in *Freedom's Journal* were just the first of many rhetorical efforts on the part of the free black population to assert its rights; these were followed in 1829 by the two incendiary manifestoes of Alexander Young and David Walker (see Stuckey), and in 1831, by Stewart, whose speeches were featured in *The Liberator*. With *Freedom's Journal*, Cornish planted in African Americans the seeds of strength and hope; Stewart nourished them. Many more efforts such as these occurred over the years both before and after the Civil War. For example, African Americans made concerted efforts to establish their constitutional rights as citizens and the ensuing implications throughout their periodicals during the latter half of the nineteenth century. In an exemplary study of these endeavors, rhetorical theorists Celeste Condit and John Lucaites demonstrate in their book, *Crafting Equality: America's Anglo-African Word*, both the slippery and conflicting uses of the terms *equality*, *equal rights*, and *liberty*; moreover, they illustrate how African Americans found ways to disarticulate these terms/concepts from their current meanings and to rearticulate them so that they would apply to *all* people, as universal ideals. Their study is limited, however, to periodicals published somewhat later in the century, including *The Colored American*, published originally as *The Weekly Advocate* in 1837; in the *Frederick Douglass' Paper* in 1854; and in the *Weekly Anglo-African* in 1859. Although their work is remarkable in that they suggest an important trend in scholarship on African American rhetorical history, I suggest here that skillful rhetorical maneuvers around these contested terms had really begun in earnest in 1827 and were first explicitly carried out in the periodical press by Stewart.

And yet, Stewart's task was not so easily undertaken. As I explained earlier, the early understanding of *citizen*, promulgated by the original framers of the Declaration, included only those who were white, male, and propertied. As the years progressed, however, the term became increasingly vulnerable to interpretation. To wit, as the American public became more "informed," they too began to assert their right to own property, to petition Congress, to hold public office, and to sit on juries (Brown 120). In order to achieve any of these rights, however, there needed to be some agreement about the term itself: Did birthright entail citizenship? Property ownership? A proper education? The latter was particularly problematic, because although most children received some education, it was far from uniform. African Americans attended Sabbath schools but did not receive the same kind of (rhetorical) instruction as did white, middle-class children; lower- and working-class children were often denied altogether, for if they worked in factories, they could not attend school at all. Although questions of wealth and property ownership (i.e., class positions) were eventually settled, race and gender were to remain contentious issues throughout the nineteenth century.

Citizenship was simply too complicated to be resolved through the acquisition of knowledge or property. Noah Webster, for example, had coined the earliest definitions of *citizen* in 1828, but under the entry of *citizen* in his dictionary, he describes five distinct *and different* senses. The fourth, had it been upheld and agreed on, would have drastically improved chances for the growing population of free blacks to be considered citizens immediately: "A native or permanent resident of a city or a country." Yet this was quickly shot down by Connecticut's Chief

Justice David Daggett, who ruled in 1833 that African Americans and Native Americans "are not citizens"; he in fact privileged Webster's fifth definition, which contradictorily referred to a citizen as a man who (already) held voting privileges and who (already) held the qualifications to purchase property (qtd in Brown 156).

Such a tautological definition did not, however, stop the growing literate population of African Americans from trying to claim equal status as citizens and to claim the right to liberty and suffrage. Thus, it is easy to see how, in this dynamic cultural climate, the first of many newspapers published specifically for African American audiences worked to cultivate a unified community dedicated to freedom, racial uplift, and most of all, morality and virtue.

It was, in fact (and perhaps ironically), a woman representing the least enfranchised group—African American women—who took up the challenge of redefining the term *citizen* and concomitantly *citizenship*, two concepts that changed as often as a particular occasion warranted. After soliciting Garrison's support for her 1831 pamphlet, the recently widowed Stewart delivered four speeches to hostile, mixed audiences in Boston in an attempt to unify her race, encourage their attention in moral matters, and urge them to "sue for [their] rights and privileges" (*Religion* 38). Significantly, her speeches could be read as politically motivated op-ed pieces, for she was the first woman to be given a byline (in African American weeklies). Clearly, Stewart was a pioneer, being the first woman to employ the periodical press to disabuse the reading public of the notion that rights, equality, and liberty pertained only to white Americans. In a city dominated by whites, and in a culture whose rules and rituals were defined by patriarchy, Stewart demonstrated not only linguistic prowess but also rhetorical acuity as she called into question the narrowly constructed meanings of *citizenship*, *equality*, and *liberty*.

One of the best illustrations of this occurs in her February 1833 Masonic Hall address, published in two subsequent *Liberator* installments. In it, Stewart facilitates the racial uplift of her community, whose success depends in large part on moral "Christian" behavior. She also urges her auditors to remember that "all is owned by the lordly white [...]." She in fact compares whites to the biblical King Solomon:

> who put neither nail nor hammer to the temple, yet received the praise; so also have the white Americans gained themselves a name, like the names of the great men that are in the earth, while in reality we have been their principle foundation and support. We have pursued the shadow, they have obtained the substance. ("An Address" Part One 68)

This example does more than remind African-Americans of their usurped right to pursue prosperity on American soil. By referring to whites as "white Americans," Stewart is purposefully differentiating white from black Americans, at the same time implying that as *Americans*, blacks deserve the same opportunities as their white counterparts. She is arguably the first to dissect this rhetoric and pave the way for other black rhetors to fight for "universal" equality, because neither Young nor Walker makes an explicit claim to be American; rather, they refer to themselves as "Ethiopian" or as "a man of colour [*sic*]," respectively. Stewart's tone in this passage also reveals her frustration at this injustice and attempts to incite more positive action by turning her auditors' attention instead to "mental and moral improvement" ("An Address" Part Two 72). If they continue in their intemperate and "frivolous" ways, Stewart warns, "God will bring you into judgment." Stewart begins and ends her "Address" by appealing to her community's presumed desire to be granted "African rights and liberty, [...] a subject that ought to fire the breast of every free man of color in these United States, and excite in his bosom a lively, deep, decided and heartfelt interest" ("An Address" Part One 68; "An Address" Part Two 72).

By reframing the meaning of *American* by explicitly attaching to it the modifier "white" and reminding the "sons of Africa" that their fathers bled and died in the Revolutionary War and fought for liberty under Jackson, Stewart led the way in reconstituting the concept and the scope of American citizenship ("An Address" Part One 68). These and other claims were meant to reinforce the notion that Africans born in America were African *American* and were entitled to—and expected to—"sign a petition to Congress to abolish slavery in the District of Columbia and grant [them] the rights and privileges of common citizens" (68). Stewart's rhetorical practice was intended to produce a perspectival shift in her audience, from regarding themselves as "objects of pity and commiseration" to identifying themselves as "fearless and brave, noble and gallant [... and] critics in useful knowledge" (68). If these methods of persuasion needed reinforcement, African Americans could (and did) insert the term "universal" in front of human rights, as Condit and Lucaites demonstrate (79-80).

Although we cannot reasonably attribute to Stewart all of the many successes the African American population earned, we must consider the increased number of rhetors who took her message to heart by preaching and practicing racial uplift; by writing books, poetry, pamphlets, editorials, and by publishing their own papers; and by speaking in public on abolition, suffrage, and equal rights. Contemporary feminist rhetorical historians have shown, through their recent work in this area (see, e.g., Campbell; Logan; Peterson; Royster), the extent to which Stewart, and others after her, contributed to the African American rhetorical tradition—one still ripe for further investigation and discovery.

NOTE

1. Sparks specifically refers to civil disobedience or to demonstrations when she exemplifies noninstitutional opposition. I have extended her example to include the political function of the Black periodical press, which did not promote violence or sanction any other unlawful activity, but did use channels of communication other than those of the dominant culture (i.e., those periodicals geared predominantly toward white—Anglo-American—audiences).

WORKS CITED

Brown, Richard D. *The Strength of a People: The Idea of an Informed Citizenry in America, 1650-1870*. Chapel Hill: U of North Carolina P, 1996.

Campbell, Karlyn Kohrs. *Women Public Speakers in the United States, 1800-1925: A Bio-Critical Sourcebook*. Westport, CT: Greenwood, 1993.

Condit, Celeste Michelle, and John Louis Lucaites. *Crafting Equality: America's Anglo-African Word*. Chicago: U of Chicago P, 1993.

Cornish, Samuel T. Editorial. *Weekly Advocate* 7 Jan. 1837: 1.

---. "Proposals and Plan of a Newspaper for the People of Color: *The Colored American.*" *Weekly Advocate* 29 Feb. 1837: 1.

---. "Proposals for Publishing the *Freedom's Journal*: Prospectus." *Freedom's Journal* 30 Mar. 1827: 12.

---, and John Russworm. Editorial. *Freedom's Journal* 16 Mar. 1827: 1.

Logan, Shirley Wilson. *We Are Coming: The Persuasive Discourse of Nineteenth-Century Black Women.* Carbondale: Southern Illinois UP, 1999.

Peterson, Carla. *Doers of the Word: African-American Women Speakers and Writers in the North (1830-1880).* New York: Oxford UP, 1995.

Royster, Jacqueline Jones. *Traces of a Stream: Literacy and Social Change Among African-American Women.* Pittsburgh: U of Pittsburgh P, 2000.

Searle, John. *"What Is a Speech Act?" The Philosophy of Language.* London: Oxford UP, 1971.

Sparks, Holloway. "Dissident Citizenship: Democratic Theory, Political Courage, and Activist Women." *Hypatia* 12 (1997): 74-109.

Stewart, Maria. "An Address, Delivered at the African Masonic Hall in Boston, February 27, 1833." Part One. *The Liberator* 27 Apr. 1833: 68.

---. "An Address, Delivered at the African Masonic Hall in Boston, February 27, 1833." Part Two. *The Liberator* 4 May 1833: 72.

---. *Religion and the Pure Principles of Morality, The Sure Foundation on Which We Must Build.* 1831. Boston: Isaac Knapp, 1879.

Stuckey, Sterling. *The Ideological Origins of Black Nationalism.* Boston: Beacon, 1972.

15

The Rhetorical Display of "Publicness" in Global Institutions

J. Robert Cox
University of North Carolina–Chapel Hill

In one of the stranger moments in the Kafkaesque world of globalization, critics who had been prevented from attending the World Trade Organization's summit in the sheikdom of Qatar were told that the 400,000 hits (monthly) on the WTO Web site revealed "a remarkable response to calls for increased transparency" (Sampson 58). The claim, coming less than a year after Western Hemisphere leaders had retreated behind old Quebec's fortress walls for the Summit of the Americas, threw into relief the dilemma facing the defenders of globalization. At the same time that "free trade" agreements, fueled by triumphal rhetorics of neoliberalism and laissez-faire capitalism, had begun to shift control of domestic markets and social welfare policy to administrative apparatuses under the WTO, NAFTA, the European Union, and the proposed Free Trade Area of the Americas (FTAA), forums for public participation and accountability of global authority were being left outside the opaque walls of these institutions. Although its defenders claimed that globalization bolstered the opportunity for economic prosperity, critics in the streets of Seattle, Prague, Washington, D.C., Quebec City, and Genoa increasingly complained of a corporate-driven global agenda, lack of transparency, and the widening disparity of income in third world nations.

Stung by charges of insularity and the undemocratic practices of global institutions, spokespersons from the Office of the U.S. Trade Representative and the WTO have pledged an increased transparency and openness to civil society organizations. U.S. Trade Representative Robert Zoellick, for example, boasted in July 2001 of an increased transparency in the negotiations for the proposed FTAA and promised "to enhance the transparency of other [trade] negotiations, such as the WTO" ("Joint Statement" 2). This move, I would argue, is not without irony. Rather than identifying meaningful procedures and spaces for public participation, global apologists have instead sought to reframe the idea of "publicness" itself. In discourses surrounding the WTO and other "free trade" agreements, I argue, this has assumed the form of a refeudalization of the principle of critical "publicity," from the consensus forged in open, critical debate to the display or representation of authority before an audience of political subjects.

THE NEOLIBERAL TURN IN ECONOMIC DISCOURSE

Although economists Friedrich Hydeck, Ludwig von Mises, and others forged the intellectual basis for a radical "neoliberal" turn in economic discourse (Aune), its robust embodiment arguably came in the multilateral trade negotiations that culminated in the World Trade Organization and such regional agreements as NAFTA and the EU. Authority to regulate trade moved from concerns at the borders over tariffs and quotas to the heartland of democratic governance. Trumpeting a "realist" rationale, these agreements began to subject fiscal as well as social welfare policy to the discipline of "market forces" and the threat of capital to migrate. Areas now subject to domestic, deliberative authority (e.g., environmental, health, and other social regulations) would increasingly be subsumed by new regimes of trade rules and closed dispute procedures. Democratic regulation of the market, under such regimes, threatened to pose "non-tariff" barriers to foreign trade and investment. (The WTO, on this basis, e.g., forced the United States to alter its implementation of the Clean Air Act. For this and other rulings, see Wallach and Sforza.)

A potentially more forceful challenge appears in rulings under an obscure provision of NAFTA for the protection of foreign corporate investment. Creating a new category of tort action, Chapter 11 declares any state or federal action that restricts foreign business operation to be "tantamount to [...] expropriation" of a firm's assets, including its expected profits (North American Free Trade Agreement). Specifically, Chapter 11 grants foreign investors the right to challenge such regulation as a nontariff barrier in NAFTA tribunals (Curtis 308; DePalma). Such tribunals, Curtis notes, extends the "Club" model of the post-World War II international economic regime that "kept outsiders out" and "insulated ministers from domestic pressures" (304-05).

As a result of such challenges to state regulatory authority, Bellman and Gerster argue, globalization has led to a "democracy deficit" or failure of popular sovereignty where "national parliaments no longer determine legislative language themselves" in areas now governed by trade agreements (31). At one level, elites view global institutions as a bulwark against intrusion of the "irrational" forces of popular will. One World Trade Organization official reflected this attitude when he conceded that, "The WTO is the place where governments collude in private against their domestic pressure groups" ("Network Guerrillas" 20).

This much, at least, has been charted by the critics of global trade and finance institutions, and I do not want simply to echo these criticisms. Instead, it is the disarming reply by defenders of the new global order to which I now turn.

REFEUDALIZING "PUBLICNESS"

Instead of constructing meaningful venues for publics, I argue, the defenders of global trade agreements have sought to reframe the idea of "publicness" itself. Even as delegates confess to using the WTO as a space to meet secretly, they have sought nonetheless to present a public face, a *representation* of publicness. I want to trace this effort briefly, both through gestures of inclusion and in apologists' reframing of the principles of "publicness" itself. Such discourses, I argue, attempt to refeudalize what Habermas termed the principle of "critical publicity," a return to the functions of rule in premodern (feudal) society in which "public" became the display of authority before an audience of political subjects (7, 10).

In *The Structural Transformation of the Public Sphere*, Habermas argued that the form of "publicness" in the High Middle Ages, specifically the attributes of lordship, was a type of display of courtly authority "publicly represented" before political subjects (7). "This *publicness* (or *publicity*) *of representation* was not constituted as a social real, that is, as a public sphere"; instead, it was something like a claim of status (7). Such a representation presumed to render visible what was hidden through the public staging of the personal attributes of the lord—in insignia and demeanor, and through a stylized rhetoric (7-8). Although the publicity of representation was staged usually at the prince's court, the people were not—indeed, if "display" was to be accomplished, *could not*—be completely excluded. "Representation was still dependent," Habermas argued, on the presence of those assembled in the streets, "before whom it was displayed" (10).

In the context of the WTO and related trade agreements, I argue, a refeudalization of the ideal of the "public" occurs in a similar deferral and legitimizing rhetoric, even as officials pledge to give parliamentary bodies and the "multitudes" new assurances of transparency and openness.

GESTURES OF "PUBLIC" INCLUSION IN TRADE AGREEMENTS

Briefly, I want to illustrate three areas in which "free trade" authority intersects potentially with civil society forces and in which critical engagement is, instead, deferred: negotiation of trade agreements, rule-making, and settlement of disputes. In each area, we are presented with the rhetorical "insignia" and actions through which trade bureaucracies represent the status of neoliberal authority.

Negotiation of Trade Agreements

Despite U.S. Trade Representative Zoellick's assurances that the ongoing FTAA negotiations are precedent setting in their transparency, actual processes for interaction with civil society forces seem aimed instead at the display of sensitivity by trade officials. In 1999, for example, Trade Ministers unveiled the FTAA's official channel for communication with civil society. The initiative, termed the "Open Invitation to Civil Society," consisted of a call for nongovernmental groups to submit their views on "trade-related" issues to a Committee of Government Representatives on the Participation of Civil Society (Shamsie 15).

Most civil society groups, however, found the FTAA's gesture disappointing. The Hemispheric Social Alliance, a confederation of more than 300 civil society groups, complained that the "Open Invitation" provided not for the engagement with trade negotiators, "but simply a one-way communication" (1). Indeed, rules for the committee's work contained no requirements for reply, shared contact, exchange, or other deliberative engagement with negotiators, government representatives, nor even by the committee itself with civil society. One Canadian critic argued that the "[c]ommittee's real role is not to listen, but to keep up the appearance of real dialogue" (Barlow 21).

Rule Making

Perhaps the most explicit evidence of a shift from engagement to the "display" of public status appears in the deferral of participatory rule making to the self-congratulatory rhetoric of the WTO's Web site. Although giving assurances of openness, officials at the same time boasted of insulating governments from their "domestic pressure groups"; entry into the WTO, they explained, locks in agreements to deregulate domestic markets (WTO 1). Still, noting there are disagreements over precisely such policies, the WTO Web site explains that "one of the most important reasons for having the system is to serve as a forum for countries to thrash out their differences on trade issues. Individuals can participate," the site confidently explains, "not directly, but through their governments" (WTO 1).

Settlement of Trade Disputes

Finally, in NAFTA's procedures for trade disputes, neoliberals' rearticulation of critical publicity is fully realized. In granting private corporations the right to challenge state regulatory authority directly, the Chapter 11 provisions radically eclipse the occasion and influence of deliberative rhetorics. Put bluntly, the outcomes of public argument in influencing state authority may be overturned *in camera;* that is, within the discretion of NAFTA's secret tribunals that arbitrate corporate-to-government claims (see NAFTA chs. 11, 20, and the summary of cases in International Institute).

One high-profile instance of such a threat is *Methanex Inc. v. United States,* a dispute over the state of California's ban on the toxic substance MTBE, a gasoline additive that the state found to be leaking into drinking water sources. Corporate briefs filed in the case explicitly invoked NAFTA's Chapter 11 authority to set aside the results of the public deliberation that led to the state's decision to end MTBE's use. The 1999 ban came "after an extensive public consultation and university-led review process" of the evidence of the leaking of MTBE into ground waters (IISD 96). In its claim, Methanex Corporation, however, argued that California could have chosen other (more expensive) ways to protect its water supplies. Rather than forging its decision on the basis of public debate and an airing of evidence, NAFTA's dispute settlement procedures *a priori* presume a right to declare such judgments to be "non-tariff barriers" or actions that are "tantamount to [...] expropriation" (See IISD 97). Similarly, Wallach and Sforza have argued that the WTO engaged in "double-speak" when, in its ruling on the Clean Air Act, it "rhetorically affirmed the right of nations to sovereignty over environmental matters while acknowledging that, in practice, countries' environmental laws must conform to WTO rules" (19).

DENYING THE "PUBLIC" STATUS OF CIVIL SOCIETY

Relatedly, I want to argue that the refeudalization of "publicity" occurs not only in pseudogestures of inclusion or the eclipse of public judgment, but in the deferral of the claims of civil society groups to speak for a "public" interest. Deploying what Hariman has called the "realist" style of political discourse—particularly in its reduction of motive to a calculus of private interests—neoliberal apologists view the criticism of globalization as a form of special pleading or an aberration of the rules of economic exchange. This comes as a challenge to the status of civil society groups themselves as non-representative and nonaccountable to a "public" that is identifiable. Writing under the auspices of Stanford University's Hoover Institution, for example, conservative economist Fiona McGillivray claims that the incentives to lobby the WTO are greater for the "losers" in economic globalization—labor unions, environmentalists, displaced workers, an so on. Opening the WTO to these civil society organizations, she argues, potentially pulls decisions of the global trade body "even further from the interests of the majority and toward the interests of unelected special interests" (15). Indeed, political activity itself, Aune argues, becomes in this view a form of "rent-seeking" behavior; pleas for protection from toxic waste or chemical exposure in the workplace, for example, are "simply an effort by special interests to gain special favors from the government" (45).

Others pose the matter more bluntly. Political theorist Jean-Luc Migué celebrates the discipline that free trade exerts on national governments, specifically the threat of capital to migrate when faced with social regulation. Such threats to "exit" national boundaries minimize what he calls political "coercion" in society (31). "Exit (mobility) is an alternative to (voice) politics. The movement of goods, capital, and people between communities [...] emerge[s] as a substitute for the political process" (31). Such "mobility," Migué argues, functions as a constraint on domestic public choice.

The defense of neoliberal moves to deregulate capital (and labor) markets begins therefore by constraining other rhetorics, marking other discourses *as* rhetorical ("voice," as Migué says). As Hariman suggests of the realist style more generally, such an assault devalues civil society precisely because its rhetors "are too discursive, too caught up in their textual designs to engage in rational calculation" (17).

Such charges, of course, deny the basis from which a public arises, in a critical engagement of rhetors with the claims of authority. The result, Friedman observes, is that once a nation puts on a "Golden Straightjacket," or adopts the rules of neoliberal deregulation, "your politics shrink" (105). The critical function of civil society necessarily is eclipsed as governments confront the threat of capital to "exit." Once a nation decides to shield its economy from its "domestic pressure groups," Friedman argues, "politics becomes just political engineering to implement decisions in the narrow space allowed you within this system" (107). Under such a regime, neoliberal hegemony need not achieve consent, Grossberg suggests: "It is a matter of containment rather than compulsion or even incorporation" (162).

Well, not quite. Although from their side, global apologists have tried to refeudalize the idea of "publicity," I want to end by arguing that they also open potential sites of a new antagonism or discursive fields that are able to unsettle the claims of a triumphal neoliberalism.

Interestingly, Hariman notes that the realist style itself ultimately is constrained by the need of its proponents to contest opposing views for continued support in the political marketplace. As a result, the "demands of establishing consensus and motivating action often require" the realist speaker to "stretch beyond the style's own limitations" (44). And, in stretching, the interests of those constituents must themselves be accommodated in some fashion. The celebration of the U.S. trade representative or WTO bureaucrats of the "unprecedented" openness of trade negotiations or administrative practices, I suggest, is one such "stretch," one that reveals vulnerability as well as necessity.

In rearticulating "openness"—to the nascent possibilities of utterance, voice, and responsiveness—the forces of an emergent global justice movement may yet be able to secure the normative spaces for a critical publicity. It is the task of rhetorical critics, I urge, to identify not only the discursive stratagems of Neoliberal apologists but also the possibilities for counterveiling rhetorics. As Aune eloquently concludes in *Selling the Free Market*, "the classical theorists of rhetoric and their twentieth-century successors knew that human beings are a composite of appetite, spiritedness (*thymos*), and reason" (170). Only an epideictic discourse that transcends the realist calculation of costs and benefits can invite political subjects into being who would create anew the desire, and the spaces, for a democratic accountability.

WORKS CITED

Aune, James Arnt. *Selling the Free Market: The Rhetoric of Economic Correctness*. New York: Guilford, 2001.

Barlow, Maude. *The Free Trade Area of the Americas: The Threat to Social Programs, Environmental Sustainability, and Social Justice*. San Francisco: International Forum on Globalization, 2001.

Bellman, Christophe, and Richard Gerster. "Accountability in the World Trade Organization." *Journal of World Trade* 30.6 (1996): 31-74.

Curtis, John H. "Trade and Civil Society: Toward Greater Transparency in the Policy Process." *Trade Policy Research 2001*. Toronto: Canadian Department of Foreign Affairs and International Trade, 2000. 301-26.

DePalma, Anthony. "Nafta's Powerful Little Secret." *New York Times* 11 Mar. 2001, Money & Business sec.: 1+.

Friedman, Thomas L. *The Lexus and the Olive Tree: Understanding Globalization*. Rev. ed. New York: Anchor, 2000.

FTAA Homepage. 5 Feb. 2001 <www.ftaa-alca.org/VIEW_e.asp>.

Grossberg, Lawrence. "History, Politics, and Postmodernism: Stuart Hall and Cultural Studies." *Stuart Hall: Critical Dialogues in Cultural Studies*. Ed. David Morley and Kuan-Hsing Chen. London: Routledge, 1996. 151-73.

Habermas, Jürgen. *The Structural Transformation of the Public Sphere: An Inquiry into a Category of Bourgeois Society*. Trans. Thomas Burger. Cambridge, MA: MIT P, 1991.

Hariman, Robert. *Political Style: The Artistry of Power*. U of Chicago P, 1995.

International Institute for Sustainable Development and World Wildlife Fund. *Private Rights, Public Problems: A Guide to NAFTA's Controversial Chapter on Investor Rights.* Winnipeg, Canada: International Institute for Sustainable Development, 2001.

"Joint Statement of the NAFTA Free Trade Commission Building on a North American Partnership." U.S. Trade Representative Press Release. Washington, DC: Office of the United States Trade Representative, 31 July 2001. <www.ustr.gov>.

McGillivray, Fiona. *Democratizing the World Trade Organization.* Hoover Institution Essays in Public Policy, No. 105. Stanford University, 2000.

Migué, Jean-Luc. *Federalism and Free Trade.* Hobart Paper 122. London: Institute of Economic Affairs, 1993.

"Network Guerrillas." *Financial Times* 30 Apr. 1998: 20.

North American Free Trade Agreement. Chap. 11, Investment; Sec. A; Art. 1110, Expropriation and Compensation.

Sampson, Gary P. "The Environmentalist Paradox: The World Trade Organization's Challenges." *Harvard International Review* (Winter 2002): 56-61.

Shamsie, Y. *Engaging with Civil Society: Lessons from the OAS, FTAA, and Summit of the Americas.* Ottowa, Can.: North-South Institute/L'Institut Nord-Sud, 2000.

Wallach, Lori, and Michelle Sforza. *Whose Trade Organization? Corporate Globalization and the Erosion of Democracy.* Washington, DC: Public Citizen, 1999.

World Trade Organization. "10 Common Misunderstandings about the WTO." 12 Feb. 2002 <http://www.wto.org/wto/about/about.htm>.

16

Civil Disobedience and the Ethical Appeal of Self-Representation

Ann Dobyns
University of Denver

In spring 2001, six Oberlin College students participated in an act of civil disobedience for which they were arraigned and stood trial on the charge of "unlawful entry." The following is from the press release they published on June 13, 2001, on Independent Media Center's Web page:

> On April 2, 2001 six Oberlin College students entered the National Guard Association Building in downtown Washington, DC, to protest at the opening session of a Sikorsky Corporation Blackhawk helicopter conference. The six young women locked their arms together inside pipes in the conference room.
>
> The six women, two of whom have recently traveled to Colombia, read a statement to the people in the conference room, including a Vice President of Sikorsky.
>
> In part, their statement read, "Plan Colombia, the $1.3 billion US aid package, is being used to enrich private corporations in the US and fuel the violence in Colombia, not to bring peace or to end the drug trade.
>
> "We target the Sikorsky Corporation today because the Sikorsky Corporation is making $221 million on 30 Blackhawk helicopters that will be sent to Colombia. We believe that helicopters and military aid will not bring an end to the 40-year civil war or the drug trade in Colombia."
>
> Sikorsky, subsidiary of United Technologies, based in Connecticut, lobbied Congress for 30 Blackhawks to be included in Plan Colombia.
>
> If convicted of unlawful entry, the six face a maximum possible sentence of six months in jail and a $100 fine. The Oberlin Six say, "We are willing to risk jail time to bring attention to the flawed priorities in the US's war on drugs. US tax dollars should be spent on drug treatment and to rebuild our communities, not to enrich private corporations, build prisons and cause suffering in Latin American countries like Colombia."

They were to stand trial in the U.S. Superior Court in Washington D.C. The prosecution offered them a pre-trial agreement that would result in a $100 fine and no jail time, and although none of them wanted to spend time in jail, they all believed that accepting the agreement was not in the spirit of their action. After much deliberation, they decided to defend themselves, or go *pro se*. They knew the long tradition of activists representing themselves in civil disobedience trials, and they believed strongly that doing so would give them more control of their own case and thus allow them to complete the action begun by their act of civil disobedience. With some trepidation, they all agreed (Bania-Dobyns).

Throughout the trial, the defendants used arguments that fell into the category of *ethos*, or the character of the speaker. With the emphasis shifted from the facts of the case to the ethics of the action, the courtroom became a forum for what James Crosswhite has called a "rhetoric of reason," or argumentation that does not rely on the determination of truth or falsity or even validity, but rather is the way to argue by making claims and giving reasons for believing them. It is, in short, argument as dialogue that has as its ends "the peaceful resolution of conflicts, meaningful social criticism, higher education, and even self-transformation" (47).

A dialogic model contrasts with the rhetoric of the typical courtroom, which enacts an agonistic model of argument. In the courtroom, the agonistic model sets up significant barriers to traditional ethical proof. Because the attorney is representing the defendants, any ethical appeal is secondhand. The attorney characterizes the defendant by calling character witnesses or using a line of questions that suggests the value system behind the defendant's action. In addition to controlling the appeal, the attorney, by his or her mere presence and centrality, infects the appeal, if you will, by his or her ethos—credibility, sincerity, or authenticity. Furthermore, the attorney retains the right to make the final decisions about how to establish the defendant's moral character.

To understand the difference between a typical trial and a *pro se* trial, it is important to know something about *pro se* litigation. Although a number of cases have ruled on the right of defendants to conduct their own defenses,[1] the landmark case was in 1975. Writing for the court, Justice Stewart argued that "The Sixth Amendment does not provide merely that a defense shall be made for the accused; it grants to the accused personally the right to make a defense" (Faretta 806). This ruling is supported by a statutory provision in the United States Code that states, "In all courts of the United States the parties may plead and conduct their own cases personally or by counsel as, by the rules of such courts, respectively, are permitted to manage and conduct causes therein" (qtd in "Nonlawyer").

The majority of *pro se* procedures involve civil litigants; however, with the rising number of arrests for acts of civil disobedience on the part of antiglobalization and antimilitary activists, we may expect an increase in *pro se* criminal litigation.[2] Such activists consider self-representation as an essential stage in their nonviolent act. As such, their choice is an ethical one, a defense that foregrounds character. The defendants acknowledge the facts of the case and accept responsibility for their actions. They acknowledge that a conventional legal defense conducted by an attorney might give them a greater chance for acquittal, but they choose instead to use the courtroom as the second stage in their action (Bania-Dobyns).

This decision is not an easy one. Codefendants must engage in dialogue and work toward cooperation. The decision must be reached through consensus. When the choice is not a consensual one, it can cause irrevocable division of the defendants, as was the case in the famous Harrisburg trial of eight antiwar activists in the early 1970s (Polner and O'Grady 292).

By having the authority to manage and construct their own cases, *pro se* defendants retain agency. As the Oberlin students planned their case, they agreed that they wanted to appeal to the goodwill of the judge and jury by arguing that their action was one of conscience. They intended to raise the issues they had addressed in their act of civil disobedience, to explain their reasons for the action, and to retain control of the direction of the case (Johnson). In other words, they wished to transform the rhetoric of the courtroom.

In addition to risking a guilty verdict and requiring a united front in a trial of codefendants, the choice for activists to go *pro se* involves a rigorous time commitment to research and preparation. In other words, the decision depends on the responsibility of all defendants. To prepare for *pro se* trials, defendants in such cases must familiarize themselves with the court system and pretrial and trial procedures. Before the trial, they will determine the terms of their own defense and participate in discovery. During the trial, they will conduct the jury selection, opening statements, cross-examination, and closing statements, for which they need to understand courtroom decorum and rules of evidence. In their preparation, they rely on educational programs established by some states, Web sites providing self-help advice, or the aid of *pro bono* standby counsel.[3]

The Oberlin students not only spent the month before the trial learning the language and procedures of the court, but also had the assistance of a *pro bono* civil liberties attorney. He provided pretrial advice and was on hand during the trial to answer procedural questions. Throughout the proceedings, however, he remained in the background so that the judge and jury would respond directly to the defendants, and so that their ethical appeal remained central.[4]

Kenneth Burke's dramatistic analysis provides a way to talk about the rhetoric of the courtroom. The scene-action ratio vividly demonstrates the challenge the six women faced. As the scene in which the drama played out, the courtroom exerted a great influence on the defendants while they presented their case. The judge, of course, sat in the front behind a raised desk with court officials to her left, immediately in front of the door to the holding area. The defendants sat behind a table along the left wall. The jury sat to the judge's right; the prosecution table was between the defendants and the jury. This configuration meant that the defendants were closer to the jail, behind a table, with no real ability to move out into the space in front of the witnesses, judge, and jury—an act the prosecutors engaged in throughout the trial. Five of them sat along the wall with their *pro bono* legal counsel, while one at a time each represented the group—making opening arguments, cross-examining witnesses, making closing arguments, and making final statements.

Within these constraints, the defendants realized that they would need to rely heavily on ethical appeals to reassert agency and attempt to reshape the scene. By choosing to go *pro se,* they retained their right to make their own arguments. Thus, as they constructed their own case, they established their moral character in a number of ways, and this appeal transformed the courtroom atmosphere. One essential consideration in a civil disobedience case is how the demeanor of the defendants might reflect the philosophical position of their action. The students had engaged in many non-violence training workshops. They brought this training into the courtroom. In their opening statements, they briefly introduced themselves as students and women of peace, asserted their commitment to nonviolence, described the action and their involvement in the peace movement, and emphasized the nonviolent nature of their action. Furthermore, as they worked to establish dialogue, they identified a different audience than they had with the action itself. Their goal was to draw attention to U.S. foreign policy that they perceived to be violating human rights. The immediate audience associated with public opinion was the jury, judge, and assembled observers, including reporters from three national newspapers.

The students also sought a ruling that might change unjust laws. They hoped to address injustices in the legal system by persuading the judge to rule on particular laws affecting civil disobedience. A more global issue they hoped the judge might address would be whether defendants in civil disobedience trials could claim that international law superseded national law. The appeal to international law has been argued in actions protesting the use of nuclear weapons through what is called the necessity defense or, "Conduct that the actor believes to be necessary to avoid harm or evil to himself or to another [which] is justifiable, provided that: [...] the harm or evil sought to be avoided by such conduct is greater than that sought to be prevented by the law defining the offense charged" (*The Model Penal Code*, qtd in Teuber).

The greater harm, the Oberlin students argued, was that because the Sikorsky Corporation was lobbying Congress for more money for helicopters, U.S. tax dollars were contributing to civil war in Colombia. This may seem like quite a risky defense, but the students knew that similar pleas had been effective in other civil disobedience trials. In 1998, for example, eight activists were acquitted against a charge of disorderly conduct for blocking traffic at the Bangor Naval Base where eight Trident submarines were docked. The jury acquitted the defendants of all charges, basing its decision on testimony about international treaties, which oblige the United States to take action on nuclear disarmament.[5]

In addition to letting their demeanor and arguments demonstrate their commitment to peace, the defendants also decided to accept the rules of court decorum. They knew from the experience of other activists that such a position might increase the chances that the judge and jury would listen with open minds to their arguments. In the Bangor Eight case, for example, one account reported, "It helped that the protesters [...] were respectful and gave intelligent and often moving testimony in court" (Parrish). Thus, in the case of the Oberlin Students, when the judge disallowed lines of argument, they apologized. When she corrected their procedure, they thanked her. When she urged them to move forward, they complied.

They also relied on ethical appeals, because they showed the care the students had used in preparing their case. They presented themselves as knowledgeable, yet not professional. They were respectful, but expressed the emotions that reflected their belief systems. When the prosecution portrayed them as dangerous enemies of the state, their intelligence, preparation, respectful demeanor, and soft-spoken manner belied that characterization. Their opening and closing arguments were simple, brief, and sincere. They showed courtesy and respect when they cross-examined witnesses. At the end, they thanked the judge for her patience and fairness.

This raises the question: Was the *pro se* choice effective? If the question concerns the verdict, the answer is no. After roughly an hour of deliberation, the jury declared the defendants guilty of unlawful entry. With this verdict, the students could have faced up to six months of jail. The prosecution then sought a weekend of jail time for each. The judge refused to give such a sentence. Instead, she fined each defendant $75.

But did they change minds? In a few (rare) cases, the ethical appeal results in the jury's choice to ignore the letter of the law and vote as their conscience dictates (a legal doctrine called *jury nullification*), but this jury ruled by the letter of the law. They did not respond to the ethical appeal, as least in determining their verdict. As the defendants watched the faces of members of the jury, however, the students believed that some of the jury members listened and responded with sympathy.

There were positive outcomes. The judge refused to send the students to jail, giving them only a small fine. In addition, before the sentencing, she engaged in dialogue with the students and expressed admiration for their commitments to their beliefs. She even shared a story from her college years when she joined a protest, and, as a result, was not allowed to go through graduation. Also, the stories in two of the three national newspapers were remarkably sympathetic and characterized the students' action as an act of conscience. In the article in the *Boston Globe*, the reporter repeated the defendants' argument that "Through [the U.S. aid given Columbia], [the] Sikorsky [corporation] will net $221 million by supplying 30 Black Hawk helicopters to accompany fumigation planes and fly American and Colombian soldiers into direct combat" (Bayot).

But, most significantly, the courtroom was different—whereas the prosecution continued to operate on an old model of argumentation, one designed to win, the defense engaged in dialogue with the judge explicitly, with the witnesses and, by implication, with the jury by anticipating their questions and concerns. Despite the guilty verdict, something had changed. The ethical appeal led not to acquittal but perhaps to the beginning of a conversation. As such, the defendants, at least in part, participated in a larger discussion about human rights.

NOTES

1. In one of the earlier decisions, the Supreme Court found in Adams v. US ex. Re. McCann (1942) that in federal trials the Constitution does not require the defendant to have an attorney. Other central cases include Harris v. Kaines (1972), Wiggins v. Estetle (1982), McKaskele v. Wiggins (1984), Ortiz v. Cornella (1989), and U.S. v. Sanchez (1996).

2. See discussions of the increase in *pro se* litigation in Gibeaut, Goldschmidt et al., and Rubin.
3. His actions were in accordance with the 1984 Supreme Court ruling that "Standby counsel must be sure she allows the defendant to 'preserve actual control over the case he chooses to present to the jury,' and she must not 'destroy the jury's perception that the defense is representing himself.'" (*McKaskle*, 465 U.S. at 178. qtd in Williams 793).
4. Helen Kim points out "Experience has shown that providing general legal information to *pro se* litigants can significantly increase their chances of success both in court and in settlement negotiations" (1642).
5. In an article in the *Seattle Weekly*, one journalist observes:

   Against these disturbing trends (the international proliferation of nuclear weapons), the international community has been mounting a strong drive in recent years toward nuclear disarmament. Key to this—and cited by the Bangor Eight in their defense—was a 1996 International Court of Justice ruling that: "The threat or use of nuclear weapons would generally be contrary to the rules of international law applicable in armed conflict, and in particular the principles and rules of humanitarian law." (Parrish)

WORKS CITED

Bania-Dobyns, Sarah. Personal interview. 1 Sept. 2001.

Bayot, Jennifer. "Verdicts Deliver Lesson to Students about Activism." *The Boston Globe* 23 June 2001. 25 June 2001 <http://www.globe.com/globe>.

Burke, Kenneth. *A Grammar of Motives*. New York: Prentice-Hall, 1945.

Crosswhite, James. *The Rhetoric of Reason: Writing and the Attractions of Argument*. Madison: U of Wisconsin P, 1996.

Faretta v. State of California, 422 U.S. 806. 1975.

Gibeaut, John. "Turning Pro Se: The Number of Unrepresented Litigants Is Growing, but Few Courts Have Developed Policies in Response." *ABA Journal* 85 (January 1999): 28.

Goldschmidt, Jona, Barry Mahoney, Harvey Solomon, and Joan Green. *Meeting the Challenge of Pro Se Litigation: A Report and Guidebook for Judges and Court Managers*. Chicago: American Judicature Society, 1998.

Johnson, Rebecca. Personal interview. 30 Sept. 2001.

Kim, Helen B. "Legal Education for the Pro Se Litigant: A Step Towards a Meaningful Right to be Heard." *The Yale Law Journal* 96.7 (1987): 1641-1660.

"Nonlawyer Activity in Law-Related Situations: A Report with Recommendations." *ABA Commission on Nonlawyer Practice* (1995). *American Bar Association. National Federation of Paralegal Associations Homepage*. 12 Mar. 2002 <http://www.paralegals.org/Development/nonlawyer.html>.

Parrish, Geor, "Busting the Feds." *Seattle Weekly* 8-14 July 1999. 12 Mar. 2002 <http://www.seattleweekly.com/features/9927/impolitics-parrish.shtml>.

Polner, Murray, and Jim O'Grady. *Disarmed and Dangerous: The Radical Life and Times of Daniel and Philip Berrigan, Brothers in Religious Faith and Civil Disobedience*. Boulder, CO: Westview, 1998.

Press Release. June 13, 2001. *Independent Media Page*. 12 Mar. 2002 <http://www.indymedia.org>.

Rubin, Howard M. "The Civil Pro Se Litigant v. The Legal System." *Loyola University Law Journal* 20.2 (1989): 999-1011.

Teuber, Andreas. "The Necessity Defense." 12 Mar. 2002 <http://www.People.brandeis.edu/~teuber/necessity.html>.

Williams, Marie Higgins. "The Pro Se Criminal Defendant, Standby Counsel, and the Judge: A Proposal for Better-Defined Roles." *University of Colorado Law Review* 71.3 (Summer 2000): 789-818.

17

The Coalition Rhetoric of Rose Schneiderman

Timothy Doherty
Rivier College

In 1912 in Manhattan, in the context of friction between suffrage and socialism, between political and industrial feminism, Rose Schneiderman, a leader of the Women's Trade Union League (WTUL), joined six other women in a forum entitled "Senators vs. Working Women." Cosponsored by both a suffrage league and a "wage earners" league, the event was prompted by the dismissive audience that New York state Senators in Albany had recently given to a committee of women arguing for suffrage referenda. Schneiderman and the others delivered their speeches that night to thousands in the Cooper Union's Great Hall of the People. Her audience of predominantly women was fractured along lines of class, ethnicity, and politics. For Schneiderman and her cospeakers, the successful passage of suffrage referenda would rest on cross-class cooperation.

In this chapter, I draw on feminist theories of adversarial discourse in order to examine the rhetorical context and strategies used by Schneiderman. My aim is to illuminate some dynamics of a militant "coalition rhetoric"—a mode of discourse aimed at achieving solidarity through, among other strategies, mock dialogue and oppositional questioning, the use of testimonials and representative anecdotes, and withering irony. Ultimately, I want to argue that Schneiderman is a fascinating figure in twentieth-century labor history, offering scholars and teachers across a variety of fields in the humanities and social sciences a vital resource for a complex coalition rhetoric.

Bridge building—a rhetoric of common ground—is valuable and necessary. Pat Bizzell argues that we should draw on "cultural archives" for examples of critical moments in American history "when different groups are contending for the right to interpret what is going on." In particular, she urges us to attend to those writers and speakers in "non-dominant American cultures but who have also set themselves to master the dominant culture, in order to build rhetorical bridges to members of this culture and effect social change" ("The 4th" 47). I want to respond to Bizzell's request by calling attention to those instances in the cultural archive of persuasion and argument conducted in perhaps narrower, more oppressive spaces.

There are of course instances when oppression is so great that open and equal disputation is not possible, or at least not with mutually consenting parties. Thus, more combative stances and alternative strategies are needed. As Catherine Lamb puts it, "[W]e have not talked much about how it can be feminist to both at times be confrontational and at other times advocate approaches that minimize confrontation" (260). Susan Jarratt and bell hooks have strongly advocated a more confrontational feminist approach to argument. In her essay "Critique of Adversarial Discourse," the philosopher Janet Farrell Smith claims that, whereas combative argument is historically masculine, women can, do, and should adopt strategies of adversarial argument in appropriate circumstances (i.e., some divorce settlements). She advocates the use of critical, oppositional questioning along with nonadversarial techniques of negotiation (71-72).

One finds adversarial, militant rhetorical strategies used by many women in the American labor movement at the turn of the century, yet several scholars see such strategies as fitting with a "feminine" or "maternal" rhetoric. Drawing on the work of Karlyn Kohrs Campbell, Mari Boor Tonn examines Mother Jones's militant rhetoric, finding in it a "feminine rhetorical style" (8). She writes:

> The most visible hallmark of Jones's dramatic rhetoric was its intense intimacy, manifested in several features: personal terms of address; inclusive pronouns; personal experience, self-disclosure and enactment as evidence; examples and stories often drawn from the workers' own lives; simulated and even occasional dialogue with audience members; and praise and insults directed at specific individuals. Such characteristics of form, coupled with the dissident content of her talk, reinforced a nurturing persona that was at once tenderly affirming and aggressively confrontational. (8-9)

Influenced by Carol Gilligan and Sara Ruddick as well, Tonn describes Mother Jones's militant rhetoric as filled with "properties [nurturing] a collective 'familial' identity for her audience and [equipping] them with skills and confidence sufficient to resist their oppression" (3). There have of course been ample critiques of such essentialist notions of the *feminine*—from Pat Bizzell ("Review"), Devoney Looser, and Joy Ritchie, to name but a few. In sum, their preference is for a self-reflective use of the term *feminist* rather than *feminine*. This debate aside, Tonn's work on Mother Jones offers a helpful framework for analyzing the rhetorical style employed by Rose Schneiderman.

In the speeches of Rose Schneiderman, one can trace a similar rhetorical approach, although without Mother Jones's overt, strategic use of the maternal trope. In Schneiderman's 1912 speech, confrontation is in the service of coalition building, of forming alliance against a common enemy who will not enter the space of disputation. What should one do when one has an argument with someone with power but who will not listen? The answer implied by Schneiderman's example is that one should build a broader coalition with those in *kindred* circumstances, build alliances, enter en masse into the historically agonistic, masculine, public domain, and create conditions in which one has to be respected. Easier said than done, especially in 1912, a period in which a growing gulf had to be bridged between socialist women labor activists and middle- and upper-class suffrage "allies."

Schneiderman's rhetorical ability was recognized early. Immigrating to the United States in 1890 from Russian Poland, Schneiderman grew up on Manhattan's Lower East Side, where poverty threw her into the workforce at age thirteen. Only four foot nine inches tall, with flaming red hair, she organized the first female local of the Jewish Socialist United Cloth Hat and Cap Makers' Union in 1903, at the age of 21. In 1907 she began to work closely with the WTUL, attempting to organize thousands of women, only three percent of whom belonged to unions. She was central to the successful shirtwaist strike in 1909 in the garment industry—"The Uprising of the 20,000"—which gave rise to the International Ladies' Garment Workers' Union. In *Common Sense and A Little Fire: Women and Working-Class Politics in the United States, 1900-1965,* Annelise Orleck writes:

> From a fire-breathing stump speaker, Schneiderman evolved into a lobbyist, a fund-raiser, and an administrator. Over several decades of activism, she moved through a range of cultural and political milieus, from the garment shops of Manhattan's Lower East Side to political offices in Albany and Washington, D.C. She counted Franklin and Eleanor Roosevelt among her friends and taught them much of what they knew about working people. She helped shape some of the major pieces of New Deal legislation [...]. By the end of her long career, Schneiderman had traveled far from the culture into which she had been born and raised. As her life changed, so too did her sense of which strategy held the most promise for working women. (3)

Schneiderman is fascinating because her persuasive speeches and writings demonstrate that she was a tireless bridge-builder, but also someone who knew limits, who knew that the powerless are difficult to unite, and that resources are hard to come by.

AUDIENCES FOR "SENATORS VS. WORKING WOMEN"

On that night in 1912, Schneiderman faced an audience primarily bifurcated between working-class women and middle- and upper-class suffragists (see Orleck, Dye). The WTUL was founded, and in the first three years its leadership dominated by, wealthy "allies" who, according to Orleck:

> tried to steer workers away from radical influences, particularly the Socialist Party. Yet Schneiderman, [one of] the League's leading working-class organizers, [was] a Socialist Party member and saw unionism as a potentially revolutionary tool [...]. Socialists distrusted their work with upper-crust women reformers. Union men were either indifferent or openly hostile to working women's attempts to become leaders in the labor movement. And the League women often seemed to Schneiderman [...] to act out of a patronizing benevolence that had little to do with real coalition building. (43)

Although they exacted their toll on Schneiderman, these conflicts were helpful in clarifying for her what mattered most to working women: "good wages, safe conditions, and shorter hours; an end to sex-based pay differentials and segregation of the labor force; equal access to education; and greater power within the labor unions. Tying these goals to the attainment of woman suffrage,

Schneiderman [...] fleshed out the contours of the industrial feminist vision" (Orleck 88-89). She advocated that vision, attempting to build broad-based support for it in oppressive conditions. Just one year earlier, she and others had been beaten on strike lines. In 1911, she witnessed the loss of 146 women in the Triangle Shirtwaist Factory fire, many of them her friends. Her socialist beliefs were beleaguered by the "allies," whose financial support and social visibility proved indispensable to the movement (indeed, violence against strikers was usually curtailed when wealthy suffrage leaders appeared on the picket lines). Finally, Schneiderman was constantly rebuffed by the male-dominated AFL. As Orleck points out, "It was an irony of the referendum movement and of the woman suffrage movement generally, that no matter how successful women organizers were at raising consciousness among women, they would win the ballot only if men voted for it" (105). With all the resources at their disposal, wealthy and middle-class allies would be crucial in the effort to persuade men. On the one hand, allies were needed; on the other, writes Orleck, asserting their difference and equality, socialist women labor leaders "argued that working women were the real experts on working women and should be given a voice in making the policies that affected them. That, they insisted, was just common sense" (88).

"SENATORS VS. WORKING WOMEN: SENTIMENTALITY OF NEW YORK SENATORS IN EQUAL SUFFRAGE DEBATE ANSWERED BY COMMON SENSE OF WORKING WOMEN"

In the very title framing the series of speeches offered by seven speakers that night of April 22, 1912, common sense would be the appeal used in all of them. As a WTUL publication of the texts of the speeches indicates, the seven speakers that night "each took a quotation from speeches by law-makers setting forth obsolete quibbles why women should not vote," and answered them (Schneiderman). As Mari Boor Tonn argues, simulated dialogue had been a feature of the militant rhetorical style of Mother Jones (8), and here too it structures Schneiderman's overall organization, a dialogical structure enacting the power to speak back. The speech is also marked by such features as inclusive pronouns and examples and stories often drawn from the workers' lives. Overall, the discourse is, as Orleck describes it, "gritty, sarcastic, and confrontational" (89), but the driving motive is an overarching sisterhood, a familial impulse that, says Tonn, becomes "defined primarily by mutual concern and group identity" (5), an identity forged through a common resistance against the "sentimental," misogynist ideology of the senators.

Schneiderman "Replies to New York Senator on Delicacy and Charm of Women"

A senator is reported to have said, "Get women into the arena of politics with its alliances and distressing contests—the delicacy is gone, the charm is gone, and you emasculize women" (Schneiderman). And Schneiderman immediately replied, "Fellow-workers, it already has been whispered to you that there is a possibility that our New York Senators don't know what they are talking about. I am here to voice the same sentiment." The use of quotation forces an opening, a kind of presence of the other that one can ventriloquize and then respond to. Dialogue that won't happen in reality can nevertheless be theatrically enacted. The entire speech is based on a dialogical structure of challenge and counter, a style of oppositional questioning advocated by Janet Farrell Smith, and which Tonn detects in the speeches of Mother Jones as well. Schneiderman states:

> When our Senators acknowledge that our political life has alliances and distressing contests which would take the charm away from women if she got into them, let me reassure the gentlemen that [woman's] great charm has always been that when she found things going wrong she has set to work to make them go right. Do our Senators fear that when women get the vote they will demand clean polling places, etc.? It seems to me that this rather gives them away. Is it their wish to keep the voters in such a condition that it is a disgrace for anybody to come in contact with them?
>
> What about the delicacy and charm of women who have to live with men in the condition of a good many male voters on election day? Perhaps the Senators would like them to keep that condition all year round; they would not demand much of their political bosses and [the bosses] could be sure that they would cast their votes for the man who gave them the most booze.

Throughout the simulated dialogue and oppositional questioning, Schneiderman is an expert ironist—one can almost hear the acidic, withering tone. The dialogical, humorous enactment, as Tonn argues in relation to Mother Jones, here enables Schneiderman to convince audiences of their own power, to use humor to relieve their psychological stress, and to model for them, as Tonn states, "the dialectical cognitive processes severely dependent workers had to emulate to seize control of their lives" (12).

Schneiderman also uses effective repetitions of the term *work*, along with the first-person plural pronoun, to underscore her solidarity with her otherwise divided audience: "We want to work, that is the thing. We are not afraid of work, and we are not ashamed to work, but we do decline to be driven; we want to work like human beings; we want to work for the welfare of the community and not for the welfare of a few." Mari Boor Tonn argues that these strategies form a powerful familial and "feminine"/feminist rhetorical aim—the nurturance of group identity and welfare. This aim informs Schneiderman's attempt to bridge the differences between women workers and "allies" in her audience, a solidarity wrought through the common sense that women must muster in answer to the Senators' misogyny.

By far the most complex moment in Schneiderman's speech comes when she makes reference to the silence women had experienced, the sense of having no audience:

> During the hearing at Albany our learned Senators listened to the opposition very carefully; they wanted to be able to justify themselves afterwards when they voted against our bill. But when the Committee, who spoke for the working women came to plead for the bill, there was only one Senator left in the room—he was the chairman—he couldn't very well get out; we had to make our arguments to the

> chairman of the Committee, all the other Senators had left [...]. What did these men care. We were voteless working women—no matter what we felt or thought we could not come back at them.

In Cooper Union that night, Schneiderman unites her class-divided audience on this common ground of silence, giving voice to their power by directly answering the imagined "Senator": "Poor Mr. Senator, you don't expect us to put any faith in you when we have seen women working in electric works, working all day with sleeves rolled up until they had developed the muscles of their arms as strong and hard as a strong man's; yet these women were intelligent and charming." Schneiderman "stages" a verbal confrontation with the absent oppressor—a kind of political theatre. She appropriates male oppressive discourse about women and quotes it, forcing it into dialogue, dramatizing it for purposes of building a women's community ethos and coalition across differences. In "Senators vs. Working Women," the tension and conflict are represented and enacted, and the lampooned patriarchal discourse creates a sense of both catharsis through ironic laughter and comfort through the empathy of common resistance.

The last section of Schneiderman's speech contains vivid anecdotes, demonstrating in detail what the Senators do not know about the industrial working life of women, but in essence obliquely providing the middle- and upper-class allies with the same information, building a bridge of information and awareness of what the vote might mean in economic terms for working women, all within a theatricalized dialogue berating the Senators' ignorance.

Schneiderman's speech on this occasion and her subsequent speeches delivered for the next eight years on behalf of the National American Woman Suffrage Association demonstrate that she faced enormous obstacles in her fight for working women and the power that might come to them through the vote. She squarely faced the resistance of male unions, and bridged barriers of language and ethnicity. Most of all, she carefully forged cross-class alliances otherwise vexed by distrust and misunderstanding. By 1913, she seems to have diluted her allegiance to socialism as a solution for women's oppression, perhaps through her seasoned pragmatism, grasping that the more effective route for that time would be through suffrage and protective legislation for women workers. Although a coalition of wealthy suffragists and socialist working women never materialized through her efforts, Schneiderman did successfully use her rhetorical skill to introduce thousands of women—"Jewish and Gentile, skilled and unskilled, socialist and conservative" (Dye 48)—to the critical linkage between women's work and suffrage. In *As Equals and as Sisters,* Nancy Schrom Dye claims that, "Without doubt, the Women's Trade Union League went further than any other American women's organization to ameliorate working women's situation and to come to terms with the problems women of different classes and ethnic backgrounds have in relating to one another" (166). Much of the credit goes to Schneiderman and her fifty years of leadership of the organization.

Schneiderman's Legacy for Coalition Rhetoric

There are several lessons one might take from an analysis of Schneiderman's speech. First, the speech and its rhetorical occasion offer glimpses into a complex dynamic created by multiple audiences. Second, one may learn much from Schneiderman's persuasive tactics used in circumstances of oppression and coalition building: dialogue, oppositional questioning, theatrical enactment, appeals to common sense, strategic use of pronouns, use of the visceral anecdote, humor, and irony. Third, one gets a deeper appreciation of the political necessity of militant rhetorical strategy—we need not just "bridge-building" texts from minority writers and speakers, but also those that reveal the lack of footings for the bridge in the first place. Such speeches allow us to explore instances when oppression is so great that fair disputation is not possible—or at least not with mutually consenting parties—in an open exchange of differences. Perhaps most of all, the speech should be added to our examples of women's discourse that show the power to be gained through coalition of the oppressed—an example of a militant, coalition rhetoric.

WORKS CITED

Bizzell, Patricia. "The 4th of July and the 22nd of December: The Function of Cultural Archives in Persuasion, as Shown by Frederick Douglass and William Apes." *College Composition and Communication* 48:1 (1997): 44-60.

---. Review of Anxious Power: Reading, Writing, and Ambivalences in Narratives by Women." *Rhetoric Review* 13 (1994): 192-96.

Dye, Nancy Schrom. *As Equals and As Sisters: Feminism, the Labor Movement, and the Women's Trade Union League of New York.* Columbia: U of Missouri P, 1980.

hooks, bell. "Toward a Revolutionary Feminist Pedagogy." *Talking Back: Thinking Feminist, Thinking Black.* Boston: South End, 1989. 49-54.

Jarratt, Susan. "Feminism and Composition: The Case for Conflict." *Contending with Words.* Ed. Patricia Harkin and John Schilb. New York: MLA, 1991. 105-23.

Lamb, Catherine. "Other Voices, Different Parties: Feminist Responses to Argument." *Perspectives on Written Argument.* Ed. Deborah Berrill. Cresskill, NJ: Hampton, 1996.

Looser, Devoney. "Composing as an 'Essentialist'? New Directions for Feminist Composition Theories." *Rhetoric Review* 12 (1993): 54-69.

Orleck, Annelise. *Common Sense and A Little Fire: Women and Working-Class Politics in the United States, 1900-1965.* Chapel Hill: U of North Carolina P, 1995.

Ritchie, Joy. "Confronting the 'Essential' Problem: Reconnecting Feminist Theory and Practice." *Journal of Advanced Composition* 10 (1990): 249-73.

Schneiderman, Rose. "Senators vs. Working Women. Miss Rose Schneiderman Cap Maker Replies to New York Senator on Delicacy and Charm of Women." 22 Apr. 1912. *Papers of the Women's Trade Union League and its Principal Leaders.* Leonora O'Reilly Papers (Collection V, M64). Schlesinger Library, Radcliffe Institute, Harvard University.

Smith, Janet Farrell. "A Critique of Adversarial Discourse: Gender as an Aspect of Cultural Difference." *Defending Diversity.* Ed. Lawrence Foster and Patricia Herzog. Amherst, MA: U of Massachusetts P, 1994. 57-82.

Tonn, Mari Boor. "Militant Motherhood: Labor's Mary Harris 'Mother' Jones." *The Quarterly Journal of Speech* 82 (1996): 1-21.

18

Identity Across *Blood Meridians*

Jay Ellis
University of Colorado

Cormac McCarthy's novel *Blood Meridian* (1985) follows someone called "the kid" in John Joel Glanton's gang of scalp hunters, through Mexican-American border violence in 1849 and 1850. Before the kid joins the Glanton gang, he is taken up briefly by a Captain White and his company of filibusterers. White is an accurate parody of several advocates for manifest destiny.[1] Marching into Mexico to take Sonora, White and company are surprised by Indians, most of whom hide behind their ponies before rising up to surprise their foes. In the three pages of violence that follow, McCarthy never uses the word *Indians* at all:

> A legion of horribles, hundreds in number, half naked or clad in costumes attic or biblical or wardrobed out of a fevered dream with the skins of animals and silk finery and pieces of uniform still tracked with the blood of prior owners, coats of slain dragoons, frogged and braided cavalry jackets, one in a stovepipe hat and one with an umbrella and one in white stockings and a bloodstained weddingveil and some headgear of cranefeathers or rawhide helmets that bore the horns of bull or buffalo and one in a pigeontailed coat worn backwards and otherwise naked and one in the armor of a spanish conquistador, the breastplate and pauldrons deeply dented with old blows of mace or sabre done in another country by men whose very bones were dust [...]. (52)

The sentence goes on, but what rhetoric of identity is already here?

At the 2000 International Conference on McCarthy in Manchester, England, John Beck juxtaposed this passage with a recollection of the Reagan era. To Beck, McCarthy's description of Indians amounts to Rambolike xenophobia and a caricature of the racial other as having no identity beyond that of animals dressed in the garb of colonial violence. In short, Beck argues that the novel is not an ambiguous depiction of violence at all, but is instead a "fundamentalist" and "reactionary" fevered dream of the New Right. I return to this argument later, but first, what happens next in the novel?

Except for nine of the company, the Indians kill everyone. The kid escapes and finds a man named Sproule. One of them asks, "What kind of Indians was them?" "I don't know," the other replies (56). Interestingly, McCarthy makes it unclear who asks this question—eliding each survivor's individuality. The Indians turn out to be Comanches, but we are told this twenty-one pages later (56 and 77). The narrator knows the tribe, but it is clear that the kid did not.

The victims of the massacre are not individualized at all. They are simply "the company." By contrast, the Comanches exhibit almost as many individual identities as their number allows. In the massacre's violence, the kid sees individual men of the company only in their dying: one man with an arrow in his neck, "bent slightly as if in prayer," another with blood running from his ears as he charges his rifle. Then the dying invaders are again grouped—in contrast to the repeated "one" referring to each individual Indian, we see the plural "some": "Among the wounded some seemed dumb and without understanding and some were pale through the masks of dust and some had fouled themselves or tottered brokenly onto the spears of the savages" (53).

That word, *savages*, might recall Beck's reading. It is typically applied by the putatively civilized to describe the uncivilized other. However, from Charles Brockden Brown's *Edgar Huntley* to this book, written nearly two hundred years later, violence of the civilized against the savage regularly turns the civilized into savages.[2] (In the Glanton gang—active killers, in contrast to the massacred company of White—markers for individuality are as ambiguous within the dictates of civilization as are markers for savageness among the attacking Comanches.)

At the height of the massacre, we have two equally impossible names for the two groups: savages, and "the unhorsed Saxons" (54). Four long sentences that take up a page and a half detail the killing and scalping and worse with almost no commas at all, until the longest sentence breaks up into individual body parts, separated by commas and blades together.

I find this scene easier to read as a white nightmare of reactionary politics *if* I read it out of context. Forget the book's title, that it mostly concerns an Indian-scalping gang as motley as the Indians and far more cruel, and focus on the violence of this massacre in odd sympathy (if I can) for this company of filibusterers—then I read this passage as a racist description of the Indian other. But closer reading reveals markers for individuality among the Comanches. The book—if not its main character and his companions—knows what kind of Indians they are: They are a group of individual Comanches. Furthermore, the ironic juxtaposition of animal feathers and hides, with clothing and armor of every European invasion from the conquistadors to a white (or Mexican, or Spanish, or mestizo) bride's wedding veil actually mocks the pretensions of Captain White to racial superiority. In a pompous speech wasted on the kid, White argues for the invasion because, in his reasoning, the Mexicans are inferior to whites because they are unable to control the further inferior Indians. So much for the inherent superiority, however, of white identity on the battlefield.

A scalp is a synecdoche for an individual's identity, and as the Glanton gang quickly find out, it is easy to trade any coarse black hair for the Indian scalps they are hired by the Chihuahuan government to collect. The gang's most notorious member is Judge Holden, a murderous child-molesting philosopher with alopecia universalis, a likely descendant of both the whale and Ahab. In one of his addresses to an odd audience of largely uneducated fellow scalp hunters, the judge claims that epistemological error is inevitable for humans:

> The truth about the world [...] is that anything is possible. [...] The universe is no narrow thing and the order within it is not constrained by any latitude in its conception to repeat what exists in one part in any other part. Even in this world more things exist without our knowledge than with it and the order in creation which you see is that which you have put there, like a string in a maze, so that you shall not lose your way. For existence has its own order and that no man's mind can compass, that mind itself being but a fact among others. (McCarthy 245)

One should expect problems then, when it comes to rhetoric of identity in this novel. McCarthy points in particular to the problem of naming identity; the narration beginning Chapter VII tells us that "[i]n this company there rode two men named Jackson, one black, one white, both forenamed John. Bad blood lay between them [...]" (81). White Jackson threatens to shoot black Jackson, who waits his turn and beheads white Jackson with a bowie knife (107). White Jackson's taunts include racist language, whereas the narration's attention to their name suggests that in fact they do not share blood, but rather the same name referring to opposite skin colors—if we may forget that there are no such things as white and black men. Indeed, those terms for skin color are distillations in reaction to one another. These two cannot share the same meridian.

Later, the judge wants to sketch a man named Webster into his notebook. Webster resists, and the judge tells him not to be afraid for his identity. "Whether in my book or not, every man is tabernacled in every other and he in exchange and so on in an endless complexity of being and witness to the uttermost edge of the world" (141). Perhaps, yet this trickster is using a spatial metaphor in connection with human identity, having already warned us that space is relative and our understanding of it limited.

The narrator slips in for the judge and tells us that "although each man among them was discrete unto himself, conjoined they made a thing that had not been before and in that communal soul were wastes hardly reckonable more than those whited regions on old maps where monsters do live and where there is nothing other of the known world save conjectural winds" (152). Again, identity is linked to topology; group identity is also forged through violence.

Violence in McCarthy is a fact of life, impossible to abolish. His novels are as apolitical as possible. Some characters embrace violence, but others suffer from it; rather than advocating for or against violence, McCarthy simply details its inevitable realization. In a rare interview, McCarthy makes his only statement outside the novels on violence:

> There's no such thing as life without bloodshed [...]. I think the notion that the species can be improved in some way, that everyone could live in harmony, is a really dangerous idea. Those who are afflicted with this notion are the first ones to give up their souls, their freedom. Your desire that it be that way will enslave you and make your life vacuous. (Woodward 29)

In *Blood Meridian*, group identity is possible only through group violence, which requires group identity, in a feedback of horror. It seems silly to insist on claims of group identity for victims, when such group identification robs particular victims of individuality. McCarthy's statement points outward, however, beyond the ambiguity afforded within a novel. He implicitly calls into question the efficacy (or even reasonableness) behind political injunctions against violence—a position most of us find abhorrent in life, even if we find it persuasive in philosophy (or at least permissible within the safe confines of fiction). McCarthy's shift in stance from "[t]hose" to "you" even implies a threat.

Is there any rhetorical use for such a novel in civic discourse? What might these ambiguities of identity tell us about definitions of identity in politics? Between August 31 and September 8, 2001, the United Nations met in Durban, South Africa, in a "World Conference against Racism, Racial Discrimination, Xenophobia and Related Intolerance." In language that (albeit before the terror attacks that followed three days later and the escalation of group violence in the Middle East) must have been carefully forged, the UN makes identity claims for oppressors and victims. In deference to the conference location, the language in the resulting "Declaration and Programme of Action" uses the word *diaspora* four times, referring only to the "the African Diaspora."[3] By doing so, the document is at pains to maintain a cohesive identity for everyone of any African heritage as a victim, including the descendants of slaves who indeed may have more European than African ancestry, but for whom the legacy of slavery constitutes a narrowing function for their identity.

The UN Declaration, and especially the 219 calls for action in its "Programme," carefully describe identities that on the one hand define people as a group; on the other hand, they attempt to account for all manner of variations in individual identity, to leave no one outside definition. The results are linguistically overdetermined. The word *victim* or *victims* occurs exactly 90 times in the document, seldom with reference to any but the most general geographic locations. Indeed, this lengthy document against intolerance only uses the term *Jewish* once—alongside *Muslim* and *Arab*[4]—the term *anti-Semitism* occurs only twice, again alongside its assumed counterpart, *Islamophobia*[5] and once with *anti-Arabism*.[6] This putative balance of language did little to ease the feelings of the Rabbi Abraham Cooper, Associate Dean of the Simon Wiesenthal Center, who complained of "physical intimidation and threats" at the conference.

The problem, of course, is that nothing is politically possible in terms of particular action when language is confined to generalities. *Whom* do we identify? It is easy to surmise that the answer to that question is the "countless human beings" named as such by the document.

How do we measure the relative strengths of the constitutive parts of a person's identity? Also in 2001, written before September 11 but translated since, Amin Maalouf's *In the Name of Identity: Violence and the Need to Belong* addresses this difficult question, arriving at a heartfelt revaluation of an idea intrinsic to humanistic thought: individualism. Maalouf sees nothing but violence resulting from eliding or obfuscating the ambiguities of identity. Complexities of personal identity serve Maalouf's argument well. Born in Lebanon, Maalouf is descended mostly from Christians. He grew up speaking Arabic, and has lived in Paris for the last several decades, publishing several well-received novels in French. Lest we still simplify his identity, Maalouf also mentions a grandfather who "was a poet, a freethinker, perhaps a freemason, and in any case violently anti-clerical" (19). There's that word, used innocently in the midst of an argument against simplistic definitions of identity:

violence. Maalouf's grandfather's identity as a non-Christian seems to have necessitated at least a violent feeling. Indeed, Maalouf admits that "[t]he identity a person lays claim to is often based, in reverse, on that of his enemy" (14).

Maalouf is uncompromising in his insistence that identity can only exist without violence in terms of individuality:

> That is precisely what characterises each individual identity: it is complex, unique and irreplaceable, not to be confused with any other. [... Otherwise,] all anyone need do to proclaim his identity is simply say he's an Arab, or French, or black, or a Serb, or a Muslim, or a Jew. Anyone who sets out, as I have done, a number of affiliations, is immediately accused of wanting to "dissolve" his identity in a kind of undifferentiated and colourless soup. (20-21)

How do these texts relate to one another? I suggest a continuum.

It would be glib simply to fall back on relativism and undecideability here, to point out with *Blood Meridian*'s kid that "People see what they want to see" (63) when it comes to identity. For someone who loves novels for their complexity, their ambiguity of expression and the ambivalent feelings they elicit, it would be tempting to say that identity in a novel is truer to life than in overtly political writing, such as the Durban Declaration and Programme. Writing about Dostoevsky criticism, the translator Richard Pevear complains that "the first complexity of [literary] criticism is that it must speak monosemantically of the polysemous" (viii). Is it rather the case that literature affords a safe space for "many meanings"? I chose Amin Maalouf's claim that identity is *always* composed of many meanings in part because of his identity as a writer of fiction. The aim of his book, however, is political even as it calls on personal definitions of individual identity that refuse monosemantic urges.

It is understandable that writing done by committee excludes markers for individualism in its definitions of group identity. The rhetorical task of the Durban Declaration and Programme is, of course, impossibly enormous. The statement purports to determine the truth of geopolitical history, to define a number of current geopolitical conflicts, and to link a historical perspective on the past and finding on the present to a call for change in the future. If the past it characterizes, let alone the present, were sufficiently polysemous in definitions of identity to better correspond to reality, to what "Programme of Action" could it possibly lead? That the UN Declaration's definitions of identity nonetheless exhibit the strains of making group identification in the face of polysemous reality, however, suggests that an appreciation for irony is integral to understanding political rhetoric.

Thus, I offer a continuum of relative degrees of ambiguity through these three texts: from the novel, to the personal statement on a political matter made by a novelist, to the statement from no one author made with the authority of an organization attempting to comprise a global identity united against the crimes of its constituent parts. From ineffable contradictions, to the most reasonable definition, to the most problematic attempt at avoiding misapprehension, this continuum moves from a text that makes no political claims, to one that does so hesitantly, to one that is nothing if not political. Finally, among novel, novelist, and committee, it is interesting to note that only in the center do we have a single voice—Maalouf, whose identity is wonderfully complicated—attempting to reconcile the warring forces of individualism and belonging. His, too, is the only situation outside of violence.

NOTES

1. Robert Jarrett identifies mimicry of several "expansionists" (70).
2. "Latin *salvāticus*, from Latin *silvāticus*, of the woods, wild, from *silva*, forest" (*American Heritage*).
3. Declaration Article 33, and Programme Articles 7, 158, and 159.
4. Declaration Article 61.
5. Declaration Article 61.
6. Article 150 of the Programme for Action.

WORKS CITED

Beck, John. "Filibusters and Fundamentalists: *Blood Meridian* and the New Right." *The Second European Conference on Cormac McCarthy*. University of Manchester, Manchester, England. 23 June 2000.

Brown, Charles Brockden. *Edgar Huntley; Or, Memoirs of a Sleep-Walker*. Ed. Norman S. Grabo. New York: Penguin, 1988.

Cooper, Rabbi Abraham. "Human Rights and Jews." Letter to the Editor, *The New York Times*, 28 May 2002: A18.

Jarrett, Robert L. *Cormac McCarthy*. New York: Twayne, 1997.

Maalouf, Amin. *In the Name of Identity: Violence and the Need to Belong*. Barbara Bray, trans. New York: Arcade, 2001.

McCarthy, Cormac. *Blood Meridian: Or, the Evening Redness in the West*. 1985. New York: Random House, 1992.

Pevear, Richard. Forward. *Crime and Punishment*. By Fyoder Dostoevsky. New York: Knopf, 1992.

"Savage." *American Heritage Dictionary*. 3rd ed. Boston: Houghton Mifflin, 1996.

Woodward, Richard B. "Cormac McCarthy's Venomous Fiction." *The New York Times Magazine*. 19 Apr. 1992: 28-31.

19

Defending the Public: Procedural Rationality and the Limits of Actually Existing Jurisprudence

Daniel L. Emery
Gustavus Adolphus College

"Actually existing jurisprudence" might seem an oxymoron, an impossible figurative connection of practical reality and theoretical ideality. My title draws from Nancy Fraser and in some ways mirrors her essay on the public sphere, expressing a fondness for Habermasian discourse ethics despite recognizing within it a series of problematic presumptions. Still, jurisprudence can be defined in two ways: the theoretical science of law on the one hand and the administration of a system of laws on the other ("Jurisprudence" 854). This dual character reflects one of the central contentions of Habermas's *Between Facts and Norms*—although notions of "the law" conspicuously imply the universalistic language of theory, the consideration of the law is never free from the materiality of its exercise. The principles of validity that make the system cohere philosophically and the factual constraints of its administrative operations are both at stake in questions of jurisprudence, for Habermas and in this chapter. Alongside an explanation of Habermas's discourse theory of law, I examine legal defense procedures for indigent defendants in New York City to demonstrate the possibilities and limits of procedural norms of justice and to consider the relation between law and democracy in the contemporary United States.

In contemporary considerations of rhetorical democracy, the role of forensic rhetoric as an element of rhetorical democracy has been deemphasized. Analysis of contentious political campaigns, mediated political spectacles, and the rhetorical construction of publics have generally overshadowed the place of courtroom rhetoric in contemporary political life. However, as the 2000 presidential election controversy and Habermas's theory of law both demonstrate, debates concerning the law and its just administration can and do determine our collective democratic future. For these and many other reasons, reconsideration of the practices of forensic rhetoric is critical to understanding the role of discourse practices in contemporary political life.

ELEMENTS OF HABERMAS'S DISCOURSE THEORY OF LAW

Between Facts and Norms (1996) can be read as Habermas's effort to translate the theory of discourse ethics articulated in *The Theory of Communicative Action* (1984, 1987) into the practical realm of political administration described in *Legitimation Crisis* (1975). Habermas suggests that normative legal theory is constantly in danger of losing contact with social reality, whereas social theory mistakenly screens out all normative content from law (7). This tension between the normative ideal expressed in the law and the practical effects of its application and administration is fundamental. For individual statements, the universalistic meaning of the claimed validity exceeds all contexts, but nevertheless only the local, binding act of acceptance enables validity claims to bear the burden of social integration for an everyday context-bound practice (21). For administration, this tension appears in the hierarchical relationship between the normative content of law and its material exercise. This undeniable tension suggests that a wider orientation to the field of law is necessary.

Among homogenous communities, the ethical application of the law was once presumed to be derived from a set of normative principles accepted by all members of the community. In contemporary complex societies, no longer supported by metaphysical guarantees of the justice of laws or sets of homogenous norms, its legitimacy encounters several difficulties. Habermas states:

> The traces of modern natural-law normativism thus get lost in a trilemma: neither in the teleology of history nor in the constitution of the human species can we find the content of practical reason once its philosophic foundation in the knowing subject is shattered, nor can we justify such content simply on the basis of the fortuitous resources of successful histories and traditions. (3)

Citizens in complex societies find themselves looking for a means to illustrate the legitimacy of particular laws without reliable universalist resources available. One effect of this gap is that legal administration can operate on the basis of interest while claiming its traditional legitimacy. According to Habermas:

> [I]n the functional imperatives of the state apparatus, the economic system, and other social subsystems, normatively unfiltered interest positions often carry the day only because they are stronger and use the legitimating force of legal forms to cloak there merely factual strength. Therefore [...] modern law remains a profoundly ambiguous medium of societal integration. (40)

For Habermas, the law's capacity for social integration is of paramount importance. More than a system of enforcement, legitimately established law is the foundation for democratic structures of governance and ethical relations between citizens. As Ciaran Cronin and Pablo De Greiff note in their introduction to *The Inclusion of the Other*, the German word *Rechsstaat*, which translates as "the rule of law," literally means "constitutional state" (265).

Habermas argues that social integration can only be achieved today on the basis of an alternate form of legitimacy that emerges from discourse ethics. Admitting that an idealist notion of discourse ethics will always be confounded at its point of application by the material exercise of communicative practice,

Habermas nonetheless seeks legitimacy of law in appeals to reasoned discourse. He begins by describing a familiar principle: just those action norms are valid to which all possibly affected persons could agree as participants in rational discourses (107). Taking this notion of validity as a measure for actually existing laws, the discourse principle establishes that only in a realm free from the intervention of the state and coercion by force or money can a principle of validity be established.

It is at this point that the connection between discourse ethics and rhetoric becomes most apparent. Rejecting the fundamentalism of an ethics based on normative contents and the anarchy of the politics of clashing interest groups, Habermas establishes a space for forensic rhetoric as a practice of civic engagement. He notes: "Starting with the general presuppositions of argumentation as the reflective form of communicative action, one can attempt to elucidate this principle in formal-pragmatic fashion [...]. For the application of moral norms to particular cases, the universalization principle is replaced by a principle of appropriateness" (109).

Discourse ethics functions as a normative constraint on the law on the basis of the construction of arguments and a standard of appropriateness. From the basis of discourse ethics, enacted by processes of argument, *Between Facts and Norms* suggests a legal code of rights derived from this discourse principle essential for the legitimacy of laws and finally posits the constitutional state as the mechanism to guarantee these rights.

The discourse theory of law has several strengths to recommend it. First, it takes seriously the relationship between discourse practices and social cohesion. Second, it recognizes the connection among practices of argument, norms of appropriateness, and democratic legitimacy, recognizing the discourse of law as civic practice. Third, Habermas's consideration displaces liberal and civic republican theories of law with a postmetaphysical notion of legitimacy—democratic legitimacy without transcendental guarantees. Finally, its procedural character is particularly applicable to the appellate court system in the United States. These benefits can be seen most clearly in the context of a legal system facing a crisis of legitimacy, which is the case for criminal defense in New York City.

INDIGENT CRIMINAL DEFENSE IN NEW YORK CITY

In 1963, the U.S. Supreme Court heard *Gideon v. Wainwright*. Gideon was tried in Florida for a noncapital offense, having allegedly broken into a pool hall. At the time, Florida provided defense attorneys only in cases of capital crimes, so despite Mr. Gideon's request for counsel, none was appointed. Pitting his Fourteenth Amendment rights against the Florida court's interpretation of the Sixth, Gideon asserted that the failure to grant him counsel denied him equal protection under the law and won a 9-0 decision. The *Gideon* case overturned the previous precedent, *Betts v. Brady* that allowed states to determine procedures for indigent criminal defense on a case by case basis. Justice Black stated in the majority opinion:

> Not only these precedents [*Avery v. Alabama* 308 U.S. 444 (1940), *Smith v. O'Grady* 312 U.S. 329 (1941)] but also reason and reflection require us to recognize that in our adversary system of criminal justice, any person hauled into court who is too poor to hire a lawyer cannot be assured a fair trial unless one is appointed for him. This seems an obvious truth [...] from the beginning our state and national constitutions and laws have laid great emphasis on procedural and substantive safeguards designed to assure fair trials before impartial juries in which each defendant stands equal before the law. That ideal cannot be realized if the poor man charged with a crime has to face his accusers without a lawyer to assist him. (4)

In establishing a right to counsel, the *Gideon* decision staked claim to the necessity of procedural guarantees to maintain a system of just laws. Unfortunately, this procedural guarantee has been significantly eroded since 1963. Although numerous examples are available, the status of indigent defense in New York provides a prime illustration.

The Legal Aid Society of New York is modeled on a dream of civil society. Rather than placing the state in the contradictory position of both prosecuting crime and defending the accused, a private corporation was established in New York for indigent defense, operating on behalf of citizens to defend them from the exercise of state's power to sanction and serving to guarantee the rights of the accused. Appeals for increased funding have consistently accompanied Legal Aid since it was established in the 1960s, but a change in the debate occurred in 1994 (Fritsch and Rohde, "Lawyers" A1). A strike of unionized Legal Aid attorneys in 1994 brought criminal prosecutions to a standstill in New York. In the wake of the strike, former prosecutor and then Mayor Rudolph Giuliani sought to break the monopoly of Legal Aid on indigent criminal defense. Justifying the shift as the creation of a competitive market, Giuliani reduced funding for Legal Aid and shifted the burden of defense to nonprofit organizations and independent attorneys (Rohde, "Decline" B1).

The defunding of Legal Aid coincided with the administration's aggressive new street crime policy. Operating on the assumption that toleration of petty crime encouraged more serious ones, the Giuliani administration took a hard-line, zero-tolerance stand on so-called "quality of life" crimes. Police officers aggressively targeted loitering, graffiti, panhandling, and other minor offenses throughout the city, and particularly in historically high-crime areas disproportionately populated by poor New Yorkers (Erzen 21). Quality-of-life policing brought new waves of indigent defendants into a system with diminishing resources. In 1998, nonprofit organizations took thirty percent of the indigent case load, yet increasing arrests meant that the Legal Aid Society handled almost exactly the same number of actual cases as it had in 1994 with only two thirds of its 1994 budget (Fritsch and Rohde, "Lawyers" A1).

The failure of the competitive market was evident by 1999. State-supported attorney's fees (unchanged in thirteen years) failed to attract independent lawyers and increasing case loads led experienced lawyers to refuse to add new clients or to quit indigent defense altogether (Rohde, "Critical" 59). The resulting shortage meant that defendants routinely waited six months and up to two years in jail awaiting trial as no lawyers were available to represent them (Rohde, "Critical" 59).

Between 1990 and 2000, the number of attorneys representing indigent defendants held constant, but the number of cases quadrupled (Mansnerus B4).

In April 2001, the *New York Times* ran its "Two Tiered Justice" series: a three-part exposé on the status of indigent defense in New York. Using a seven-month analysis of court records from the year 2000, the *Times* reported an alarming series of statistics:

- In 137 homicide cases, lawyers in a third of cases billed the city for less than one week's work. In only twelve of the cases did attorneys spend 200 hours preparing a case, which the standard experts asserted was evidence of appropriate diligence.
- Defense attorneys visited the crime scene in only thirty-one percent of cases, another standard considered necessary for adequate defense.
- Only thirty-six percent of lawyers visited Rikers Island to meet with their clients prior to trial.
- Only thirty-seven percent employed investigators to look for witnesses, check records, or investigate police accounts of the crime, although the city would have covered the costs.
- Only twenty-four percent requested expert witnesses, again despite the fact that the city would cover costs. (Fritsch and Rohde, "Lawyers" A1)

By 2000, Legal Aid was representing less than half of indigent defendants, eighteen percent were represented by nonprofits, and the remainder where given over to independent lawyers hired by the state (Fritsch and Rohde, "For Poor" A1). Without caps on case loads, the backlog of cases in the system created an excess of potential clients for lawyers eager to maximize their earnings and minimize their labor. In 2000, attorney Sean P. Sullivan personally represented 1,600 clients, with the twenty busiest attorneys representing 9,000 clients past arraignment and hundreds more in plea agreements (Fritsch and Rohde, "For the Poor" A1).

In June 2001, the New York County Lawyers Association sued the state of New York, arguing that the system of indigent defense in criminal and family court violated the Sixth Amendment, demanding increased fees for work inside and outside of court (Mansnerus B4). Under pressure, Governor George Pataki promised reforms to the system and higher fees to attract more competent attorneys. By December, Pataki had retreated from his pledge, citing the fiscal impacts of September 11 on the state budget (Fritsch F1).

The detrimental effects of weak defense falls disproportionately on the poor, whereas public attention to injustice in New York City falls disproportionately on those involved in law enforcement. Prior to their heroic portrayals in post 9/11 discussion, the New York Police Department was recognized most often for the tragedies resulting from Zero Tolerance policies (e.g., the shooting of Amadou Diallo), or for their track record of deliberate violence (e.g., the sexual assault of Abner Louima). The public outcry that has followed from these and other instances of police violence have led many in New York and nationwide to criticize the quality-of-life campaign. Much less public attention has been afforded to the crisis of legal defense in New York. I argue that Habermas's discourse theory of law suggests that these crises be considered differently to address the legitimacy of policing, crime prevention, and the law in New York City.

On Habermas's view, state authority hides behind outmoded notions of legitimacy to mask its interested enforcement of the law. The quality-of-life campaign draws its rhetoric quite explicitly from the tradition of civic republicanism and an explicit appeal of a good life. At the same time, critiques of the campaign draw their legitimacy from liberal arguments based on principles of human rights. As Habermas notes, these positions have always been in competition and are never complementary. As a result, the debate over crime policy in New York traces a well-worn path.

As public debate most often centers on police injustices, misrecognition of the wider problem of the legitimacy of law results. Defenders of crime control assume that the common good of crime control mitigates against police abuses—for example, the argument that Diallo's unfortunate death is the price we pay to fight crime. Critics of the police treat the activities of individual officers as a synecdoche for the police department and criminal justice as a whole—for example, that Louima's assault was merely an extension of official police policy. By emphasizing attention on good and bad instances of enforcement, the legitimacy of the system remains unconsidered; supporters implicitly confirm its absolute legitimacy whereas critics presume the precise opposite. By addressing the issue of legitimacy more directly, the problems in New York take on a new cast.

For Habermas, law loses its social integrating power if it is merely a system of regulation without a normative basis in legitimacy. Attention to the crisis of indigent defense in New York reveals a systemic procedural failure of justice in New York City, one that cannot be dismissed as isolated or inconsequential for advocates of law and order policies. Nevertheless, the critique of the system of indigent defense implicitly supports the legitimacy of law—if procedures were administered appropriately, then just outcomes might ensue. By focusing attention on the systemic procedures of criminal defense, the legitimacy of law can be considered with due attention to the role of law in social integration. To the degree that the quality-of-life campaign has had the effect of exacerbating the procedural crisis, its negative consequences might be addressed without suggesting that critiques of policing imply the corruption of the entire system. Critics of police brutality can admit the desirability of living in safe environments and the necessity for policing, while law and order advocates can admit that the desire for safety is not equivalent to a demand for racial profiling, patdowns, and police brutality. Attention to procedural justifications offers a chance to critique the system of justice without abandoning it, and to defend the need for policing without excusing its abuses.

CONCLUSION

Habermas concludes *Between Facts and Norms* stating: "[The] secularization of the spiritual bases of government authority, by now long underway, suffers from a deficit in implementation that is overdue. If this deficit is not met by more extensive democratization, the constitutional state itself will be endangered" (443-44). Although critics of Habermas fault the normative emptiness of procedural rationality (Ball 75-79), the impossibility of procedural equality without material redistribution on the other (Marsh 177-87), and the affirmative dependence of the criminal justice system on inequality (Cole 5), the theory of discourse ethics provides an invaluable resource for the reconsideration of forensic rhetoric in this and in similar instances. Although these critiques merit consideration and illustrate the problems of blind faith in formal norms, the procedural character of contemporary forensic rhetoric and the procedural failures of New York City suggest that attention to the legitimacy of formal legal procedure is both tactically expedient and strategically critical for sustaining, or perhaps reviving, a critical element of our rhetorical democracy. Although the success of a coherent (if contingent) formal foundation to law will always be mitigated by the limits of its material exercise, mindfulness of the procedural character of practices of contemporary forensic rhetoric are of clear merit. Attending to its function in social integration as well as its procedural norms, Habermas's discourse theory of the law places rhetorical theorists and critics in a more discerning and judicious relationship with the civic practices of forensic rhetoric and democratic legitimacy more broadly. What could be a more fitting tribute to rhetorical democracy?

WORKS CITED

Ball, Peter. "Discourse Ethics and Human Rights in Criminal Procedure." *Habermas, Modernity, and Law*. Ed. Mathieu Deflam and David W. Rasmussen. London: Sage, 1996. 75-81.

Cole, David. *No Equal Justice: Race and Class in the American Criminal Justice System*. New York: New Press, 1999.

Cronin, Ciaran, and Pablo De Greiff. "Editor's Introduction." *The Inclusion of the Other*. By Jürgen Habermas. Cambridge, MA: MIT P, 1998. vii-xxxii.

Erzen, Tanya. "Turnstile Jumpers and Broken Windows." *Zero Tolerance: Quality of Life and the New Police Brutality in New York City*. New York: NYU P, 2001. 19-49.

Fraser, Nancy. "Rethinking the Public Sphere: A Contribution to the Critique of Actually Existing Democracy." *Habermas and the Public Sphere*. Ed. Craig Calhoun. Cambridge, MA: MIT P, 1992. 109-42.

Fritsch, Jane. "For the Poor, A Lawyer With 1600 Clients." *New York Times* 9 Apr. 2001, late ed.: A1.

---. "Lawyers Often Fail New York's Poor." *New York Times* 8 Apr. 2001, late ed.: A1.

---. "Pataki Rethinks His Promise of a Raise for Lawyers to the Indigent." *New York Times* 24 Dec. 2001, late ed.: F1.

---, and Rohde. "For Poor, Appeals Are Luck of the Draw." *New York Times* 10 Apr. 2001, late ed.: A1.

Gideon v. Wainwright. 372 U.S. 335. U.S. Supreme Court, 1963.

Habermas, Jürgen. *Between Facts and Norms: A Discourse Theory of Law and Democracy*. Cambridge, MA: MIT P, 1996.

---. *Legitimation Crisis*. Trans. Thomas McCarthy. Boston: Beacon, 1975.

---. *The Theory of Communicative Action*. 2 Vols. Trans. Thomas McCarthy. Boston: Beacon, 1984-1987.

"Jurisprudence." *Black's Law Dictionary*. 6th ed. 1990.

Mansnerus, Laura. "Saying Courts Fail the Poor, Lawyers' Group Sues the State." *New York Times* 2 June 2001, late ed.: B4.

Marsh, James L. *Unjust Legality: A Critique of Habermas's Philosophy of Law.* Lanham, MD: Rowan, 2001.

Rohde, David. "Critical Shortage of Lawyers for Poor Seen." *New York Times* 12 Dec. 1999, late ed., sect. 1: 59.

---. "Decline Is Seen in Legal Help for City's Poor." *New York Times* 26 Aug. 1998, late ed.: B1.

20

Between Sympathy and Self-Interest: A Reframing of Adam Smith's Economic Rhetoric

David Charles Gore
Texas A&M University

"The Adam Smith problem," the issue of reconciling Smith's altruistic approach to public affairs in *The Theory of Moral Sentiments* (*TMS*) with the more egoistic self-interest approach found in *An Inquiry Into the Nature and Causes of the Wealth of Nations* (*WN*)—has captivated scholars for years (see Dickey). Jerry Z. Muller believes that "to recover Smith's thought we must attend to the rhetorical elements of his writing and to his intended audience. For Smith wanted not merely to inform and enlighten his readers but to *influence* them" (9). Such a rhetorical view of Smith's work reveals that his aim was to design a decent society, a society that enjoyed economic prosperity as well as moral strength.

Sympathy, and not self-interest, actually serves as the foundation of the decent society, but Smith recognized that a concern for others through communication needed to be tempered with the other human reality of concern for self. In so doing, Smith prefigured several theories of democratic involvement that focus on the human desire to assist others, while still protecting the self and those most important to it. The tendency to divorce the concepts of sympathy and self-interest in Smith's writings has lead to corrupted versions of his approach to capitalism, unfortunate definitions of humankind as primarily selfish wealth-maximizers, and the all-too-often neglect of communication theory as central to moral behavior.

SELF-INTEREST

> It is not from the benevolence of the butcher, the brewer, or the baker, that we expect our dinner, but from their regard to their own self-interest. We address ourselves, not to their humanity but to their self-love, and never talk to them of our own necessities but of their advantages.
>
> —Smith (*WN* 27)

Perhaps the most oft-quoted and most quotable of all of Smith's writings, this passage is usually employed in support of the "there's no such thing as a free lunch" doctrine. Economists build on this claim by implying that humans are always out for their own self-interest, and that by nature we always seek to maximize our personal profit. This argument is *ad hominem,* an attack on the character of the audience (McCloskey 26). Such an *ad hominem,* however, has only gained in popularity as public choice theorists and others who advocate like tenets have defined human nature as primarily selfish. It is a safe and easy explanation to argue that humans are motivated solely by self-interest. It is more difficult to place constraints on self-interest that still capture what it means to be a self, but at the same time do not destroy the origin of the self in other selves, or that the self should recognize its political and social obligations to the group.

Once a reader works his or her way through several pages on the price of corn in the eighteenth century, variations in the value of silver, and long discourses on the division of labor in pin factories, the reader finds that the doctrine of self-interest comprises a very small portion of the *Wealth of Nations.* McCloskey's *Rhetoric of Economics,* Hirschman's *Rhetoric of Reaction,* and Aune's *Selling the Free Market* constitute the early beginnings of studies in the rhetorical construction of self-interest.

We should recognize that studying self-interest does improve our comprehension of conflict. However, admitting that we act in self-interested ways does not require us to abandon any notion that we can be altruistic or cooperate. Smith's ethical doctrines combine Stoic and Christian virtues, resulting in a golden rule of Smithian ethics: "[A]s to love our neighbour as we love ourselves is the great law of Christianity, so it is the great precept of nature to love ourselves only as we love our neighbour, or what comes to the same thing, as our neighbour is capable of loving us" (*TMS* 25). If we take the preceding statement as Smith's golden rule of ethics, we see that within his system, love of self comes from the love of others. Or, in other words, we love ourselves only as much as our neighbors love us. This puts a new twist on Christian and Stoic ethics because within this system self-love is a collective affair. Self-love requires the love of others in society, and this necessitates that we work together to achieve common goals because we live together and because our self-love is dependent on it.

The traditional economic reading of Smith suggests that self-interested acts always have positive consequences for others. In actuality, often these acts have a negative effect, or even no effect on others. The negative effects often result from situations in which our self-interest collides with the self-interest of others, but can also be a result of our self-interest causing them direct harm. Such disagreement as to the virtue of self-interest is complicated if we see it as the *only* regulation of our public behavior. Surely nothing was further from Smith's thinking. However, some economists and political scientists, particularly the public choice variety, have been arguing for years that political and public decisions would be more effective if they were based on market principles, the chief principle of economics being self-interest. This is a conception of self-interest without sympathy. Fortunately, we still make most decisions in the public sphere based on evidence that is more than economic and more than self-interested. However, it is not difficult to find political leaders and theorists who argue that the self-interest-governed market should guide all public decisions. This thinking grows from arguments about self-interest that claim to trace their origin to Smith's writings, but ignore a holistic view of his work.

Self-interest, when viewed in conjunction with Smith's metaphor of the invisible hand, was to motivate us for economic reasons. Self-interest as it applies to policy, in Smith's system, always accompanies sympathy. In other words, self-interest cannot serve as our sole motivation in public affairs because sympathy underwrites all of Smithian philosophy. Smith's self-interest is part of a larger argument suggesting that people, when given the liberty to choose, will make choices that are of the greatest benefit to themselves economically. To suggest that Smith's work is meant to argue for self-interest in political, moral, and social matters is disingenuous, especially when it considers self-interest as a philosophical and social end. Furthermore, it has the unfortunate effect of divorcing public decisions from ethics, something Smith would likely have found abhorrent.

Smith's self-interest is coupled with the metaphor of the invisible hand in order to ensure good outcomes from self-interested behavior. The invisible hand is quite mystical, in part because we do not know anything about the arm to which the hand is attached. Those in policy positions who argue that self-interest should be the sole motivator in public affairs advocate moral decisions based on the self-interest-driven market, but they ignore the larger implications of Smith's writings by allowing self-interest to reign supreme in their system of politics, which is also their system of morality, which is really economics. In other words, they make moral decisions but call them market decisions, and they transform Smith's intentions for self-interest as a means to self-interest as an end.

Kurt Baier, in *The Moral Point of View*, argues that the position of all-out self-interest can be universally adopted without self-contradiction (Kant's categorical imperative), but it does not necessarily follow that such a system is moral because a consistent egoist adopts for all occasions the principle of "everyone for him/herself." The "softer ways," of morality, as Baier calls them, have no place within such a system. And a system so designed is self-contradictory, especially when self-interests collide, or when so-called markets fail. Baier writes:

> This is obviously absurd. For morality is designed to apply in just such cases, namely, those where interests conflict [...] when there are conflicts of interest, we always look for a "higher" point of view, one from which such conflicts can be settled. Consistent egoism makes everyone's private interest the "highest court of appeal." But by 'the moral point of view' we mean a point of view which is a court of appeal for conflicts of interest. Hence it cannot (logically) be identical with the point of view of self-interest. (190)

Conflicting self-interests necessitate and constitute morality. If we subscribe to a theory in which all actors are self-interested beings, where is the room for rhetoric? Persuasion is simply relegated to a minor, almost nonexistent role. When interests conflict, a system of politics and morality based solely on personal interests is not equipped to respond. On a larger scale, because of their realist style, self-interested systems lack the rhetorical skills necessary to respond to crisis (Aune

42). Furthermore, as Baier writes, the solutions that self-interested systems provide to conflict can never be moral because interests direct and guide what is right and wrong.

There is in humanity a desire to improve situations, to improve society, and to improve one's talents. Self-interest is useful as a means of encouraging us to participate in politics and can be considered virtuous only when its ends are good, which is why I think Smith invoked the invisible hand metaphor. Furthermore, Smith wrote about the contribution of self-interest to the improvement of society, not just the economy:

> If you would implant public virtue in the breast of him who seems heedless of the interest of his country, it will often be to no purpose to tell him, what superior advantages the subjects of a well-governed state enjoy; that they are better lodged, that they are better clothed, that they are better fed [...]. You will be more likely to persuade, if you describe the great system of public police which procures these advantages, if you explain the connexions and dependencies of its several parts, their mutual subordination to one another, and their general subserviency to the happiness of the society; if you show how this system might be introduced into his own country, what it is that hinders it from taking place there at present [...] and all the several wheels of the machine of government be made to move with more harmony and smoothness [...]. It is scarce possible that a man should listen to a discourse of this kind, and not feel himself animated to some degree of public spirit. (*TMS* 186)

Self-interest is a key motivation to animate our feelings of public spirit, and its greatest contribution to society occurs when it encourages individuals to consider how to improve the public policy. It does little good to appeal to his sympathy with the benefits that others enjoy, Smith tells us. It is far more effectual to show him how the improvements can be introduced into his own country, what prevents those benefits from being there already, and how harmony can be accomplished in the system of policy. Notice the language, "if you would implant virtue in the breast of him who seems heedless of the interest of his country." Smith never goes so far as to say that self-interest alone is virtuous. Instead, he maneuvers means and ends to show that self-interest can be a means of implanting public virtue and awaking a concern for others. Notice further that the virtue imparted by self-interest is "public" in nature. Self-interest becomes the means for public moral sentiment, but it never attains the status of an end in Smith's writings.

SYMPATHY

Sympathy represents the ability to experience vicariously the feelings of another, feelings that could be either positive or negative, but that could be accessed vicariously only through observation and imagination. Smith writes: "By the imagination we place ourselves in his situation, we conceive ourselves enduring all the same torment, we enter as it were into his body, and become in some measure the same person with him, and thence form some idea of his sensations, and even feel something which, though weaker in degree, is not altogether unlike them"

(*TMS* 9). The sentiment experienced through sympathy in the imagination is weaker in degree to the sentiment actually felt by the observed, but it is similar.

Sympathy arises more from the situation that excites the feeling than from the feeling or the view of the passion itself, which is why its prerequisite is interaction. When a graduate student declares openly before class that she is frustrated with her marriage, the feeling of impropriety that may come to her classmates through sympathy would arise more from the declaration than from her frustration. This explains why we feel embarrassed at "the impudence and rudeness of another, though he himself seems to have no sense of the impropriety of his own behavior," according to Smith (*TMS* 12).

Social scientists and interpersonal communication theorists have expended tremendous effort on the argument regarding the similarities and dissimilarities of sympathy and empathy. Thomas Steinfatt writes, "that empathy is different from sympathy. Empathy is the ability to 'get inside' of another person—the ability to predict accurately the other's internal states. Sympathy refers to the feelings associated with an attempt at empathy" (Steinfatt 232). Steinfatt argues further that either empathy or sympathy can occur without the other, but that they generally occur together. One of the myths of relationships is that it is possible to see things precisely as the other person does. Smith's sympathy differs from empathy in a similar way because it is not an exact duplicate of emotion, but rather manifests itself through interaction and imagination. In this way, sympathy is more rhetorical or communicative by nature than empathy because of its dependence on a mediated understanding.

John Durham Peters writes, "sympathy [...] is not a matching of emotions, a heart-to-heart transfer from one person to another, but a judgment made by an observer, an act of interpretation. There is, for Smith, no transcendence of subjective experience. We are naturally limited, he says, in our ability to sympathize; nature has given us 'a dull sensibility to the afflictions of others'" (660). We insert ourselves into their place through an act of interpretation. We can sympathize with a lunatic who is singing and laughing, and this can make us miserable, not because the lunatic has miserable feelings to impart, but because we would feel miserable if we, being sane, were found in his or her place. Peters continues, "Smith has no angst about the unbridgeable distance between individual minds: the human ability to match feelings is 'sufficient for the harmony of society. Though they will never be unisons, they may be concords, and this is all that is wanted or required'" (661). Because Smith is using sympathy at the level of society, he is not writing about interpersonal communication or personal morals per se. Instead, his focus is on what effect our interactions have on our ability to function in the public sphere. The closest we may be able to come to another's feelings is to change "places in fancy with the sufferer," writes Smith (*TMS* 10). But this is more than enough when viewed at the societal level, as opposed to the interpersonal, because our public concern for others will always, and necessarily should always, be less than our private concern for those closest to us. Yet, it is only through sympathy that we understand both the needs of those in our family and the needs of those in our community. Sympathy is the communicative center of

Smith's decent society and through it we come to appreciate the feelings, desires, and needs of those around us.

CONCLUDING REMARKS

Stephen J. McKenna argues that, for Smith, communication theory underwrites ethical theory because communication is prior to moral consciousness (58). Smith wanted communication and ethics at the center of his decent society, and this is why we are not justified in reading Smith's later work as a violation of these central tenets. Smith's sympathy suggests that he was acutely aware of the needs of others and wanted to keep moral sentiment as the foundation of human behavior and motives. However, he also recognized that in order for us to be motivated to public interest, we had to be reached through our private interests. Self-interest is not the basest of motivations, for through it we seek to improve our own condition and the condition of others, and it serves as a *topos* of persuasion that allows us to implant virtue in the hearts of persons who otherwise would not participate in the public forum. The public forum constitutes public virtue, and sympathy and self-interest function rhetorically to increase public virtue. Viewing sympathy and self-interest together allows us to capture Smith's intentions and approach a decent society.

WORKS CITED

Aune, James Arnt. *Selling the Free Market: The Rhetoric of Economic Correctness*. New York: Guilford, 2001.

Baier, Kurt. *The Moral Point of View: A Rational Basis of Ethics.* 6th ed. Ithaca, NY: Cornell UP, 1969.

Dickey, Laurence. "Historicizing the 'Adam Smith Problem': Conceptual, Historiographical, and Textual Issues." *Journal of Modern History* 58 (Sept. 1986): 579-609.

Hirschman, Albert O. *The Rhetoric of Reaction: Futility, Perversity, Jeopardy*. Cambridge, MA: Harvard UP, 1991.

McCloskey, Deirdre N. *The Rhetoric of Economics*. 2nd ed. Madison: U of Wisconsin P, 1998.

McKenna, Stephen J. "Fitting Words: Propriety in Adam Smith's Rhetoric and Ethics." *Scottish Rhetoric and Its Influences*. Ed. Lynee Lewis Gaillet. Mahwah, NJ: Erlbaum, 1998. 57-65.

Muller, Jerry Z. *Adam Smith in His Time and Ours*. Princeton, NJ: Princeton UP, 1993.

Peters, John Durham. "Publicity and Pain: Self-Abstraction in Adam Smith's Theory of Moral Sentiments." *Public Culture* 7 (1995): 657-84.

Smith, Adam. *An Inquiry Into the Nature and Causes of the Wealth of Nations*. Ed. R. H. Campbell and A. S. Skinner. Indianapolis: Liberty Fund, 1981.

---. *The Theory of Moral Sentiments*. Ed. D. D. Raphael and A. L. Macfie. Indianapolis: Liberty Fund, 1984.

Steinfatt, Thomas M. *Human Communication: An Interpersonal Introduction*. Indianapolis: Bobbs-Merrill, 1977.

21

The Concept of Global Citizenship in Michael Hardt and Antonio Negri's *Empire*: A Challenge to Three Ideas of Rhetorical Mediation

Ronald Walter Greene
University of Minnesota–Twin Cities

In the human sciences, the concept of citizenship is emerging as a future object of study for interdisciplinary work. Due to the energy of this research, I have argued that citizenship—and, in particular, its role alongside the processes of globalization—provides a possible site for the ongoing encounter between deliberative rhetoric (argumentation studies) and cultural studies (Greene, "Citizenship). However, as Cindy Patton and Robert Caserio point out, the ongoing reinvestment in citizenship brings with it a desire to overcome "the inevitable exclusiveness of citizenship" (1). One of the most contested sites for investigating the exclusiveness of citizenship concerns its relationship to immigration.

The modern legacy of citizenship locates the citizen within the political space of the nation-state whereas the circulation of immigrants constantly transgresses these borders.[1] In so doing, immigrants are often vulnerable to intense anxieties about how their arrival disrupts the national imaginary. Lisa Lowe, for example, argues that in the United States, the "legal categories of 'legal' and 'illegal,' 'citizen and non-citizen,' and '[U.S.] born and permanent resident' sustains the figuration of the Asian immigrant as a transgressive and corrupting foreignness that continues to make 'Asians' an object of law, the political sphere, as well as national culture" (19). Lauren Berlant argues that even when U.S. public discourse embraces an optimistic rhetoric about immigration, these rhetorics serve the purpose of shoring up "national vanity" by transforming immigrants into "prima facie evidence that freedom and democracy exist in the United States" (196). For both Lisa Lowe and Lauren Berlant, the current anxiety over immigration in the United States includes a fear over the racial makeup of the United States, at the same time as immigrant labor becomes increasingly important to the needs of capitalism. It is with an eye toward the link between migrant labor and the current stage of global capital that motivates Michael Hardt and Antonio Negri's advocacy of global citizenship for all forms of migrant labor.

This chapter uses Hardt and Negri's concept of global citizenship as a point of departure for exploring the possibility of commonality, communication, and community in the wake of globalization. One of the most radical claims underwriting their brand of postmodern republicanism is the abandonment of modern forms of mediation. In this chapter, I argue that Hardt and Negri's abandonment of mediation poses a significant challenge to how rhetorical studies imagines the role of citizenship. In particular, Hardt and Negri suggest that nationality, an autonomous political space, and representation are three forms of mediation that rhetorical studies should abandon. To make visible this challenge to rhetorical studies, I first outline the material ontology that is advanced in *Empire*, and then highlight how this material ontology threatens rhetorical investments in modern forms of mediation. I conclude by suggesting some warnings about the appropriation of Hardt and Negri's work in rhetorical studies.

THE MULTITUDE OR HUMAN COMMUNITY WITHOUT MEDIATION

In *Empire*, Michael Hardt and Antonio Negri advance a materialist ontology for understanding the rupture from modernity to postmodernity. This materialist ontology requires the recognition of a plane of immanence; that is, a situation in which social being no longer needs an outside moral authority, or transcendental unity, to guide human history. In their hands, *Empire* is the name of the form of sovereignty, or logic of command and rule, that is currently governing the process of globalization. At the center of this process is the ability of capital to extend its reach both extensively across the globe and intensively into the very fabric of life. What marks the rupture of postmodern capitalism is the culmination of the process described by Marx as the *real subsumption of labor*, which implies that capital no longer relies on an outside to find a market to capitalize value, but instead integrates labor "ever more completely" within the logics of capital.

However, the real subsumption of labor also relies on a shift in how capitalism creates value. Capitalism is thoroughly invested in the production of life itself, creating a new terrain of biopolitical production. Recall that, for Foucault, biopower describes the process by which power works less as a repressive force that threatens life, but increasingly works to protect and promote life (135-59). In other words, power becomes productive in the sense that it generates capabilities and harnesses the potential of individuals and populations to perform tasks that promote the welfare of its subjects. Although taking Foucault's insight into the production of life and subjectivity as a point of departure and picking up Delueze and Guattari's refashioning of materialist thought around the production of social being for their materialist ontology, Hardt and Negri nonetheless believe that Foucault as well as Deleuze and Guattari underappreciate the interaction among biopower, social production, and capitalism. To put it bluntly, capitalism is fully implicated in producing life and social being.

One of the consequences of this biopolitical terrain of production is that it becomes necessary to rethink the nature of productive labor. At this point, Hardt and Negri, drawing on work done in Italy, suggest that the tendency of productive labor is to "become increasingly immaterial" (29). *Immaterial labor* describes how surplus value increasingly depends on the exploitation of intellectual, communicative, and affective forms of production disrupting the older division between manual and intellectual labor. What the idea of immaterial labor requires is both "a new theory of value [and] a new theory of subjectivity [...] that operates primarily through knowledge, communication and language" (29). However, what must be resisted is an exclusive focus "on the horizon of language and communication," for to do so risks an overly intellectual and incorporeal understanding of value and subjectivity (29). For Hardt and Negri, the intellectual and communicative aspects of biopolitical production must also include "the productivity of bodies and the value of affect" (30). Empire describes the process by which the terrain of biopolitical production leaves behind the nation-state and the disciplinary society for a global "control society" whereby "power reaches down to the ganglia of the social structure and its process of development [... it] extends throughout the depths of the con-sciousnesses and bodies of the population—at the same time across the entirety of social relations" (24). Hardt and Negri provide a scary diagnosis.

However, the process of globalization and the new logic of command that Empire names is not the effect of the abstract laws of capital. Globalization is not, as it is for David Harvey, a temporal and spatial fix to the internal contradictions of capital.[2] The real actors pushing the processes of globalization are the multitude. Empire is an apparatus of capture reacting to the demands of the multitude to escape the disciplinary logics of modernity. What ensues in the name of Empire is a new form of command that attempts to control the strength of the multitude. Empire is parasitic, a constitutional form that lives off of the productive power of the multitude. The multitude created the new form of imperial power at the same time as imperial power must rely on the labor of the multitude without losing control of its ability to extract value. It is the terrain of biopolitical production that provides the key to understanding the past and future of the multitude.

Although modernity allowed the ability to make distinctions between productive labor and social labor, or base and superstructure, or forces of production and relations of production, these distinctions were obliterated by the multitude's challenge to modernity and the invention of Empire. For Hardt and Negri, "the passage to postmodernity and Empire immediately presents communication, production and life as one complex whole." This social body is an "open site of conflict" (404). Empire's increasing reliance on valorizing the multitude's immaterial labor disrupts the stability of capitalism. From the perspective of the multitude, the present situation offers a "more radical and profound commonality than has ever been experienced in the history of capitalism" (302). For Hardt and Negri, biopolitical production "increasingly means constructing cooperative and communicative commonalities" (302). As such, a new concept of the commons can be wrestled away from its private appropriation and the "the spatial dimension of ontology today is demonstrated through the multitude's concrete processes of globalization, or really, the making common, of the desire for human community" (362).

Empire runs over the nation-state, but puts it to work of its own purposes. For Hardt and Negri, "Empire must restrict and isolate the spatial movements of the multitude to stop them from gaining political legitimacy" (398). One of the most powerful concrete forces of globalization is the mass migration of human beings. What the movement of peoples requires is not a rebirth of national identity or new tactics of assimilation, but instead global citizenship. For Hardt and Negri, "global citizenship is not a call for the cosmopolitical state, but a common species" (362). What the circulation of the multitude entails is a process by which "human community is constituted" (362). It is through circulation, movement, nomadism, and miscegenation that "the multitude re-appropriates space and constitutes itself as an active subject" (362). According to Hardt and Negri, it is a "struggle against the slavery of belonging to a nation, an identity, and a people, and thus the desertion from sovereignty and the limits it places on subjectivity [...]. Nomadism and miscegenation appear here as figure of virtue, as the first ethical practices on the terrain of Empire" (361-62).

In terms of the pragmatic struggle of concrete immigrants living and working within the territory of nation-states global citizenship means that "all should have the full rights of citizenship in the county where they live and work" (400). To work is to generate value, and this productive capacity is to be rewarded with political, economic, and cultural citizenship rights. The more abstract claim for global citizenship is the ability of the multitude to assert control over the spatial ontology of production. In this way, "the general right to control its own movement is the multitude's ultimate demand for global citizenship [...]. Global citizenship is the multitude's power to re-appropriate control over space and thus to design a new cartography" (400). Hardt and Negri advance the idea of global citizenship to highlight the commonality of the multitude and its desire for human community. The commonality of the multitude is not a transcendental unity, but instead is a singularity, a productive multiplicity that desires a real democracy.

THE MULTITUDE AND THE CHALLENGES TO RHETORICAL CITIZENSHIP

Empire is a paper tiger. It is ontologically empty. It lives off of the multitude's constituent power, an ontological power that generates value, and produces life and the desire for human community. For Hardt and Negri, now is not the time for pessimism, nor is it the time to furnish Empire with the mechanisms of mediation that might allow it to displace the terms of the conflict between imperial power and the multitude. The dialectical legacy of modernity is disappearing because "capitalist development faces the multitude directly without mediation" (236). The challenge that Hardt and Negri pose to the idea of rhetorical citizenship, then, is a world without mediation. The historic relationship between rhetoric and politics, however, has a tendency toward a view of citizenship built on the principles of mediation. I want to focus briefly on three: nationality, political space, and representation.

Although the nation-state does not disappear, it is increasingly harnessed to the needs of Empire. Whereas Hardt and Negri offer a postmodern theory of capital, it should not be confused with advocating a "politics of difference." For Hardt and Negri, the nation-state functions as part of a network of command that Empire uses to feed off of differences among the multitude at the same time as it segments and manages that difference. The nomadic flows of people across the spatial terrain of Empire points to the inability of national culture to offer a solution to the demands of capitalism without reinforcing forms of segmentation and the management of difference. When James Aune appeals to the fragility of republics and a call to strengthen national patriotism to resist globalization, he inadvertently contributes to the cultural policing of new immigrants (149). In this way, immigrants are always unstable citizens, and represent a threat to national culture, even a culture that claims to value immigrants. For Hardt and Negri, the challenge of the multitude for rhetorical citizenship is to resist the mediation of the nation. It is important to resist a desire to "reinforce the walls of nation, ethnicity, race, people and the like" for to do so "can be regressive and even fascistic when they oppose circulation and mixture" (362).

The withering away of national sovereignty disrupts the effectiveness of relying on the autonomy of the political. First, communication industries evaporate the public sphere through the image economy of a spectacular society. For Hardt and Negri, the society of spectacle operates through the communication of fear and increasingly takes away the ground for traditional notions of political exchange and participation (322-23). Second, incorporation of communication networks, communication industries, and communicative labor disables the Habermasian distinction between the instrumental rationality of the economy and the communicative rationality of the life world. Communication has been thoroughly subsumed into the terrain of biopolitical production (404). Third, the loss of an autonomous political space also means that civil society can no longer serve the role of mediating the relationship between state and capital (328). Capital has swallowed the state. When Gerard Hauser calls for a newly improved civil society, he offers capital a new mechanism to manage the conflicts it produces. Nor can the concept of civil society be rewritten on a global scale—for Hardt and Negri, a global civil society relies on an outdated domestic analogy that transfers a mechanism for managing national conflict onto an international terrain (7-8). Empire already takes advantage of an emerging global civil society of nongovernmental organizations to represent the interests of the multitude in supranational institutions (35-37). The solution is not a new autonomous political space resembling national public spheres or civil societies, but instead a recognition of how the biopolitical space of production has merged the political, the social, and the economic. This is the space that best "explains the ability of [the multitude's] desire to confront the crisis" (387).

The constitution of Empire only gains political legitimacy through the representational logics of a global civil society. The problems of representation associated with global civil society point to the third challenge to rhetorical citizenship without mediation. The tendency of many forms of ideological critique is to conceptualize the rhetorical citizen as a representative of a particular interest (epistemological, axiological, or economic). Similarly, civic republicans tend to refashion the rhetorical citizen as an ethical representative of his or her community.[3] Hardt and Negri appeal to the militant as "the one who best expresses the life of the multitude" (413). The militant, however, is not envisioned as a representative of the community or even "the fundamental needs of the exploited" (413). A new revolutionary militancy must avoid representational politics and "re-discover its constituent power"—in other words, its strength to make and remake the world through struggle and organization. A central part of the struggle of the multitude will be a battle over "linguistic sense and meaning and the networks of communication" (411). However, this struggle is part of the struggle to wrestle the value of cooperation away from the parasitic grasp of Empire. It is not a struggle for representation, ethically or politically, on the terrain of Empire. As I have argued elsewhere, what is at stake in a new materialism is not the struggle over representational politics, but a struggle over modes of governance (Greene, "Another").

CONCLUSION

What Hardt and Negri and rhetorical studies have in common is an affirmative investment in human innovation and invention. I see no reason why rhetorical action, refigured as part of the governance of biopolitical production, is not part of the constituent power, or productive labor of the multitude. But to fully appreciate this dimension of rhetorical action requires the abandonment of the modern legacy of mediation that imagines that the multitude needs a nation, a public sphere, or a representative. To rethink rhetorical action at the level of biopolitical production suggests that we focus our attention on the multitude's becoming, and their new innovations as forms of experience and experimentation in the desire for human community.

Although I suspect the debate over mediation has barely begun in rhetorical studies, works like *Empire* do pose a particular problem for textual criticism.[4] As Meaghan Morris points out, "blockbuster theories of history" tend to make the mundane work of historical analysis seemingly irrelevant. For Meaghan Morris, and I suspect Michael Leff would agree, all brands of textual criticism are threatened by "great schematic sweeps through time." This is so because the object of analysis becomes manageable only as a "symptom of a broader cultural logic, a social condition, or epochal moment." In such a situation "there is little room for historical practice—or unsettling empirical surprises—of any kind" (Morris 2).[5] There is no way of getting around the fact that Hardt and Negri's *Empire* is just such an historical epic. Its rhetorical force depends on the rupture they represent as postmodern sovereignty, and its optimistic tone is dependent on embracing the experiences and experimentations of the multitude. For this reason, we should be careful not to reduce every form of rhetorical action into a symptom of the multitude's creative force, nor of Empire's power of capture. But we must also resist the temptation of forms of mediation that disrupt the desire for human community by defending new apparatuses of segmentation, representation, and division. We need to use cultural criticism to position our students directly into the debates taking place on the terrain of biopolitical production. Rhetorical citizenship requires that students learn how to communicate their interests, desires, and values so that they might invent and solve social problems. If the goal of rhetorical citizenship is the production of citizen critics, in Rosa Eberly's provocative prose, let them be global citizens, in the future becoming of democracy.

NOTES

1. Arjun Appadurai argues that we should approach the vast numbers and types of "moving groups and individuals," including "tourists, immigrants, refugees, exiles, guestworkers" and others, as making up the flow of the global cultural economy he calls the "ethnoscape." For a closer reading of Appadurai's position see, *Modernity at Large: Cultural Dimensions of Globalization.* Minneapolis: U of Minnesota P, 1996. 27-48.
2. David Harvey, *The Condition of Postmodernity.* Oxford, UK: Blackwell, 1989. It should be pointed out that Hardt and Negri are more often than not in agreement with many of Harvey's claims.
3. For an example of ideological criticism, see Dana Cloud, "The Rhetoric of <Family Values>: Scapegoating, Utopia, and the Privatization of Social Responsibility." *Western Journal of Communication* 62 (1998): 387-407. For a civic republican version of the orator as ethical representative of the community, see Michael Leff ("Cicero's *Pro Murena* and the Strong Case for Rhetoric").
4. It should be noted that Aune strongly defends mediation as a concept and a necessity for rhetorical studies (46-49).
5. For a recent outline of Michael Leff's investment in the concrete situation of rhetorical action and the need to avoid abstract theoretical hammers, see "Cicero's *Pro Murena.*"

WORKS CITED

Aune, James Arnt. *Rhetoric and Marxism.* Boulder, CO: Westview, 1993.

Berlant, Lauren. *The Queen of America Goes to Washington City; Essays On Sex and Citizenship.* Durham, NC: Duke UP, 1997.

Deleuze, Gilles, and Felix Guattari. *A Thousand Plateaus: Capitalism and Schizophrenia.* Trans. Brian Massumi. Minneapolis: U of Minnesota P, 1987.

Eberly, Rosa. *Citizen Critics: Literary Public Spheres.* Urbana: U of Illinois P, 2000.

Foucault, Michel. *History of Sexuality, Volume 1: An Introduction.* Trans. Robert Hurely. New York: Vintage, 1980.

Greene, Ronald Walter. "Another Materialist Rhetoric." *Critical Studies in Mass Communication* 15 (1998): 20-41.

---. "Citizenship in a Global Context; Towards a Future Beginning for a Cultural Studies Inspired Argumentation Theory." *Arguing Communication and Culture: Selected papers of the 12th NCA/AFA Conference on Argumentation Volume 1.* Ed. G. Thomas Goodnight. Washington, DC: National Communication Association, 2002. 97-103.

Hardt, Michael, and Antonio Negri. *Empire.* Cambridge, MA, Harvard UP, 2000.

Hauser, Gerard. *Vernacular Voices: The Rhetorics of Publics and Public Spheres.* Columbia: U of South Carolina P, 1999.

Leff, Michael. "Cicero's *Pro Murena* and the Strong Case for Rhetoric." *Rhetoric and Public Affairs* 1 (1998): 61-88.

Lowe, Lisa. *Immigrant Acts: On Asian American Cultural Politics.* Durham, NC: Duke UP, 1996.

Morris, Meaghan. *Too Soon Too Later: History in Popular Culture.* Bloomington: Indiana UP, 1998.

Patton, Cindy, and Robert Caserio. "Introduction Citizenship 2000." *Cultural Studies* 14 (2000): 1.

22

Rhetoric of Globalization: A Social Movement Defines Its Collective Identity in America

Shawn Hellman
University of Arizona

Concurrent with the presentation recounted in this chapter was a panel presentation just around the corner that continues the dialogue begun by Steven Mailloux in the Spring 2000 issue of *Rhetoric Society Quarterly*. Mailloux's essay introduced the possibility of a synthesis that would unite rhetoricians in English and Communication departments. Responding articles by William Keith, Michael Leff, and Thomas Miller discussed the feasibility of this interdisciplinary work. That was a session I really wanted to attend, because my research illustrates the possibility of such work. As rhetoricians in English expand their research beyond the study of academic discourse, they can look toward their colleagues in Communication. One area of shared interest—an area that can support Mailloux's vision of uniting rhetoricians in different departments—is work in social movements.

Social movements are basically communities of people who articulate shared beliefs and values and appeal to shared experiences as a means to foster identifications and forge shared purposes. Studying social movements can help us understand how communities constitute and maintain shared beliefs and values and frame shared experiences to create collective identities. This chapter focuses on how one community uses its shared knowledge to define its situation and create its collective identity. I explore the relationship between the community's rhetorical discourse and the rhetorical situation, and examine how the community representatives use language to shape and appeal to the audience's beliefs and values. Kenneth Burke's work on identification and terministic screens is especially useful when looking at how a community develops a collective identity because it accounts for the interactive—or what Burke termed "dramatistic"—process involved in constructing shared perspectives. Chaim Perelman's work is helpful when looking at how a community creates a sense of presence for the audience by using concrete and abstract values. Thus, as a rhetorician in English borrowing from Communication, I examine how a religious movement within Judaism engaged its community to define and redefine its collective identity.

The Reform Movement in Judaism created and revised the collective identity of Reform Jews against changing conceptions of American identity, and documented its collective identity in its platforms. The Reform Movement in America is the only denomination in Judaism that has created statements or platforms at different points in time to define itself. The Central Conference of American Rabbis (CCAR) in the Reform Movement has created three platforms: the 1885 "Declaration of Principles," the 1937 "Guiding Principles of Reform Judaism," and the 1999 "Statement of Principles for Reform Judaism." These historical artifacts provide an opportunity to trace the development of the movement's collective identity and how its well-orchestrated writing process for each platform reflected the collective identity.

Individually, these three platforms redefine the Reform Movement at specific points in time in response to changing realities by interpreting the shared experience of the community, constituting a shared understanding of that experience, and "framing" the collective identity of Reform Jews. Borrowing from Erving Goffman and David Snow (and Snow's work with Robert Benford and others), I consider a *frame* to be a categorizing system that functions to organize experience and influences how people interpret and describe issues and events. Influential authors in the Reform Movement used their interpretation of the historical situation for evidence to justify their conception of the world and support their conceived collective identity in America. Together, these platforms illustrate how collective identity is a creative social construction that is both continuously reinvented over time and grounded in changing social experiences. In my work, I examine how the authors of these documents interpreted and organized relevant events and experiences, articulated shared values and assumptions in socially acceptable ways, and revised their collective identity to address changing needs and adapt to broader contexts.

The Reform Movement documented its process of constructing the platforms and saved those documents at the Jacob Rader Marcus Center of the American Jewish Archives in Cincinnati. As a Research Fellow at the American Jewish Archives, I looked at the CCAR official conference proceedings, annual conventions' transcripts, and platform committee statements, as well as relevant newspaper articles and CCAR rabbis' correspondences. My goal was to understand how the Reform Movement defined the situation so I could understand how a response was considered fitting to the community. I examined the authors' interpretive framework of the situation, how they assigned meaning to relevant experiences, spoke to their community's shared knowledge and experience to construct a collective identity, and wrote these platforms. Using my researched materials, I reconstructed the writing process for each document, which changed considerably through time. I examined how the Reform Movement articulated shared values and assumptions in ways that spoke to the current situation and lived experiences of the audience, and I explain how the authors of these documents depend on the accepted knowledge of the time to construct a collective identity. Based on my research, I present a quick overview of the CCAR's understanding of the situational context for each platform, the articulated shared beliefs and values, the frame in the platform, and the writing process.

Reform Judaism officially began in the United States in 1885, with the issuance of "The Declaration of Principles," commonly referred to now as "The Pittsburgh Platform." The Pittsburgh Platform spoke to Jewish immigrants at a time of strong public sentiment against foreigners and restrictive immigration and naturalization laws. In America, Jewish immigrants who adhered to their religious practices could not avoid being identified as foreigners, so creating a Jewish American identity was problematic. The Pittsburgh Platform combined the community's concern about appearing foreign and its belief in the value of modernity to frame the historical situation as an opportunity to revise Judaism. Based on this interpretation, the platform presented traditional ceremonies and customs as "primitive" and "foreign" (CCAR Pittsburgh). The platform suggested that the values that traditional Judaism promoted no longer fit with the Reform Movement's constituents because they were reasonable, modern American Jews. The platform used "the views and habits of modern civilization" as the measuring stick with which to evaluate Judaism, and it defined traditional practices as outdated and apt to obstruct rather than further "modern spiritual elevation" (CCAR Pittsburgh). The platform thereby reflected Reform Jews' desire to appear "modern"—a term used often in the document, but never defined.

The 1885 platform, written entirely in English, demonstrated to new immigrants that they could be accepted as Jewish Americans by modernizing themselves and giving up outmoded Mosaic and rabbinical laws and practices. In addition to describing what Jews were no longer obligated to do, the Pittsburgh Platform framed Jewish identity as not a nation, but a religious community—a community of reasonable, modern, and progressive people—terms that reflected the values of the Progressive era. Finally, the Reform Movement amplified Reform Jews' belief in the democratic right to be an individual in America, a belief that was salient to new immigrants who wanted to be part of the American community. The platform suggested that as modern Americans, Reform Jews could choose which Jewish laws and traditions to observe.

The 1885 platform was essentially written by one German rabbi, Kaufmann Kohler. Kohler came to the conference with a previously prepared draft, which was ratified by a committee of five like-minded German rabbis whom he had invited. The writing process of the 1885 platform was not consistent with the assumptions of the Reform Movement, because Kohler authoritatively decreed the platform while he declared that individual autonomy was fundamental to making Judaism modern. Consequently, this prescriptive platform was quickly outdated.

In 1937, the Reform Movement revised its collective identity once again and wrote a new platform. Several factors contributed to revising Reform thinking in the 1937 platform: the enormous influx of Eastern European Jewish immigrants had changed the makeup of the Reform Movement, which now represented a larger variety of belief systems about what Reform Judaism was and what it should be. Additionally, the increase of anti-Semitism in America and abroad, the rise of Nazism, and a new definition of Zionism led to a concern about Jewish continuity. The belief in the need to evacuate Jews from Eastern Europe altered the definition of Zionism from the notion of creating a place in which to segregate Jewish people because Jews couldn't fit in elsewhere to the idea of creating a Jewish state because a Jewish homeland was needed for refugees and for cultural and spiritual stability. In the 1930s, modernity and national loyalty were no longer salient issues to Reform Jews, who had been modern Americans for generations. The important issue of the time was a concern for the continuity of the Jewish people, which the writers of the 1937 document used as the dominant frame for the 1937 platform. The 1937 Columbus platform reframed the Reform tradition and adopted new metaphors for its identity. It defined Judaism as a collective "historical religious experience" and framed Jews as "a people" with common foundations, ethics, and religious practices (CCAR Columbus). This platform argued for individuals to make decisions about Jewish practices by considering the community.

For the writing of this platform, a committee was created to represent the two major factions in the movement—Zionists and non-Zionists—and each faction created a draft. Using Chaim Perelman's ideas, I looked at how each draft created *presence* (in the French sense of being made present) in the minds of those addressed, and how each used abstract or concrete values in their arguments. The author of the non-Zionist draft used concrete negative images that did not fit with the constituents' experiences when discussing his conception of Jews in the world, and he used abstractions when discussing his vision of the future view of Jews in the world. This draft was not successful, because it ignored the current situation and the constituents' concerns, it characterized Reform Judaism as a conceptual abstraction, and it did not speak to or attract readers' attention. The platform committee deemed this draft unacceptable. The Zionists' draft presented an argument that articulated concrete claims and provided concrete evidence that drew from and made sense of the community's history. It framed Reform Judaism as a community and spoke to the community's current concerns about the threat to Jewish continuity.

The writing situation in the 1937 platform was influenced by tensions between the Zionist and the non-Zionists rabbis and the majority's belief that Jewish survival meant that they couldn't afford to exclude any Jews. This belief gave rise to a writing process that was consistent with the assumptions of the group. To strengthen the shared sense of collective identity, the entire membership of the CCAR was asked to read and respond to a draft of the platform so that the rabbis' comments could be incorporated into the final version. The long, arduous writing process of the 1937 platform illustrated the difficulty in both maintaining a coherence of beliefs within multiple interpretive communities and collaboratively writing an inclusive collective identity.

In 1998, the CCAR president decided to write a new platform for the impending new century. In this case, the process of writing the platform instigated a new understanding of the community's beliefs and values. The third draft of the platform was printed in *Reform Judaism* magazine and posted on the CCAR and the *Reform Judaism* Web sites to allow all Reform Movement members, not just Reform rabbis, to read the draft. The publication of these documents stimulated a movementwide discussion. In response, people wrote a record number of letters to the editor, hundreds of people responded individually to the draft and read other's responses on the *Reform Judaism* Web page, people created online discussion groups, Reform rabbis created forums in their synagogues in which congregants examined the third draft, and Reform rabbis discussed the draft on a closed listserv. The use of computers in this process permitted the inclusion of many more participants—even from the periphery of the community.

Response from rabbis, lay leaders, and congregants focused on the concern that the draft represented a narrow conception of beliefs and actions and did not reflect the diversity of beliefs and practices in the Reform Movement. Because of the tremendous response from the constituents, leaders of the Reform Movement determined that evaluating and reorienting the beliefs and practices of the movement must actively involve others and not just rabbis in the process if it were to have any impact in the Reform Movement. The CCAR president created a committee made up of eight Reform rabbis from across the ideological spectrum, two Hebrew Union College faculty members, a rabbinic student, and three national Reform lay leaders to revise the draft. The new, inclusive writing process was consistent with the group's beliefs and assumptions that everyone can participate in the creation of knowledge. The platform was recast as a teaching opportunity for rabbis and an opportunity for Reform Jews to reflect on their beliefs and practices. The new committee envisioned the revised platform as a template of governing conceptual paradigms in the Reform Movement that rabbis and lay people could use when discussing their own ideas on where they stand on issues. The role of the rabbi was shifted in this document from one of authority to facilitator, because religious authority was decentralized away from the rabbis and into the hands of the lay people. The platform illustrated an understanding that meaning is not confined to the narrow intentions of the author or rabbi, but rather is generated within the experience of each reader or congregant interacting with the text. This platform framed the Reform Movement as made up of people who interpret for themselves and contribute to knowledge.

The Reform Movement engaged its community to define its collective identity in the 1885, 1937, and 1999 platforms. Successful articulations were created through a writing process that physically manifested the community's beliefs. The writing processes of these platforms included the ideas of one Reform rabbi in 1885, input from all Reform rabbis in 1937, and input from all Reform Jews in 1999, reflecting the movement's evolving belief that the collective identity of Reform Jews is not monolithic, but includes multiple interpretations. Creating a collective identity is a dynamic, recursive process, and I hope I have shown that a social movement can be a fascinating site to examine how a community creates its collective identity. By examining historical situations, the writing situations, and the writing processes, researchers can theorize how influential authors in social movements frame collective identities. Studying the historical construction of a community's shared beliefs and values is an important new area of study for rhetoricians in English, as it has been for rhetoricians in Communication, and it can provide an interesting site to bridge our disciplines.

WORKS CITED

Burke, Kenneth. *A Grammar of Motives.* Berkeley: U of California P, 1969.
---. *Language as Symbolic Action.* Berkeley: U of California P, 1966.
---. *Permanence and Change.* Berkeley: U of California P, 1954.
---. *A Rhetoric of Motives.* Berkeley: U of California P, 1969.
Central Conference of American Rabbis. "Declaration of Principles." Pittsburgh, 1885. 14 Feb. 2000 <http://ccarnet.org/platforms/pittsburgh.html>.
---. "The Guiding Principles of Reform Judaism." Columbus, 1937. 14 Feb. 2000 <http://ccarnet.org/platforms/columbus.html>.
---. "A Statement of Principles for Reform Judaism." Pittsburgh, 1999. 14 Feb. 2000 <http://ccarnet.org/platforms/principles.html>.
Goffman, Erving. *Frame Analysis: An Essay on the Organization of Experience.* Cambridge, MA: Harvard UP, 1974.
Keith, William. "Identities, Rhetoric, and Myth: A Response to Mailloux and Leff." *Rhetoric Society Quarterly* 30.4 (2000): 95-106.
Leff, Michael. "Rhetorical Disciplines and Rhetorical Disciplinarity: A Response to Mailloux." *Rhetoric Society Quarterly* 30.4 (2000): 83-93.
Mailloux, Steven. "Disciplinary Identities: On the Rhetorical Paths between English and Communication Studies." *Rhetoric Society Quarterly* 30.2 (2000): 5-29.
Miller, Thomas. "Disciplinary Identifications/Public Identities: A Response to Mailloux, Leff, and Keith." *Rhetoric Society Quarterly* 31.3 (2001): 105-17.
Perelman, Chaim. *The Realm of Rhetoric.* London: U of Notre Dame P, 1982.
Snow, David A., et al. "Frame Alignment Processes, Micromobilization, and Movement Participation." *American Sociological Review* 51 (1986): 464-81.
Snow, David A., and Robert D. Benford. "Clarifying the Relationship between Framing and Ideology." *Mobilization* 5.1 (2000): 55-60.
---. "Framing Processes and Social Movements: An Overview and an Assessment." *Annual Review in Sociology* 26 (2000): 611-39.
---. "Ideology, Frame Resonance, and Participant Mobilization." *International Social Movement Research* 1 (1988): 198-217.

23

Strategies of Objection in the Trial of the Chicago Eight

David B. Hingstman
University of Iowa

Reading extended arguments offers a difficult challenge to the rhetorical critic. The tools of traditional argumentative analysis, handed down from Aristotle through the Scholastics to modern social science and composition, require that conversational gestures be bracketed within a framework of speech acts of assertion and refutation regulated by deliberative norms. Extended arguments—in which the practices and norms themselves are generated and tested through social learning processes—fit uncomfortably, if at all, into this framework. Faced with this challenge, then, critics may inclined either to challenge the outlying discourses for their failure to adhere to standards of discursive rationality implied in the argumentative model, or to classify these discourses as wholly outside or beyond argument, as aesthetic gestures of opposition. Either way, the discourses are said not to participate in the dominant argumentative framework.

The trial of the Chicago Eight in 1969 and 1970, can be, and has been, read these ways. The federal government charged eight leftist activists with conspiring to incite violence at the August 1968 Democratic National Convention in Chicago. Lindsay Tanner, a reporter for the *Sunday Rutland Herald*, colorfully described the discourses twenty years later: "The 4½-month theatrics featured wild-haired defendants whose antics included wearing judicial robes to court, taking them off and stomping on them; and a 74-year-old judge who refused to allow Seale his own attorney and ordered him bound and gagged in the courtroom when he protested (1)." Numerous books and chapters by journalists, writers, and political scientists either laud or excoriate these tactics as calculated to disrupt the functioning of adjudicative institutions (see, e.g, Dee, Epstein, Lukas, Schuetz and Snedaker, Schultz, St. John).

Another reading of these discourses looks to a speech act much in evidence in the trial transcript—the objection—and what objections do in the context of trial arguments. In one sense, objections participate in the institutionally protected invention and judgment of legal arguments. If a participant in the practical reasoning connected with the making of claims and taking of proofs violates a norm of adjudicative reasoning, another participant can raise an objection that asks that intervention be made to vindicate the norm. Thus, the objection can reaffirm attribution of intersubjective understanding or procedural regularity of convention. Reasons for opposition can exist within a domain of prudence, propriety, regularity, or certified legitimacy. You can agree to argue within an official, well-recognized, and established way of articulating difference.

But the objection also inflects the relationship of the objector to the other participants in the trial, and cannot be launched or withheld without consequences for the communicative relationship. The objection is an unpredictable interruption of ordinary argumentative interaction, which may fail to be accepted by the trial participants because it seems to fall outside the conventional domain. Nevertheless, the objection is made because the agreed rules seem to exclude modes of expression that call for alternative discursive arrangements. In this sense, the objection looks to the intervention of an appellate court to refigure the communicative relationship between the litigants, perhaps by ordering a new trial. Hence, through gesture, an objection has a second function of creating an oppositional argument that tests and stretches the bounds of consensus. The objection serves as a gesture or act that disrupts communicative expectations and calls into question propriety conditions, rule regularities, procedural aptness, or capacity.

This chapter argues that the trial of the Chicago Eight can be read usefully as an extended argument or dialogue, in which Judge Hoffman, the prosecution, and the defense participate actively. The reading finds sensitivity in the speech acts to the doubling quality of the objection, and the constitutive and oppositional strategies afforded by its prevalence in the trial setting.

YOU'VE GOT TO SHUT THEM DOWN, JUDGE —OBJECTIONS AT PRETRIAL

The pretrial discourses of the participants in the Chicago Eight trial seemed far removed communicatively from the highly technical exchanges in the courtroom itself. Judicial institutions claim legitimacy in part from their ability to resolve difficult technical issues for which partisan deliberation and personal conversation are felt to be inadequate. But the demands of technical modes of proof exchange do not monopolize all discursive interactions among the parties in court. Those who attend to pretrial and procedural discussions have noticed that the communicative norms often take on the more spacious qualities of personal exchange. Attorneys are named by the institutions as their "officers," and the officers are expected to reach accommodations with the judge on these issues away from the jury's ears.

Bargaining typically occurs over the amount and conditions for bail, requests are made to bend the strict interpretation of appearances by legal counsel, the appropriate location for the trial is hammered out, the range of questions that can be asked of potential jurors is determined, and the conditions under which defendants are represented. American judicial institutions confer the discretion on the judge to resolve these exchanges within the overall interests of cordiality, fairness, and expeditiousness.

Perhaps because he had been forewarned by the FBI wiretaps that the defendants might seek to disrupt his trial, Judge Hoffman acted in objection to these argumentative norms during the pretrial proceedings. These objections were performed in the doubled sense that I described earlier. The judge claimed on the one hand that the defense attorneys had taken excessive advantage, which needed to be recognized, of opportunities for flexibility in representing their clients, and on the other hand that their new requests were unacceptable for technical concerns about expediting the trial. Thus, it was ambiguous as to whether the judge's position called for the reinforcement or supersession of the ordinary informal way of resolving such complaints.

In one sense, Judge Hoffman's actions can be framed as arbitrary suspension of the usual concessions that judges make to bend over backwards, so as to protect the rights of defendants. As Goldberg noted, "Judge Hoffman began the trial with a refusal to grant a six-week continuance to the defendants while Charles Garry, attorney for Bobby Seale and lead counsel for the eight defendants, recuperated from gall bladder surgery" (35). Instead, Judge Hoffman jailed without bail two lawyers who were handling pretrial motions, saying that the defendants had too many lawyers already and that the trial was being delayed. Then Judge Hoffman refused to allow Bobby Seale to proceed *pro se* (on his own, without a lawyer). Motions for a change of venue and for leniency on the scope of questions to potential jurors were denied summarily.

But Judge Hoffman accompanied his rulings with allegations of bad faith that might be persuasive in appellate review. There had been several substitutions of attorneys by the defense during the earliest stages of the legal proceedings, done in ways that spoke either to dilatory tactics or to the precarious lives of the defendants. The defense attorneys asked potential jurors long, convoluted questions that could either inform the selection or prejudice the respondent. The judge could clothe otherwise arbitrary rulings in the mantle of prudent repair work to the defendants' duplicities in the interests of expeditiousness and fairness.

Judge Hoffman's objection to the informal procedural arguments of the defense was risky from the point of view of ordinary legal communicative relationships. If the Seventh Circuit appellate court found, as it did later, that the judge did not have the discretion to redress the pretrial balance of favors between the defense and the prosecution, and that the technical reasons for failing to consider seriously the defense requests were too flimsy, then his objection would be met with an order for a new trial. Moreover, the objection risked alienating the legal community, which responded to the jailing of the lawyers with an uproar of protest.

However, the judge's objection also had the possibility of opening up space for Hoffman to serve as protector of the American political majority from subversion. If the FBI's interpretation of the wiretaps was accurate, then the government was soon to be the victim of subversive tactics by anarchistic radicals who were hoping to accomplish at trial what they could not accomplish during the Democratic convention: the violent overthrow of the American government. Although the judge's speech acts could be interpreted as partisan, they were perhaps a justified response to the partisan subversion of the judicial process by the defendants.

LOOKING DOWN THE GUN BARRELS—OBJECTIONS AT TRIAL

There was more at stake for the defendants than how they looked in cameo appearances before the national media; from legal advisor and now professor Jon Waltz: "Beneath the theatricality, it was tense. They were looking down the gun barrels of a long prison sentence and they knew it." Waltz recalls telling the defendants before the trial that they "could expect to go to prison for a long time, and no one would remember who they were when they got out," if they opted for theatrics (Goldberg 33). Thus, the defendants could win in the court of public opinion and still lose their arguments at trial if they were not careful.

Any appellate court review of the pretrial and trial arguments would interpret the fairness of the proceedings by taking the measure of the judge's rulings and statements recorded in the written trial transcript; but Judge Hoffman's objection anticipated such interpretative practices. Law professor Harry Kalven notes shortly after the trial that Judge Hoffman's communicative style traded on the ambiguity of interpretations of motive: "Judge Hoffman is, as a matter of style, often elliptical in his rulings and does not feel it necessary to explain. There is the chance always present, therefore, that any given episode read in the context of the full transcript would leave a somewhat different impression than we can garner here from the excerpts the judge has selected" (xvi). In short, Judge Hoffman could issue his rulings in a manner that conveys technical proficiency and impartiality on the printed page, or he could be interpreted as assuming the persona of a rabid partisan. What conditions at trial would create opportunities for the defense to color his discursive acts?

Whatever objections the defense offered at trial needed to reflect back on the interpretation of the fairness of the argumentative procedures in the trial as a whole. If, for example, Judge Hoffman were provoked into exercising his disciplinary powers at trial arbitrarily and harshly, continuity could be established between the events of pretrial and trial. The power of a judge to physically restrain defendants and to hold trial participants in summary contempt is accompanied by discursive expectations that are similar to those that shape pretrial and procedural rulings. Attorneys once again are expected to mediate among clients, judges, and each other, and personal relationships are drawn on to ground and structure the discourses. As well, judges are expected to exercise that power to keep the proceedings moving, not to punish the participants. If Judge Hoffman's pretrial rulings substituted partisan for interpersonal style because he feared that the defendants would disrupt the truth-seeking process at trial, then in some sense the defendants' discourses needed to fulfill his expectations to encourage the overexercise of disciplinary powers.

Yet, the defendants' discourses also required framing within the discursive conventions of the truth-seeking process. Their objection to the trial process had to be framed within the context of the arguments that Judge Hoffman rejected in the informal pretrial proceedings. They needed to argue, in effect, that had Judge

Hoffman not prejudiced the truth-seeking process by his partisan approach to the pretrial and procedural issues, they would have been prepared to participate fully in the truth-seeking process.

Most interpretations of the Chicago Eight trial emphasize the boundary-testing aspects of the defendants' interruptions and statements, and neglect the rigorous fidelity of the defendants and their attorneys to the larger technical discursive conventions of the trial. As Kalven observes, the "circus atmosphere" of the trial is not fully conveyed by the written trial transcript. However, the adherence to procedure is.

Consider, for example, what Judge Hoffman considered to be the most contumacious behavior at trial: the frequent interruptions by defendant Bobby Seale of the attorneys and the witnesses. Hoffman's actions of binding and gagging Seale, and then ultimately of removing him from the courtroom, imply that Seale was irrational. However, examination of the statements in the trial transcript lead elsewhere. Seale did not interrupt Hoffman at random. Each time he stopped the judge, it was to make a single point that always provided the content and the occasion for his efforts to speak. His performance, including the questioning of witnesses, was an extended argument about the denial of his right to choice of counsel and to represent himself, and the consequences of that ruling (Kalven xxiv-xxv; see Seale, 323-37). Because Judge Hoffman never stated the reasons for ruling that Bobby Seale could only be represented by William Kunstler, the only reasoned appeal in the transcript was that made by Seale. No other participants made any effort, formal or informal, to adjust the proceedings to deal with Seale's problems of representation.

Although Seale was making an objection to the judge's orders and thus was literally interfering with the progress of the truth-seeking process as constituted by the previous decisions, he was also offering to improve the truth-seeking process by increasing the quality of argumentative tests of the witnesses—either by his own questioning or by that of his preferred attorney. Had Hoffman been willing to negotiate with Seale according to the conventional personal discursive expectations, Seale's appeal might have failed. Instead, Seale's objections encouraged Hoffman to memorialize his partisan intransigence in rope and expulsion.

Similar considerations seemed to inflect the speaking moments of other defendants. Kalven suggests that the exploitation of particular incidents by the defendants "never clearly reached the level of literal heckling that would make it impossible for the trial to proceed" (xxvii). Many of the interruptions were performative arguments, even if crudely phrased, about the fairness of the trial and the judge. The disruptive effects of some other comments were minimized because they were mimetic in form, imitating the judge's ordinary conversational tone of one-line jokes and bolt-out-of-the-blue observations. This is part of what Schuetz and Snedeker interpret as "mocking" without marking similar speech acts by the judge. Abbie Hoffman even engaged Judge Hoffman in an extended dialogue about Jewish ethnicity. If the judge used this tone, an appellate court might reason, surely the defendants could do so as well. Finally, the overt efforts to turn the trial into a political forum, noted by Dee, were relatively minor and quickly abandoned—such as trying to stop the trial to read names of Vietnam War dead or seeking an adjournment to attend outside rallies.

Judge Hoffman resolved his interpretation of the defendants' objections in favor of a disruptive intent. In support of his view, Hoffman imposed 175 total summary contempt citations against the eight defendants, with jail terms far in excess of what such citations normally involve. But appellate court Judge Gignoux, in reviewing these contempt charges, preserved the ambiguous legacy of the objections lodged by the defendants. Although he agreed that the speech acts of the defendants disrupted the trial process, he refused to ratify punishment for them because Judge Hoffman's acts had placed him in partisan opposition to the defense to the detriment of the right of fair trial.

CONCLUSION

Whether metaphorical or metonymical, the speech act of objection affords a critical perspective that recognizes the possibilities for both engaging and challenging deliberative norms in particular discursive contexts. The legal objection should be read both as a juridical model and as a history of argument practice. The objection is the juncture at which alternative discourses are born and take on a life of their own in the sense of being conventionalized, having certain roles and functions to play. However, such objections are not guaranteed to succeed in the sense of realizing some intention of the objector. For Judge Hoffman, the objection to informal pretrial bargaining earned him a visit with President Nixon in Miami Beach after the trial, but also professional oblivion after appellate review reversed his errors and took away his discretion to jail the defendants for their disrespect. For the defendants, the objections to the conduct of the trial itself earned them freedom when the appellate courts ordered new trials and suspended the contempt citations. But the style of the objections was cited in support of the belief that countercultural protest could not participate in civil discourses, and that physical force must be met with physical force when disagreements persisted.

WORKS CITED

Dee, Juliet. "Constraints on Persuasion in the Chicago Seven Trial." *Popular Trials: Rhetoric Mass Media, and the Law.* Ed. Robert Hariman. Tuscaloosa: U Alabama P, 1990. 86-113.

Epstein, Jason. *The Great Conspiracy Trial: An Essay on Law, Liberty and the Constitution.* New York: Random, 1970.

Goldberg, Stephanie B. "Lessons of the '60s: 'We'd Do It Again,' Say the Chicago Seven's Lawyers." *American Bar Association Journal* 15 May 1987: 32-39.

Kalven, Harry. "Introduction: Confrontation and Contempt." *Contempt: Transcript of Contempt Citations, Sentences, and Responses.* Chicago: Swallow, 1970. ix-xxiv.

Lukas, J. Anthony. *The Barnyard Epithet and Other Obscenities: Notes on the Chicago Conspiracy Trial.* New York: Harper, 1970.

Schuetz, Janice, and Kathryn Holmes Snedaker. "Courtroom Drama: The Trial of the Chicago Eight." *Communication and Litigation: Case Studies of Famous Trials.* Carbondale: Southern Illinois UP, 1988. 217-46.

Schultz, John. *The Chicago Conspiracy Trial.* Updated ed. New York: Da Capo, 1993.

Seale, Bobby. *Seize the Time: The Story of the Black Panther Party and Huey P. Newton.* New York: Random, 1970.

St. John, Jeffrey. *Countdown to Chaos.* Los Angeles: Nash, 1969.

Tanner, Lindsay. "The Sixties in Vermont: Now Middle-Aged, Chicago 7 Remain Committed Activists." *The Sunday Rutland Herald* and *The Sunday Times Argus*, 10 July 1988. 10 Sept. 2001 <http://www.uvm.edu/~jmoore/sixtiesonline/chicagosevennow.html>.

24

Figuration of Moral Reform in the Rhetoric of Theodore Dwight Weld

Robert S. Iltis
Oregon State University

As an abolitionist agent, a trainer of agents, a researcher and anonymous author of *The Bible Against Slavery* and *American Slavery As It Is,* Theodore Dwight Weld was one of the most important American moral reformers of the mid-nineteenth century. In that work, Weld evolved from a religious moral crusader to pietist to educator. In his rhetoric throughout that career, Weld's configuration of the objectives of moral reform, as well as the enemies and advocates of such reform, reveals dynamics of what Russell Hanson calls "the tensive relationship between liberty and democracy" in the public, moral sphere (34-35).

Operating from a background of Weld's view of moral reform as he developed it in his letters and early publications, this chapter discloses Weld's stylistic and argumentative configuration of moral reform as he presented it late in life in epideictic addresses on the pro-slavery politician Senator John C. Calhoun, on the abolitionist William Lloyd Garrison, and on the subject "The Cost of Reform." His figurations of moral reform in these addresses and his other works treat social evil as an encrusted aggregate of destabilizing actions, the stripping away of which is essential, inherently destructive, and ironically portentous of new evils. Weld's figurations build on the religious foundations of his audience to develop a conscience for moral reform. Weld's figuration of slavery in particular not only raised consciousness regarding slavery; for those with reform sentiments, it roused conscience.

I employ in this argument Mark Johnson's position that moral reasoning is "imaginative through and through" (11). Johnson argues that contemporary studies in narrative, "basic-level experience," metaphor, frame semantics, and the theory of prototypes point to the ways a "'cognitive science of moral imagination'" can deepen our analysis of both commonsense and philosophical moral theories. The "meaning, relevance and guidance" a person's moral principles extend "depends ultimately (though perhaps not always immediately) upon the narrative settings in which they have emerged and to which they are being applied" (160). Metaphor is an essential aspect of the moral imagination. Johnson does not argue that all mental concepts are metaphorical, nor does he believe that all thinking is metaphoric. Instead, he maintains that we define major ethical concepts metaphorically, and that we define concrete situations with systematic metaphoric mappings and clusters (52-53).

In 1855, the abolitionist Charles Stuart described Weld as "one of the most melancholy and anomalous objects that could be presented to me" (Dumond II 1170). A devoted friend and fellow abolitionist, Stuart was concerned with the condition of Weld's soul as Weld moved away from his evangelical faith. Yet Stuart's description could apply as well to Weld's career as an abolitionist. He began as an evangelical exponent of moral suasion using revivalist methods. Disillusioned by the egos of some abolitionists and the un-Christian rancor in abolitionist ranks over politics and the "woman question," by the early 1840s, he turned to his farm, to his family, to pietism, and ultimately to a personal faith akin to Swedenborgianism. Through the 1840s and 1850s, Weld was torn about the nature of reform and his place in it. He remained out of the fray for most of that time. He reemerged from the farm during the Civil War to advocate the Federal cause. After the war, drawing on the nationalist assumptions that grounded many abolitionists, Weld advocated the need for federal authority to enforce civil rights and social reform.

As Robert Abzug observes, Theodore Dwight Weld is "one of the most extraordinary little-known men in American history" (ix). Despite his remarkable contribution to abolition as an agent, trainer, and author—a contribution acknowledged by contemporaries ranging from William Lloyd Garrison to Frederick Douglass—Weld remains obscure, in part because he shied from public recognition of his work. Apart from his work as a lecturer, he sought anonymity: He refused offices in abolitionist organizations; he avoided abolitionist conventions as places for mere mutual admiration; he retained few notes of his abolition lectures, and he published anonymously. Yet *Slavery As It Is* was reported to be "the best-selling book" in the country in 1839 (Barnes I xiii). Harriet Beecher Stowe acknowledged the book's influence on her as she conceived *Uncle Tom's Cabin*. It served as a reference work for antislavery agents at that time. Equally important, as Barnes and Dumond point out, *Slavery As It Is*—along with *The Bible Against Slavery* and Weld's other anonymous writings—replaced agents in areas already covered by them as sources of abolitionist thought (I xiii). Weld's biographers, however, note that few scholars apart from historians know his work (Abzug, Thomas).

Despite the facts that Weld's work in reform was through rhetoric, and that his rhetoric achieved powerful effects, we know little about the workings of that rhetoric. Stephen Browne attempts a corrective in his treatment of Weld's *American Slavery As It Is*. He argues that this work is a form of sentimentality, that "depends not on conclusions reached or actions prompted, but on images rendered and emotions exacted." The referent was no longer slavery, but the reader and the reader's emotions. Browne argues that such sentimentality weakens moral reform because it confuses "spectatorship with moral action" (291). Although Browne's interpretation points to a problem in the construction and reception of evil in moral reform, as an account of Weld's texts in particular it is incomplete. *Slavery As It Is*, along with all of Weld's works, must be read in their religious context, which Browne does not do. Viewing them in this context shows that Weld integrated into the sentimentality of his texts a calling toward moral obligation for action.

Weld himself expressly stated that gathering Christians to abolitionism was his chief goal. He claimed in *Slavery and the Internal Slave Trade* that arousing "professed Christians to testify, both in their individual and associated capacities, against the sin of oppression" was "a prominent object" for American abolitionists (*IST* 131). "American churches," he wrote, "were mainly answerable for the continuance of American slavery" (*IST* 131). Abzug points out that "abolitionists tapped the same vein of discontent that sparked earlier and contemporaneous revivals of religion." In tapping this vein, abolitionists engaged the "conversion aspect of commitment to abolition" (129). As Timothy Smith argues, revivalist awakenings between 1828 and 1836 "required a moral platform." Abolition "was the one most ready to hand" (181). The revivals of the 1830s, unlike those of the 1740s or 1800s, sought to save the world through moral reform. Earlier revivals had focused on personal salvation; those of the 1830s focused on issues of social morality (Cole 77).

Conversion into a cause such as temperance or abolition brought to the converted the prospect of action for the cause. Thousands of church members throughout the North embraced abolition, even when pastors did not. For example, in the late 1830s New England and New York Methodist conferences were torn over abolition. When Bishop Elijah Hedding brought charges at the 1838 Methodist conference against Orange Scott (the popular abolitionist pastor from Lowell, Massachusetts, who had become an agent for the American Antislavery Society) the conference rebuked Hedding by declaring Scott not guilty. Prior to 1840, when aversion to Garrisonianism caused disaffection among some of the faithful, three hundred Eastern district Methodist churches expressed commitment to abolition. Indeed, that the Methodists, the Presbyterians, the Baptists, and evangelicals in general split over Garrisonianism shows the deep connection, and the deeper conflict, between Protestant belief and the issue of slavery (Smith 184-85).

Weld's rhetoric worked to change the world for the religious among his audience by breaking through the encrustation and formalism that facilitated, if not encouraged, evil practice. His metaphoric treatment of slavery and other evils clusters around structures imposed on nature, and on encrustations formed by habit and by time. Late in life, Weld reflected on the nature of reform and its costs in ways that shed light on his work as a reformer generally, and his abolition work specifically. In the lecture "The Cost of Reform" he argued, "to reform is literally, to form again, to give another form, not a better, not a worse, but a different form. That was once its only meaning; now to reform, means to give an improved form, in common speech, a *betterment* [...]. The new form springs from an experience of perceived defects." Social reform seeks first "to push something out of the way that a better something may take its place" ("Reform" n.p.) Thus, wrote Weld:

> the first thing to be done, is to *undo*; to *destroy*, not to construct; to tear down, not build up the good. Their [reformers'] *immediate* object is not [to] direct moral culture, but to uproot the causes that thwart it; not to plant corn, but kill out weeds; not to break up the ground, but to blast rock and wrench out stumps, not to irrigate crops, but to drain swamps; not to sow and reap, but to grub up roots and strip off under growths, thus uncovering to the sun, before turning up the soil to drink in its rays. ("Reform" n.p.)

There is a convoluted metaphorical world here. Nature must be perfected. It is the human lot in life to do so, given the Christian assumptions of Weld and his audience, by the sweat of the brow. Yet this reforming of nature can only be done in coordination with nature. The reformer strips away, then turns things over, then lets the sun do its work. Here, the sun takes on the same divine attributes as do winds and storms in Weld's reflection on South Carolina Senator John C. Calhoun after the war:

> Now, in this lull of the elements, [just] as the storm-burst has swept by and baffled treason [with its allies, routed everywhere, crouches and slinks away]; now, when the spent winds and waves lie hushed, is the time to [drop our fathom line and] sound the depths, and bring up thence those truths of our immortal Declaration which, paralysed by slavery lay there for half a century dormant and drowned. ("Calhoun" n.p.)

In both passages, great forces of nature represent powers beyond human control to which humans must align themselves. Human institutions imposed contrary to these powers must fall, whereas those aligned with them will endure. Thus, between the Declaration of Independence and slavery (both human institutions), only the "immortal Declaration" remained after the war's storm.

An early letter further supports this Emersonian complaint about encrustration and arid forms. In 1828 Weld expressed his concern that the great evangelist Charles Grandison Finney, who had taught Weld the revivalist tactics he used in abolition, was succumbing to the ease of formalism. Weld believed that sin lay in a person"s actions tending to become mere formality. Only "personal holiness" could resist this temptation. He then told Finney that having seen his revivals in Stephenstown, and in having read Finney's letters, he worried:

> that *revivals* have become with you matters of such every day commonness as scarcely to throw over you the least tinge of solemnity. I fear they are fast becoming with you a sort of trade, to be worked at so many hours every day and then laid aside. Dear brother do you not find yourself running into *formality*, a round of formality in the management of revivals? I mean of feeling. The machinery all moves on, every wheel and spring and chord [*sic*] in place; but isn't the *main spring* waxing weaker? (Barnes I 15)

Suggested here is that habit and lack of vigilance incline the person to mere formalism. Weld complained here only of the dangers of personal formalism. When he applied the same basic metaphor to society and people merely functioning within that society, he again opened the conceptual space for the reformer's action in stripping away social forms.

In his lecture on William Lloyd Garrison, Weld depicted him as surveying slavery and seeing it as "the one [all] over shadowing power in the nation. [Monopolizing and] absorbing into itself all its [efficient] forces leaving captive at its will its entire civilization, its states, its professions, its commerce, its manufactures its whole trade and traffic." Garrison, "Bible before him . . . consecrates his life" to its abolition. Garrison knew "that though passions lash[ed] the soul's surface, still depths sleep beneath unstirred by the storms that burst above them and that in those clear depths there lie unerring touchstones of truth and right *institutions* divinely planted there" ("Garrison" n.p.). As he did with the Declaration of Independence in the lecture on Calhoun, here Weld deployed the ocean as both an organic and a structural metaphor to delineate the superficial institutions that humans impose from those emerging from divine sources. He used the ocean again in a lecture titled "The Cost of Reform," as he contrasted the superficial attractions of reform for those who record history to the more important causes of reform:

> As history has, hitherto, dealt mainly with results, and their immediate antecedents, their superficial sources, and the mechanisms that have driven them, *ultimate* causes, processes and motives, the means with which they wrought, and their reactions upon the workers, their coadjutors, their antagonists and their times, lie without its general scope. Whatever heaves to the surface, and froths there, makes the record. The realities, that act below, lie all unchronicled. ("Reform" n.p.)

In *Slavery and the Internal Slave Trade,* Weld deployed structural metaphors to account for churches' silence on the licentiousness of slavery. Indeed, he saw the slave "system," the institution, as the direct cause of this licentiousness, which was "especially prevalent and indiscriminate where *slave-breeding*" was "done as a business" (*IST* 33). Licentiousness, he reasoned, "grows directly out of this system, and is inseparable from it" (*IST* 32). Evidence lay in "the swarming tribes of light hued slaves in city, town, and country" (*IST* 34). Profits of the system linked "cupidity" to lust. Thus, although in slave-holding, productive agricultural states "licentiousness" was "a passion," in the withered lands of the slave-breeding states, the sin was "both a passion and a pursuit, [...] a branch of a flourishing trade" (*IST* 32). Especially odious was that whereas increases in one's slave population brought an owner gains, slaves of "mixed blood" brought "a considerably higher price." Such temptation, he concluded, so often overcame "both the virtue and the pride of white men" that one doubted that "there [was] much of either left" (*IST* 32-33). On this issue, final evidence of the hardening of virtues and conscience was the silence of the churches on such licentiousness:

> Extensive, however, as this amalgamation unquestionably is, the professed ministers of the gospel dare not expose or rebuke it any more than they dare to denounce slave-breeding or selling. It is a *part of the system*, a *branch of the 'institution'*; one department of the craft by which slaveholders have their gains. If it were solely a lustful indulgence it might be spoken against, but being a *business transaction* it is unimpeachable and inviolable. (34)

Here the superficial institution, the part of the system, cut even religious leaders from the roots of shame that would expose right action, so that the products and profits of the system—the "business transaction"—can be sustained.

In this treatment of licentiousness Weld revealed a double-edged truth for the religious among his readers about the nature of slavery. In the opening of *The Bible Against Slavery,* Weld laid bare his charge against the institution. Slavery, he wrote, was the reduction of persons to things (17). Although the major thrust of his work was to prove this reduction for the slaves themselves, the important subtext of the material was the way slavery enslaved the master, and thus symbolically reduced him or her to being owned by passion and sin. Slavery made the owner ultimately subject to her or his passions: "convenience, lust of domination, of sensual gratification, of pride and ostentation" (*Bible* 21-22). Slavery subsumed a slave owner's reason under such passions, and thus reduced his or her ability to act in general as a responsible moral agent. Weld made this point clear in a different context as he responded to a letter from Lewis Tappan on February 6, 1844, regarding the case of their friend, Russell

Judd, a minister in Brooklyn who had molested ten girls: "J's vile lusts [...] have really been, and it would seem *habitually*, his *permanent masters*, leading him captive at their will. It is one of the most monstrous and humiliating developements [*sic*] of this age of horrible revelations." Yet Weld took a message from this episode instructive to him, and, by extension, instructive to our understanding of Weld's rhetoric to those of religious sentiment. "'Cease from man,'" he wrote:

> 'Cease from man' is the sermon God is preaching everywhere just now. Ministers are by the mass of professors put in the place of God, and God is showing them that if they put them there He will cast them headlong [...]. Whoever consents to be exalted by the professing church, in any such sense as almost the entire ministry do consent to be, and do aim at and strive for, him will God cast down and those who conspire them to exalt he will utterly confound. (Barnes II 994-95).

Charles Grandison Finney's views on conversion and preaching, from which Weld drew methods and inspiration, held that sentiment, and—as thought more generally—led to action. Finney believed that teaching doctrine should always be done to regulate a person's practices in daily living. Indeed, distinguishing doctrinal preaching from practical was "a device of the devil." This delineation was especially diabolical because it justified a limited conversion of the mind, whereas—as scripture taught clearly in 2 Timothy 3:16-17—doctrinal instruction must lead to the perfection of man by "thoroughly furnishing unto all good works." Finney taught that "the very design of doctrine is to regulate practice. Any preaching that has not this tendency is not the gospel" (198). To emphasize the point of the Christian's duty to work for moral reform, particularly for abolition, Weld provided on the cover to *American Slavery As It Is* two cautionary biblical passages:

> Behold the wicked abominations that they do.
>
> —Ezekial 8: 9
>
> The Righteous CONSIDERETH the cause of the poor; but the wicked regardeth not to know it.
>
> —Prov. 29: 7

It is safe to assume that thousands among Weld's readers both beheld the horror of slavery and considered the cause of the slave—witness the splits among the congregations of the faithful. And although at this point it is foolhardy to argue for the definitive influence of Weld's metaphoric and argumentative figurations on these faithful, that his rhetoric was used so much by them, and that it drew on their religious sensibilities through metaphor, suggests that this rhetoric not only hit chords of sentiment and emotion, it also stirred them to act. The sensitized, sensible, and informed audience believed, and acted, as Weld believed and acted—in the faith that faith without work is dead.

WORKS CITED

Abzug, Robert. *Passionate Liberator: Theodore Dwight Weld and the Dilemma of Reform.* New York: Oxford UP, 1980.

Barnes, Gilbert H., and Dwight L. Dumond, eds. *Letters of Theodore Dwight Weld, Angelina Grimke Weld and Sarah Grimke, 1822-1844.* 1934. 2 vols. Gloucester, MA: Peter Smith, 1965.

Browne, Stephen H. "'Like Gory Spectres': Representing Evil in Theodore Weld's American Slavery As It Is." *Quarterly Journal of Speech* 80 (1994): 277-92.

Cole, Charles C., Jr. *The Social Ideas of the Northern Evangelists.* New York: Octagon, 1966.

Dumond, Dwight L., ed. *Letters of James Gillespie Birney, 1831-1857.* 1938. 2 vols. Gloucester, MA: Peter Smith, 1966.

Finney, Charles G. *Lectures on Revivals of Religion.* Ed. William G. McLoughlin. Cambridge, MA: Harvard UP, 1960. [The sermon "How to Preach the Gospel" was first printed in the *New York Evangelist,* 21 Feb. 1835.]

Hanson, Russell. *The Democratic Imagination in America: Conversations with Our Past.* Princeton, NJ: Princeton UP, 1985.

Johnson, Mark. *Moral Imagination: Implications of Cognitive Science for Ethics.* Chicago: U of Chicago P, 1993.

Smith, Timothy L. *Revivalism and Social Reform: American Protestantism on the Eve of the Civil War.* 1957. New York: Harper, 1965.

Thomas, Benjamin P. *Theodore Weld: Crusader for Freedom.* New Brunswick, NJ: Rutgers UP, 1950.

Weld, Theodore Dwight. *American Slavery As It Is; Testimony of a Thousand Witnesses.* New York: American Anti-Slavery Society, 1839.

---. *The Bible Against Slavery.* 1837. Detroit: Negro History Press, 1970.

---. "Calhoun." Unpublished ms. Weld Manuscripts, William C. Clemens Library, University of Michigan.

---. "The Cost of Reform" Unpublished ms. Weld Manuscripts, William C. Clemens Library, University of Michigan.

---. *Slavery and the Internal Slave Trade in the United States.* 1841. New York: Arno, 1967. [Referred to as *IST.*]

---. "William Lloyd Garrison" Unpublished ms. Weld Manuscripts, William C. Clemens Library, University of Michigan.

25

The Alphabet as Ethics: A Rhetorical Basis for Moral Reality in Hebrew Letters

Steven B. Katz
North Carolina State University

The title of this volume—*Rhetorical Democracy: Discursive Practices of Civic Engagement*—can be understood to reflect our fundamental belief that societies are rhetorically constructed in and through discourse, and that the nature of such discourse shapes civic and political interaction. Generally, we also assume that the power of discourse to shape social interaction is related to the epistemic power of language to create and shape meaning and culture. In this chapter we explore how the power of discourse to shape meaning and culture can be understood to be grounded in the physical substance of language itself. That is, we explore not only how societies are constructed through discursive practices that depend on civic engagement, but also how these discursive practices—how civic engagement itself—might be regarded as grounded in the alphabet.

It is a commonplace idea now that the invention of writing made language a material object. But the Western rhetorical tradition has conceived of writing as an imitation of an imitation and thus of no "substance" (Plato), as forms ideally but rarely rational and empirical that are necessary owing to a defect in our hearers (Aristotle), or as sensuous forms that that create experience and knowledge through language by deceiving the senses (the sophists). In the twentieth century, the philosopher Ernst Cassirer examined in depth the nature of language as a sensuous form in consciousness, and literary and rhetorical theorists as diverse as Bakhtin, Burke, Perelman, and Cixous have in different ways taken into account the materiality of language in relation to ideology, motivation, argumentation, and gender.

In all of this work, the stylistic focus is on the word (or sign), syntax, and social construction. But in the Western rhetorical tradition, there is an alternative philosophy of rhetoric that until recently has been relatively neglected, in which the letters of the alphabet themselves as forms become the entire focus of experience and interpretation. That is, the alphabet becomes the physical basis of discursive practices of civic engagement—in this case, ethics. Continuing in a different vein from my earlier work in rhetoric and ethics ("Ethic of Expediency"; "Aristotle's Rhetoric"), this chapter briefly overviews the Jewish mystical rhetorical tradition of the alefbet as a basis of morality. In this rhetorical tradition, unlike Aristotle's, the substance of the letters rather than expediency is the basis of deliberative discourse.

In "The Epistemology of the Kabbalah: Toward a Jewish Philosophy of Rhetoric," I explored how Jewish Kabbalah, a collection of mystical texts composed between the twelfth and sixteenth centuries, instantiates a material philosophy of language and knowledge grounded in the interpretation of and meditation on the Hebrew alphabet. I also attempted to demonstrate that within the classical rhetorical tradition of the West, this philosophy, epistemologically if not chronologically, seems to fall somewhere between Platonic and sophistic philosophies. Generally, Platonists assume that essence, true knowledge, exists outside language, and thus rhetoric cannot be used to attain it; the sophists denied the possibility of knowing essence, thus making rhetorical persuasion the basis of all knowledge. The philosophy of language and knowledge underlying Kabbalah seems to assume that essence is embodied in the material substance of language itself, in the shapes, sounds, numerical equivalents, sequential positions, and permutations of the Hebrew letters. That is, the rhetorical epistemology of Jewish mysticism appears to posit a direct connection between the substance of language and the moral physical world. If language is regarded as the basis of "reality," by which we usually mean social reality but in Jewish mysticism also means physical reality, the letters of the alphabet are the moral atoms that constitute it.

In Jewish mysticism, the letters of the alefbet are understood as moral as well as material essences, and are combined and interpreted according to hermeneutic principles to constitute an ethical rhetorical reality—an ethical rhetorical reality rooted in the very substance of language itself. In fact, the application of these principles to sacred texts represents the beginning of a "democratization" of what was in earlier history cult knowledge possessed only by high priests. I do not have space here to examine at any length the principles that govern the interpretation of the alefbet, the later *baraita* (literally "outside"—the Mishnah) of the thirty-two rules developed in the Rabbinic age (roughly 100 BCE to 400 CE). These hermeneutic principles govern the permutation and interpretation of letters, spellings, and vocalizations (or "vowelizations") of Hebrew words. Rather, I only touch on these in an attempt to begin to suggest some ethical ligaments of the letters.

The first phenomenon to comment on is the attention paid to the Hebrew letters in contemporary Jewish religious practice and culture. Let's begin by looking at a part of a sermon by Rabbi Lucy Dinner on the Shema, a prayer that is the cornerstone of Judaism and in which congregates declare the unity of and their covenant with God (please remember that Hebrew is read right to left):

שמע ישראל יהוה אלהינו יהוה אחד.

And so by way of interpretation we have these questions and possible answers:

> Why are the last letters of שמע [shema] and אחד [echad] written large in all Torah scrolls? We no longer know the reason, but the following have been suggested: To remind us to concentrate on the thought that lies between the ע [ayin] and the ד [dalet]; the large ע [ayin]: so that one should read שמע [shema; "hear"] and not שמא [shemhah; "Perhaps, O Israel"]; The large ד [dalet]: so that one should read אחד [echad; "one"] and not אחר [achair; "another"]; Together, ע [ayin] and ד [dalet] read עד [aid; ed, witness], to emphasize that the Jew who pronounces the Shema witnesses to the Holy One. (Dinner)

Beyond a simple matter of emphasis (like boldface), one notices that the size of the letters is assumed be significant, and that significance (signification, really) is ethical. There is good reason to believe these and all letters to be significant: Every Torah scroll in the world is still written painstakingly by hand on parchment by *sopherim* (scribes), and every Torah must be the same to be valid. In addition to size, one notices the application of several of the later *baraita* of the thirty-two rules. According to Hermann Strack's compendium of them, these *baraita* include: *ma'al* (paronomasia), the relation of words based on similar sound—or in the case of Hebrew, the same consonants; *athbash*, systematically changing the order of letters in a word or substituting other letters to arrive at other, and in this case undesirable words in interpretation; *notarikon*, whereby each letter of a word is read as standing for the first letter of another word (i.e., the whole word is signified and embodied by that letter)—anagrams or acrostics are similar examples—and the splitting of a word into two; and, not used here, *gematria*, the calculation of the numerical value of Hebrew letters to discover hidden relations and meanings. On two oversized letters and a few *baraita* an entire moral world is derived and maintained.

This *drash* on the Shema begins to hint at how the application of the later *baraita* provide a hermeneutic basis for understanding the alefbet as an ethical rhetorical system, and are in fact a part of that system. These later *baraita* read the letters of Torah as an alphabet of ethics, revealing a complex and epistemologically different rhetoric *rooted in the substance of language itself.*

There's a related hermeneutic system begun in a story found in the Babylonian and Jerusalem Talmud, that also is contained in several *midrashim*, and fully realized in the influential Kabbalistic *Zohar* (Book of Splendor) of Moses de Leon in the thirteenth century. This hermeneutic system uses *notarikon* to lead to other levels of interpretation based on the letters. The basic story is that four rabbis entered *pardes*, but only one, Rabbi Akiva, "left in peace." In Kabbalah, *pardes* (literally "orchard" or "paradise") is also an anagram for four levels of interpreting Torah represented by the Hebrew letters פ [pey], ר [resh], ד [dalet], ס [samech]—פרדס (PaRDeS): פ - peschat (plain, or simple meaning), ר remez (hint, or allegorical meaning), ד drash (dig, interpreted meaning, as in the Talmud and Midrash), and ס sod (secret, or hidden meaning). For example, the first answer to the question in the sermon on the Shema can be considered an example of *peschat*, the second two perhaps of *remez*, and the last of *drash*. But PaRDeS is both a "physical" and an "orthographic" place—physical because orthographic—a site of discursive practice located in the substance of language itself. As a method of interpretation—as a hermeneutic mode of civic engagement—PaRDeS often moves beyond *notarikon*, to become a mystical gloss on Torah as *sod*—as a hidden ethical world materially manifested in the letters of the alefbet themselves.

We also can see the *baraita* applied at all levels of PaRDeS, as well as *sod*, not only in Kabbalah, but also in more recent books with titles like *The Alef-Bet: Jewish Thought Revealed through the Hebrew Letters*, *The Inner Meaning of the Hebrew Letters*, and *The Wisdom of the Hebrew Alphabet* by contemporary Rabbis and mystics Yitzchak Ginsburgh, Robert Haralick, and Michael Munk, respectively. These authors all believe that hermeneutics of the Hebrew letters constitute a code of ethics—indeed, are the very foundation of those ethics. For the purpose of this chapter, I'm going to relay some of their contemporary *midrashim* on one Hebrew letter—really a speck: the letter י [yud].

Focusing on size and shape again, from Rabbi Munk we learn that the yud, the tenth letter in the Hebrew alefbet, "is barely larger than a dot and cannot be divided into component parts" (125). Because of its size, for Munk and Haralick it represents humility. Yet, says Munk, yud also "represents the metaphysical, and alludes to HASHEM Who is One and Indivisible": the yud "consists of 3 parts: a prong pointing upwards to the One above, a prong directed downwards to earth and the middle part uniting both" (126-27). "[T]he tiniest letter," says Munk, yud "represents and safeguards the concept of greatness" (132).

Based on *gematria*, Rabbi Munk also derives the following ethical lesson:

> [S]ince the number ten may be viewed as a unit, any instance in which ten plays a significant role should be viewed as a whole comprising ten parts; the set of ten represents completion [...]. It took ten generations from Adam to Noah to *complete* the breakdown of morality [...]. From Noah's time, God waited ten more generations until Abraham evolved as the potential father of the Jewish people [...] with ten utterances God created the world—these correspond to the Ten Commandments on whose observance the world's existence depends [...] ten miracles [i.e., the plagues] were performed in Egypt. (126-28)

Biblical history is not only contained but also created in the smallest letter.

Drawing from Midrash, Munk also employs *athbash* and *gematria* in discussing the changing of Abraham's name from **אברם** [Avram], father of Aram, to **אברהם** [Abraham], father of nations, and **שרי** [Sarai], <u>*my*</u> *princess*, to **שרה** [Sarah], *princess* "by splitting the י [yud] (=10) of Sarai into two ה's (ה = 5), which were then added to the names of Abram and Sarai" (131). Munk also discusses a permutation involving the addition of a yud to form the future tense of *pa-al* verbs (in third person singular): "After the Israelites had successfully crossed the Sea of Reeds, Moses sang a song of praise and thanksgiving to God. Instead of describing this in the past tense—**שר** [shar], *he sang*—the Torah uses the future tense: **ישיר משה** [yasheer Mosheh], *Then Moses sang* [lit. *will sing*] (*Exodus* 15:1)" (126). In these examples, the letter yud is related directly to historical processes and events as an active, creative agent.

Haralick uses *ma'al* in discussing yud:

> **יוד** [yod] is related to the word **יד** [yad], which has the common meaning of *hand*, but also means *handle, monument, place, power, strength, share,* or *portion*. It also

> is related to the root ידע [yeedah], which means to *introduce* or to *specify*, and the root ידע [yadah], which means to *know, perceive, understand, discern, comprehend, be aware of*, and to *have sexual intercourse with*. (141)

In fact, yud is the first letter of one of the names of God. "The most important word beginning with a י," says Haralick, "is the Tetragrammaton יהוה [yud-hey-vov-hey]" (156). Because the letters are not merely symbols of reality, but rather the basis of reality, the Tetragrammaton is the manifestation of the energy of God into the physical world. י is:

> the state of concealment and obscurity, before it develops into a state of expansion and revelation in comprehension and understanding. When the "point" evolves into a state of expansion and revelation [...] it is then contained and represented in the letter ה [hey]. The shape of the letter ה has dimension, expansion, breadth [...] to indicate extension and flow downward to the concealed worlds. In the next stage this extension and flow are drawn still lower into the revealed worlds [...]. This stage of extension is contained and represented in the final letters ו [vov] and ה [hey ...]. ו [vov], in shape a vertical line, indicates downward extension. (Zalman qtd in Haralick 156)

Thus, the letters of the Tetragrammaton themselves are understood not only to act as a bridge between the divine-spiritual and the material-physical worlds, but also to be the foundation of those worlds. Haralick concludes:

> י brings into physical manifestation and being that which unites heaven and earth. ה [hey] is the eternal life above, the life in the spiritual realm [...]. ו [vov] is the connection between above and below. And the final ה [hey] is the transitory life below, the life in the physical realm. Thus, [yud-hey-vov-hey] is the source which brings into being all existence. (157)

Literally. For as Haralick points out, the *Zohar* asserts that "the י is the symbol of the head of all creatures; the two ה [heys] represent the five fingers of the right hand and the left; the ו [vov] is the symbol of the body" (qtd in Haralick 156). Further, in the view of the Kabbalists, the Tetragrammaton is the ethical form of both God and human, as shown in Fig. 25.1.

FIG. 25.1 Adam in the likeness of his maker (Halevi 185).

In addition to the application of the *baraita,* then, in *sod* the letters are obviously understood by mystics as ontological ethical entities—as material as well as moral atoms. The rhetoric of *sod*—"secret" knowledge of the letter yud—furthers our understanding of the ontological status accorded to the alefbet as ethical atoms from which the entire moral and material universe is created. We see how the material shape and position of the letters in the alefbet are read not only as symbols, but also as ethical reality. Rabbi Yitzchak Ginsburgh's account of the Biblical moment of creation using yud, the first letter of the Tetragrammaton, illustrates the expansion of the letter into ethical reality:

> The letter *Yud,* a small suspended point, reveals the spark of essential good [...]. Subsequent to the initial [...] contraction of G-d's Infinite light in order to make a "place" for Creation, there remained [...] a single, potential point or "impression." The secret of this point is the power of the Infinite to contain finite phenomena within Himself and express them to apparent external reality. Finite manifestation begins from a zero-dimensional point, thereafter developing into a one-dimensional line and two-dimensional surface [...] which reflects itself as the Infinite potential of the point to develop and express itself in all of the manifold finite phenomena of time and space. (154)
>
> From within this point of limitation is revealed the secret of the ten *sefirot,* the Divine channels of light through which G-d continually brings His world into being. Ten, the numerical value of *Yud,* is also the number of commandments (literally "statements") revealed by G-d to His people Israel at Sinai. All the commandments, and in fact every letter of Torah, possess the power of the "little that holds much"; each is a channel for the revelation of G-d's Infinite Light in finite reality. (154)

What is most significant here is that space and time are not only defined by but also contained within the alefbet as moral substance. In this particular discursive practice of civic engagement, the moral and physical universe is constructed in and through the letters. We thus have in Kabbalistic rhetoric an account of the rhetorical origins of the material and moral universe, one not grounded in the *peschat* of the Creationist movement, but on a "big bang theory" that predates our own. We watch as the letters (and *sefirot)* as "atoms" expand into a rhetorical-ethical universe, as shown in Fig. 25.2.

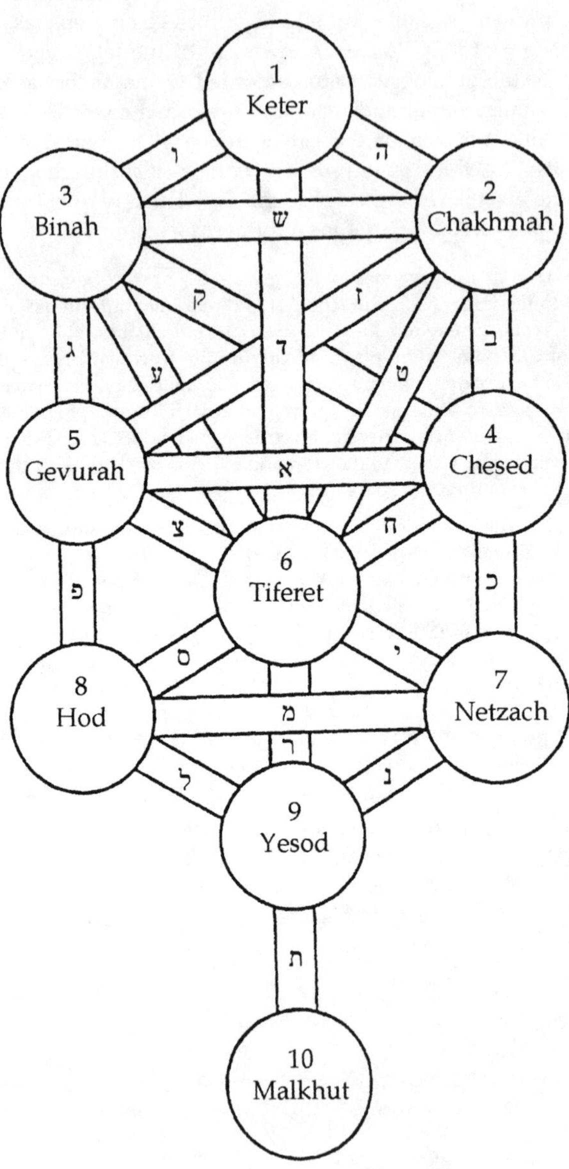

FIG. 25.2 The thirty-two paths of wisdom (Kaplan 155).

It is obvious that this discursive practice of civic engagement—this system of rhetorical ethics—is based on a philosophy of language and knowledge that is quite different from that of Plato and Aristotle or the sophists. It is different from Christian traditions of Biblical exegesis as well. No doubt it is perhaps because of dominant rational and empirical philosophies—and as Walter Burkert argues perhaps the bias of nineteenth-century German scholars working in the classical period against oriental influences on ancient Greece—that the Jewish philosophy of the alefbet has been ignored in Western rhetoric. This is a rhetoric that bases its epistemology on a belief in the ontological status of letters.

Although this may seem farfetched to us, the progeny of Plato and Aristotle who use the Latin alphabet, a recent spate of books on the origin, history, and mythology of the Roman alphabet (e.g., Firmage) and on writing systems generally (Daniels and Bright) might indicate a growing interest in this material dimension of language and meaning in our culture. The interpretation of our alphabet might represent a democratization of what is now hidden design knowledge. In fact, the rhetorical philosophy explored here is not only predominant in the hermeneutics of Jewish sermons, but also in our own popular culture (Mr. Spock's "live long and prosper" sign, e.g., is actually the priestly benediction, which is in the shape of the Hebrew letter ש [shin], the first letter of one of the names of God). But more important, in a Web culture where language design and graphics literally become the spaces we inhabit (Moskow and Katz), interpretation of our own invisible alphabet at least may become a more apparently physical if not ethical rhetorical democracy, a site of discursive practice and civic engagement grounded in the substance of language itself.

WORKS CITED

Aristotle. *The Rhetoric.* Vol 2. Trans. W. Rhys Roberts. *The Complete Works of Aristotle.* 2 vols. Ed. Jonathan Barnes. Princeton, NJ: Princeton UP, 1984. 2152-269.

Bakhtin, Mikhail. "Marxism and the Philosophy of Language." Trans. Ladislav Matejka and I. R. Titunik. *The Rhetorical Tradition: Readings from Classical Times to the Present.* Ed. Patricia Bizzell and Bruce Herzberg. Boston: Bedford, 1990. 928-44.

Burke, Kenneth. *Rhetoric of Motives.* NY: Prentice-Hall, 1952.

Burkert, Walter. *The Orientalizing Revolution: Near Eastern Influence on Greek Culture in the Early Archaic Age.* Trans. Margaret E. Pinder and Walter Burkert. Cambridge, MA: Harvard UP, 1992.

Cassirer, Ernst. *The Philosophy of Symbolic Forms. Vol. 1: Language.* Trans. Ralph Manheim. 3 vols. New Haven, CT: Yale UP, 1955.

Cixous, Helene. *The Laugh of the Medusa.* Trans. Keith Cohen and Paula Cohen. *SIGNS* 1.4 (1976): 875-93.

Daniels, Peter T., and William Bright. *The World's Writing Systems.* New York: Oxford UP, 1996.

de Leon, Moses. *Zohar: The Book of Splendor.* Trans. Gershom Sholem. *Basic Readings from the Kabbalah.* New York: Schocken, 1949.

Dinner, Rabbi Lucy. Sermon on the "Shema." Temple Beth Or, Raleigh, NC. Nov. 1996.

Firmage, Richard A. *The Alphabet Abecedarium: Some Notes on the Letters.* Boston: Godine, 1993.

Ginsburgh, Yitzchak. *The Alef-Bet: Jewish Thought Revealed Through the Hebrew Letters.* Northvale, NJ: Aronson, 1995.

Halevi, Z'ev ben Shimon. *The Way of Kabbalah*. London: Rider, 1976. 185.
Haralick, Robert M. *The Inner Meaning of the Hebrew Alphabet*. Northvale, NJ: Aronson, 1995.
Kaplan, Aryeh. *The Bahir*. Northvale, NJ: Aronson, 1995.
Katz, Steven B. "Aristotle's Rhetoric, Hitler's Program, and the Ideological Problem of *Praxis* Power, and Professional Discourse as a Social Construction of Knowledge." Special Issue on Power and Professional Discourse, *Journal of Business and Technical Communication* (Jan. 1993): 37-62.
---. "The Epistemology of the Kabbalah: Toward a Jewish Philosophy of Rhetoric." *Rhetoric Society Quarterly* 25 (1995): 107-22.
---. "The Ethic of Expediency: Classical Rhetoric, Technology, and the Holocaust." *College English* 54 (March 1992): 255-75.
Moskow, Michal Anne, and Steven B. Katz. "Re-Building Life in Cyberspace: Ethnography of Rhetoric in Post-Holocaust Discussion Lists in Germany and United States." 12th Biennial International Society for the History of Rhetoric Conference, Warsaw, Poland, 26 July 2001.
Munk, Rabbi Michael L. *The Wisdom in the Hebrew Alphabet: The Sacred Letters as a Guide to Jewish Deed and Thought*. New York: Mesorah, 1983.
Perelman, Chaim. *The Realm of Rhetoric*. Trans. William Kluback. Notre Dame, IN: U of Notre Dame P, 1982.
Plato. "Phaedrus." Trans. R. Hackforth. *The Collected Dialogues of Plato*. Ed. Edith Hamilton and Huntington Cairns. New York: Bollingen Foundation-Pantheon, 1961. 475-525.
Strack, L. Hermann. *Introduction to the Talmud and Midrash*. New York: Jewish Publication Society of America, 1931.
Zalman, Shneur. "Igeret Hateshuvah." *Likkutei Amarim-Tanya*. Bi-lingual ed. Brooklyn, NY: Kehot Publication Society, 1993. 363.

26

Dewey, Discussion, and Democracy in Speech Pedagogy

William Keith
University of Wisconsin–Milwaukee

> I know of no miracle so wonderful as the sudden unfolding of a man's mind or the glorious blossoming of a womanly spirit, and I am filled with gratitude that I am permitted to behold these things, and with humility that I should be, in even so small a degree, a contributor to the awakening. With these rich gifts, we salute thee, O America! These are our offerings to the Democracy of the Future!
>
> —Wells ("Coaching Debates" 173)

From the founding of the discipline in 1914, Speech Communication teachers have claimed, at least in part, a civic mission for their pedagogy: They held themselves responsible for training students in the skills of public, democratic life. As they made the transition from oratory and declamation to public speaking and debate during the founding of the field, they rethought the political context of their pedagogy. Primarily within a Progressivist notion of democracy, debate instruction emerges, falls short, and thus gives birth (with John Dewey's help) to a new pedagogy, *discussion*, which explicitly embodies the political ideals which debate fails to achieve. This chapter charts the evolution of discussion within a distinctly Deweyan framework.

HOW DO WE TEACH DEMOCRACY?

"Debating," in something like the form we now know it, began as an intercollegiate sport in the 1890s. Literary societies at Ivy League colleges, which until then had featured debates only among members, began to arrange debates with other universities; at this point there was no faculty involvement, and no curricular presence for debate. Baird and Cowperthwaite claim that the first decade of the twentieth century saw the emergence of both faculty coaches and courses in debate (which allowed debaters to get credit for what they were doing). As a focus for school rivalries and an activity in which individuals could excel, debate became wildly popular, resulting in predictable, and familiar, problems. Critics accused debaters of being superficial, obsessed with the glory of winning, and willing to bend evidence and logic to do so.

Although these criticisms are familiar, the ground for making them may not be. Critics of debate judged it relative to its value for civic education; these problems were problems with preparing students for real deliberative and political contexts. In some cases, this connection is established by mapping the activity closely onto the corresponding institution, as in the case of parliamentary debate and moot court. But the point can be made more generally; most students are not going to the legislature, but that doesn't excuse the debasement of debate. William Hawley Davis, in response to James O'Neill's argument that debate is a sport that sharpens the mind, claims a very broad territory for the democratic purpose of debate training: "The opposite conception of debating, which I find myself compelled humbly and insistently to advocate, is that of training for the wise disposition of important matters in legislatures, public gatherings, club and society meetings—wherever men collect, as they must constantly be doing, at least in a democracy, for counsel and effective action" (173). As we would say nowadays, debating should aspire to be, or at least mimic, *deliberation*.

In the first ten years of the *Quarterly Journal of Speech*, scholars explored debate as a contested ground, caught between academic and political goals. Critics expressed their general dissatisfactions with debate—it is too competitive, unscrupulous, and generally poor training in democracy—as fairly technical points about debate practice. In particular, three elements of debate practice became points of contention. First, should students debate both sides of the question? That depends on whether we (as teachers or coaches) are training flexible arguers or honest people; certainly, we'd like to think that deliberators argue their convictions, not their convenience. A second problem concerned the so-called expert judge; originally, debates were public affairs, judged by prominent members of the community. By 1920, however, professional judges (coaches and debate teachers) were preferred for their ability to see the finer points of debate technique. For some, the professionalization of the speech field was at stake: If you could bring in Judge Smith or Reverend Jones to judge a debate, then there was nothing particularly professional or technical about teaching debate (which, of course, had been exactly the case one hundred years earlier). For those who wanted external judges, led by Hugh Wells of USC, the civic context of speech instruction was at stake: If we didn't mimic the form *and* content of civic occasions by holding students responsible to real audiences (i.e., members of the community), then debate became a game with no substantive connection to civic life.

Judging criteria provoked the angriest confrontations. Should debates be judged on the debate, or the question? The sides were clear. If we judge the debate, then we get technically better and more skillful arguers. Or maybe we just get slick and cynical sophists. If we judge the question, then we'll get better citizens later on, or maybe we cheat students by having them stoop to local politics rather than learning superior debate skills. The debate community took these criticisms quite seriously. Baird and Cowperthwaite claim:

> Although the competitive elements continued to evoke enthusiasm among superior debaters [...] the education[al] values of the forensic program for the functions and purposes of a democratic society were recognized as playing an indispensable role in the struggle for survival. If free speech, basic to the American system, is to serve democracy properly, discussion and debate will continue as essential education disciplines. (275)

In response to these criticisms, debate teachers and coaches experimented with reforms in the 1920s, including audience-judged debates and decisionless debates. Although these experiments didn't cause significant changes in debate practice, they did result in new developments. Midwestern coaches in particular experimented with decisionless debating, but concluded that it presented too many motivational problems as a student activity. However, those in the profession noticed that the decisionless debate embodied many *politically* attractive features; in particular, it seemed to instantiate a Deweyan approach to democratic life that captured exactly the *zeitgeist* of the moment.

DEWEY AND THE TURN TO DISCUSSION

Argumentation combines a mode of communication with a mode of reasoning; both communication and reasoning can embody various political principles. Different combinations yield types of argumentation adapted to different forms of political life, from demagoguery in an authoritarian context to Isocrates's citizens persuading each other. In the 1920s, a particular picture of democratic life came together with emerging insights about communicative forms of reason to produce a compelling vision of civic pedagogy, a vision centered around the term *discussion*. Discussion emerged as a cooperative, problem-solving activity, as opposed to the conflictive, resolution-passing activity of debate. The advantages of discussion were both rational (debate often seemed merely strategic) and political (debate embodied an outmoded conception of democratic communication). Here I focus mainly on the political justifications for turning to discussion.

Whereas traditional training in debate and declamation presumed fixed democratic institutions toward which educators could direct pedagogy, discussion focused on *general* deliberative modes of communication, independent of the institutional constraints of parliamentary practice. Although it mattered whether or not the requirements of discussion actually conflicted with the requirements of legislative practice, it mattered less than the project of rethinking democratic communication in a single stroke. The boldness of this move—its bootstrapping quality—is easy to miss, because the terms that framed the change are by now so familiar to us.

The most important influence on discussion is undoubtedly John Dewey. His work provided an account of reasoning (what Baird liked to call "the New Logic") as well as a vision of democracy that made communicative practices, rather than institutional settings, definitive. Two features of Dewey's philosophy inform discussion pedagogy: the relation of democracy and science, and the tools for argument/thinking. For Dewey, democracy is ubiquitous, not confined to legislatures or parliamentary settings. Any occasion for joint action that requires decision making is a potential site of democracy, or what Robert Westbrook calls "the consummatory moment." In "Philosophy and Democracy," Dewey points out that in the broadest sense philosophy is continuous with science, and also with democracy; the democratic moment and the epistemic moment are one and the same (see also Dewey's "The Inclusive Philosophic Idea").

Pragmatism tied thinking to action in a deep way. Dewey's pragmatism had no place for thought independent of action, and hence merely shuffling categories (as in syllogisms) could not account for the character of thought. And Dewey fully historicized action; the solitary thinker (or doubter) found no place in his philosophy. Human action, and thinking, are thus social, and hence embody some form of politics. Hence, Dewey believed the search for knowledge, whether in philosophy, science, or public policy, responded better to democratic forms than other political types. For Speech Communication teachers, this view permitted a realignment of democracy and pedagogy. The democracy for which they trained students could go beyond simple participation in the dominant political institutions (which required a conflictive and apparently undemocratic mode of communication) and embrace any "actional" situation.

To flesh out this vision of democracy pedagogically, speech teachers needed a way to define the relevant situations, and so they appealed to Dewey's 1910 *How We Think*. Dewey identified thinking with problem solving: The world resists us in some way; hence we require knowledge of it for an action/decision, and so we attempt "experimentally" to work out the right course of action. Dewey deftly wove the experimental method of science together with everyday practical concerns, and succeeded in moving "thinking" out of peoples' heads and into the predicaments in which they find themselves. This approach would have seemed entirely natural to debate and argument instructors, because it represented (from their vantage point) a generalization of the parliamentary situation, in which resolutions are potential actions, adopted or not depending on whether the assembly decides these actions would solve the problem (cf. Bitzer for an explicit statement of this generalization). Hence, Dewey's "logic" was a logic of deliberative situations that dovetailed perfectly with the argumentative traditions of debate instruction. In addition, debate by this time was structured around a kind of problem/solution logic known as the "stock issues." These points of stasis (significance, inherence, plan, solvency) allowed the affirmative and negative teams to plan their cases in advance, because each side knew in general what points would be argued. Dewey's steps of problem solving were nearly the same (perceived difficulty, definition of the difficulty, possible solution, reasoned examination of solutions, and experimental corroboration) and thus, with little effort, the debate tradition faded into a conception of discussion based on Deweyan principles.

How do discussion textbooks embody these Deweyan principles? Two texts help illustrate: one early text, and one from the mature period of discussion pedagogy (circa 1940). Alfred Sheffield's 1922 *Joining Public Discussion* launched the project boldly and clearly. Sheffield turned the conceptual tables on debate, and explicitly tied democratic practice to *cooperation*, rather than conflict (as in parliamentary and legal contexts). Specifically, he challenged the assumptions undergirding the oratorical model of argument and persuasion. At a time when the debate community focused on argument as alternating speeches, he presented discussion as a political methodology: "A man's ambition to speak tempts his mind to picture the group as a passive audience with himself in action before it as a platform orator. That picture is a 'wishful day-dream,' beguiling his attention away from the realities of his problem [...]. He must begin mastering the technique of *Discussion*—by which the whole group is maneuvered into co-operative thinking and speaking" (v).

Even with the context of years of experimentation with decisionless debate and audience involvement, Sheffield was making a bold leap here. He rejected the political implication of one-to-many communication: the "one" who can lead/control the "many," the group, overwhelming them with argument or persuasion. The passive audience is not a democratic audience. Democratic communication finds a home in cooperative, rather than competitive, groups. Given the long-established traditions of deliberation as parliamentary (the resolution is proposed, then the sides engage, presumption and burden of proof operate), this is an astonishing reversal. Sheffield thought that adopting his method could have far-reaching consequences: "The real technicians of modern democracy are those who win insight into the forces of thought and feeling that can be touched into activity when people sit down together. The student of discussion, therefore, should picture a deliberative meeting as a sort of field of magnetic forces wherein his mind can conspire with other minds to organize socially advantageous currents [...]" (v).

The "marketplace of ideas" had no place here. Rather than surrendering to a Hobbesian chaos or Mill's economic competition, we should be putting our heads together. The phrase "technician of democracy" is particularly resonant. Like Dewey, Sheffield was not exclusively interested in the institutions of democracy, but in democracy as a way of life and a cultural moment.

James McBurney and Kenneth Hance delivered on the promise of Sheffield's work in 1939, with *The Principles and Methods of Discussion*. They characterized discussion as the "reflective deliberation of problems" (10) and give an interesting history (15 ff.) of the development of discussion, moving from *ekklesia* and the Roman forum to dialectic ("a group of people discussing things together 'in the spirit of inquiry' "), to Bacon and the scientific method, to Dewey's oft-quoted remark in *The Public and Its Problems* that "the essential need [today] is the improvement of the methods and conditions of debate, discussion and persuasion" (qtd in McBurney and Hance 18). Modestly, they forward the suggestion that "the principles and methods of discussion attempt to bring the problems of practical policy in our society under the surveillance of an approach comparable in many ways with the methods of science" (18). McBurney and Hance then connect this method to democratic politics:

> If democracy means anything, it must mean the active participation of the individual in the choices and policies of the group. In its best sense, it means action of this sort on the highest possible plane of intelligence with relative freedom from exploitation and violence. Democracy by its very nature must place a premium on group intelligence, since its values are realized in the degree that the members of the group participate competently in the solution of group problems [...]. Democracy is thwarted in the degree that passivity and domination supplant such intelligent participation. (20)

For further clarification, in an appendix they reprinted an essay on "Discussion in the Democratic Process" by one of Dewey's colleagues at Columbia, Lyman Bryson. Bryson begins with an historical sketch leading up to the "challenges" to democracy posed by "industrialism" (roughly, the cult of efficiency and the rationalization of labor). He then goes on to argue that discussion and democracy are virtually identical; technical questions can be settled by discussions among experts, but "all the really important questions are still left to be decided" (qtd in McBurney and Hance 432), because values and political positions can't be *authoritatively* settled—in a democracy.

CONCLUSION: CONCEPTIONS OF DEMOCRACY IN SPEECH PEDAGOGY

Speech Communication teachers did not reinvent democracy in a vacuum. The early twentieth century saw the influence of the Progressive movement. James Morone characterizes the Progressive Era as part of a recurring cycle in U.S. history: As the country grows along with burgeoning bureaucracies and the expanding reach of public policy, the "democratic wish" asserts itself in a renewal of populist democracy; this fell out of favor after WWII, replaced by interest group politics. Morone identifies two characteristics of Progressivist reforms, populism and science. Populism expressed itself in the attempt to make more of the growing government bureaucracy directly accountable to popular vote; the scientific aspect of progressivism emerged as a faith (mostly clearly expressed by Croly and Lippmann) that sufficient knowledge and expertise could solve public policy problems. As Morone points out, unexpected consequences torpedoed each of these. "Populism" either wilted in the face of wealthy and influential lobbyists or devolved into a tyranny of petty local interests, even as entrenched interests and a failure to account for goals stymied "scientific management" by experts.

The conception of democracy emerging from discussion pedagogy embodied both of these Progressive dimensions, but also moved beyond them. The populist roots of this pedagogy emerge in its focus on face-to-face participation, privileging interpersonal deliberative contexts, recalling the myth of the town meeting. The problems with populism as localism, although not confronted explicitly, are addressed in the connection of discussion to the Forum Movement, which sought to link public forums to the continuing civic education of voters. The scientific dimension is clear, since groups are the engine that generates knowledge. However, discussion addressed a deep flaw in Progressivism—its reliance on a cadre of experts in public policy—by incorporating democratic structures into the notion of expertise. As Sheffield emphasizes, expertise is not a body of knowledge that a few people carry around in their heads, but instead is the critical attention of all the people who have an interest in a decision or policy. Negotiating goals and interests is a central part of the discussion process, and ensures the democratic character of expertise.

Clearly, discussion is the forerunner of much of the sophisticated work that is now being done on mediation and conflict resolution. But whether its lessons are profitable for public speaking courses, which are rapidly becoming business presentation courses (e.g., Daly and Engleberg), or argument courses, which bill themselves as critical thinking courses (even Freely's durable text now features critical thinking), remains to be seen.

WORKS CITED

Baird, A. C. *Public Discussion and Debate*. Boston: Ginn, 1928.

Baird, A. C., and L. L. Cowperthwaite. "Intercollegiate Debating." *A History of Speech Education in America*. Ed. K. Wallace. New York: Appleton-Century-Crofts, 1954. 259-76.

Bitzer, Lloyd. "The Rhetorical Situation." *Philosophy and Rhetoric* 1 (1968): 1-11.

Croly, Herbert David. *The Promise of American Life*. Ed. Arthur M. Schlesinger, Jr. Belknap of Harvard UP, 1965.

Daly, J. A., and I. Engleberg. *Presentations in Everyday Life*. Boston: Houghton, 2000.

Davis, W. H. "Is Debating Primarily a Game? *Quarterly Journal of Speech* 2 (1916): 171-79.

Dewey, J. *How We Think*. Boston: Heath, 1910.

---. "The Inclusive Philosophic Idea." 1919. Reprinted in *The Essential Dewey, Volume I*. Ed. Larry A. Hickman and Thomas M. Alexander. Bloomington: Indiana UP, 1998. 308-15.

---. "Philosophy and Democracy." 1919. Reprinted in *The Essential Dewey, Volume I*. Eds. Larry A. Hickman and Thomas M. Alexander. Bloomington: Indiana UP, 1998. 71-78.

Freely, A. J., and D. Steinberg. *Argumentation & Debate—Critical Thinking for Reasoned Decision Making*. 10th ed. New York: Wadsworth, 2000.

Lippmann, Walter. *Drift and Mastery; An Attempt to Diagnose the Current Unrest*. New York: M. Kennerly, 1914.

McBurney, J. H., and K. G. Hance. *The Principles and Methods of Discussion*. New York: Harpers, 1939.

Morone, J. *The Democratic Wish*. New Haven, CT: Yale UP, 1998.

Sheffield, A. *Joining in Public Discussion: A Study of Effective Speechmaking for Members of Labor Unions, Conferences, Forums and Other Discussion Groups*. New York: George H. Doran, 1922.

Wells, H. N. "Coaching Debates: Purpose and Method." *Quarterly Journal of Speech* 4 (1918): 170-83.

Westbrook, R. *John Dewey and American Democracy*. Ithaca, NY: Cornell UP, 1991.

27

Homepages, Blogs, and the Chronotopic Dimensions of Personal Civic (Dis-)Engagement

John B. Killoran
University of Colorado–Denver

Optimistic predictions spawned during the Web's euphoric 1990s boom that ordinary citizens would now have a virtual printing press for personal civic engagement have been tempered recently by a growing recognition of the disjunction between the Web's technical potentials and its rhetorical actualities. Although the technical potentials may offer unprecedented democratic engagement by ordinary citizen publishers, the rhetorical actualities of civic engagement do not emerge from a discursive vacuum but rather from a legacy of discursive action propagated through genres. In looking to the Web for civic engagement by citizen publishers, it would thus behoove us to look at the emerging Web genres available for adoption by ordinary citizens.

This chapter contrasts the two primary genres that have been popularized for personal Web publishing: the personal homepage and the Weblog. I illustrate how the personal homepage has not developed a reputation for civic engagement, whereas the Weblog thrives on such a reputation. I explain this divergence by drawing on Bakhtin's concept of the chronotope to point out how the different chronotopes underlying these two genres support different discursive actions.

GENRES AND CHRONOTOPES

In her seminal article "Genre as Social Action," Carolyn Miller observes that social action, such as the action of civic engagement, is rooted not just in the private motivations of individuals, such as singular Web publishers, but in "the typical joint rhetorical actions available at any given point in history and culture" (158) through the discursive model of genres. To determine the kinds of social action enabled at this point in the Web's history and culture by different Web genres, one key variable to examine is what Bakhtin characterizes as a genre's *chronotope*, its "time-space" background. The chronotopic background "provides the ground essential for the showing-forth, the representability of events" (250) in the foreground. Certain chronotopic backgrounds will show forth certain kinds of discursive events. As genre researcher Catherine Schryer explains, "[E]very genre expresses space/time relations that reflect current social beliefs regarding the placement of human individuals in space and time and the kind of action permitted within that time/space" (83). The potential for social action and, more specifically, civic engagement by individuals in their unprecedented placement as producers in a worldwide medium may thereby be traced in Web genres' chronotopes. Next, we look in turn at two distinct genres of personal Web publishing—the personal homepage and the Weblog—to examine how their different chronotopes have positioned them as, respectively, potential inhibitors of and potential facilitators of civic engagement.

PERSONAL HOMEPAGE GENRE

The personal homepage was the first of the two genres to emerge and seemed to hit its peak of fashionability in the mid-1990s. Although the idiosyncracy of individual personal homepages frustrates our apprehension of any single generic homepage archetype, a sense of genre is nevertheless commonly perceived in the homepage's public relations function (Killoran), in which the author is exhibited either directly through his or her background and personal experiences, family and genealogy, education and career, or indirectly through his or her personal and professional interests and creative achievements.

Because everyone has some such material, everyone could, in principle, become a personal homepage publisher—seemingly a boon for the Web's potential for participatory democracy. The scale of the undertaking, however, may discourage potential publishers. In a 1997 survey of over one hundred personal homepage publishers, I found that most envisioned their homepage to be an ongoing project, with several explaining that their homepage development was a labor-intensive product of their own personal development. As such a finding suggests, the long-term horizon of the project would prompt representations that are projected to be equally long term, such that the previous season's work would still be relevant in the current season and the next season and would thereby not have to be scrapped. The personal homepage, even with the familiar "under construction" notice, typically aspires to permanence.

Many also explained that their homepage development was a product of their access to viable content, content perceived to be worthy of being maintained in the public eye over the long term without the risk of social embarrassment or disapproval; such content turns out to be a surprisingly scarce resource. Such scarcity is exacerbated by the need to package content into discrete "spaces" ample enough to be worth linking to, at least ample enough to fill out a computer screen. Apart from content copied from other published sources, not always with regard to copyright, such content typically drew selectively from personal information and experience, because such sources offered content that my survey respondents said they already had or knew well enough to create from scratch and, moreover, because such content may enable their site to occupy a unique niche on the Web. For instance, common in my sample of personal homepages were quasi-official representations of participants' family, genealogy, career, and so forth, as well as socially safe information about innocuous hobbies and displays of personal creativity. Tellingly, almost all sites in my sample had a title rooted in the name of the site publisher.

Such an assemblage of personal information and experience posits a chronotope that can support a site's network of discrete virtual spaces accompanied by interconnecting navigation. The resulting site architecture may be elaborate enough to orient the site toward equilibrium, relatively unresponsive to changes in current events that would in turn compel the labor of architectural redesign or navigational rewiring. Instead, and in conjunction with the long-term horizon of the genre, the personal homepage chronotope more readily sustains information and experience marked not by their mutability but by their durability, and hence may set the personal homepage to a conservative orientation.

The personal homepage's conservative orientation raises the possibility that the genre may lack viability with its fast-changing, outward-looking, new media environment. Tim Berners-Lee, the inventor of the Web, has observed how the personal homepage has evolved in a way that was unanticipated in his earlier vision of the Web's potential for personal and family domains: "[T]he personal home page is [...] not really home. They may call it a home page, but it's more like the gnome in somebody's front yard than the home itself" ("Tim Berners-Lee"). Tim Berners-Lee's vision of the gnome suggests a homepage posture that is relatively immobile and unresponsive, perhaps a consequence of hitherto private citizens envisioning their long-term public posture on a worldwide stage and responding with a bit of stage fright. As such, the stance taken on the personal homepage may be more defensive and less engaged than the corresponding stances taken within the home itself or within the local community. The gnome genre models the act of publishing on the Web as one of safe public relations, not of dynamic civic engagement.

WEBLOG GENRE

The second popular genre of personal Web publishing is the Weblog, also known within the Web's counter-culture as a *blog*. A blog typically consists of a series of brief text-only postings or annotated links to other Web sites, organized in reverse chronological order.

Whereas personal homepages emerged and gained popularity in the mid-1990s, blogs only emerged in the late 1990s. Rebecca Blood, doyenne of the blog community and author and editor of two books about blogs, points out that, as of early 1999, the then-nascent bloggers community was composed of only 23 known bloggers. Later that year, the genre had gained enough of a profile that *Chicago Tribune* journalist Julia Keller could characterize the growing community of bloggers as "relentlessly verbal, fiendishly well-read, usually subversive folks who relish tying together the shoelaces of the stiffly homogenized corporate world

[…]." Three years later, in 2002, blogs were estimated to number over half a million (Eakin) and their collective "intellectual cyberspace" had received its own fashionable designation: *blogosphere*, derived in part from the root *logos* (Quick).

The genre's booming popularity has been bolstered by the facilitative role of technologies such as Blogger, which offer interfaces that automate the formatting and posting of blog updates. Technology journalist Neil McIntosh credits Blogger for rescuing personal Web publishing from the decay of the personal homepage, a genre that offers "little more than a CV and pet pictures," and is now recognized only for its "dormancy" ("A Tale"):

> A few years ago, home pages were almost universally dull, because creating them was a fiddle that made it just too tempting to post and forget. Most became sleepy relics. Then came Blogger and, suddenly, it was easy to create a dynamic, constantly changing website. The creative talents of people who otherwise couldn't be bothered with web authoring were set loose. (McIntosh et al. "The Seven Wonders")

In contrast with that fading novelty of personal homepages, the thriving phenomenon of blogging regularly receives coverage in such prominent mainstream media as the *New York Times*.

Blogs constitute what *Salon* columnist Scott Rosenberg describes as "a new and fertile niche in the Web's information ecology." In contrast with the longer, static set pieces typical of many Web sites, this niche favors a guerillalike approach to Web publishing marked by brief but frequent postings, and in contrast with the appearance of objectivity aspired to by much Web data and information, this niche brandishes authors' own openly subjective perspectives. "Blogs express opinion," writes Judith Shulevitz in the *New York Times*. "They're one-person pundit shows, replete with the stridency and looniness usually edited off TV." She contrasts the genre favorably with other journalism genres: compared with traditional journalism, blogs evince "greater looseness of spirit; openness to more points of view; a more conversational tone; and a compulsive honesty […]." Technology journalist Henry Jenkins likewise contrasts the new genre with other, more familiar genres: "Blogs are […] more dynamic than older-style home pages, more permanent than posts to a Net discussion list. They are more private and personal than traditional journalism, more public than diaries."

Recognition of such distinction from other genres, and in particular from more established, settled Web *sites* or *homepages*, accrues in part from the distinctiveness of the designation *Weblogs* and its hipper truncated form *blogs*. Credit for the usage *Weblog* apparently goes to Jorn Barger, a blogger who introduced the term in late 1997 with his "Robot Wisdom Weblog" (Barger). Weblogs, a designation akin to such computer usages as *server logs, http logs, usage logs,* and *log files* (Barger) and also reminiscent of such precomputer genres as ships' logs, originally took root in the nomadic, wanderlust behavior of surfing. The genesis of the discourse emerging out of such activity is unclear, having been traced to the practice of e-mailing family and friends about interesting Web sites (Outing) or to the 1994 emergence of online diarists (Tweney). Such discourses tend to be as frequent and short as the variable activities they represent, and likewise the typical blog entry is often only a fleeting comment and link to a just-read article on another Web site.

Such discursive behavior illustrates how the genre is based on a chronotope that values immediacy, with a time horizon typically no more enduring than that of a daily newspaper. Like newspaper stories, to which they are often hyperlinked, blog entries are normally dated and thereby highlight both their currency with the day's events and also their much shorter shelf life. Unlike the permanence projected by the personal homepage, which preserves the past in the form of old photos, genealogical trees, and résumés, the past in a blog, exemplified by older postings that get pushed down the page with each new update and that eventually get archived, quickly fades from view and from relevance; the top screen of a blog orients readers to its most recent posting, its freshness. Moreover, blogs are rarely overtly "under construction," a metaphor that betrays how personal homepages may be conceived to be completed, a state beyond which they become static. Whereas a blog, like a homepage, may be abandoned, a blog cannot by definition be completed as, in its dynamic constitution, it always projects new postings into the future. Unlike the elaborate architectures and page displays of Web *sites* or Web *homes*, which, as their designations metaphorically suggest, invoke virtual spaces fortified with the Web's visual and multimodal decor, blogs favor plainer but quicker text-only contributions laid out in a one-dimensional linear sequence. Hence, in contrast with the conservative orientation of the personal homepage chronotope, the blog chronotope, endlessly resituating the blog ahead to the next development, may set the genre to a radical orientation.

Blogs, because of their means of production and their collaborative ethos, provide ordinary citizens with a viable model of civic engagement. First, because of their means of production, blogs are better able to sustain the swift, responsive free speech that ordinary citizens can best offer to public discourse. Unlike personal homepages, which favor stable displays of information, blog entries (especially in the genre's original incarnation) are frequently based on a timely link to another Web site, often a news item, annotated with a brief comment or opinion, none of which are scarce commodities. Again, unlike personal homepages, which draw on the Web's multimedia resources, blogs' generic kinship with such short, verbal genres as e-mail postings and conversational turns better adapts them to the longer-established and more prolific literacies of their authors. Blogs emerge from their authors' daily engagement with news and events, a source that accommodates the genre to people's daily work schedules and that thereby offers people a viable way to participate discursively in the daily events and issues of their society.

Second, because of their collaborative ethos, blogs are a genre better suited than personal homepages to encourage participation in a collective effort. Unlike personal homepages, which tend to be a product of a solo effort oriented toward a solo public relations function, and unlike corporate journalistic discourses, which are civic-oriented but collaborative only within house, blogs tend to be read zealously by other bloggers and interlinked with related blogs, thereby promoting responsive models of social relations that nurture publishers' and readers' personal commitment to each other. Technology journalist John Ellis explains that by maintaining such a network of contacts, bloggers can draw on the labor of others for new, publishable items. He thereby makes a distinction between blogs and mainstream media by the different attitudes and assumptions creators hold toward their readers: unlike mainstream journalists, "bloggers assume that their readers are as smart as they are, if not smarter." Indeed, some blogs thrive on e-mailed submissions from devoted readers, such as the long-running memepool blog (www.memepool.com).

Such a fast-growing discursive practice illustrates how social action can be enabled by the leadership of a genre, which models, for a new class of media producers, how to "mediat[e] private intentions and [the] social exigence" of their new civic forum by "connecting the private with the public" (Miller 163). In a forum that otherwise shares many similarities with the impersonal mass media, blogs, more so than personal homepages, create visibility for individuals' distinctive Web role alongside the Web presences of the traditional, mainstream media. Rebecca Blood sees in the genre "the power [...] to transform both writers and readers from 'audience' to 'public' and from 'consumer' to 'creator,'" thereby offering agency to a media class hitherto cast as passive.

CONCLUSION

In conclusion, we have observed that, although individuals have published on the Web on their own behalf since its inception over a decade ago, the private intentions of singular individuals alone cannot explain the past trends and future promise of personal Web-mediated civic engagement. It is not just a new medium per se that encourages our meaningful participation, but rather the model of a meaningful way, a discursive way, to participate in that medium.

Over the past decade, two different genres of personal Web publishing have experienced different histories and offer different promise for popular participation. These genres posit different chronotopes, which in turn sustain different discursive actions. The orientation of the personal homepage chronotope, because of its long-term temporal support of publishers' public relations and its elaborate virtual architecture, is the more conservative, whereas the orientation of the blog chronotope, because of its responsiveness to current events and its simple, forward-looking spatial configuration, is the more radical. In the new media environment favoring currency and enabling easy contact among citizen publishers, it is, of these two genres, the blog that may better sustain a more distinctive, more socially responsive means of civic engagement.

WORKS CITED

Bakhtin, Mikhail M. "Forms of Time and of the Chronotope in the Novel." *The Dialogic Imagination*. Ed. Michael Holquist. Trans. Caryl Emerson and Michael Holquist. Austin: U of Texas P, 1981. 84-258.

Barger, Jorn. *Weblog Resources FAQ* Sept. 2000. 30 April 2002 <http://www.robotwisdom.com/weblogs/>.

Blood, Rebecca. *Weblogs: A History and Perspective*. 7 Sept. 2000. 27 August 2001 <http://www.rebeccablood.net/essays/weblog_history.html>.

Eakin, Emily, "The Ancient Art of Haranguing Has Moved to the Internet." *The New York Times* 10 Aug. 2002. 10 Aug. 2002 <http://www.nytimes.com/2002/08/10/arts/10TANK.html?ex=1030006279&ei=1&en=c86db33994e4c358>.

Ellis, John. "All the News That's Fit to Blog." *Fast Company* 57 (April 2002): 112. 29 Apr. 2002 <http://www.fastcompany.com/online/57/jellis.html>.

Jenkins, Henry. "Blog This: Online Diarists Rule an Internet Strewn with Failed Dot Coms." *Technology Review* March 2002. 14 May 2002 <http://www.technologyreview.com/articles/jenkins0302.asp>.

Keller, Julia. "She Has Seen the Future and It Is—Weblogs." *Chicago Tribune* 7 Sept. 1999. 18 Feb. 2001 <http://chicagotribune.com/leisure/tempo/printedition/article/0,2669,SAV_9909070005,FF.html>.

Killoran, John B. "Under Construction: A 'PR' Department for Private Citizens." *Business Communication Quarterly* 62.2 (June 1999): 101-04.

McIntosh, Neil. "A Tale of One Man and his Blog." *The Guardian* 31 Jan. 2002. 26 Apr. 2002 <http://www.guardian.co.uk/online/story/0,3605,641742,00.html>.

---, et al. "The Seven Wonders of the Web." *Guardian Unlimited* 27 Dec. 2001. 26 Apr. 2002 <http://www.guardian.co.uk/Archive/Article/0,4273,4326023,00.html>.

Miller, Carolyn R. "Genre as Social Action." *Quarterly Journal of Speech* 70 (1984): 151-67.

Outing, Steve. "Weblogs: From Underground to Mainstream." *Editor and Publisher Online*. 8 Mar. 2000. 18 Feb. 2001 <http://www.mediainfo.com/ephome/news/newshtm/stop/st030800.htm>.

Quick, William. *Daily Pundit*. Blog posting. 1 Jan. 2002. 9 May 2002 <http://www.iw3p.com/DailyPundit/2001_12_30_dailypundit_archive.html#8315120>.

Rosenberg, Scott. "Fear of Links." *Salon* 28 May 1999. 18 Feb. 2001 <http://www.salon.com/tech/col/rose/1999/05/28/weblogs/index.html>.

Schryer, Catherine F. "Genre Time/Space: Chronotopic Strategies in the Experimental Article." *Journal of Advanced Composition* 19.1 (1999): 81-89.

Shulevitz, Judith. "At Large in the Blogosphere." *The New York Times* 5 May 2002. 5 May 2002 <http://www.nytimes.com/2002/05/05/books/review/05SHULEVT.html?ex=1021657365&ei=1&en=db334b94404e97c8>.

"Tim Berners-Lee: On Simplicity, Standards, and 'Intercreativity.'" *World Wide Web Journal* 1.3 (Summer 1996). 14 Aug. 1997 <http://www.w3j.com/3/s1.interview.html>.

Tweney, Dylan. "Weblogs Make the Web Work for You." *Business 2.0* 14 Feb. 2002. 26 Apr. 2002 <http://www.business2.com/articles/web/0,1653,37974,FF.html>.

28

Civic Education and Republican Judgment: The Stem Cell Research Discourse of George W. Bush

Stephen A. Klien
Augustana College

President George W. Bush's televised address of August 9, 2001, on the subject of federal funding for embryonic stem cell research, was anticipated by many observers as "a defining moment for his presidency, as political allies and foes sized up his ability to grasp a complex medical issue and balance the competing demands of science and politics on an emotional issue that has split his own party. He knew that whatever he did, he would infuriate many Americans" (Keen). The response of the Bush White House demonstrated not only a sensitivity to the ethical complexities of the policy decision, but also a need to educate the American public on the relevant information, issues, and competing positions in a clear, accessible, and fair manner. Bush and his representatives enacted, in short, a public character of civic education. This chapter examines the ways in which the performances of Bush and his official representatives appropriated the rhetorical style and normative ideals of civic republican education.

"REPUBLICANISM" AS A PERFORMATIVE TRADITION IN AMERICAN POLITICAL RHETORIC

Scholars of political rhetoric have identified "civic republicanism" as a recurrent performative tradition that enacts the ideals of deliberative democracy via prudential judgment. A key element of civic republicanism is the constitution of an active, informed, interested, and community-oriented public via the public rhetor's performance of an ideal "interpretive framework" for political judgments (Murphy 316).

Murphy identifies three primary elements that define republicanism in the American tradition: first, an emphasis on the "public good" as the paramount goal; second, the performance of "virtuous power," typified by a demonstration of prudent judgment; and third, a reinforcement of governing institutions as "political architecture," establishing an appropriate distance between the leader's judgment on the one hand, and the political pressures of interested parties on the other (Murphy 314-16). However, the public exercise of republican judgment has the potential to run counter to popular expectations for leadership: "The language that embodies such a perspective—complex, careful, and dispassionate—can easily be taken [...] as indecisive and condescending. The conceptual, moral, and linguistic clarity that have come to be taken as hallmarks of presidential leadership [...] are seldom available to a republican rhetor (326-27). One important question, then: How can a political leader appropriate the republican tradition while still maintaining the persona of a strong, decisive leader?

A relatively small body of work in criticism of American political rhetoric discusses the public character of political actors as "teachers" or "educators," an ethos providing a potential answer to the republican/leader paradox. Antczak describes "democratic education" as a process by which public rhetors promote the development of public character in the citizenry with a distinctive set of ethical norms and principles. He argues that democratic education is possible only if the teacher holds a paradoxical, simultaneous position of authority sufficient to command the attention and compliance of the audience (6-7) and a position of egalitarian social representation. Nineteenth-century "democratic educators" used identification strategies to solve this problem: "Americans identified with, granted authority to those like them; in the full capabilities and virtues his discipline gave him, an Emerson or Twain or James *could be representative of them—like them, only more so*" (Antczak 200-01, emphasis added).

Thus, the republican teacher constructs a position of ethical authority that stems not from the exercise of political power per se but from the ability to identify with and instruct the audience in such a way that he becomes an example to attend to and emulate. The somewhat unusual performance of the Bush White House in early August 2001 suggests that we examine political performances of republicanism from this neglected angle: To what extent can public rhetors not only embody republican virtue, but also actively educate public audiences on the complexities of policy issues that require deliberation, judgment, and action?

ANALYSIS OF THE BUSH WHITE HOUSE'S "STEM CELL DECISION"

The Bush White House's stem cell decision discourse between August 9 and August 11, 2001, used three significant strategies, roughly paralleling the three elements of republican performance delineated by Murphy, but involving rhetorical strategies that may have avoided (for many observers, anyway) the appearance of weak leadership style to which Adlai Stevenson fell victim in 1952.

Republican Morality: Placing the Public Good First

In his addresses, President Bush consistently applied a utilitarian "greatest good for the greatest many" reasoning. On the one hand, Bush used such reasoning to defend the use of federal funds in order to advance "the greatest public good" ("Remarks by the President"). On the other hand, Bush also deployed utilitarian reasoning to express the need for ethical caution in pursuing research: "As I thought through this issue, I kept returning to two fundamental questions: First, are these frozen embryos human life, and therefore, something precious to be protected? And second, if they're going to be destroyed anyway, shouldn't they be used for a greater good, for research that has the potential to save and improve other lives?" ("Remarks by the President"). This strategy enabled Bush to maneuver among factions opposed on the issue by linking two warrants presumably shared by them: that life should be protected, and that the most good for the greatest number is a morally sound premise for policy.

The Bush White House made a concerted effort to feature the commonweal as the president's first priority. Such was declared by senior adviser Karen Hughes after the televised address: "[The President] said this is not a political decision, that this is a public policy decision, this is an ethical decision. [... T]hroughout this process he wanted to come to a decision that he personally felt comfortable with, based on his recognition of the important public policy ramifications and on his own core convictions and his own moral compass" ("Karen Hughes Press Conference"). This point not only established the public good as Bush's primary goal, but also underscored Bush's exercise of virtuous republican power by relying on deliberate, balanced judgment of the available issues and arguments.

Republican Virtue: Exercising Power via Prudent Deliberation

A constant theme throughout the decision discourse of the Bush White House was the manner in which the President weighed the opinions of a diverse body of opposing opinions from credible sources before making an intellectually and morally defensible decision. Press Secretary Scott McClellan described the President's approach to the issue as "deliberate and thoughtful," with the decision made having "carefully considered all the scientific and ethical issues involved." McClellan and Hughes also placed special, repeated emphasis on the "complexity" of the problem: "[T]his is an issue that [...] many Americans find the more they learn about it, the more complex it is" (McClellan). Bush emphasized the same points, injecting a word on his own process of exploration: "I've asked those questions and others of scientists, scholars, bioethicists, religious leaders, doctors, researchers, members of Congress, my Cabinet, and my friends. I have read heartfelt letters from many Americans. I have given this issue a great deal of thought, prayer and considerable reflection. And I have found widespread disagreement" ("Remarks by the President"). This comment introduced a central theme of Bush's televised remarks: that he found disagreement and contrary positions taken within as well as between those who emphasize "scientific" and "moral" perspectives. This move, which problematizes the common tendency at the time to simplify the issue into a "science versus religious morality" binary, enabled the President to avoid charges of simplifying the issue and choosing one set of decision criteria at the expense of the other.

In order to develop this position, both of the presidential addresses and a *Fact Sheet* published on the White House's official Web Site lay out not only the specific planks of the Bush policy on research funding, but also a brief, accessible explanation of relevant medical and ethical background information for the American audience. Bush defines and describes embryonic stem cells and where they come from, contrasts them against adult stem cells, emphasizes the potential for cures available by researching both types, explains the difference between using existing stem cell lines for research (which his policy will fund) and creating new embryos for research purposes (which his policy will not fund), and compares and contrasts stem cell research with that of human cloning (which he vehemently opposes). With accessible language, Bush provides a brief yet clear and easily understood summary of an admittedly complex area of medical research and bioethics ("Remarks by the President").

To address the key point of stasis—how does one negotiate the need for medical research with the need for protecting the sanctity of all forms of life—Bush positioned himself as one who must judge the case based on core beliefs he shares with the American people:

> My position on these issues is shaped by deeply held beliefs. I'm a strong supporter of science and technology, and believe they have the potential for incredible good—to improve lives, to save life, to conquer disease. [...] I also believe human life is a sacred gift from our Creator. I worry about a culture that devalues life, and believe as your President I have an important obligation to foster and encourage respect for life in America and throughout the world. ("Remarks by the President")

Note that Bush's articulation of virtuous judgment is not that of a disinterested, dispassionate judge of arguments. Rather, by continually using such language as "I have great hope" and "I worry" ("Remarks by the President"), Bush discloses his own feelings as well as his thought process, establishing a more intimate relationship with the American audience. He closed both his televised and radio remarks with a final moment of identification closing the distance between himself and the American people: "As we go forward, I hope we will always be guided by both intellect and heart, by both our capabilities and our conscience. I have made this decision with great care, and I pray it is the right one" ("Remarks by the President," "Radio Address").

Redefining the Relationship between Political Institutions and the People

The Bush White House took a novel approach to establishing the "political architecture" surrounding the decision by presenting it with personal—even homey—intimacy, rather than by increasing the distance between institutions and the public. At least two significant strategies were used to this end.

First, McClellan and Hughes provided what many noted was an unusual move for Bush and his White House. McClellan referred to the Hughes postaddress briefing as a "tick-tocking," an exhaustive account of the President's meetings with advisers and advocates to describe "how the President reached this decision." Hughes described a process consisting of both a battery of "formal meetings" with advocacy groups, scientists, and bioethicists, and a large number of less formal conversations at events ranging from conferences on the Patients' Bill of Rights to a "birthday get-together" for members of the White House medical unit (Hughes). Throughout this period, Bush engaged "almost everyone who works at the White House" ("Karen Hughes Press Conference"): "[N]ot only did he ask your opinion, but he also asked really probing questions [...]. He didn't stop at knowing what you thought about this issue; he wanted to know the moral underpinnings, the rationale, the reasons that you held that position" ("Karen Hughes Press Conference").

Hughes also described a timeline of discussions to give the impression that Bush had consulted a large number and variety of individuals and groups. Of these, according to Hughes, only two groups acted as "advocates": representatives of National Right to Life, and representatives of the Juvenile Diabetes Research Foundation ("Karen Hughes Press Conference"). These groups seem to represent the "two opposing sides" in the controversy, illustrating the balanced attention Bush gave to the issues. Everyone else, apparently, served as providers of insight and sounding boards to "guide the President" in his decision-making without advocating specific policy recommendations.

However, press accounts noted some omissions in the Hughes "tick-tocking." Among those individuals Bush did not consult were Jamie Thomson, the researcher who discovered stem cells in 1998, Senator William Frist, the only doctor in the U.S. Senate; and prominent Democratic senators. In addition, among the communications omitted in Hughes's account include several supportive exchanges between the White House and "pro-life" conservatives who oppose stem cell research (Kornblut). It is, finally, a curiosity that despite the significance of this briefing emphasized by McClellan on August 9, a transcript of the Hughes briefing has not been made available on the White House's official online archive of press releases and transcripts (at least as of the writing of this chapter) since the briefing was held.

Nevertheless, the "rare" (Kornblut) Hughes briefing provided insight into the policy deliberation process of the Bush White House that was previously unprecedented. This move opened up the President's decision-making process to public examination and scrutiny in a way that many simply did not expect.

A second strategy to make Bush's decision more intimate was the location of the decision discourse: Crawford, Texas, site of the Bush family ranch that has been dubbed "the Western White House." McClellan explained the decision thusly: "He will be sitting in a chair in front of a window that will show some of the landscape of the ranch [...]. This is a decision that [the American people are] discussing in the heartland, and the President believes that there is no more appropriate place to do this than at his ranch, where he is in the heartland" (McClellan).

Bush briefly alludes to this point at the start of his address:

> The issue of research involving stem cells derived from human embryos is increasingly the subject of a national debate *and dinner table discussions*. The issue is confronted every day in laboratories as scientists ponder the ethical ramifications of their work. *It is agonized over by parents and many couples as they try to have*

> *children, or to save children already born.* ("Remarks by the President," emphasis added)

The Bush White House, by visual setting and by use of the "dinner table discussion" metonym, established the political architecture of the stem cell decision as intimate, personal, and family oriented rather than distant, impersonal, and institutional.

In brief, the end result of these three strategies—the assertion of utilitarian public good, the demonstration of prudential judgment, and an atypically intimate political architecture for the decision—was an admittedly imperfect but surprisingly effective example of civic republican education on an important public policy controversy.

CONCLUSIONS: A TELEVISUAL REPUBLICANISM TO ENGAGE THE AMERICAN COMMUNITY?

Many have argued that the advent of televisual politics has resulted in a dumbing-down of public policy discourse. Scheuer maintains, for instance, that television inherently simplifies complex ideas into emotional, self-oriented, and conservative moral and political impulses, and therefore impedes truly democratic public consideration of complexity, ambiguity and connectedness in political and social issues (Scheuer 10-11).

The discourse of the Bush White House surrounding the stem cell decision suggests that televisual emphases on dramatic narrative, visual imagery, individual personality, and increased perceptions of intimacy between leaders and those whom they lead have the potential to refigure civic republican judgment in productive directions. Harris public opinion data released the Monday following the decision are perhaps informative on this point. Sixty percent of Americans approved of Bush's decision regarding stem cell research, up 10% from the previous Thursday. Moreover—and more importantly—78% of Americans deemed the issue important, up from 62% the previous week ("Poll: Public Responds to Bush Stem Cell Decision").

This case is by no means consistently promotive of citizen education; one need only look to the ambiguities surrounding the Hughes "tick-tock" briefing as evidence of democratic shortfall in this effort. Poll data also suggest that most Americans may not have taken the discourse at face value. Fifty-two percent of those polled believed that the decision was made "mostly because of political reasons," with only 36% believing it was based "mostly because of his deeply held beliefs" ("Poll: Public Responds to Bush Stem Cell Decision"). In any event, more critical work should be done to examine the ways in which public policy discourse in a televisual political age may effectively exercise its potential to engage the American political community.

WORKS CITED

Antczak, Frederick J. *Thought and Character: The Rhetoric of Democratic Education.* Ames: Iowa State UP, 1985.

Bush, George W. "Remarks by the President on Stem Cell Research." The White House Official Web Site 9 Aug. 2001 Transcript. 12 Sept. 2001 <http://www.whitehouse.gov/news/releases/2001/ 08/print/ 20010809-2.html>.

Bush, George W. "Radio Address by the President to the Nation." The White House Official Web Site 11 Aug. 2001. Transcript. 12 Sept. 2001 <http://www.whitehouse.gov/news/releases/ 2001/ 08/print/ 20010811-1.html>.

Fact Sheet: Embryonic Stem Cell Research. The White House Official Web Site 9 Aug. 2001. 12 Sept. 2001 <http://www.whitehouse.gov/news/releases/2001/08/print/ 20010809-1.html>.

"Karen Hughes Press Conference." *Online NewsHour Extra.* 14 Aug. 2001. Transcript. 12 Sept. 2001 <http://audio.pbs.org:8080/ramgen/newshour/expansion/2001/08/10/ hughes_qa.rm?altplay=hughes_qa.rm>.

Keen, Judy. "Reading, Reflection Brought Bush to Decision." *USA Today* 10 Aug. 2001, first edition: 4A. 20 May 2002 < http://web.lexis-nexis.com/ universe>.

Kornblut, Anne E. "Aides Say President Doggedly Sought Data." *Boston Globe* 11 Aug. 2001, third edition: A1. 20 May 2002 < http://web.lexis-nexis.com/ universe>.

McClellan, Scott. "Press Briefing by Scott McClellan." The White House Official Web Site 9 Aug. 2001. Transcript. 12 Sept. 2001 <http://www.whitehouse.gov/news/briefings/ print/ 20010809.html>.

Murphy, John M. "Civic Republicanism in the Modern Age: Adlai Stevenson in the 1952 Presidential Campaign." *Quarterly Journal of Speech* 80 (1994): 313-28.

"Poll: Public Responds to Bush Stem Cell Decision." *CNN.com AllPolitics* 13 Aug. 2001. 12 Sept. 2001 <http://www.cnn.com/2001/ALLPOLITICS/08/13/stem.cell.poll/>.

Scheuer, Jeffrey. *The Sound Bite Society: Television and the American Mind.* New York: Four Walls Eight Windows, 1999.

29

Panoramic Memories: Realism, Agency, and the Remembrance of Japanese American Internment

Brian Lain
University of North Texas

In his 1984 testimony about the World War II internment of Japanese Americans, John Tateishi, then National Redress Director of the Japanese American Citizens League, told the U.S. Senate:

> That injustice was visited upon the lives of individuals who believed in this country and its ideals and who have faith that the United States will live up to its promises [...]. We are talking about people like those you see in this room who went through the experience, and who suffered personal tragedies. We are talking about people like a woman I know, named Mary Tsukamota who has an extreme case of arthritis and is in pain every time she puts her hand up to her chest, but that woman stands there, extremely proud to be able to recite the pledge of allegiance, or to hear the national anthem, and every time she does either, her eyes fill with tears. We are talking about someone like a man named Tom Watanabe in Chicago who lost his twin daughters and wife at childbirth at Manzanar because of the lack of medical facilities, and, for forty years, all he wanted to do was find their graves because he was never told what happened to their bodies [...]. We are talking about individuals here, and not some vague group that can easily be forgotten. (10)

One could not make a more apt summary of the politics of remembering internment. Tateishi's brief statement, a single moment amid what eventually became eight years of debate and discussion in the U.S. Congress, signals the joining of historically produced politicized identities invested in what Wendy Brown calls its "wounded attachments" and the reliance on logics of difference, individuality, and temporality that Lawrence Grossberg sees as constitutive of contemporary identity politics. Tateishi's statement also marks the intersection of identity politics, national memory, and contemporary nationalism. Here, ethnic suffering buttresses the national imaginary by re-calling the citizenry to the obligations of the great promises of the American nation while at the same time displaying exceptional patriotism in the face of remembered exile and racism.[1]

Finally, this statement displays an often-overlooked feature of contemporary identity politics: its reliance on a logic of realism. The presence or absence, recognition or misrecognition of "real" identities ground the politics of remembering internment, as well as most contemporary race politics. Tateishi's remarks illustrate rhetorical democracy's reliance on a logic of identity that views individuals as unchanging and values a natural connotation between the character of injured groups and rhetoric about them. Political power is accrued because of singularity, stability, continuity, homogeneity, and authenticity. Jinqi Ling has noted that Asian American literature succeeds or fails according to its ability to pass through a series of "authentication strategies" that serve as technologies of realism, popularly accepted modes of corresponding to "reality" (148-52). Tateishi's statement would have little force were we not to imagine the very real presence of people like Mary Tsukamota and Tom Watanabe.

It would be nice to imagine that the politics of remembering internment were limited to one debate in a government setting concerning only one group of citizens. That, however, is not the case. Tateishi's statement is but one instance of individual political participation based on Japanese American identity. Not only is the figure of the Japanese American as an injured identity everywhere in American culture—circulating through local museums, the Smithsonian, a new monument on the National Mall, the *New York Times* bestseller list, and in recently formed departments of Asian and American Studies in universities across the country—but also it is marking quite complex changes in the functioning of American nationalism. Whereas once the presentations of the "model minority" were used to limit the possibilities of Asian American citizenship and discipline other minority workers,[2] contemporary uses of Japanese American subjectivity utilize both ethnic and national identifications to produce the new technologies of "multicultural citizenship."[3]

Although there has certainly been some degree of payoff, literally when speaking of reparations, Japanese American politics have also been assimilated into different forms of realist nationalism. Internment remembrance, as with many identity politics, has "run out of steam" and "become a style" because rather than opening up political opportunities, people are "spoken by it" (Bailey and Hall 15). What, then, are the possibilities of locating agency if we are no longer talking about rhetorical agency as a "robust force located in the subject" (Butler 30)? Is there any possibility for a politics of remembering internment that does not rely on these logics that are easily assimilated into American nationalism? What would the politics of remembering internment look like if, instead of conceiving of civic engagement as individual participation in political practices, scholars attended the relationships established between the cultural object and the historical codes of reading those objects as rhetorically engaging the citizenry? To examine one possibility for a politics of remembering internment that does not rely on the logic of identity, and to make a case for the civic engagement of the object, I turn to Masumi Hayashi's panoramic photo collages "American Concentration Camps" to argue that they offer a perspective by incongruity that can provoke questions about realism and the process of recognizing the figure of the Japanese American.

Masumi Hayashi, professor of Art and Photography at Cleveland State University, has constructed an unusual presentation of internment memories. Her collection "American Concentration Camps" is a series of images presenting the landscapes, ruined buildings, and monuments left at the ten former internment camp sites.[4] The images in "American Concentration Camps" are all panoramic photo-collages. Over one hundred separate photographs taken by a 55-mm camera are pasted together on a large piece of foamboard. Steven Litt describes the process by noting:

> She picks a site, plants her tripod and Nikon FM camera, and then takes a series of shots scanning horizontally in every direction, moving her 55 millimeter lens roughly 22 degrees each time. The process takes about an hour. After having color prints processed by a professional lab, Hayashi returns to the studio and has assistants assemble the snapshot-sized photographs in a grid matrix. The images are then drymounted on 4-by-8-foot sheets of foamcore. (3I)

The result is an image reminiscent of David Hockney's photo-collages except that Hayashi's images are panoramic and, unlike Hockney's collages that fabricate a single perspective with pictures from different locations, Hayashi's display distortion from a single point in space.[5]

Hayashi's panoramic photo-collages mark the intersection of three systems of sense-making in a single form: The images display a panoramic view, photographs construct that view, and the whole image is arranged as a collage. Whereas the panorama, the photograph, and the collage, as individual forms of visualization, all subscribe to specific, historical codes of connotation, Hayashi's panoramic photo collages produce an intersection that place these very different economies of discourse into conversation with one another. That intersection visually displays a tension between connoting reality and presenting a different version of the world.

Taking the collection as a perspective, one on memory and internment, opens up new possibilities for civic engagement. More than simply questioning whether the collages themselves are realistic presentations of the internment camp sites (e.g., are they accurate or complete) the juxtaposition of photography with cubist and panoramic practices offers a different perspective on practices of remembrance. Questions about the world the images create thus become paramount. Kenneth Burke calls the view generated by merging categories once felt to be mutually exclusive, within a general economy of statements, a perspective by incongruity (69). Burke's historic, linguistic examples demonstrate the combination of: Spengler's "decadent athleticism" and Veblen's "trained incapacity" (90-91). It is "violating the proprieties of the word in its previous linkages" that creates the incongruous perspective (91). In each case, the juxtaposition of two seemingly incompatible terms creates new meanings that break the previous frame or reference. The perspective itself allows new practices that problematize the trained incapacities of convention.

As a concept metaphor for rethinking national memory, Hayashi's images trouble the narrative that requires assimilating Japanese American internment remembrances on two levels. First, Hayashi's panoramic photo collages offer a visual perspective by incongruity that unsettles the realist logic of identity politics.

Second, the collages disrupt the logic of recognition based on the internee as a stable, homogenous identity.

Hayashi's images provoke questions over the connotation between photography and reality. These collages are assemblage panoramas: Assembling a series of frames into a whole constructs the image. However, unlike other assemblages, Hayashi's images do not attempt to create a seamless depiction of the real world. The lines and edges where snapshots meet are accentuated, not smoothed over or erased. In *Manzanar Monument*, for example, the circular foundation of the monument is rendered as a series of jagged triangles, calling attention to the place where one photo ends and another begins. In *Heart Mountain Hospital*, a furnace tower ascends toward the sky with a single base, yet its top is split into two as slightly different perspectives of the tower record the light at different angles.

Another feature that departs from traditional photographic techniques is the presentation of different temporalities in the same image. The collages are composed of at least three horizontal rows of frames. These horizontal rows are often the combination of several separate "passes" of the camera. Thus, images beside one another are often taken at different times. This temporal quality is preserved in the collage as photographs displaying different color shades, different shadows, or, in some cases, different clouds or suns, are joined together in one collage. *Manzanar Guard Gate* contains two suns, one on each side of the image, and the center of the image displays a different set of shadows from the top and bottom portion.

The jagged edges and the different temporalities in the images accentuate the seams or fissures that lie between the individual snapshots. In this sense, the images retain a collage effect. Collages, Shapiro argues, denaturalize the photograph because they present seams in what is supposedly a seamless medium. Photography normally functions by supposing the seamlessness of reality (Krauss 28). The photo collage is "disruptive, intervening in the process through which the viewer's interpretive codes accord a representational quality to photographs" (Shapiro 146). Rather than efface the techniques of production, Hayashi's collages call attention to their own constructedness.

Hayashi's images also make use of the panoramic form. They attempt to allow the viewer to "see all" by providing a view that is wider than the eye can regularly observe. Each image "unwraps" the natural world in order to render features in front of, to each side, and even behind the point of perspective onto a flat two-dimensional surface that can be observed at once. Hayashi's panoramas, however, overwhelm the viewer due to the extensive visual distortion. These collages are not just panoramic; they are hyper-panoramic. In many images, towers, doorways, even trees are placed within the frame twice making the perspective more than 360 degrees. *Manzanar Guard Gate* presents two gates framing an entrance. That framed entryway, however, is a construct of the image. Repeating pictures of a single guardhouse creates the collage's gateway. There is no such entryway at Manzanar. In *Tule Lake Stockade*, the collage is centered at an intersection of three hallways. Yet, the reproduction of the hallways on each side produces five hallways intersecting in the point of view of the image. This distortion removes the possibility of a single viewpoint within the image. The viewer gets lost because there is no way to make the image conform to what is accepted as the real world.

The variations in Hayashi's camera angle from a position parallel to the object's plane, tilted down, tilted up, or placed very close to the landscape produce distortions altering the size of parts of the same object or altering relationships between objects. The "cigar effect" distortion, the "end of the earth" distortion, and the "bowl effect" distortion are all present in Hayashi's work (see Meehan 63-72). In collages such as *Heart Mountain Blue Room*, the room itself appears warped due to the merging of multiple frames from different angles. Some art critics have noted that this hyperpanoramic view even distorts personal memory of firsthand observation making "familiar places seem very strange" (Litt).

The panoramic photo collages also disrupt the logic of recognition. In contrast to traditional photographic remembrances of internment that feature internees in camp settings, there is no Japanese American subject within Hayashi's frame.[6] Instead, the internee frames the landscape. As Homi Bhabha says, "There is no native informant here." Rather than give in to dominant constructions of internees as either resistant or oppressed, the emphasis on the "disjunctive present of the utterance" allows a view of subaltern agency based on "relocation and reinscription" (63). The ruins of internment are presented instead. In the same way that the images call attention to their own constructedness, as practices of remembrance, they also call attention to the reconstructedness of all memory. Hayashi offers a personal, experiential perspective of the way she sees the camps. Instead of focusing on the moments in time caught by documentary photography, she presents the leftover spaces from internment, the remainder. The lasting trace of internment, however, is made visible. Despite their absence from the frame, internees are somehow present in this once inhabited landscape, haunting the ruins to remind the viewer of their history.

The many distortions of the collages contribute to the disruption of recognition. Without a stable position from which to view the collage, the landscape itself becomes unrecognizable. *Gila River Monument*, for example, prevents the viewer from finding any reference points within the frame whatsoever. Shadows crisscross. Straight lines bend. Circles flatten. The multiple temporalities even prevent the viewer from establishing the "time" that they are to view the scene. In short, the location itself, as a space of American history, becomes foreign to the eye.

Rather than present a perspective based on the reality of a stable identity, the "perspective" Hayashi's images perform is the impossibility of any stable perspective. Viewers are only centered insofar as they must lose the perspective of their own subjectivity in order to find a location from which to make sense of the images. That location, however, is denied and the result is the presentation of the danger of multiculturalism: the loss of stable identity. The collages perform the limit of the dominant mode of sense making in identity politics.

When commenting on the New Times politics, Stuart Hall asserted that if ethnicity is to have any political force, it must be conceived of as a place, not as a delimitable identity. He notes:

> By "ethnicity" we mean the astonishing return to the political agenda of all those points of attachment which give the individual some sense of 'place' and position in the world, whether these be in relation to particular communities, localities, territories, languages, religions, or cultures [...]. The question of ethnicity reminds us that everybody comes from some place—even if it is only an "imagined community"—and needs some sense of identification and belonging. (236-37)

Hayashi's panoramic photo collages construct Japanese American, not as a stable subjectivity, but as the name for a place. Within the frame of Hayashi's collages, Japanese American becomes a position founded on the multiperspectival nature of memory. In contrast to individual practices of civic engagement based on identity, such as John Tateishi's, "American Concentration Camps" visualizes a politics in which the object is engaging individuals. Hayashi's images provoke questions about realism, remembrance, and visualization by disrupting the processes of connotation and recognition on which American multiculturalism relies.

Viewing Hayashi's photo collages as generating a perspective by incongruity poses the possibility of new practices of remembrance not limited to recognition politics. In other words, to deal with a question raised by Jinqi Ling, Hayashi's images take *advantage of* the contradictions and contingencies of remembering to insist on their own politics, while avoiding nationalized identities.

NOTES

1. The politics of remembering internment also supplied a number of examples of heroic patriotism. The many performances of World War II Japanese American veterans provided multiple acquiescent, patriotic subjects that displayed loyalty in the face of injustice. For a discussion of the importance of this performance to Japanese American cultural politics, see Brian Lain, "Performing Japanese American Citizenship: The Case of Congressional Reparations Hearings."
2. Although there are many investigations of the circulation of model minority discourses, for an excellent discussion of the deployment of the model minority myth to discipline Asians, Hispanics, and Black workers, see David Palumbo-Liu, especially "Part III: Modeling the Nation" (149-215).
3. I take the term *multicultural citizenship* from Will Kymlicka's investigations on the political possibilities for democracy based on minority group rights. For a brief summary of the use of the figure of the Japanese American to mark the articulation of ethnic to national imaginaries (and vice versa), see Brian Lain, "The Trauma of Multiculturalism." That essay argues that "the Japanese American National Museum [...] marks a more general cultural ambivalence about the relationship between ethnicity and nationalism [...] The JANM attempts to produce a convergence between the hyphenated 'other' of multiculturalism, the nation, and the technologies of exhibition" (662).
4. All images are from Masumi Hayashi's webpage <www.masumihayashi.com>.
5. For more on Hockney, see his website at the Getty Museum <www.getty.edu/ artsednet/resources/Look/Landscape/hockney.html>. For a viewer, Hockney's point of view is itself an illusion whereas Hayashi's work demonstrates the instability of any single viewpoint.

6. Here I am referring to documentary photography's many encounters with internees. Ansel Adams's "Suffering Under a Great Injustice," currently housed in the Smithsonian's American Memory Project, is one of many examples. See <memory.loc.gov/ammem/aamhtml/>.

WORKS CITED

Bailey, David, and Stuart Hall et al., eds. "The Vertigo of Displacement: Shifts within Black Documentary Practices." *Ten.8: Critical Decade: Black British Photography in the 80s* Birmingham, UK: Ten.8, 1992 [Vol. 2 (3); Spring].

Bhabha, Homi K. "Postcolonial Authority and Postmodern Guilt." *Cultural Studies.* Ed. Lawrence Grossberg, Cary Nelson, and Paula A. Treichler. New York: Routledge, 1992. 56-68.

Brown, Wendy. *States of Injury: Power and Freedom in Late Modernity.* Princeton, NJ: Princeton UP, 1995.

Burke, Kenneth. *Permanence and Change: An Anatomy of Purpose.* 3rd ed. Berkeley: U of California P, 1954.

Butler, Judith. "Agencies of Style for a Liminal Subject." *Without Guarantees: In Honour of Stuart Hall.* Ed. Paul Gilroy, Lawrence Grossberg, and Angela McRobbie. London: Verso, 2000. 30-37.

Grossberg, Lawrence. "Identity and Cultural Studies—Is That All There Is?" *Questions of Cultural Identity.* Ed. Stuart Hall and Paul du Gay. Thousand Oaks, CA: Sage, 1996. 87-107.

Hall, Stuart. "The Meaning of New Times." *Stuart Hall: Critical Dialogues in Cultural Studies.* Ed. David Morley and Kuan-Hsing Chen. New York: Routledge, 1996. 223-37.

Krauss, Rosalind. "Photography in the Service of Surrealism." *L'Amour Fou: Photography and Surrealism.* Ed. Rosalind Krauss and Jane Livingston. New York: Abbeville, 1985. 15-54.

Kymlicka, Will. *Multicultural Citizenship: A Liberal Theory of Minority Rights.* Oxford, UK: Clarendon Press, 1995.

Lain, Brian. "Performing Japanese American Citizenship: The Case of Congressional Reparations Hearings." *An Imperfect World: Resonance from the Nation's Violence, International Association of Asian Studies 2002 Race Relations Monograph Series.* Ed. Lemuel Berry. Houston, TX: Moorhead State UP, 2002. 55-84.

---. "The Trauma of Multiculturalism: Ethnic and National Memory Practices in the Japanese American National Museum." *Arguing Communication and Culture. Selected Papers from the Twelfth NCA/AFA Conference on Argumentation.* Vol. 2. Ed. G. Thomas Goodnight. Alta, UT: NCA Press, 2001. 661-67.

Ling, Jinqi. *Narrating Nationalisms: Ideology and Form in Asian American Literature.* New York: Oxford UP, 1998.

Litt, Steven. "Panoramic Presentation: Hayashi Exhibit Hints She's Trapped in Specialty." *Plain Dealer* 23 Nov. 1997, sec. Arts: 3I.

Meehan, Joseph. *Panoramic Photography.* New York: AMPHOTO, 1990.

Palumbo-Liu, David. *Asian/American: Historical Crossing of a Racial Frontier.* Stanford, CA: Stanford UP, 1999.

Shapiro, Michael J. *The Politics of Representation: Writing Practices in Biography, Photography, and Policy Analysis.* Madison: U of Wisconsin P, 1988.

Tateishi, John. "Testimony before Subcommittee." *Recommendations of the Commission on Wartime Internment and Relocation of Citizens: Committee on Governmental Affairs, Subcommittee on Civil Service, Post Office, and General Services, U. S. Senate. 98th Cong., 2d Sess.* Washington DC: U.S. Government Printing Office, 1984. 6-11 .

30

Rhetorics of Subversion and Silence: The Naming of Illinois State University's Student Union

Jeff Ludwig
Illinois State University

> In all honesty and certainty it can be stated that I wish nothing but freedom, justice and equality: life, liberty, and the pursuit of happiness—for all people.
>
> —Malcolm X (*Malcolm X Speaks* 59)

> But put identification and division ambiguously together, so that you cannot know for certain where one ends and the other begins, and you have the characteristic invitation to rhetoric.
>
> —Kenneth Burke (*Rhetoric of Motives* 25)

Illinois State University's *Student Handbook* (2001) proclaims, "Behind the name of each campus building is a story told in brick and stone in memory of one of the university's founding fathers, a former president, a professor, or important event in the school's history" (5). Such a "story" occurred in the winter of 1969-1970. Spurred by a climate of civil rights and the deaths of black leaders, the Black Student Association (BSA) demanded that the university promote the interests of black students to fight racist ideologies on campus. One way was to rename the university's union after Malcolm X. After a lengthy democratic process, the Illinois Board of Regents voted to support President Samuel E. Braden's disapproval of the renaming because the "message received from Malcolm X seems to emphasize our differences and therefore is inappropriate to the University as a community" (Braden "Memorandum").

After the veto, over 200 of ISU's black students barricaded themselves in the union in a nonviolent protest. That evening (March 3, 1970), Braden held a "campus rally" to explain his decision. Proclaiming that he had "studied" *The Autobiography of Malcolm X* and black perspectives on the leader, Braden closed his speech by saying: "The issue is how we get along in our education [...]. We can't and we won't put up with things that tear us apart and don't help us solve our problems, which are the problems of getting along with one another" (qtd in Champagne 71).

This chapter explores the rhetorical dynamics of the longer narrative of the 1969-1970 events at ISU—one erased in ISU's history. Using Kenneth Burke's general theory of "identification," I argue that ISU's marginalized student voices enacted a rhetoric of subversion, forcing administrators to confront campus racism. The BSA's efforts were silenced, however, by a color blind rhetoric of unity from the university's administration and its figurehead, President Braden. Whereas the BSA's rhetoric of subversion was an attempt to mark publicly the importance of racial difference in the university, the administration's rhetoric of unity elided racial "division" by seeking "identification" with the dissenting group, arguing that racial problems are problems of "unification." This site is also appropriate for examining how, in public discourses, types of *ethos* are enacted for political gain. Although the BSA enacted an *ethos* "from the margins" (Reynolds 326), ISU's administration relied on a classical Aristotelian *ethos* that foregrounded their efforts to maintain "good will," and work for "unity" rather than "division."

This chapter looks closely at the erasure of race at this moment in ISU history to counter such elision. Thus, articles from ISU's student newspaper, the Bloomington-Normal *Pantagraph*, and historical documents from ISU's archives form the rhetorical narrative of these events, explaining how universalized discourses work in political rhetorics of race.

For Burke, rhetoric pertains to the study of symbolic actions between divided groups that examines the dialectic of identification and division: "Identification is affirmed with earnestness precisely because there is division. Identification is compensatory to division. If men were not apart from one another, there would be no need to proclaim their unity" (*Rhetoric* 22).

In this trope of "unity," Burke locates the give and take of symbol-using beings and as governing ideology and materiality. The proclamation of unity in a situation of division, Burke posits in *Language as Symbolic Action*, is also a "selection of reality": "Even if any given terminology is a reflection of reality, by its very nature as a terminology it must be a *selection* of reality; and to this extent it must function also as a *deflection* of reality" (45). If language stems from a selection of reality, then such selections are contingent on who holds power to select what "reality" to identify. Although the BSA successfully identified racial division and erasure on their campus, the public statements and actions made by Braden simply reinforce then-dominant ideologies of racial consciousness.

Instigated by the murders of Black Panther leaders Fred Hampton and Mark Clark, on December 5, 1969, the BSA lowered the American flag on ISU's quad. Afterward, they issued demands to the university. In addition to demanding that "a major campus building facility be named after a black leader," the BSA called for reforms to communication media, funding for a "black arts festival in memory of black leaders," and representation on ISU's entertainment board.[1] With these demands, the black students enacted their "rhetoric of subversion." Seeking a revised conception of being "marked" in a university controlled by white structures, the BSA made efforts to meet their needs as "othered" language users. Although the lowering of the flag shows those in the center that American heroes exist in the margins, their demands of those lowering the flag vocalize the need for recognition in the dominant/dominating structures of the university.

They were successful in that President Braden immediately responded. But how did the BSA gain a voice in this situation? Adopting Nedra Reynolds's discussion of *ethos* situated in "the margins," we see that the BSA, in their attempt to change exclusionary structures, based their *ethos* in their own marginality. Reynolds writes: "These writers [and speakers] earn their rhetorical authority by [...] stating explicitly their identities, positions or locations, and political goals"; they recognize that, "'it *does* matter who is speaking or writing'" (331). This conception of *ethos* illustrates that the BSA recognized how particularized conceptions of "race" and racial division constitute an authority to come to voice. Their demands are a way of using a marginalized position to subvert hegemonic structures of a white university. The insistence to be heard in public forums are obvious attempts to reconstitute their voice, but the demand to rename a "major" building after a black leader was an attempt to carve out a space for themselves in the university, altering its ideological and material infrastructures. Lastly, this demand dominated the climate of racial relations at ISU for over four months.

In his December 10 letter "To the University Community" (rather than the BSA), President Braden sets up an *ethos* of sincerity in his efforts to "improve the position of minority groups on this campus." He makes it clear that ISU is ready to change its tradition of naming buildings, insists that all students offer suggestions to improve ISU's "learning community," and stresses his "own personal commitment to act constructively [...] to accord black and all other students the dignity which is their due." Braden makes important rhetorical moves toward "unification" countering the subversive *ethos* of ISU's black students—placing that power in the hands of the university, and by caveat, himself. By addressing his response "To the University Community," Braden implicitly makes the demands of "the black students" the demands of the university as a whole. By asking that the proposal go through the "proper channels" of the university (black students, the University Council, and the Student Senate) empowers Braden as the "good man" to bring the proposed name before the Illinois Board of Regents.

The *ethos* of Braden's announcement is an appeal that asserts unification over subversion and community over difference, and can be situated in the classical sense that Aristotle defined as the purpose of rhetoric: persuasion that benefited the "good" of the community through a rhetor inherently "good" him- or herself. To James S. Baumlin, however, an Aristotelian (or Quintilian) *ethos* "asserts the sufficiency of *seeming* good" (xv), and this "good man" is a construction of self that is convincing because of its connection to the ideological and cultural structures of the larger community. Thus, President Braden establishes his authority as a morally upright and sympathetic agent attempting to help change ISU's racial structures for the benefit of all.

Braden's most remarkable move was two letters published to the students in the December 16 issue of *The Vidette*—one was addressed to "the black students of ISU," and the other to "the white students of ISU." To the black students, Braden states that his own actions would depend on what name was presented through ISU's bureaucratic structures. He concludes by attempting to unite his own motives for ending racism with those of the black students: "I hope each of you will consider how best we can reach the goals to which we aspire. I can't do it alone. Your actions will tell the University whether you intend to help" ("Braden Issues" 1). This statement asks for an end to the BSA's subversive efforts and for a measure of "good will." Braden thanks the white students of ISU for their "self-discipline" in the face of "tactics of exasperation which have sorely tried your tolerance" throughout December (1). These letters make abundantly clear that Braden equates the ethical appeal for unification with actions of "good will" from everyone in the university. Ironically Braden's appeal to unification separates black from white, asking cooperation from one while praising the other for its perseverance in the face of adversity: an appeal that authorizes Braden as the "good man" to diplomatically end division.

Beginning in January, the BSA lost power when it allowed the university-formed Task Force on Intergroup Relations to voice their demands. The Task Force became the first universalizing strategy of ISU's administration, forcing the BSA to "integrate" its own voice with one authorized by administration. On January 6, 1970, the Task Force forwarded a resolution to ISU's University Council to have ISU's union be renamed the "Malcolm X Memorial Union." It passed through Braden's "appropriate channels" (the University Council and the Student Senate) in early February. At the same time, however, the predominately white Bloomington-Normal community voiced its opposition to the resolution. Common arguments against the renaming, although various, were that Malcolm X did not appropriately represent black Americans or the institution of education. However, what the name Malcolm X "means" became more important than Braden's own recognition that ISU's black students "should identify their own heroes [... for] memorialization" (Braden "To the University Council"). To the larger community, Malcolm X signified a racial division that flew in the face of American civil rights. One anonymous community member stated: "I cannot accept the designation of 'American Hero' to one who preached racial hatred" ("Letter to President Braden"). As the tenor of the debate changed to what Malcolm X would mean for the community, the subversive *ethos* of the BSA was rendered powerless to the larger community's authority to name the terms of the debate.

Indeed, the center of power in this narrative shifted to the various, and often elite, voices that would take up the renaming. At their February 1 meeting, with Braden in attendance, the Illinois Board of Regents decided to no longer "remain silent." Chairman Gordon Millar suggested that the name selected "must necessarily have some association with the educational process" (Mastler 97-98). Dr. Percy Julian, the only African American member of the Board, agreed, and added: "I would turn over in my grave if my grandchildren or great grandchildren [...] would have to turn back and say, 'Our granddad—was he not able to find any other recipient than Malcolm X?'" (98). Julian remained stolid in his assertion that "Malcolm X is no name for a building in the university of our state or any state of the union" (98). Certainly the cogency of Julian's stance against Malcolm X, especially considering his status as a respected member of the black community, would influence Braden in his later dealings with the issue.

Another group who controlled the debate was ISU's faculty, who held a meeting on February 19 to vote on the Council's recommendation. In the opening speech of the meeting, President Braden made an appeal to reason in a time of emotion—to "unify" in a time of division—erasing the subversive voice of ISU's black students. Braden first suggested that the "freedom on this campus has been inhibited" by those who question the "appropriateness to the educational community of Malcolm X's message" ("Statement to the Faculty" 1). These people had "estopped" a "collegial analysis" of the issue, which includes: "The desirability of seeking the truth, the superiority of peaceful over violent means of conflict resolution, the preference for the use of reason as a scholarly method, and indeed the concept of the importance of academic freedom [...]" (1). Masked in an appeal to "good reason" as well as a "liberal" ideology of democratic freedom, Braden identifies the BSA's recommendation as "emotional" (1), subjective, and therefore unreasonable and destructive to structures of "truth" and "objectivity" that he assumes are the goals of higher education. In assuming this privilege, Braden reinforces the universalizing ideology of liberal humanism that suggests that truths are always universal because they go beyond—indeed erase—subjective experiences. Braden concludes that the university cannot give a "reasoned consensus" on the naming, and should work as a "community of scholars" to "avoid polarization" and "crystallize dissension" on the issue (2). Despite the faculty's vote in favor of the resolution, representing the campus as "divided" is Braden's ace in the hole.

In his February 24 statement to the ISU community, Braden asserts that, although he is obligated to present the recommendation to the Board of Regents, he does so with his "disapproval": "At the same time I take this action, I reaffirm my position that we should be free to name buildings for blacks, and that we should direct our attention to the campus conditions that are conducive to the successful education of all students" ("Memorandum"). Here we see a version of Julian's stance, as well as the appeal to "education" that characterizes his February 19 statement to ISU's faculty. Braden is explicit in his liberal belief that an acknowledgment of race is vital to his vision of a campus "community." Because Malcolm X does not fit this idealized vision, a name more "appropriate" must be determined. Stating that the university must work toward the "goal of racial equality and reconciliation," Braden is unwilling to "abdicate the authority and responsibility of [his] office to any group [...] which in [his] opinion may lead the University in another direction" ("Memorandum"). On March 1, 1970, when Braden's veto reaches the Board, and after hearing statements from both sides, the Board voted unanimously to support Braden's veto, and went on with its usual business.

Trusting in the "good will" of a university president who consistently proclaimed dedication to building "community" and having "whites understand blacks and [...] blacks understand whites" (Braden "Statement to the Faculty"), the BSA surrendered their "voice from the margins" to go through the "regular channels" of the university. In a vain attempt to explain his veto, Braden stated at an all-campus rally: "The issue of Malcolm X is not the real issue we have before us. The real issue [...] is how we get along with one another and how we get on with our education" (qtd in Salinger A-3). Attempting to reconcile warring ideologies, Braden reveals that the real issue of racial difference is not in a multiplicity of voices, but instead in a univocal—"universalized"—voice that speaks the truths of education. Braden's statements attempt, finally, to eliminate division in the name of identification—one that presupposes a monocultural "we."

This is not the entire narrative of the renaming of ISU's student union. Today, the same building that the black students of ISU tried to name as a marker of "brotherhood" and racial renewal now stands as the "Bone Student Center" and the "Braden Auditorium," and somehow this history was erased from the record books. Here, the words of Burke remind me that, with this case, two distinct definitions of "identification" and "division" are placed together in this particular historical and political moment. For the black students of ISU, "identification" literally means to be identified. Given their position in a context that privileges white as the universal, their fight was for recognition. The BSA embraced the *ethos* of their marginality and attempted to mark campus with the name Malcolm X—a leader who preached unity only to the extent of recognizing that being separate is equally vital in eliminating ideological essentialism. For the administration of ISU, as embodied in President Braden, "identification" means "unity" and erasure of difference. The irony of this narrative is that the union is not named after any "black heroes," but after a man who successfully erased racial difference on his own campus: President Samuel E. Braden.[2]

NOTES

1. From: "RALLY: COALITION OF CONCERNED CITIZENS," a flyer distributed December 8, 1969 (Illinois State University Archives, 1 page).
2. Thanks to Lori Ostergaard for pointing out this irony and her dedicated support. Thanks also to Mike Martin and Kenneth Lindblom for help with this narrative.

WORKS CITED

Anonymous. Letter to President Braden. Normal, IL: Illinois State University Archives, 18 Jan. 1970.

Baumlin, James S. "Introduction: Positioning *Ethos* in Historical and Contemporary Theory." In *Ethos: New Essays New Essays in Rhetorical and Critical Theory*. Ed. James S. Baumlin and Tita French Baumlin. Dallas: Southern Methodist UP. 1994. xi-xxvii.

Braden, Samuel E. "Memorandum." Normal, IL: Illinois State University Archives, 24 Feb. 1970.

---. "Statement to the Faculty." Normal, IL: Illinois State University Archives, 19 Feb. 1970.

---. "To the University Community." Normal, IL: Illinois State University Archives, 10 Dec. 1969.

---. "To the University Council," Normal, IL: Illinois State University Archives, 15 Dec. 1969.

"Braden Issues Letters to Black, White Students." *The Vidette*. 16 Dec. 1969: 1.

Burke, Kenneth. *A Rhetoric of Motives*. Berkeley: U of California P, 1969.

---. *Language as Symbolic Action*. Berkeley: U of California P, 1969.

Champagne, Roger J. *A Place of Education: Illinois State University, 1967-1977*. Normal, IL: Illinois State University Foundation, 1978.

Illinois State University Student Handbook. 2001-2002 ed. Normal, IL: Illinois State University, 2001.

Mastler, Franklin G. "Minutes of the Meeting of the Board of Regents." Chicago, IL. Normal, IL: Illinois State University Archives, 1 Feb. 1970.

Reynolds, Nedra. "*Ethos* as Location: New Sites for Understanding Discursive Authority." *Rhetoric Review* 11 (1993): 325-38.

Salinger, Hank. "Malcolm X Not Real Issue." *The Pantagraph* 5 Mar. 1970: A-3.

X, Malcolm. *Malcolm X Speaks: Selected Speeches and Statements*. Ed. George Breitman. New York: Grove Weidenfeld, 1965.

31

Tyrannical Technology and Thin Democracy

Ken S. McAllister
University of Arizona

There is an often-told story about Josef Stalin that well captures the complexity of a tyrant's work. The story goes that when Stalin was on his deathbed, he called in two likely successors to test which one of them had a better knack for ruling the country. He ordered two birds to be brought in and presented one bird to each of the two candidates. The first candidate took a bird, but was so afraid that it would free itself from his grip and fly away that he squeezed his hand too tightly and, when he opened his palm, the bird was dead. Seeing the disapproving look on Stalin's face and being afraid to repeat his rival's mistake, the second candidate loosened his grip so much that his bird freed itself and flew away. Stalin looked at both of them scornfully. "Bring me a bird!" he ordered. And they did. Stalin took the bird by its legs and one by one he plucked all the feathers from the bird's little body. Then he opened his palm. The bird was lying there naked, shivering, and helpless. Stalin looked at the bird, smiled gently and said, "You see? And it is even thankful for the warmth coming from my palm" ("Stalin").

It is easy to see in this story an illustration of what comes to mind when we think about tyrants: the megalomaniac who captures and maintains power through a coercive program of torture and terror. But there is more to this illustration than a caricature of a brutal politician. Stalin's bird, it's important to note, is not simply cruelly disabled; it has been so mutilated that not only can it *not* fly, it doesn't *want* to fly. So expert is Stalin's tyranny, the candidates learn, that its victims forget the past and take refuge in their oppressor's incidental warmth and disingenuous smile.

The first half of this chapter's title is "tyrannical technology," a designation that is now perhaps a bit more fleshed out in your mind than it was a minute or two ago. But the image of tyrants has not always been so one-dimensional, so... evil.

In the old days, back at the dawn of Western democracy, tyrants were fairly common and did not necessarily have the kind of bad reputation that tyrants of the twentieth century earned. There were, in fact, many "good" tyrants, people who ruled over their subjects more or less benevolently, even though they came to power by means other than requisite bloodlines or legal decree. A tyrant in those days, in fact, *depended* on the support of the masses in order to grab and stay in power.

Peisistratos, for example, became Tyrant of Athens in about 546 BCE, and drew strong support from the impoverished peasantry by instituting a uniform five percent tax (lower than what peasants usually paid and much higher than what the wealthiest citizens were used to). He also established a judicial system that paid judges to travel to outlying areas rather than forcing peasants to travel to the city center for redress of their grievances, and he extended numerous agricultural loans. Peisistratos—and his sons who ruled after him—supported the arts, constructed many public buildings and religious temples, and, according to some accounts, revived the tradition of public recitations of Homer, what might be considered a sort of protoliteracy training ("Peisistratos").[1]

Even such benevolent tyranny was not, however, without its vicious side. Alongside his acts of public welfare, Peisistratos also covertly eliminated his detractors and rivals, and imposed his rule on numerous small cities with the help of his growing army. What we learn from these stories of Stalin and Peisistratos, then, is that tyrants are more complicated than their smiles and good deeds suggest, and that their "happy" subjects may be willfully deluded.

* * * * *

Political scientist Benjamin Barber has been concerned for the past twenty years or so with articulating a detailed critique of representative democracy—what he calls "thin democracy." This system, of course, has its clearest nation-state manifestation in the United States. "Thin democracy," writes Barber, is a system of governance "whose democratic values are prudential and thus provisional, optional, and conditional—[it is a] means to exclusively individualistic and private ends." Barber goes on to say that "From this precarious foundation, no firm theory of citizenship, participation, public goods, or civic virtue can be expected to arise" (*Strong Democracy* 4). Barber summarizes this critique with a reference to Ambrose Bierce, who, in his *Devil's Dictionary*, defines *politics* as "the conduct of public affairs for private advantage" (95).

Barber contrasts thin democracy with "strong democracy," a system of governance that enacts "substantive political equality and [...] citizens' active engagement in political discourse" (Sclove 26). Strong democracy "envisions extensive opportunities for citizens to participate in important decisions that affect them" (Sclove 26). Barber makes considerable efforts to explain the implications of these two kinds of democracy—two among many, by the way—discussing what, for instance, constitutes "active engagement," "important decisions," and "substantive political equality."

Rather than review these clarifications here, I refer you to his book *Strong Democracy*, but one clarification I do want to make is that Barber is arguing for a much more deliberative and participatory system of governance than we currently practice in the United States, one in which all issues that might have a broad social impact are first debated locally, then slowly proceed—and the word *slowly* is important to Barber—outward to increasingly broad communal deliberative structures. Such painstaking deliberation, says Barber, is much more likely to ensure thoughtful public discussion and debate than in thin democracy where, he says, "Once a year the voter is free, she votes and then goes home and watches and waits [...]"("Ambiguous" 3).

Speaking specifically of digital telecommunications technologies' role in thin democracy, Barber observes that they intervene in it along seven axes: speed, simplicity, solitude, pictoriality, lateralness, informationality, and segmentation. Each of these characteristics has ambiguous implications for democracy, says Barber.

These ambiguous axes or characteristics are worth examining, partly because they stand as an excellent compilation of the most salient critiques that have been made about digital technology, and partly because I am interested in how these critiques extend beyond the framework of thin democracy about which Barber is concerned, and well into democracy of any kind.

The *speed* (Axis 1)[2] of digital telecommunications discourages thoughtful deliberation, but allows people to be more quickly apprised of world events that could make their deliberations—were they to take the time to engage in them—more informed. In conforming to this speed, Barber says, we find ourselves compelled by immediacy rather than patience, short-term personal gratification rather than long-term social transformation.

Digital technologies can also encourage *simplistic thinking* (Axis 2), allowing people to meet the complexity of the world around them with reductive and reactionary responses, but also making it easier for them to be aware of more information.

Because digital technology tends to be designed for one user at a time, it also tends to *isolate* (Axis 3) them from deliberative communities, which often leads to uncritical thinking. Most people don't challenge themselves to think differently, and, in virtual communities, isolationism is made manifest in ideologically homogeneous "chats." But, Barber concedes, there are significant exceptions to this tendency, for instance the Pnyx (pronounced "nicks") Unchat web application (www.unchat.com).[3]

The trend toward *pictoriality* (Axis 4)—visual culture—is another ambiguous effect that digital technology has on democracy. Images are powerful persuaders and most people have not yet evolved a habit to question photos and computer-generated drawings and illustrations, even though they are now just as malleable as words. This makes their use in argumentation ethically complicated, argues Barber, especially because international media conglomerates exercise the most control over the distribution and interpretation of images.

Lateralness (Axis 5), or the ability of digital technologies to link one person to another, has the advantage, says Barber, of allowing people to connect without the mediation of "masters and manipulators." On the other hand, it has the disadvantage of allowing people to connect on matters of substance without the mediation of "educators and tutors" (e.g., talk radio and newsgroups). Although

Barber generally appreciates lateralness, he expresses concern that "unmediated conversation" runs the risk of being "undisciplined," "prejudiced," "private," "polarizing," and "unproductive" ("Ambiguous" 8).

Similarly, Barber questions digital technology's tendency to make *information* (Axis 6) seem more important than wisdom. Information is "raw, unmediated, undigested, data—meaningless noise," he says. Wisdom, however, is information that has been thoughtfully considered in particular contexts, which again is generally discouraged by the speed and immediacy factors: "The problem of modern democratic societies in the global era is not [...] too little information or too little access to information, but too much information out of which we make far too little sense" ("Ambiguous" 8).

Finally, Barber puzzles over the *use* of digital technologies by corporations to *segment* (Axis 7) the population according to their roles as consumers rather than citizens. The capability of digital technologies to provide a few broad channels of communications that could serve to bring people together on important issues is being replaced, Barber argues, by thousands of narrow channels that attempt to capture with highly specific rhetorics citizen-consumers who have been oriented to think of themselves as unique and possessing few shared interests with their neighbors, coworkers, and compatriots.

Ultimately, Barber sees globalization as becoming increasingly instrumental in the control over potentially democratic technologies. His view of technology, in fact, could be fairly characterized as instrumental: The Internet, he would say, is inherently neither pro- nor antidemocratic; it merely tends in the direction of those who control it.

On almost all of these points I agree with Barber. Where I disagree with him, as I suggested earlier, is in his decision to situate these critiques of technology within the confines of thin democracy alone. But strong democracy (or any other kind of democracy), I suggest, is also subject to these critiques.

Democracy of any stripe is necessarily rights based, and requires that some people have rights (people who are granted the title "citizen"), whereas others do not (people who are labeled "foreigners," "aliens," "noncitizens," "illegals," or "slaves"). This is not to say that noncitizens are disallowed from participation in a democratic society; quite the reverse. Democratic societies *depend* on noncitizens to make citizenship valuable, to provide labor that citizens would not do, and to perpetuate economies that can only function when the majority of the world's population is compelled—by hegemony or might—to sell its labor to those few who control the means of production. Democracy, in other words, is inherently divisive along class lines, no matter how much deliberation and participation is permitted among its citizenry.

Jacques Ellul, writes in his book *Propaganda* that because democracy is founded on principles that require the exclusion of some people—and some peoples' rights—that it must constantly make such exclusions seem reasonable, to both citizens and noncitizens alike. This is the work, says Ellul, of propaganda. Noam Chomsky makes a similar point in his book *Necessary Illusions: Thought Control in Democratic Societies,* observing that the greatest challenge for propagandists is not to persuade people to think in new ways, but rather to persuade people to appreciate their bondage. Chomsky writes that one of the great success stories of democratic U.S. propaganda is that it has worked to make many people see doctrines that define the conditions for what is reasonably thinkable not as constraining but as evidence "that freedom reigns" (48).

The primary tool of this democratic propaganda is, of course, technology. In all the ways that Barber notes—speed, simplicity, isolation, pictoriality, lateralness, informationality, and segmentation—digital telecommunications technology effects social organization. But Barber does not look beyond his model of *democratic* citizenship, and thus he does not account for the ways in which democracy's oppressive character—a character clearly evident in a perusal of history—is reliant on technology to blur the difference between *opp*ression and *prog*ression.

Political scientist Richard Sclove argues that:

> Technologies function politically and culturally as social structures by coercing physical compliance; prompting subconscious compliance; constituting systems of social relations; establishing opportunities and constraints for action and self-realization; promoting the evolution of background conditions; affecting nonusers; shaping communication, psychological development, and culture generally; and constituting much of the world within which lives unfold. (17)

When democracy guides technology to function in these ways, in essence, as Sclove says, not only affecting society but also constituting a large portion of it, then "democratic technology" must be viewed with great wariness, as a smiling tyrant whose warm hand, generous gifts, and gentle smile mask motives of personal power and domination.

NOTES

1. Rhetoricians might also be interested to know that Peisistratos was a highly accomplished orator who became Tyrant of Athens by engineering a plot to overthrow Solon, the much-praised democratic reformer. See Aristotle's *Athenian Constitution* (Ch. XIV) for a detailed account.
2. The numbers ascribed to the seven technological axes (e.g. "Axis 1") are denominative, not hierarchical. All the axes simultaneously penetrate and transform democracy in relatively equal ways.
3. The Pnyx Unchat web-based software application applies:

   > "the ideas of democratic debate and deliberation that have enriched and deepened traditional off-line conversation from ancient Greek democracy to modern business and learning transactions. Put to use in civic and political debates, learning and educational development, community building and non-profit communications, corporate meetings and knowledge management, our software will enhance discussion, nurture deliberation and facilitate the arbitration of differences and the quest for common ground."

4. For more information, go to <www.unchat.com>.

WORKS CITED

Aristotle. *Athenian Constitution*. 7 Sept. 2002 <http://perseus.mpiwg-berlin.mpg.de/cgi-bin/ptext?doc=Perseus%3Atext%3A1999.01.0046&query=head%3D%2316>.

Barber, Benjamin. "The Ambiguous Effects of Digital Technology on Democracy in a Globalizing World." Talk given to Heinrich Boll Stiftung. 7 Sept. 2002 <http://www.wissensgesellschaft.org/ themen/demokratie/democratic.html>.

---. *Strong Democracy*. Berkeley: U of California P, 1984.

Bierce, Ambrose. *The Devil's Dictionary*. New York: Dover, 1993.

Chomsky, Noam. *Necessary Illusions: Thought Control in Democratic Societies*. Boston: South End, 1989.

Ellul, Jacques. *Propaganda*. New York: Vintage, 1965.

"Peisistratos." Web page in the Museum Project, University of Natal, Durban. 7 Sept. 2002 <http://www.classics.und.ac.za/projects/democracy/Peisistratos.htm>.

"Pnyx Unchat." Web-based discussion software. 7 Sept. 2002 <www.unchat.com>.

Sclove, Richard. *Democracy and Technology*. New York: Guilford, 1995.

"Stalin." Web Page on the History of the Russian Revolution. 7 Sept. 2002 <http://home.earthlink.net/~gqsmith/revolution/stalin.htm>.

32

How Medium Clarifies Message in Emerson's "Divinity School Address"

Michael Moghtader
University of New Mexico

Scholars of Ralph Waldo Emerson regard the "Divinity School Address" as his first serious attempt to test the viability of a lecture career. As Stephen Railton remarks, the 1837 Phi Beta Kappa address ("The American Scholar") helped Emerson to understand "the problem of his vocation [...], [although] he did not solve it" (33). But it is with the 1838 Divinity School Address that we see Emerson attempting to find that solution. As we know from the work of scholars like biographer Robert D. Richardson, the dilemma that Emerson hoped to confront with the Divinity School Address stemmed from his own "personal religious consciousness" to interpret the significance of Christ's acts—like that of taking communion—rather than to passively rely on the formal religious ceremonies of organized Christianity (288–89). The Address, in other words, was a "farewell"; it was, as Richardson puts it, "Emerson's last face-off with formal or organized religion" (291).

What Lawrence Buell and others like Wesley T. Mott have said about the Address is that it was Emerson's first intentional public attempt to reveal the emptiness of institutionalized religion and, simultaneously, to assert the viability of a secular individual religion—transcendentalism. Mott tells us that, with the Address, "Emerson finds himself 'in a moment of transition,' [as] religious institutions and 'forms' [have] lost their power to inspire, but with nothing worthy having arisen [to take] their place" (182–83). Buell and Henry Nash Smith both paint a similar picture of Emerson's problem but with a much broader stroke, by grouping together Emerson's struggle with those of other transcendentalists. According to Buell, "[T]here was no institutionalized outlet for [their] ambitions [...], no socially recognized name for what they wanted to do. They were going through the most severe crisis of identity ('vocation' was their word for it) that New England had seen" (50).

As influential as these scholars have been to our literary study of Emerson, they overlook the influence that the formalized modes of rhetoric had on transcendentalists like Emerson, whose writings grew from his many lectures. Moreover, the conventional interpretations of Emerson's Address that have been established by prominent scholars like Buell and Smith ignore the effect that the venue where Emerson's oration took place had on the way his transcendental ideas were received. Such studies have long determined how students and scholars alike should appreciate the Address and, more important, the notorious controversy it stirred among Emerson's contemporaries.[1] Although the ensuing controversy has caused scholars to describe the Address as a "failure" that "chilled [Emerson's] hopes for an instant 'conversion of the world'" (Railton 45), scholars like Buell, Smith, Mott, and others have nonetheless explained it as a natural by-product of Emerson's determination to change vocations and, symbolically, to further the new philosophical direction he had to take following his rejection of Unitarianism some six years earlier.

My intent, however, is not to rehearse the orthodox interpretations of the controversy that have shaped our understanding of Emerson and his transcendental expression. Instead, I want to give us some ideas about how we might understand the controversy in ways that open the door to more rhetorical-based protocols to studying canonical works of American literature such as Emerson's Address. Of course, in one sense, my approach gives us yet another way of thinking about the Address. But in another, broader sense, my argument suggests a need to think more interdisciplinarily about texts that we have narrowly defined as "literary."

With this purpose in mind, I want to suggest that the controversy surrounding the Address tells us much more than something about Emerson's struggle with the scholar's "problem of Action *versus* Contemplation," as Smith suggests, or about the early buds of Emerson's transcendental aesthetic, as Buell contends. Taking a more rhetorical approach to the controversy reveals how the forum for Emerson's discourse—the Divinity School Chapel—might account for much of the consternation that his Address caused. Delivered to the Senior Class and their families in Divinity College, Cambridge, July 15, 1838, the Address was so controversial not just because Emerson vilified some of the Unitarians' most cherished ideas but also because he challenged audience expectations of an oration delivered in such a discursive forum. The graduates, their families, and the most noted Unitarians of the day were not sufficiently prepared for the kind of rhetoric Emerson was using to preach his secular ideas. As a result, Emerson necessarily encountered problems with the way his audience interpreted his ideas because of the kinds of rhetorical modes—in particular, "sermonic oratory"—that the Divinity School audience expected speakers to use in such addresses. The controversy ensued because Emerson was preaching a message in a more "popular" oratorical mode, one appropriate not for the Unitarian Church but, rather, for a more secular, public discursive forum—such as the Lyceum—that had not yet solidified.

Scholars have generally agreed that Emerson as both preacher and lecturer was concerned about his audience. As Stephen Railton has shown, however, most characterize this concern as one of disappointment and condescension (33).[2] Invariably, these scholars focus on the contempt Emerson harbored toward his audience; rarely, however, do they discuss the forces that conditioned Emerson's audience to expect his ideas to take a particular rhetorical shape. We might begin such a discussion, then, with the central question Railton poses about the Address—"What reaction had [Emerson] hoped to provoke" in his Divinity School audience—but move on to ask a more interesting question: What were the rhetorical forces that kept Emerson's audience from reacting the way he *wanted* them to?

One way to understand the confusion and public outcry that ensued with Emerson's Address is to show how his search for a suitable forum for public discourse coincides with his attempt to break out of the established rhetorical modes he was taught while he was a student at Harvard under the instruction of Edward Channing, Andrews Norton, and others. A study of the audience reaction to the Address, then, becomes important for what it says about Emerson's attempt to wrestle with established forms of oratory that caused audiences to mishear what he was trying to say. From the work that theorists like Steven Mailloux, Stanley Fish, and others have done into the study of reception, we know how meaning is profoundly shaped by the way historical audiences receive, interpret, and judge both the written and oral texts of their time. By encouraging us to look at the preformed beliefs and expectations that existing audiences bring to a text, studies of reception animate the overlooked forces at play in the Divinity School controversy—forces other than Emerson's elusive style or what Emerson's contemporary Andrews Norton termed, the "heretical" content of his Address. Specifically, Emerson knew what *he* meant; but to an audience or interpretive community that operated under conventional assumptions about oratory, what Emerson intended to say is not what his audience heard. In a sense, we might see Emerson as the initial member of an emerging interpretive community whose assumptions about oratory would transcend the "sermonic" mode toward an incipient "popular" mode—one that would not be formalized until the latter part of the nineteenth century.[3]

Fortunately, a number of scholars have begun the work for the kind of study I'm suggesting. With their help, we can see the significance of the Divinity School Address to lie in how it contributes to our understanding of nineteenth-century rhetoric and the role that the audience played in Emerson's oratory. Stephen Railton, for example, has argued that the "specific theme and immediate rhetorical context are what give the address its dramatic prominence" (34). This sentiment is echoed in the introduction to Gregory Clark and Michael Halloran's *Oratorical Culture in Nineteenth-Century America*. Like Railton, they acknowledge Emerson's self-reliant philosophy in the Address, but they find such addresses "particularly instructive in the development of the ideology of liberal individualism to a point where it always left the community behind" (11). With its focus on individuation, Emerson's speech exemplifies what Clark and Halloran see as a "general shift of the public realm" of discourse and "the increasing secularism—or at least the decreasing practice of traditional, formal religion—of a people who insisted upon assigning moral responsibility to conscience alone" (13). Although "Emerson was aware that his views would not be universally applauded," particularly given the oratorical expectations of audiences at the time, he approached the Address with the "underlying confidence that if he could disassociate himself from any sectarian motives, if he could speak 'simple truth without any bias, [without] any foreign interest in the matter,' [then] any possible controversy could be overshadowed" (Robinson 124).

Unfortunately, Emerson underestimated the power of those forces beyond his control that made such disassociation impossible. First, he had broken from the traditional sermonic oratory that, given the occasion for his Address, the interpretive community at the Divinity School chapel expected. Second, this community's preconceived notions about what speakers *should* address given the nature of the rhetorical occasion colored their interpretation of what they heard Emerson say. As

David Robinson has written, Emerson "had taken his message to an audience somewhat different from his usual, and had preached it in a somewhat special place on a special occasion" (125). As a result, Railton adds, although the Address was an "assault on the values of his immediate audience, [...] it nonetheless points up how anxiously [Emerson] sought a home for his words among the 'brothers' [...] and 'friends' [...] he rhetorically gestures to" (44). With these observations about "seeking a home" or place for one's ideas, we begin to see the important role that Emerson's audience played in determining the success of his Address. As Sarah Wider has argued, "To re-create what [Emerson's audience] heard was in large part to create what they thought Emerson had said" (1).

It is important to recall the fundamental canons of rhetoric that, during Emerson's time, identified the sermon as a distinct form of oratory—one that educated audiences easily would have distinguished from other modes of oratory that were established between 1800 to 1880. As Robinson has suggested, despite the fact that the "sermon form was in a state of rapid transition during Emerson's ministry," it was firmly established in the educational curricula at the time when Emerson entered the ministry; in fact, he adds, "the sermon had been for two centuries the major channel for American thought and literary expression" (48). Clearly, then, Emerson would have based his sermonic form on the New Rhetoricism he learned while a student at the Divinity School—particularly the form promoted by Hugh Blair. Indeed, Blair was among the New Rhetoricians who most influenced the oratorical training students received in their formal education. Emerson first encountered Blair's rhetoric as a student at Harvard. Reading Blair's *Lectures on Rhetoric and Belles Lettres* (1783), Emerson became well acquainted with the New Rhetoric. In fact, according to Sheldon W. Leibman, he studied Blair's work intensely (179-80). As a result, Emerson felt the legacy of those formative years of study as he composed his sermons, particularly those "written in the late 1820s and early 1830s" that "follow the traditional sermon form, roughly in agreement with Blair's suggestions on oratory" (188).

With the publication of Nan Johnson's important book *Nineteenth-Century Rhetoric in North America,* we now have a good idea what oratorical categories Emerson had studied and imitated during the early years of his formal education at Harvard. Johnson identifies the dominant "three-mode scheme" of oratory division, which paralleled the one Blair had popularized between 1800 and 1880. Formally educated speakers and audiences were conditioned to see oratory as "judicial," "deliberative," or "sacred" (157). Of the three that Johnson lists, "sacred oratory" is the form that Emerson's audience would have expected his Address to take:

> Sacred oratory
>
> Subject: explication of sacred texts and lessons on moral conduct before a congregation
>
> General aim: instruction in scriptural truth and exhortation to moral conduct
>
> Dominant rhetorical strategy: persuasion; argumentative techniques of exposition, narration, and description often required. (157)

From the "Subject" and "General aim" of sacred or sermonic oratory, we can begin to see why Emerson's audience considered his Address so inappropriate. For example, Emerson's outright attack on the value of biblical scripture as "truth" itself—on the formalistic rituals and ceremonies that established Christianity had embraced—clearly was not the kind of "explication of sacred texts" his audience was expecting. Ironically, Emerson was explicating those texts to show how *dangerous* their uncritical acceptance could be. Similarly, contrary to the expectations of his audience, Emerson's "general aim" was not to inculcate "scriptural truth" into the passive listener but, rather, to revitalize "truth" by relocating it in the individual's intuition as part and parcel of the Divine living within himself. Finally, one can hear Emerson's "exhortation of moral conduct" in the Address; but it was not the *kind* of conduct his audience was led to expect from their conservative understanding of sacred oratory.

From Johnson's work, we begin to see the Divinity School Address as Emerson's attempt to test the elasticity of the unyielding oratorical modes that were taught in schools at the time before an audience who was resistant to that search. And, considering who made up the audience, this resistance comes as little surprise. In addition to the faculty of the school were the graduating students who had invited Emerson to speak, but these were students who had also spent the past several years immersed in a rhetorical training that centered around textbooks like Blair's *Lectures*. Competing for the minds of these students, then, were two very different teachers of rhetoric: the Emersonian one that sought to refigure the conventional modes of oratory established in the Harvard curriculum; and the Nortonian one that upheld the teaching of these established rhetorical modes. As Railton reminds us, it was clear from which "school" these students chose to graduate: "After encountering their teachers' frowns, the students who had invited Emerson subsequently sought to distance themselves from his address" (40).[4] Clearly, such reactions showed Emerson that he still had a long road ahead of him.

And that road was long, indeed. What intensified Emerson's vocational problem was the tenaciousness of the New Rhetoric legacy—a legacy that regulated what an orator could say and how the orator could say it without the audience recoiling, as Emerson's audience had during and after his Address. Emerson needed a more secular venue to enable him to leave behind the institution and rhetorical associations of the church and to preach his own ideas of self-reliance and experience. However, in 1838, there were no established forums to allow him to do so. In other words, Emerson's vocational search was so challenging because he literally had no rhetorically accommodating place to conduct that search.

It would not be until the "last decades of the century," Johnson tells us, that popular oratory became formalized as

> a distinct mode of secular oratory separate from political speaking. The formalization of popular oratory as a species extended the range of oratory beyond the three-mode scheme outlined by the New Rhetoricians to a four-mode scheme: judicial, deliberative, popular, and sacred oratory. The creation of this new division—popular oratory—reflected the prominence that public lectures and platform speakers had achieved by the latter part of the nineteenth-century and the proliferation in the nineteenth-century North American society of communal occasions at which platform speaking was a central activity. (156)

For Emerson, however, the cultural acceptance of this new oratorical mode and the rising popularity of the public lecture came years after his Address and his long struggle with the oratorical conventions of his time. As Robinson has said, "What

[Emerson] needed was an audience" (71)—but an audience whose interpretive grid could decipher his transcendental ideas. Not until the establishment of the American Lyceum would this grid exist—and, with it, the "opportunity for Emerson to embrace the more literary side of the ministerial vocation, leaving aside its pastoral aspects" (Robinson 71). Just as a venue had complicated his relationship with his audience soon after leaving the pulpit, so too did a venue provide the opportunity for his transformation into the successful lecturer that Emerson eventually became.

NOTES

1. For representative reactions to the Address, see Robinson and Miller.
2. Most of these opinions are formed by reading Emerson's journals from 1838 to 1839. In particular, see John H. Sloan's article, which focuses on Emerson's often strained relationship with his audience and Emerson's reluctance to adapt his rhetoric to their expectations.
3. Specifically, "between 1880–1900" (Johnson 157).
4. In addition to what it tells us about audience expectations, Emerson's Address is important for what it says about Emerson's desire to redefine the forms of oratory that, much like institutionalized religion, had shackled the collective mind of his audience. In fact, Leibman reminds us, Emerson's attempt to break away from such constricting, institutionalized modes of oratory began as early as 1835, acting on his own impulses for a more popular mode of oratory and also on Carlyle's advice in 1834 to "'leave [...] Blair's lectures quite behind'" (qtd in Leibman 189).

WORKS CITED

Buell, Lawrence. *Literary Transcendentalism: Style and Vision in the American Renaissance.* Ithaca: Cornell UP, 1973.

Clark, Gregory, and S. Michael Halloran. *Oratorical Culture in Nineteenth–Century America: Transformations in the Theory and Practice of Rhetoric.* Carbondale: Southern Illinois UP, 1993.

Emerson, Ralph Waldo. "The Divinity School Address." 1837. *Ralph Waldo Emerson.* Ed. Richard Poirier. Oxford, UK: Oxford UP, 1990. 53-67.

Johnson, Nan. *Nineteenth–Century Rhetoric in North America.* Carbondale: Southern Illinois UP, 1991.

Leibman, Sheldon W. "The Development of Emerson's Theory of Rhetoric, 1821–1836." *American Literature* 41.2 (1969): 178–206.

Miller, Perry, ed. *The Transcendentalists.* Cambridge, MA: Harvard UP, 1978.

Mott, Wesley T. *"The Strains of Eloquence": Emerson and His Sermons.* University Park: Pennsylvania State UP, 1989.

Railton, Stephen. "'Assume an Identity of Sentiment': Rhetoric and Audience in Emerson's 'Divinity School Address.'" *Prospects* 9 (1984): 31–47.

Richardson, Robert D. *Emerson: The Mind on Fire.* Berkeley: U of California P, 1995.

Robinson, David. *Apostle of Culture: Emerson as Preacher and Lecturer.* Philadelphia: U of Pennsylvania P, 1982.

Sloan, John H. "'The Miraculous Uplifting': Emerson's Relationship with His Audience." *Quarterly Journal of Speech* 52.1 (1966): 10–15.

Smith, Henry Nash. "Emerson's Problem of Vocation." *New England Quarterly* 12 (1939): 52–67.

Wider, Sarah. "What Did the Minister Mean: Emerson's Sermons and Their Audience." *ESQ* 34.1-2 (1988): 1-21.

33

Desire and Performance at the Classroom Door: Discursive Laminations of Academic and Civic Engagement

Rolf Norgaard
University of Colorado

Janus-faced in its very name, the field of Rhetoric and Composition is driven by an effort to connect terms and traditions, among them the academic and the civic. Troubled by its early and close association with the writing classroom, and indeed with one specific undergraduate course, the field has of late sought to connect with broader rhetorical, social, and civic concerns.

The very language of book titles and conference themes can serve as a convenient barometer of that desire. Christian Weisser's recently published study *Moving beyond Academic Discourse: Composition Studies and the Public Sphere* captures in its very title how we have historically constructed academic-civic relationships, even as it argues that we rethink our work. With its announced theme "Connecting the Text and the Street," the 2002 meeting of the Conference on College Composition and Communication served as an extended expression of a desire to connect what was thought to have been separated. "Text and Street" may well be the announced terms, but they readily offer up metonymies in a series of symbolic substitutions: writing and reality, classroom and agora, the academic and the civic. Implicit in these pairings is a desire that can be variously named, but that tends ineluctably toward courtship, seduction, and marriage. Yet implicit in these pairings is desire's twin, its other: fear. And so, the pairings also speak, double-voiced as they are, of estrangement, rejection, and divorce. Our desire for connection is driven by, responds to, and represses that fear.

I wish to question the figural logic implicit in how we tend to describe linkages between the academic and the civic, and to suggest that we look more closely at, and perhaps reframe, our desire to connect text and street. To do so, I invite you to take up, along with me, a position at the threshold between the terms involved. Let us position ourselves, then, at the classroom door, a good vantage point from which we can view the traffic between text and street, the academic and civic, and how rhetoric and composition "traffics" in those terms.

My argument moves through three stages. We would do well to begin by exploring the roots of our desire to connect text and street, or academic and civic, and the model that this desire presupposes. This model has us think of these terms along a continuum or spectrum, one that invites us to seek a connection between its poles, or to move beyond one and toward the other. Then, I'd like to explore an alternative model, one that proceeds not from a received binary but from what I would like to think of as a necessary and variously constructed "lamination" of text and street, academic and civic. That is, drawing in part on the work of Erving Goffman, I propose that text and street, the academic and the civic, necessarily coexist and mingle as complex laminations of each other, the admixture of the two always varying according the activity footing involved and the perspective in play. I close by contemplating what it might mean to "perform" our laminated academic and civic roles, given the genre expectations of our classroom, professional, and civic lives.

DESIRE AT THE CLASSROOM DOOR

Renewed interest in and desire for civic discourse has led some compositionists to rediscover their own intellectual roots in rhetoric, given rhetoric's historical grounding in civic engagement. However, it has encouraged many more by far to connect teaching and student writing with concerns beyond the classroom door. Anchoring this interest are scholarly studies, to be sure. The work of Susan Wells on public writing, Rosa Eberly on citizen critics, and Anne Gere on composition's extracurriculum are the first of many to come to mind. But concrete curricular innovations and actual classroom practice probably do more both to reflect and to drive this interest in linking text and street. Those innovations range from service learning programs to ethnographic work in and beyond the classroom to first-year writing assignments and textbooks that engage the genres of civic action. Captured well in the title of an article by Diana George, our desire is to attend to "the word on the street" in an effort to use public discourse to answer what is seen as a "culture of disconnect."

Underlying much of the interest in shifting classroom discourse to civic discourse is the presumption that what seems constrained in the academy—the student's own agency—becomes real and unfettered on the street or in the various fora of civic life. The rhetoric of civic celebration, of singing the praises of the street, suggests that we should welcome the civic as a departure from, and counterbalance to, the classroom. Composition's current love affair with the civic (we are, after all, speaking of desire and an impulse to "connect") urges that we try to escape the four classroom walls and, moving out beyond the classroom door, have students write in ways that make their work live and breathe in a public sphere. Nevertheless, the epideictic tenor of the project, its tacit deployment of praise and blame, should itself give us pause, and invite us to consider the arguments afoot and the models they presume.

Our desire—we might think of it as composition's "civic fantasy"—springs from the odd ways in which the academic and the civic have been isolated and reified. Despite the fact that we should know better, we persist in assuming academic discourse as a given, as something that exists apart from the ongoing instantiations and approximations of that discourse offered by ourselves and our students. We also persist in separating the academic from other discourses that do not fit neatly into that box, the languages of the town hall and street, among them. A similar foundationalist notion haunts our sense of the civic, at least as we view the civic from inside the writing classroom looking out. We assume the civic to be a kind of given, a natural—and naturalizing—discursive space that corrects in some measure the unnatural acts of academic writing. We often define these civic areas in ways that support our underlying fantasy—a fantasy of self-creation that would have us believe that we can create and enter these discursive spaces in a virgin and immediately productive way. Likewise, we try to repress the many ways in which we are already implicated in and controlled by these spaces. These desires and fantasies construct a model of academic and civic interaction that places the two on a spectrum or continuum, with pure forms on either end, and with "connection" being the celebrated goal.

The difficulties inherent in this model, and the paradoxes rooted in our desire, become evident as we find ourselves at the classroom door. If students struggle in their classroom writing to enter and "perform" the university, they must likewise now enter and "perform," in ways no less confusing, the civic or public sphere and, what is more, puzzle out its connections to the classroom. We must not congratulate ourselves too quickly when we turn the traditional academic essay into an op-ed piece, proposal, or a letter to an elected official. Instead, we and our students might reflect on the paradoxes of that desire.

LAMINATIONS OF CLASSROOM AND CIVIC CHRONOTOPES

As a way out of this impasse, let me suggest that we consider an alternative model. Instead of viewing text and street, or academic and civic, as poles constituting a continuum, we might consider how they necessarily coexist and mingle as complex "laminations" of each other. The concept of lamination has entered rhetoric and composition studies through, among others, Paul Prior, who himself draws on sociologist Erving Goffman. In his study of face-to-face interaction, Goffman resists the kind of homogeneity that has plagued our own conceptualizations of discourse communities by thinking of these interactions as laminated and heterogeneous. More recently, Goffman has helped us see "context" as mutable, dynamic configurations of foregrounded and backgrounded elements. Drawing on this work, as does Paul Prior, I am suggesting that socioliterate activities such as writing are inherently "laminated," that multiple such activities coexist, and are immanent, in any situation. Although one or more activity footings (writing in the classroom, writing in the public sphere) may be foregrounded at any one particular time, the background activities still exert influence. Moreover, such laminations are perspectival in nature. Laminations may present themselves differently, depending on who is viewing them and how we wish to be seen. As Paul Prior reminds us, "Viewing activity as laminated and perspectival makes it clear that neither situated activity nor systems of activity can occur in autonomous spaces" (24).

This concept of "lamination" is a helpful corrective to our misplaced desire to connect autonomous or pure forms of the academic and the civic. Stationed as we are, for the moment, at the classroom door, the concept of lamination seems apt indeed. When students enter our classrooms, and write in terms of that activity footing, they don't leave behind or shed other socioliterate activities. Likewise, when they write as involved citizens far from campus, we certainly hope that our classroom instruction has a place in and an influence on their work, even if it is not explicitly foregrounded. Little do we realize, when we ask students to write on the civic as they write in and for the classroom, that we are already dealing with connections that are immanent and ongoing. These connections are also deeply predetermined, yet subject to opportune reconfiguration.

Out of what cultural material are these laminations formed? What is the glue, so to speak, that bonds that material together? Here, Bakhtin's notion of the chronotope and his approach to speech genres might prove valuable. We can think of chronotopes as recognizable, therefore typifiable configurations of time and space that project a world of relationships and norms. Chronotopes are sites where "time, as it were, thickens," and space becomes "charged and responsive to the movements of time, plot, and history" ("Forms" 84). Classrooms themselves function as chronotopes, sites where highly genred discursive activities become congealed in time and space. Likewise, the town hall meeting or the rally or the press conference might be seen as civic chronotopes, ways in which public discourse becomes congealed in time and space. Moreover, Bakhtin argues that chronotopes have "intrinsic generic significance" ("Forms" 84-85). Chronotopes represent how genres become congealed in and grow out of time and space, a formulation that echoes how Carolyn Miller has encouraged us to rethink genre: as "typified rhetorical actions based in recurrent situations" (159). Chronotopes, then, are sites in time and space determinative of certain kids of utterances that take their generic character from several variables: the roles adopted, the tasks engaged, and the discursive interactions permitted.

Laminations always show themselves in distinctive and particular ways, depending on the activity footing involved and on the one or more perspectives in play. Then, too, we have the manner in which each person has appropriated, experienced, and shaped these discursive cultural materials. Although the notion of lamination might suggest otherwise (what to say of any analogies to plywood), each instantiation of laminated academic/civic activity is constructed out of a distinctive selection and weighting of elements. The new emerges through an opportune lamination of the traditional. We carry with us, and carry forward, a layered history of the changing laminations of academic and civic. Always opportune—which is to say, always rhetorical—laminations carry inherent kairotic potential.

PERFORMANCE AT THE CLASSROOM DOOR

Given that laminations are inevitably rhetorical, it is only fitting to close by considering the performative aspects of our laminated academic and civic activities at the threshold of the classroom. That is, I'd like to explore what it might mean to perform discursive laminations of academic and civic engagement.

Such performances have both their burdens and their potential. This should come as no surprise, especially given the considerable interest that now accompanies what Mary Francis Hopkins calls the "performance turn" in Communication and more broadly in humanistic studies, one that parallels in some sense the rhetorical turn. Taking, as does Richard Bauman, a performance-centered perspective on language as a social and cultural system, we find that our laminated forms of engagement have themselves two sides, much in the same way that performance theory itself draws from two competing traditions of social description. In the context of one tradition, performance signifies the reproduction of the social. Performance implies repetition. It suggests typified action in recurrent situations, precisely those considerations that mark our notion of genre. Indeed, performance, repeated over time and situated in place, develops the very chronotopes that shape the laminations of activity. In the context of another tradition, however, performance represents a dynamic of change, a means of altering the social. Here, performance suggests departure, not repetition. A richly conceived approach to performance, and more particularly to the laminations of academic and civic, would need to draw on both traditions, the imitative and the inventive.

Our laminations of the academic and civic exist only in so far as they are performed. And of course, in having our own students address the civic in the context of a writing classroom, we ourselves are asking them to perform a discursive lamination of their own academic and civic roles. Such performances bring to light three tensions or paradoxes that might contribute to our own more informed practice in the civic oriented classroom.

The first of these tensions or paradoxes has to do with agency. The attractions of the civic stem in good measure from the presumption that what seems constrained in the academy—the student's own agency—becomes unfettered on the street. Yet, a performative take on our laminations of the academic and civic would suggest that agency inevitably draws on the imitative and the inventive, the conventional and the kairotic, and is never simply out there, ready to be seized on the other side of the classroom door. Similarly, I worry that appeals to activism will ring hollow unless we take account of the complex laminations of socioliterate activity in which action must perforce be grounded. Moreover, because socioliterate activity is always a laminate of several domains, some foregrounded and others not, I believe we have unduly narrowed the arena for civic activity if we think merely in terms of advocacy or political participation.

A second set of tensions or paradoxes can be found around the notions of invention and the rhetorical commonplace. Performance trades on the commonplace, even as it uses the commonplace as an inventive moment. As we work with variously constructed laminations of the academic and civic at the classroom door, we might explore the rich interplay between commonplace and invention. Yet the received and artificial binary of academic and civic tends to undermine that interplay, because the liberatory, activist, and radical impulses that motivate and accompany our celebration of the street tend to dismiss the commonplace and the conventional. That is unfortunate. If our performances of various laminations of the academic and civic can make a difference—and I believe they can—that difference might lie in finding and celebrating our common places.

A final tension or paradox can be seen at work in our notions of genre. A model that places the academic and the civic at opposite ends of a spectrum shortchanges the ways in which genre can become a very flexible and useful tool by which to explore the discursive laminations of academic and civic. When some of our colleagues ask students to write in the supposed genres of civic engagement (the op-ed piece, the proposal, the letter to elected officials), and link the civic too closely to those genres, we unduly narrow the range of genres that can come into play as we perform distinctive laminations of academic and civic activity. We should likewise distrust distinctions between school genres and 'real' genres, distinctions that fail to capture the complexities of our laminated work. Finally, insofar as genre itself captures the interplay between imitation and invention, the conventional and the freshly opportune, genre becomes an apt vehicle for exploring the conceptual richness of performance as a means for understanding and enacting the discursive laminations of the academic and civic.

Let us, then, reframe rhetoric and composition's desire for the civic as a desire to appreciate the many ways that the academic and civic already lead highly intertwined and laminated lives, as our own discursive performances, on either side of the classroom door, surely bear out.

WORKS CITED

Bakhtin, M. M. "Forms of Time and of the Chronotope in the Novel." *The Dialogic Imagination.* Ed. Michael Holquist. Trans. Caryl Emerson and Michael Holquist. Austin: U of Texas P, 1981. 84-258.

---. *Speech Genres and Other Late Essays.* Ed. Caryl Emerson and Michael Holquist. Trans. Vern W. McGee. Austin: U of Texas P, 1986.

Bauman, Richard. *Story, Performance, and Event: Contextual Studies of Oral Narrative.* Cambridge, UK: Cambridge UP, 1986.

Eberly, Rosa. *Citizen Critics: Literary Public Spheres.* Urbana: U of Illinois P, 2000.

George, Diana. "The Word on the Street: Public Discourse in a Culture of Disconnect." *Reflections: A Journal of Writing, Service-Learning, and Community Literacy* 2.2 (Spring 2002): 5-18.

Gere, Anne. "Kitchen Tables and Rented Rooms: The Extracurriculum of Composition." *College Composition and Communication* 45 (1994): 75-92.

Goffman, Erving. *Forms of Talk.* Philadelphia: U of Pennsylvania P, 1981.

Goffman, Erving and Alessandro Duranti. "Rethinking Context: An Introduction." *Rethinking Context: Language as an Interactive Phenomenon.* Ed. Alessandro Duranti and Charles Goodwin. Cambridge, UK: Cambridge UP, 1992. 1-42.

Hopkins, Mary Frances. "The Performance Turn—and Toss." *Quarterly Journal of Speech* 81 (1995): 228-36.

Miller, Carolyn. "Genre as Social Action." *Quarterly Journal of Speech* 70 (1984): 151-67.

Prior, Paul A. *Writing/Disciplinarity: A Sociohistoric Account of Literate Activity in the Academy.* Mahwah, NJ: Erlbaum, 1998.

Weisser, Christian R. *Moving beyond Academic Discourse: Composition Studies and the Public Sphere.* Carbondale: Southern Illinois UP, 2002.

Wells, Susan. "Rogue Cops and Health Care: What Do We Want from Public Writing?" *College Composition and Communication* 47.3 (October 1996): 325-41.

34

Sisyphus at Starbucks: Complicity Through Resistance in the Satire of *Liberties*

Omedi Ochieng
Bowling Green State University

This chapter, grounded in Antonio Gramsci's theory of hegemony, examines how the satiric genre's ambiguities and contradictoriness make the genre particularly suited to the sustenance of ruling class hegemony. Specifically, I argue that Maureen Dowd's satiric column, *Liberties,* although manifestly resistant to ruling class hegemony, was latently complicit in sustaining and legitimating elite hegemony during the 2000 presidential election impasse. I attempt to demonstrate how the limits of the satiric genre as well as the complexities of ruling class hegemony functioned to domesticate and appropriate Dowd's rhetoric toward the interests of the elite. This chapter has three sections: The first section situates the politics of satire in its historical context; the second section discusses Gramsci's theory of hegemony; and the last section presents this study's findings.

SATIRE'S DOUBLE-EDGED FORM

Fredric V. Bogel argues that traditional definitions of satire have contained a number of assumptions about the nature of the genre. The first assumption is that satire "is a full-fledged artistic mode ("literary"), not merely a symptom of ill humor or personal spite or something else" (1). Thus, this assumption implies that even though satire is "undeniably [...] an intervention in personal or literary or political quarrels, as a literary mode it cannot simply be reduced to those quarrels or their motives" (1). The second assumption holds that "the originating moment of satire is the satirist's perception of an object that exists anterior to the satiric attack" (2). These assumptions imply that there is a clear and unambiguous distinction between the satirist, who in a sense represents the forces of Good, and the object of the satire, who is depicted as the representative of Evil. Moreover, "[t]he reader's position [...] is expected to be aligned with the satirist's, and the reader to share in the condemnation of the satiric object that this identification entails [...]" (2).

Bogel challenges these traditional assumptions that underlie theories of satiric rhetoric in his book *The Difference Satire Makes: Rhetoric and Reading from Jonson to Byron*. According to Bogel, the satirist is situated in that uncertain intersection between division and identification that Kenneth Burke says rhetoric occupies. As Bogel succinctly puts it, "Satire [...] is a rhetorical means to the production of difference in the face of a potentially compromising similarity, not the articulation of differences already securely in place" (42).

The double-edgedness of satire is rooted in two aspects of the genre: its form and content. Connery and Combe describe the "militant disunity" of satire, arguing that "[p]erhaps more than any other genre, satire is constructed or structured on the basis of oppositions [which are] represented in their extremes to achieve maximum tension" (6). This contrariness of satire is due to the fact that the "most common rhetorical figures of satire—irony, paradox, and oxymoron [are] based upon opposites [...]" (6). Connery and Combe draw attention to Mary Clare Randolph's analysis of formal verse satire, which noted the juxtaposition of extreme vice and extreme virtue in satire, made even more pronounced by the satirist's emphasis on vice. Similarly, they cite Joseph Addison's evocative imagery: "Satire had Smiles in her look, and a Dagger under her Garment" (6).

Historically, political leaders have sought to domesticate satirists to serve the elite's interests. The British elite in the late eighteenth and nineteenth centuries, for example, gendered satire a masculine preserve. According to Gary Dyer, the British elite declared the genre "a most improper study for them [women]" (150), whereas others "denied that women were capable of the scurrility endemic to [satire]" (150). Women who defied elite-instituted conventions and wrote satirical articles were peremptorily branded "'masculine,' lacking the feminine 'soft sensibility'" (151). In an indication that form was as important as satiric content, the British ruling class gendered certain forms of satire masculine and other forms feminine. Thus, Juvenalian satire—satire "meant to induce fear and [was] uncompromisingly harsh and moralistic" (39)—was gendered masculine, and ascribed an essentialist British and upper-class distinction. In contrast, Horatian satire—satire that "aim[ed] at laughter or amusement, its poetic speaker [...] presented as mild, amicable, almost conciliatory" (39)—was gendered feminine. The consequence, Dyer reports, was that "those writers with only weak or qualified ties to the dominant classes were less likely to write in the Juvenalian manner" (53).

The gendered history of satire—a political act rooted in contestations for power—raises interesting questions about women's uses of satire in the present-day United States. Moreover, there is yet a more compelling reason to examine its uses in contemporary society. Although the United States's ruling class exercises dominance through the cultivation of the virulent strains of patriarchy obtained in eighteenth-century Britain, this domination differs considerably from its historical antecedent. The difference lies in the form of dominance: Whereas the British elite often employed raw political power to maintain control, the ruling class in the United States sustain their dominance by a far subtler form of political control. This control has been identified, by a section of political theorists, as hegemony. The next section discusses the nature and form of hegemony in greater detail.

HEGEMONY IN THE 2000 ELECTIONS: CONSENT THROUGH CONTRADICTORY CONSCIOUSNESS

The theory of hegemony was developed by Antonio Gramsci. According to Gramsci, hegemony is "the 'spontaneous' consent given by the great masses of the population to the general direction imposed on social life by the dominant fundamental group; this consent is 'historically' caused by the prestige (and consequent confidence) which the dominant group enjoys because of its position and function in the world of production" (12).

Previous scholarship on Gramsci's theory has, however, either misinterpreted the nature of Gramsci's conceptualization of consent or overemphasized the extent to which the elite in society are responsible for the manufacture of that consent (Lears). In fact, as Lears notes in his lucid clarification of Gramsci's theory, consent, as it was developed by Gramsci, does not take one form. Although Gramsci allowed that certain workers' consent follows the form of active and enthusiastic support for elite rule, his theory of hegemony posited a formulation of consent that was more nuanced. According to Gramsci, consent may take the form of:

> Two theoretical consciousness (or one contradictory consciousness): one which is implicit in his activity and which in reality unites him with all his fellow-workers in the practical transform of the real world; and one, superficially explicit or verbal, which he has inherited from the past and uncritically absorbed. But this verbal conception is not without consequences. It holds together a specific social group, it influences moral conduct and the direction of the will, with varying efficacity but often powerfully enough to produce a situation in which the contradictory state of consciousness does not permit of any action, any decision or any choice, and produces a condition of moral and political passivity. (333)

This formulation of consent is thus a thorough revision of the orthodox Marxist concept of false consciousness. In Gramsci's view, the working classes are not always or even necessarily sleepwalking through a fog of ignorance and lies manufactured by the ruling class. In certain contexts, the workers may be quite conscious of certain injustices, and may even consider overt resistance against these injustices. Nevertheless, it is the genius of the elite to circumscribe *the range of alternatives* available to the workers. According to Lears, this is partly achieved through language. He points out that "the available vocabulary helps mark the boundaries of permissible discourse, discourages the clarification of social alternatives, and makes it difficult for the dispossessed to locate the source of their unease, let alone remedy" (570).

This chapter examines the rhetoric of Maureen Dowd, a columnist of the *New York Times,* for resistance and complicity with ruling-class hegemony. It next examines the articles that Dowd wrote in her column, *Liberties,* during the 2000 presidential election impasse. The first section documents some of the ways that Dowd resisted elite hegemony, and the second section interrogates some of the ways that her satire worked in the interests of the ruling class. The upshot of

Dowd's contradictory consciousness, this chapter posits, was to bolster ruling-class hegemony.

DOWD'S RESISTANCE

Enactment

The history of satire in the Anglo-American context in which the ruling class has gendered satire a masculine genre demonstrates that Dowd's adoption of satire as a mode of political communication was *in itself* a significant form of resistance. Dowd adopted a rhetorical form that Karlyn Kohrs Campbell and Kathleen Hall Jamieson have termed *enactment*: a rhetorical form "in which the speaker incarnates the argument, is the proof of the truth of what is said" (9). She, on occasion, inserted herself into her columns, drawing attention to her role as a satiric persona. For example, Dowd said of George W. Bush: "W. [Bush] is starting to weird me out" ("Ahab" par. 2). She also mocked Al Gore by comparing herself favorably to the Democratic presidential candidate, likening his efforts to dispute the election results to Sisyphus's futile hard work: "Seeing Al [Gore] trudging up the hill in the cold, just 537 votes short of his prize, Sisyphus pushing his burden to Starbucks, instantly put my petty problems in perspective" ("Sisyphus" par. 7). Dowd thus inverted the hierarchy of power existing between her and the powerful politicians—a significant act of empowerment. She also positioned herself as a subject in possession of agency and power by referring to herself in the first-person pronoun *I* ("Beginning").

Dowd's resistance to the ruling class through her relentless criticism of public officials and the position she staked out as a female satirist was manifest. Yet, her criticism was hardly radical because it was developed from the premises of the dominant ideology. The following section explores the various manifestations of Dowd's complicity.

DOWD'S COMPLICITY

The Ideology of the Elite

As Lears has noted, opposition to ruling class hegemony does not translate into immunity from elite ideologies. Dowd's denunciation of the corruption of the ruling class was, for all its venom, domesticated by a fundamental conformity to the basic tenets of elite ideology. A close reading of Dowd's column revealed that her ideology was permeated with ruling-class myths that have come to be taken as commonsense notions of American identity. These commonsense notions are bound up within the resonant narrative of the American Dream and can be summed up in two threads: first, the ideology of rugged individualism; and second (but closely related to the first), the Darwinian ethic of the survival of the fittest.

Paradoxically, the ruling-class ideology of rugged individualism was imbricated even within the very terms of Dowd's resistance to this discourse. That is, in enacting the role of the satiric persona, Dowd, quite probably unwittingly, constructed herself as *the* quintessential libertarian agent: individuated and transcendental. Ultimately, this ideology prevented Dowd from articulating collective forms of resistance to ruling-class hegemony that hold possibilities for substantive structural changes.

This limitation, latent within Dowd's satire, emerges more clearly in a close reading of her criticism of public officials. Although her criticism was uncompromisingly harsh in assailing the political leaders at the center of the election controversy, it was nevertheless aimed at individuals and not the political system that sustained and legitimized ruling-class hegemony. Dowd's critique thus appeared more as a criticism of public officials for personal moral failures or personal eccentricities than as a critique of the political system. For example, Dowd charged that the election impasse had taken place because "the matched set of dauphins [the presidential candidates] were [...] inadequate" ("Unelection," par. 4). In the same article, she blamed the outgoing president, Bill Clinton, for the election stalemate (pars. 12, 13). Dowd went further, implying that all that was wrong about the election impasse could be blamed on the two presidential candidates' flawed personalities. For example, Dowd stated: "It is not the tie, but the grating behavior of the contenders in the tie, that is trying American patience" ("Mistrust" par. 22). Yet in focusing on the election as a clash of personalities, Dowd failed to articulate the systemic underpinnings of the election impasse—political corruption and cronyism, institutionalized voter disenfranchisement and neglect, and the historical foundations of political oppression (Anderson).

Dowd's creed of individualism was joined at the hip by a judgment informed by the Darwinian survival of the fittest ethic—fitness, in this context, measured by a politician's ability to beat a rival, his or her standing in the opinion polls, or even the politician's ability to get away with wrongdoing. The result was the subordination of principle to strategy, or a fixation with product over process. For example, Dowd concluded that the presidential candidates were "inadequate" ("Unelection" par. 4) because Al Gore was "a pol who can't even carry his own home state" (par. 5), and George W. Bush failed "to win the popular vote against a Democrat referred to in his own party as 'Eat Your Spinach'" (par. 6). Even Dowd's powerful critique of the unethical activities of the Supreme Court justices resorted to the invocation of the opinion polls as an arbiter of fairness. Dowd concluded the article with a purported pronouncement from Chief Justice Rehnquist: "*We're dropping in the polls* [italics mine] on the question of our fairness, but we still need to anoint Bush president" ("Bloom" par. 16). Similarly, Dowd conflated successful image management—the strategy for success in the American political arena—with right action. For example, she said of Bush: "Republicans sanguinely compare him to Ronald Reagan, but at least President Reagan had the gift of reassurance before the camera" ("Ahab" par. 16).

Irony

Dowd employed the trope of irony in most of her articles during the election impasse. Her solution to the election impasse, for example, was the ironic "Oh, heck, let's just keep Clinton" ("Unelection" par. 1). Most of her articles were suffused in an ironic tone that simultaneously ridiculed politicians even as she entertained her readers. It is for that reason that Dowd's irony was a particularly striking illustration of contradictory consciousness. Although she masterfully expressed her unease with the two presidential candidates, she at the same time undermined her critique by an ironic tone that, primarily through trivialization, denied her readers agency.

Dowd's irony was in many ways analogous to a presentation of the reader as a witness to a mudbath. The reader was likely to be repelled by the mudbath, perhaps just a touch amused, but hardly likely to feel inclined to *intervene*. Dowd's irony did not so much expose the evils of the political system as it did the buffoonery of the politicians. A lengthy quotation of Dowd's ironic putdown of Bush illustrates this point: "During the campaign, W. [Bush] had a swagger, a John Wayne gunslinger pose. But now when he comes out to face the cameras he blinks and shrinks, looking tremulous and frightened, dwarfed by American flags" ("Ahab" par. 14).

As the previous example shows, although Dowd was undoubtedly successful in documenting the flaws of politicians, these are, ultimately, flaws that encouraged the reader to smirk, not those that were likely to make the reader quiver with moral indignation. To borrow Dyer's phrase, "'Lessening' people does not 'lesson' them or us about anything except our shared humanity—an effect that is ultimately comic, not satiric" (160).

It may be argued that Dowd's irony is the trope that well describes the American polity—the opposition to elite hegemony ubiquitous but fragmented; the workers paralyzed by divided loyalties; the status quo in place in spite of so much "resistance." But that is precisely the point. At best, Dowd's irony became a device to chronicle the workings of ruling-class hegemony, not to resist it. Hers was the voice that Schudson speaks of so poignantly: "Irony is the attitude of the observer, the person who has seen it all, the person for whom *plus ca change, plus c'est la meme chose*, the person whose sense of history is one of eternal recurrence rather than direction" (105). In other words, the voice of the status quo.

CONCLUSION

The ultimate irony of Dowd's satire was that in resisting elite hegemony, it fed and strengthened it. Hers was not so much *resistance* as it was *complicity through token resistance*. In sneering at Al Gore's attempts to dispute the Florida election results, Dowd was proven right in likening his efforts to the futile exertion of Sisyphus. What she did not realize was how her own resistance evoked the vivid image of a lone and tormented figure, laboring hopelessly to push up a rock that would inevitably roll down. Of course, this does not therefore mean that resistance per se is not necessary, nor that it is doomed to failure. It requires a problematization of the means by which resistance is conducted. A more robust form of resistance is clearly attested to by the previous analysis.

WORKS CITED

Anderson, Perry. "Testing Formula Two." *New Left Review* (8 March/April 2001): 5-22.

Bogel, Fredric. V. *The Difference Satire Makes: Rhetoric and Reading from Jonson to Byron.* Ithaca: Cornell UP, 2001.

Campbell, Karlyn K., and Kathleen H. Jamieson. "Form and Genre in Rhetorical Criticism: An Introduction." *Form and Genre: Shaping Rhetorical Action.* Ed. Karlyn K. Campbell and Kathleen H. Jamieson. Falls Church, VA: Speech Communication Assn., 1976. 9-32.

Connery, Brian A., and Kirk Combe. "Theorizing Satire: A Retrospective and Introduction." *Theorizing Satire: Essays in Literary Criticism.* Ed. Brian A. Connery and Kirk Combe. New York: St. Martin's, 1995. 1-15.

Dowd, Maureen. "Ahab vs. the Waco Whale." *New York Times* 29 Nov. 2000, late ed.: A35+.

---. "The Beginning of the End? Or the End of the Beginning?" *New York Times* 10 Dec. 2000, late ed.: A15+.

---. "The Bloom Is Off the Robe." *New York Times* 13 Dec. 2000, late ed.: A35+.

---. "Mistrust in the Trust." *New York Times* 15 Nov. 2000, late ed.: A29+.

---. "Sisyphus at Starbucks." *New York Times* 6 Dec. 2000, late ed.: A33+.

---. "The Unelection Day." *New York Times* 9 Nov. 2000, late ed.: A23+.

Dyer, Gary. *British Satire and the Politics of Style: 1789-1839.* Cambridge, UK: Cambridge UP, 1997.

Gramsci, Antonio. *Selections from the Prison Notebooks.* Trans. Quentin Hoare and Geoffrey N. Smith. New York: Intl. Publishers, 1971.

Lears, Jackson T. J. "The Concept of Cultural Hegemony: Problems and Possibilities." *The American Historical Review* 90 (1985): 567-93.

Schudson, M. "When? Deadlines, Datelines, and History." *Reading the News.* Ed. Robert K. Manoff and Michael Schudson. New York: Pantheon, 1986. 79-108.

35

Learning to Be Civil: Citizen *Judith* and Old English Culture

Dana M. Oswald
Ohio State University

Women in Old English literature are notoriously silent. In *Beowulf*, the only woman who speaks is Queen Wealhtheow, to plead for her sons' rights to her husband Hrothgar's throne. Although women's actions are not as limited as their speech, we are offered only two alternatives: A woman may be a peaceweaver, one who carries the cup, serves the warriors, and is conveniently and passively married off (Olsen 312); or she can be monstrous and physically violent, like Grendel's mother, arguably Beowulf's most threatening foe. We also have little material evidence about Anglo-Saxon women but, as Clare Lees and Gillian Overing announce in their recent book, *Double Agents*, these silences and absences "tend to reinforce a general (and erroneous) perception that Anglo-Saxon culture has nothing of value to contribute to the history of women and gender in the West or, worse, that there were somehow no women in the Anglo-Saxon period" (6). The Old English *Judith*, then, is striking because in it we see a valorous and publicly respected woman who is capable of calculated speech, effective gesture, and physical violence. Judith, the protagonist of the Old English poem, must use her *metis*, that is, her cunning intelligence (Detienne and Vernant), to defeat the Assyrian military leader, Holofernes, on his own ground. She uses the kind of tactics Michel de Certeau describes in his book, *The Practice of Everyday Life*, not only while she is in the camp of her enemy, but also after her return home, when she must exhort the Bethulian warriors to accomplish their victory.

The poem of *Judith* is a tactical one, much like its heroine. It does the tricky work of creating a powerful woman capable of violent physical action whose careful rhetoric renders her a warrior. Scholars argue over the poem's purpose: Feminists extol it as a text that celebrates the power of woman, religious scholars mark it as an allegory for God's condemnation of impurity and victory over evil, and comparative scholars define it in terms of its Latin Vulgate source. These approaches, however, fail to account for one of the most remarkable characteristics of Judith: She is able to adapt her rhetoric to perform effectively for various audiences. In this chapter, I define *rhetoric* as the art of persuasion through speech and gesture. Furthermore, her tactical adaptations correspond to her physical movement out of and into her own city. Because Judith's physical location determines her ability to act and speak, the poem informed a listening Anglo-Saxon audience of both genders about the proper ways for women to perform within the confines of their communities. Although the poem features Judith as its heroine, it does not encourage women to take violent action against the men who threaten them. Instead, Anglo-Saxon women are persuaded to act as Judith does within the confines of her city. She is a civic model to both the warriors inside the text, and the men and women in the poem's listening audience.

Judith is successful in both words and works, an important quality in a Germanic warrior; together, her words and works ensure the protection of her city. But we must bear in mind that Judith is not, and cannot be, a warrior like Beowulf. She uses tactics, not strategies, according to Michel de Certeau's definitions. Strategy "postulates a *place* that can be delimited as its *own* and serve as a base from which relations with an *exteriority* composed of targets or threats can be managed" (35-36; emphasis in original). A tactic, alternately, "is a calculated action determined by the absence of a proper locus [...] it operates in isolated actions, blow by blow. It takes advantage of 'opportunities' and depends on them, being without any base where it could stockpile its winnings, build up its own position, and plan raids. What it wins, it cannot keep [...] in short, a tactic is an art of the weak" (37). Most Old English warriors, like Holofernes and Beowulf, make use of strategy; they wear armor and carry swords. But Judith uses tactics; she is wise and quick thinking. Rather than just being *shearp*, sharp as Beowulf is warned to be, Judith is consistently called *gleaw*, prudent (13b, 171a, 333b); *snotor*, shrewd (55a, 125a); and *searoðoncol*, discerning (145a, 330b). These words, although rarely used to define women, are also rarely used to define warriors.

Let us next turn to the poem with these categories in mind. Judith's works take place in Holofernes' camp. She, a Bethulian widow, is away from her kingdom and the safety of her walls and warriors. But she could not accomplish what she does within the security of such restraints; she must use her dislocation to take Holofernes unaware *because* he is in a strategic position. He is in his own camp and she is a guest there. Because this manuscript is fragmentary, we do not know in this poem how Judith came into the camp, but it is clear that she does not have her own space. She is indeed carried, *læden*, from the warrior feast to Holofernes' tent. Once inside, however, Judith controls the space of his golden flynetted tent from which one can see, but cannot be seen; his panopticon. It is the very place Holofernes uses to watch his own men without their knowledge:

þær wæs eallgyldan
fleohnet fæger *ond ymbe þæs folctogan*
bed ahongen *þæt se bealofulla*
mihte wlitan þurh *wigena baldor*
on æghwylcne *þe ðær inne com*. (46b-50b)

(There was a fair flynet, all golden, hanging around the commander's bed so that the baleful one, the prince of warriors, might look through on anyone who came by there.)[1]

In some sense here, Judith opportunistically attains the strategic position Holofernes has given up; she knows when he is about to enter the tent and she can be prepared. Furthermore, her actions will be hidden from any of Holofernes's retinue by the golden flynet. Moreover, her tactical position, that of a "weak" woman, enables Holofernes to give up his defenses.

When Holofernes is carried into his tent and passes out in a drunken stupor, he is convinced of his own safety and well-being in a space he has always controlled. Judith is not the creator of the privacy Holofernes would have used to shield her rape from the eyes of his soldiers. Instead, she is afforded a moment before Holofernes awakens, and she must think quickly about how she can best use his space. She is thoroughly, or vigorously, mindful (*"þearle gemyndig"* [74b]) about what she must do to defeat Holofernes. Holofernes's belief that he is safe and invulnerable can be used as a weapon against him. She prays, but not for an answer to her problem; instead, she prays for the strength to perform the act she has already decided on (83a-93b). When she drags him from the bed by his hair, she does not struggle; rather, she handles him *"fæste,"* firmly (99a); *"bysmerlice,"* ignominiously (100a); and *"listum,"* skillfully (101a). She does not carry a sword of her own, so she uses what is available to her—his own sword—to decapitate him. Because she is in his space instead of her own, she must use the mobility of tactics and, as de Certeau says, "accept the chance offerings of the moment" (37). When one blow is not enough, she strikes again without fear or revulsion. Her handmaid places his head into their foodsack and off they go, back to her people. Because Judith is in a position of tactics, she cannot, and does not want to, keep this space of his. Although tactics have won this victory for her, Judith's *metis*—her "good eye"—keeps her focus on her ultimate goal: a Hebrew victory over all Assyrians.

Judith willingly abandons the physical space she has won in order to invoke the powerful rhetorical move she has just made. Although this beheading is a very physical act, she performs it simultaneously for its symbolic and motivational power. She beheads Holofernes so that she may return home to inspire her own warriors to victory. Unlike Beowulf, Judith's beheadings do not follow a purpose solely physical or for personal glory. Despite the fact that Beowulf takes Grendel's head to Hrothgar's court, much as Judith takes Holofernes's head, Beowulf's gesture does nothing to inspire action in his audience, just admiration and gratitude. It is neither, for him, a tactic nor a strategy; rather, it is a symbol that Mary Godfrey claims "generates his version of the battle" (4). Judith, on the other hand, will not simply use the head to prove that she has fought a battle bravely; she will use her enemy's decapitated head as a symbol to achieve her goal and motivate her people. Therefore, Judith's tactics are not just employed against Holofernes, but are exercised in the exhortation to her own people as well.

On Judith's return to her kingdom, her ability to act alters significantly. The woman who could drag a drunken warrior from his bed by his hair now can only speak, exhort, and accept. She does not carry Holofernes's head herself, or display it as soon as she reaches her kingdom. In fact, while standing at the gate of her city, she gives an entry speech without offering any specific information, particularly leaving out her own agency: "'*Ic eow secgan mæg, þoncwyrðe þing,*'" ("I can tell you about a worthy deed"; 152b-153a). But she does not yet tell them of this deed, although her citizens are all present to hear. In fact, she chooses not to enter the city until she has given the speech that tells them she has good news. I suggest this is another of Judith's tactics, and an important part of her delivery. Judith is still in the space of the other, outside her own kingdom. Although, as Godfrey says, "like Beowulf, she is triumphant; her approach sends the Hebrews running 'in throngs' out to meet her" (17), unlike Beowulf, she does not come stalking into the city, bearing Holofernes's head in clear sight. She relies on the dramatic moment of revealing the head in order to persuade her army of their imminent victory.

To say that Judith's re-entry to her city allows her to shift from tactics to strategy would be far too simple. Although she has returned to her own "locus of power"—her position as a beloved noblewoman and widow in her kingdom—Judith's success relies on her effective manipulation of time and words. Instead of relying on her own established position within the city, she must combine the stability of strategy (her fixed position within the community) with the *metis* of tactic (the clever use of time and appropriation of material) so that she may meet her goal. Therefore, once the Bethulians have welcomed Judith back into her city, she can reveal her agency in the "good news." Although she uses Holofernes's head as a symbol, she does not unveil it or touch it herself; rather, she commands her servant woman to do it for her:

þa seo gleawe het,   golde gefrætewod,
hyre ðinenne   þancolmode
þæs herewæðan   heafod onwriðan
ond hyt to behðe   blodig ætywan
þam burhleodum,   hu hyre æt beaduwe gespeow. (171a-175b)

(Then the prudent woman decorated with gold commanded her thoughtful handmaid to unwrap the head of the warrior and to display it to the townspeople as a bloody sign of how she succeeded at battle.)

Before Judith even speaks, she makes clear what has happened. Judith is, in a sense, not moving into strategy and power by returning to her people, but instead into a different position of weakness. Whereas in Holofernes's kingdom she was at the mercy of his leadership, in her own, in order to persuade her warriors into victory, she must abide by the social limitations placed on women.

Only after this rhetorical sign of her victory and of the beheading of the Assyrian army can Judith offer a second speech. She begins:

"Her ge magon sweotole,   si gerofe hæleð,
leoda ræswan,   on ðæs laðestan
hæðenes heaðorinces   heafod starian,
Holofernus,   unlyfigendes." (177a-180b)

("Triumphant men, leaders of the people, here you may openly gaze upon the head of the most hated heathen warrior, the dead Holofernes.")

and ends:

> *"Fynd syndon eowere*
> *gedemed to deaðe ond ge dom agon,*
> *tir æt tohtan, swa eow getacnod hafað*
> *mihtig dryhten þurh mine hand."* (195b-199b)

> ("Your enemies are condemned to death and you will have renown and glory at battle, just as the mighty lord has betokened for you through my hand.")

Although Judith's audience is her citizens, both male and female, she addresses men, *"hæleð,"* specifically. She directs their gaze at the revealed head; Godfrey claims that this "display of the head is an opportunity to direct and structure the behavior of the Hebrews—urging them to fight, assuring them of victory" (19). She invokes the symbol of her rhetorical and physical decapitation and rearticulates the reason for Holofernes's demise as well as builds a nationalistic fervor. She finishes by drawing attention to her own success at a microcosmic battle and urges her soldiers forward, discarding any shred of doubt about their victory. Her action of beheading, as a woman, both shames and inspires her soldiers into action. Judith's words alone could not persuade the warriors of their ensured success, nor could the head of Holofernes. Judith must interpret for them the significance of the symbol—although she does not physically make the gesture, it is unintelligible without her words. But most telling of Judith's inability to act within the confines of her kingdom, she cannot lead her men into battle. Even though she has been capable of espionage and tactics—and in fact, murder—she cannot leave the safety of her kingdom to fight in a "real" battle. Although Christopher Fee sees her absence on the battlefield as a sign that "she, like any ideal Anglo-Saxon noblewoman, must in the end rely upon the agency of masculine military might in order to validate her right to rule" (406), David Chamberlain argues that her absence suggests "a 'national' rather than a 'personal' quality in the triumph, although it is Judith who makes the victory possible" (154).

Just as Judith's decapitation of Holofernes's can be used as a rhetorical move to spur her men into action, it also motivates Holofernes' men in the opposite way. Once they discover the headless body in the golden flynetted tent, they despair, and, without a leader, are unable to function. The Assyrian who discovers Holofernes's body cries:

> *"Her ys geswutelod ure sylfra forwyrd,*
> *toweard getacnod, þæt þære tide ys*
> *mid niðum neah geðrungen* [...]." (285a-287a)

> ("Here is revealed our own destruction, imminently betokened, that the time is hastened together with troubles.")

The word *getacnod*—betokened, made manifest, symbolized—is the strongest indicator of this parallel reaction to the symbolic decapitation: It appears only twice in the entire text of *Judith*. The first mention is in her motivational speech to her soldiers, and the second is here, in the Assyrians' speech of despair. Victory is betokened for the Hebrews by Holofernes's head, whereas doom is betokened for the Assyrians by its absence. Judith's single gesture creates the victory and doom that drives this entire text: Holofernes's actual presence or absence is not of importance, but the presence and absence of what he represents is.

Judith is subject to different sets of rules. She is a shrewd and brave noblewoman to whom her fellow citizens look for leadership, and thus she must behave as befits a ruler or a king. But she is also a woman who must defend and maintain her purity. These two sets of rules conflict as one urges her to set out to defeat Holofernes, whereas the other requires that she stay at home. Judith, then, is an anomaly. She is a leader in a time of war, and she behaves accordingly for the length of time that she is outside her city's walls. Once she has returned, however, she adopts the traditional position of a woman. With these female roles having been articulated, what could an audience of Anglo-Saxon women and men have learned from a text as confusing and shifting as *Judith*? I suggest that Judith's use of tactic and strategy offers a way into the text for its oral audience. Judith's physical tactics only occur outside her traditional location within city walls: When Judith is marginal to the city, so is she marginal to its social expectations. But rarely was an Anglo-Saxon woman so completely marginal to a social structure. Instead, Judith's example inside the city walls is a model for women. In fact, her major physical action has a rhetorical rather than simply a violent purpose. Thus, although no woman would have been encouraged to appropriate an attacker's sword and cut off his head, she would have learned what sorts of tactics and strategies were open to her. Judith must carefully negotiate between her use of tactics and strategy. Although her identity as a woman marks her as "weak," and thus a candidate for the use of tactics, so does the fixedness of her physical location establish her ability to use strategy. In carefully shifting between the stability of the hearth and the flexibility of weak social position—"the space of the other"—women's voices could be powerfully heard.

Judith is not a poem about liberating the woman confined to traditional roles. Whereas Anglo-Saxon men must learn to balance their words and works, women are covertly instructed not to "work" and to use words only sparingly. It rearticulates the exclusive nature of Anglo-Saxon society by making clear that Judith herself, despite her socially powerful role, must shift her behavior in order to achieve her ultimate goal. The borders of the city clearly show Anglo-Saxon women where their own borders are and the lines they cannot cross. Furthermore, Anglo-Saxon men also see the compliance of a powerful woman to social expectations. Gender codes are here reiterated in Judith's inability to fight in the war that results from her own motivating gesture. One fact, however, remains: An Old English maxim poem tells us that "the shield shall be for the warrior, the shaft for the spoiler, the bracelet shall be for the bride" (Gordon 344). When Judith's men return victorious from battle:

Hi to mede hyre
of ðam siðfate sylfre brohton,
eorlas æscrofe, Holofernes
sweord on swatigne helm, swylce eac side byrnan
gerenode readum golde. (334b-338a)

(The spear-brave men brought, as a reward for her from the expedition, Holofernes' sword and bloody helmet, as well as his vast mailcoat adorned with red gold.)

Judith receives the comitatus due a king: She cannot wear the armor into battle, as she might wear a bracelet in the hall. But these trappings of war are a fitting gesture in response to Judith's *taken*, or symbol—the head of its wearer.

NOTE

1. Translations mine.

WORKS CITED

Beowulf. Ed. Bruce Mitchell and Fred C. Robinson. Oxford, UK: Blackwell, 1998.

Chamberlain, David. "*Judith*: A Fragmentary and Political Poem." *Anglo-Saxon Poetry: Essays in Appreciation for John C. McGalliard.* Ed. Lewis E. Nicholson and Dolores Warwick Frese. Notre Dame, IN: U of Notre Dame P, 1975. 135-59.

de Certeau, Michel. *The Practice of Everyday Life.* Berkeley: U of California P, 1984.

Detienne, Marcel, and Jean-Pierre Vernant. *Cunning Intelligence in Greek Culture.* Sussex, UK: Harvester P, 1978.

Fee, Christopher. "Judith and the Rhetoric of Heroism in Anglo-Saxon England." *English Studies* 78.5 (1997): 401-06.

Godfrey, Mary Flavia. "*Beowulf* and *Judith*: Thematizing Decapitation in Old English Poetry." *Texas Studies in Literature and Language* 35.1 (1993): 1-43.

Gordon, R. K., ed. and trans. "Gnomic Poetry." *Anglo-Saxon Poetry.* London: Dent, 1926. 341-47.

Judith. Ed. Mark Griffith. Exeter, UK: U of Exeter P, 1997.

Lees, Clare, and Gillian R. Overing. *Double Agents: Women and Clerical Culture in Anglo-Saxon England.* Philadelphia: U of Pennsylvania P, 2001.

Olsen, Alexandra Hennessey. "Gender Roles." *A Beowulf Handbook.* Lincoln: U of Nebraska P, 1997. 311-24.

36

Memory, Narrative, and Myth in the Construction of National Identity: A Rhetorical Analysis of the Senate Debate Over Reparations for Japanese Americans

Maegan Parker
University of Puget Sound[1]

Japanese American incarceration was the prescription of FDR's Executive Order 9066, issued on February 19, 1942. The order gave military generals authority to create restricted military zones and evacuate Japanese Americans from those areas. General De Witt designated the West Coast as a restricted military zone, ordering the evacuation of all American citizens and resident aliens of Japanese ancestry. Japanese Americans from the West Coast were taken to assembly centers and later incarcerated in camps across Middle America for three years. Since the issuance of Executive Order 9066, Japanese and other Americans have been protesting the blatant civil rights deprivation it permitted. In 1980, President Jimmy Carter established an official commission to research the circumstances surrounding the incarceration. In 1983, the commission issued a report entitled *Personal Justice Denied*, concluding that incarceration was motivated by "race prejudice, wartime hysteria, and a failure of political leadership" (5). The commission recommended that a letter of apology, signed by the President and accompanied by 20,000 dollars, be given to each surviving Japanese American who had been incarcerated during World War II. In 1988, the Senate debated the issuance of these provisions. Their debate also dealt with the way in which our nation will officially remember the Japanese American incarceration as a period in our shared American history. More broadly, the 1988 Senate debate over reparations for Japanese Americans incarcerated during World War II demonstrates the societal struggle over collective memory of the past.

The Senate debate over reparations is best understood when analyzed through a conceptual framework comprised of collective memory, narrative, and mythical studies. "Collective" or "social" memory's relationship to history can be described simply: History is, whereas memory does.[2] The relationship need not be one of opposition, because the two concepts complement one another. History seeks to offer a record of past occurrences, while collective memory constructs a selective interpretation of those occurrences. Embedded within the essence of collective memory is contemporary motivation: History is interpreted subjectively to urge a perspective, advocate a position, or argue a policy. However, collective memory cannot exist in an antithetical position to history, because it is intrinsically anchored by factual record.[3] Collective memory is viewed as a persuasive medium by which the past is linked to the present. Implicit within the understanding of memory, as distinguished from history, is the recognition of memory's usability. Advocates *use* memory because history is mute: It simply *is*, and therefore relies on the human construct of collective memory to speak for it.

Collective memory is more than a social process of reconstructing the past; it is argumentative in the sense that public memory is evoked both selectively and purposefully. Marouf Hasian and Robert Frank offer three important products of the working relationship between history and collective memory. Together "[t]hey help us create our individual and collective identities, maintain our traditions, and allow us to forget [...]" (98). As depicted here, history and collective memory play an important role in the formation of societal understanding. More figuratively, David Thelen describes the process of molding collective memory as analogous to the framing of an image that a society wishes to reflect (1122). Accordingly, this image would embody those principles and perceptions that help define the collective—utilizing events from the past as a reflection of contemporary values. Theodore O. Prosise believes that constructing a collective memory may reaffirm or challenge the existing self-perceptions of a social organization (316-47).

A description of collective memory's attributes reflects its potential utility. But *how* does a socially reconstructed memory, anchored by historical occurrence and public contestation, define and challenge values, self-perceptions, or policy proposals? What elements of collective memory's composition enable the act of reconstruction to attain persuasive ends? Collective memory's reliance on the narrative form to deliver and challenge individual memory in the public realm accounts for its usability.

Narrativization describes the process of linking the past to the present, because during the process of storytelling historical events are represented in a purposeful manner. Meaning is what differentiates narrative from a mere temporal organization of events. Collective memory is constructed through individual narratives of historical occurrences presented to the public realm wherein they are negotiated and validated, constructing a cohesive social perception of the past.

Through the narrative form, the leadership of a collective engages in evaluative negotiations wherein pieces of the past are both illuminated and repressed, constructing a version of history that responds to contemporary needs and allows for prescriptive resolution. Narrativization enables individual and collective memory to link the past to the present in a manner that prescribes future action.[4]

Through the social process of remembering, past events are shaped and constructed in such a manner that encourages a particular response from the audience to which the narrative is related. Narrative's ability to inspire agency can be largely attributed to its connection with myth. This relationship is one characterized by necessary interdependence. Narratives are most persuasive when, as individual stories, they can attach themselves to long-standing myths, which are effective in the evocation of sentiment from a particular culture holding shared values and experiences. Thelen recognizes that the leadership of the collective often transforms memory into myth so that it may be easily packaged and consumed by the populous. For example, Lewis writes of President Ronald Reagan's rhetoric: "In the same way in which Reagan's stories give meaning to America, they define what it means to be American" (284). Through his observation, Lewis is demonstrating the interdependent relationship—myth informs the stories that further perpetuate a larger mythical framework.

Robert Scholes and Robert Kellogg maintain that myth becomes meaningful through two basic characteristics of narrative: motif and theme (28). Motif describes the representation of the external world within myths, while theme refers to the ideas and concepts embedded in its story. To Scholes and Kellogg's basic characteristics, a third discussed by Michael Osborn is worthy of mention. *Culturetypes,* Osborn claims, are "The counterpart of archetypes, [they] are culture-specific symbols that resonate important values [...]. Culturetypes remind us of what it means to be American, archetypes of what it means to be human" (123). Culturetypes, like archetypes, provide a simple narrative with persuasive poignancy; both have the ability to tap into wells of sentiment concerning nationality or humanity, respectively. Through an attachment to long-standing values and beliefs that connect seemingly autonomous narratives to mythical tradition, deliberative narratives become most persuasive.

To illustrate the interconnection among memory, narrative, and myth more concretely, I turn to the 1988 Senate debate concerning redress for Japanese Americans incarcerated during World War II. Within the debate, two clear positions arose. I labeled the contrasting positions the "narrative of advocacy" and that of "opposition to the bill." The narrative of advocacy was built by seventeen speeches from a bipartisan representation of narrators, including eleven Democrats and six Republicans.[5] The narrative of opposition consisted of eight speeches delivered by one Democrat and seven Republicans. Each side attempted to reconstruct the circumstances surrounding Japanese American incarceration in a manner that justified their present position on the reparation issue. Individual memories were shared via narrativization, highlighting certain events, characters, and themes. These individual memories conglomerated, creating a larger story that functioned persuasively to either advocate or oppose the legislation in question.

The first notable point of contention is the two narratives' clash in temporal sequence. The narrative of advocacy constructed their "story" in a manner that emphasized the need for reparations by minimizing past attempts at redress and maximizing the suffering of the incarcerated Japanese Americans. The scars from the injustice of incarceration were reported by the narrative of advocacy to be permanent. As Senator Matsunaga related, "For Americans of Japanese Ancestry who are over the age of 45, the single most traumatic event, the one which has shaped the rest of their lives, is the wholesale relocation and incarceration" (S4269). Conversely, the narrative of opposition paid little attention to the incarceration experience and instead focused their account on America's past and present apologetic attempts. In direct contrast to the narrative of advocacy, the narrative of opposition concluded their story happily, claiming that Japanese Americans have elevated themselves to the status of a privileged class. Senator Helms read from a letter written by former Senator Hayakawa during his final speech opposing reparations: "We are living today at a time when Japanese Americans are almost a privileged class, with their notorious scholastic aptitude, their industriousness, and their team spirit in whatever occupation they find themselves."[6]

Each side's depiction of "characters" highlighted discrepancies within their constructed memory as well. For instance, the way in which the narrative of advocacy characterized Japanese Americans as innocent victims of racism and injustice, permanently scarred by incarceration, differs drastically from the narrative of opposition's characterization. Matsunaga shared the story of a World War I. Veteran who committed suicide rather than being branded disloyal (S4326). References to the 442nd Regiment are also frequent, because the highly decorated Japanese American soldiers clearly demonstrate the loyalty of their people. In the opposition's story, Japanese Americans were characterized far differently. The narrative of opposition portrayed resident aliens and citizens of Japanese ancestry as both privileged and protected by internment. For example, former Senator Hayakawa argues that many of the youth incarcerated during World War II were released from camps to attend colleges on the East Coast, asserting that if they had not been interned then attendance at these colleges would have been less likely.[7] In addition, Senator Hecht described his memory of a lynch mob that was approaching a Japanese couple before officials came to incarcerate them (S4328). Most controversially, the narrative of opposition depicts these citizens and resident aliens of Japanese descent, alive during World War II, as potential spies, questioning their loyalty and innocence with "evidence" of fifth column activity.[8]

Additionally, the major themes emphasized by each narrative warrant attention. One major conflicting theme dealt with the issue of causation. Was Executive Order 9066 motivated by racism or military necessity? The narrative of advocacy asserts that racism was the sole catalyst for incarceration. They attempted to prove this by arguing that there was no military necessity behind the Japanese American evacuation. First, the narrative of advocacy claims that Japanese Americans posed no real threat to national security. Next, they argue that if there had been a threat, the FBI and Office of Naval Intelligence were capable of individually incarcerating any spies or saboteurs. Finally, the narrative of advocacy recalls the Battle at Midway in 1942 as ending any possible threat from the empire of Japan. Senator Cranston cited a letter from Attorney General Francis Biddle to Secretary Stimson opposing the incarceration, "stating that the War Department and the FBI had found no danger of imminent attack or evidence of planned sabotage" (S4279).

In direct contrast, the narrative of opposition claimed that the incarceration was motivated by a national security emergency. Senator Helms's statements alluding to instances of espionage on the West Coast bolstered this assertion, while Senator Hollings and Senator Wallop both argued that there was no way to determine Japanese American loyalty. Furthermore, Senator Crassley contended that the state of national security during the height of World War II mandated drastic measures. Quoting Justice Hugo Black, Crassley attempted to illustrate the emergency our nation was facing: "Compulsory exclusion of large groups of citizens from their homes, except under circumstances of direct emergency, is inconsistent with our basic governmental institutions. But when under conditions of modern warfare our shores are threatened, the power to protect must be commensurate with the threatened danger" (S4400). The opposition remembered the state of national security at the height of World War II as frightening, and this frame of remembrance helped to solidify their argument for the necessity of incarceration.

Another controversial theme prevalent in the debates was a struggle over the issue of precedent setting. The narrative of advocacy argued that the reparations bill would prevent future civil rights deprivation,[9] be demonstrative of a lesson learned,[10] and, most important, serve as a "remedy" to this abhorrent episode in American history.[11] In contrast, the narrative of opposition constructed a "philosophical objection" to reparations, claiming that they are a materialist solution and as such add further shame to a disgraceful episode in American history.[12] The essence of the philosophical objection fashioned by the narrators in opposition to reparations was succinctly stated by Senator Wallop when he claimed, "America's honor is not for sale and it is not for purchase, in either direction. Monetary policy does not buy it, nor can it be sold."[13] The narrators in opposition did not believe that offering reparations to Japanese Americans would remedy the mistakes of the past; quite conversely, they feared offering reparations would set a dangerous precedent.

Lastly, the dominant motifs reflected by each narrative are integral to the essence of the competing memories. As noted previously, motifs, or dominant themes, often link individual narratives to long-standing myths within a culture. Accordingly, the narrative of advocacy adopted a position of idealism by employing culturetypes that described America as being bound by the Constitution,[14] as well as being a proud nation that prizes patriotism and loyalty.[15] Senator Cranston argued that Japanese American incarceration "was a terrible affront to the ideals for which our nation stands" (S4278), and Senator Reid contended that incarceration "is a scourge on American history" (S4331). These statements represented the harm that the proposed reparations intended to remedy. Drawing on patriotic fervor, rejuvenated by the bicentennial celebration for the signing of the Constitution, the narrative of advocacy proposed a reaffirmation to American ideals: "This bill reinforces the strength of our Constitution by reaffirming our commitment to upholding the constitutional rights of all our citizens" (Inouye 4324).

Passage of the bill was further motivated by an emphasis on particular characteristics that America ideally embodies, such as our position as a civil rights leader among nations (Glenn S4268). The loyalty of the 442nd Battalion was another piece of history used by the narrative of advocacy to demonstrate the tragic irony that incarceration posed. Senator Exon urged, "we can cleanse our souls for the sin that the Government of the United States committed against American citizens of Japanese origin that were just as good, if not better, Americans, as many of them proved in World War II."[16] Finally, the narrative of advocacy reminded the Senate that America is a country that was built by and welcomes immigrants. Senator Wilson spoke of "the good fortune of the United States in being able to welcome to our shores the sons and daughters of immigrants who perhaps understand better than many of us who are native born the meaning of this country"(S4387).[17]

In contrast, the narrative opposing reparations used culturetypes to represent America as a nation that is reasonable, and has honor that cannot be restored by money from another generation. Essentially, the narrative of opposition used a position of realism to contrast the idealist nostalgia disseminated by the narrative of advocacy. America's realist nature was demonstrated through statements like Senator Warner's opening remark, "I feel obligated to rise and [...] defend the Members of this Chamber [...] who at the time [...] felt they were rendering the best judgment they could on behalf of this nation" (S4330). The narrative of opposition purports the seemingly noble intentions of past political leadership, which minimizes the need for reparations. Furthermore, Senator Crassley argued that America's honor is not for sale or purchase: "I don't understand how giving $20,000 to each survivor of the internment camps will help to restore their honor or that of the United States" (S4400). In conjunction, these attempts to connect the narrative of opposition with a larger "American Story" reflect an image of America that is prudent and reasonable. Although logical in its own right, the narrative of opposition failed to tap into long-standing sentiment through the utilization of attractive culturetypes, like those ideals that the narrative of advocacy reflected.

The Senate debate ended in a 69-27 vote in favor of reparations. Every Japanese American incarcerated during World War II who was still alive at the beginning of George H. Bush's presidency was mailed a letter containing an official apology and a check for $20,000. Although America officially apologized, the public debate over the way in which our society will remember this period in our shared history continues. For instance, in 1998, when the movie *Snow Falling on Cedars* was first released, the *Seattle Times* featured an ongoing "Letters to the Editor" dispute regarding the causes and conditions of the incarceration—nearly 56 years later. Furthermore, the recent treatment of Arab Americans following the September 11 attacks evokes intriguing parallels between these two instances of civil rights deprivation during wartime.

Moreover, analysis of the 1988 Senate debates over reparations for Japanese Americans offers a glimpse into how societies remember events collectively. This instance demonstrates how past events can be defined in a manner that persuades present understanding and thus prescribes future policy action. The narratives embedded within the Senate debate are most persuasive when they raise the question of identity, meaning simply that the culturetypes each side expresses, in attempts to define Americanism, relate to individual perceptions of our national identity. Senators constructing the positions advocating and opposing redress justify their stances with regards to the frame they construct, which reflects the ideology to which they adhere. If Americanism is a matter of maintaining ideals, then we, as Americans, must repair the injustice of the past. However, if Americanism is built by responsibility and pragmatism, then it would prove imprudent, even futile, to apologize for the wrongs of yesterday in light of the problems plaguing America today. In this way, we can see the relationship among collective memory, narrative, and myth demonstrated succinctly: Individual memory is related to the public sphere via the convention of narrative, which is informed by and further perpetuates myth.

NOTES

1. This chapter was made possible by the Carol Read Summer Research Grant awarded by the University of Puget Sound's Enrichment Committee and the mentorship of Jim Jasinski.
2. This dynamic is further described by Thelen, Schudson, Prosise, and Markovits and Reich.
3. Barry Schwartz introduces this notion in his article, "The Social Context of Commemoration: A Study in Collective Memory."
4. Sources consulted on narrative include Robert L. Scott and James Jasinski.
5. When analyzing the narratives, I included only speech acts that set forth an argument, a memory, or offered refutation to the opposing narrative.
6. Reading from the Hayakawa letter, Senator Helms ("Wartime Relocation of Civilians").
7. Again, reading from the Hayakawa letter, Senator Helms ("Wartime Relocation of Civilians").
8. Senator Helms and Senator Wallop are the two most vociferous narrators on this issue. Helms read from a transcript he claims to be a recorded conversation between spies in a Japanese Consulate in Seattle to Tokyo (S4408). Wallop read from a letter written by a constituent claiming to have met a Japanese spy overseas during the war (S4392; "Wartime Relocation of Civilians").
9. The narrative of advocacy uses this argument throughout the debate, most notably in the speeches of Senator Glenn (S4268), Senator Simon (S4274), Senator Cranston (S4278 and 4280), Senator Exon (S4387), Senator Evans (S4387), and Senator DeConcini (S4401; "Wartime Relocation of Civilians").
10. Senators such as Senator Inouye (S4324), Senator Wilson (S4325), and Senator Domenici (4399) use this logic ("Wartime Relocation of Civilians").
11. The remedy metaphor can be found in the speeches of Senator Matsunaga (S4269), Senator Adams (S4277), Senator Wilson (S4325), Senator Stevens (S4327), and Senator Evans (S4387; "Wartime Relocation of Civilians").
12. Wallop uses the words of his constituents to articulate this argument, which is echoed by many other narrators in opposition (S4393; "Wartime Relocation of Civilians").
13. The philosophical objection represented here by Wallop's comment on S4393 can also be seen in the speeches of Senator Hollings (S4280), Senator Hecht (S4328), Senator Chaffee (S4334 and S4335), and Senator Helms (S4400; "Wartime Relocation of Civilians").
14. Senator Matsunaga (S4269), Senator Adams (S4277), Senator Cranston (S4278), Senator Inouye (S4323 and S4324), and Senator Reid (S4331; "Wartime Relocation of Civilians").
15. America is portrayed as a nation "civilized and proud" by Senator Glenn (S4268), Senator Inouye (S4324), Senator Wilson (S4325), Senator Reid (S4332), Senator Evans (S4387), and Senator Dole (S4400; "Wartime Relocation of Civilians").
16. Specific quotes from Senator Exon (S4387). Others related to this include Senator Glenn (S4268 and 4269), Senator Adams (S4277), Senator Inouye (S4324), and Senator Matsunaga (S4326; "Wartime Relocation of Civilians").
17. Specific quote from Senator Wilson (S4387). Others related to this include Senator Wilson (S4325) and Senator Evans (S4387; "Wartime Relocation of Civilians").

WORKS CITED

Hasian, Marouf, Jr., and Robert E. Frank. "Rhetoric, History, and Collective Memory: Decoding the Goldhagen Debates." *Western Journal of Communication* 63 (1999): 95-114.

Jasinski, Jim. *Sourcebook on Rhetoric: Key Concepts in Contemporary Rhetorical Studies.* Thousand Oaks, CA: Sage, 2001.

Lewis, William F. "Telling America's Story: Narrative Form and the Reagan Presidency." *Quarterly Journal of Speech* 73 (1987): 280-302.

Markovits, Andrei S., and Simon Reich. "The Contemporary Power of Memory: The Dilemmas for German Foreign Policy." *The Communication Review* 2 (1997): 89-119.

Osborn, Michael. "In Defense of Broad Mythic Criticism—A Reply to Rowland." *Communication Studies* 41 (1990): 121-27.

Prosise, Theodore O. "The Collective Memory of the Atomic Bombings Misrecognized as Objective History: The Case of the Public Opposition to the National Air and Space Museum's Atom Bomb Exhibit." *Western Journal of Communication* 62 (1998): 316-47.

Report of the Commission on Wartime Relocation and Internment of Civilians, *Personal Justice Denied.* Part I: Report/ Part II: Recommendations. Washington, DC: U.S. Government Printing Office, 1983.

Scholes, Robert, and Robert Kellogg. *The Nature of Narrative.* New York: Oxford UP, 1966.

Schudson, Michael. "Dynamics of Distortion in Collective Memory." *Memory Distortion.* Ed. D. Schachter. Cambridge, MA: Harvard UP, 1995. 346-64.

Schwartz, Barry. "The Social Context of Commemoration: A Study in Collective Memory." *Social Forces* 61.20 (1982): 374-402.

Scott, Robert L. "Narrative Theory and Communication Research." *Quarterly Journal of Speech 70 (1984): 197-221.*

Thelen, David. "Memory and American History." *Journal of American History* 75 (1989): 1117-29.

"Wartime Relocation of Civilians" (134 Cong. Vol. 51 Rec. S4267- 4420). 11 Apr. 1988. 1 June 2001 <http://web.lexis-nexis.com/congcomp/document?_mc35ef67fr54e8b2110c93c6c597abfb&>.

37

Oral Mind in Civic Engagement: Common Sense and Rhetorical Action

Anne Pym
California State University–Hayward

In this age of "postmodernism," deconstruction of common sense and radicalization of the taken for granted go hand in hand with the dismissal of the author. What is "in" is critique (rooted in literacy), and what is "out" is common sense (rooted in orality). Drawing on research in oral traditions of rhetoric, I argue for the centrality of common sense as the condition of possibility for civic engagement. To do so, I explain the split between orality and literacy, then address civic engagement from the perspective of orality.

As Walter Ong attests, writing has more than any other single invention "transformed human consciousness" (78), making it the biggest cultural difference we experience. Most of us take writing for granted; yet writing is not without limitations. Whenever literate folks enter on the scene of oral folks, a crisis occurs (whether Romans on Britons or developers on country). Trying to identify the nature of the crisis, Rousseau considers whether the written word works as "'enslavement' of the natural spirit of man, or merely a neutral reporter and reflector of the various stages of man's departure from nature" (Havelock 36). According to Havelock, however, "Rousseau had failed to perceive the true source of the 'catastrophe'—the reduction of language to text, where an 'interior' consciousness has been forced outward and virtually destroyed" (50).

One of the results of forcing consciousness outward is consciousness that creates the individual as "separate from" (Havelock 114, Ong 46), because in literacy we remove ourselves from the fabric of oral interaction and enter into possibilities for reflection and conceptualization. Engaging only the sense of outward-projected sight (Havelock 50, Ong 72), literacy endows us with abstraction, analytical thinking, definition, self-reflexivity, fixity, and alienation one from another. Orality, on the other hand, engages the sense of sound as well as sight, smell, motion, and touch. It is fluid, analogical, traditional, situated, active, communal, and performative. In Pennick's words, "Oral myth lives in action, word and image" (159)—in the moment, and through participation.

The nature and scope of the shift from orality to literacy are enormous, and one earning barely a nod in civic engagement literature. The shift is not, however, an either/or proposition—few truly oral cultures (Ong's "primary orality" 11)[1] remain from the march to spread literacy. Rather, people exist on a continuum from orality to literacy. Those engaging modes of talk in which they are significantly committed to oral traditions, underpinned by oral consciousness (although living within the bounds of literacy), I refer to as being of oral tradition. Oral tradition in this sense flourishes today especially among working people, such as long-haul truckers, fishermen, forklift drivers, waitresses, loggers, and farmers. This is different from Ong's "secondary orality of present-day high technology culture, in which a new orality is sustained by telephone, radio, television, and other electronic devices that depend for their existence and functioning on writing and print" (11). He suggests these audiovisual devices sustain "the mind-set of primary orality," which I do not believe, given that none but the telephone are even interactive (and the telephone is limited to voice alone). No, those significantly committed to oral traditions are committed to a life world of person-to-person storytelling, myth, and metaphor grounded in physical action bound by tradition. They live in a culture whose *nomos* is preserved and transmitted orally, albeit within a larger context of literacy and society administered via alphabetic codes (Hauser e-mail). Oral tradition, as Albert Lord notes, can exist within literacy with no necessary effect (134-50), but that is to the degree its participants are not corrupted by commitment to schooling (132). Electronic media thrust oral tradition further and further into the background because they, like writing, are invested in schooling and viewing, not oral interaction.

From the abstracting and alienating nature of literacy, we forget to remember the nature of things; but, as people of oral mind know, that does not mean they do not exist. It is literacy that provides education outside of, separate from the knowing of acting with others (human and nonhuman), making for what those of oral mind experience as "college-educated idiots" or those "educated beyond their intelligence"—people who have forgotten common sense,[2] as commonality grounded in sensory action. At the risk of being unforgivably anti-intellectual (read illiterate), let me suggest we consider their contributions.

Taking action as the basis for consideration of the role of common sense in civic engagement, I engage ideas of Gerard Hauser and Richard Sennett, because both urge us to engage in significantly oral forms of communication: dialogue and acting. Both reject rationality as the ideal and acceptable norm of public discourse that Habermas espouses. Neither displaces the rhetor as a determined *it*. Both understand the existence of publics to be eventful versus philosophical or personal (Sennett 24, 28ff) and as processes versus entities (Hauser, *Vernacular* 64), linking them with oral commitments to action.

At the same time, although Hauser and Sennett make significantly "oral" turns, both undermine possibilities for civic engagement they encourage. Considering both, I argue for the centrality of the oral *activity* of common sense, grounded in sensory inter-action, as the condition of possibility for civic engagement.

Hauser explains "vernacular voices" making up the reticulate structure of the overall public sphere as "a web of discursive arenas, spread across society" (*Vernacular* 71), in the "process of public conversation that provides a backdrop of rhetorical resources for creative use by public advocates" (*Vernacular* 65). He offers vernacular voices as *background, change* as the end of publics, and civil society at its heart "concerned with relationships among *diverse groups and interests*" (*Vernacular* 22, emphasis added).

According to the *Oxford English Dictionary,* the term *vernacular* means native or indigenous as opposed to literary or learned. It is not, however, those truly vernacular voices who historically sustain either the interest or time to enter into publics whose end is change or who take particular interest in issues of diversity when working together to get a job done—they remain in the vernacular *background*. But change, for Hauser, is a condition of publics, one he contrasts with "premodern," outmoded "consensus goals" (*Vernacular* 55) of the likes of the oral mind. Emphasizing change and diversity compromises possibilities for what Chantal Mouffe refers to as constructing a "'we,' making it difficult to distinguish between differences that exist but should not exist and differences that do not exist but should exist" (39).

I do not mean to suggest that Hauser is against commonality. To address common problems or issues in publics, Hauser believes we must form common meaning: "[A] public's members must share a web of significant meanings that define a *reference world* of common actions, celebrations, and feelings" (*Vernacular* 69). At the same time, he writes, "[T]he bond of common meaning is not shared values and meanings but *the sharing of the shared world,* commonly understood even if differently lived" (*Vernacular* 102). His point is to invite folks to join in common discursive action, across permeable boundaries, without presumption of common beliefs, values, ideals, or expectation of consensus, joining in civic engagement around shared concerns, coming from a diversity of positions, to forge "agreements of common understanding [...] always specific, never universal" (100), that remain permeable to future alteration. Put briefly, Hauser advocates engaging orally around common problems carrying the *telos* of shared interests (*Vernacular* 69).

Such a perspective is beautifully aligned with oral mind in its fluid, changeable, shared nature of oral action among people, both in day-to-day conversation and in the processes of deciding together in publics. Let us proceed to enactment. Hannah Arendt writes of common sense as the way by which we may judge reality (208). It is "the one sense that fits into reality as a whole our five strictly individual senses and the strictly particular data they perceive. It is by virtue of common sense that the other sense perceptions are known to disclose reality and are not merely felt as irritations of our nerves or resistance sensations of our bodies" (208-09). Not surprisingly, Arendt notes, it is most commonly laborers who most suffer from being in a world where common sense is absent (209). Significantly oral folks, generally workers, speak of common sense in the sense of "what everybody knows" through shared experience; for example, if you want the job done you know you must hire hardworking people with the ability to do it well. Thus, if in a public discussion some wanted to set criteria for hiring based on abstractions of "under representation" or "oppression," incommensurability would result between them.

Grounding common sense in action directs us to break abstractions down into parts that can be tested through fact and action. Abstracting words from action (a wholly literate notion), words become floating signifiers. To say, for example, that women are "oppressed" requires, if we are to move beyond "ismic" ideological determinism, that we define what we mean by the term, consider what women, in what circumstances, in what time and place, experience what kinds of actions, by whom. It is at that point when participants can apprehend common sense, for they can "see" (sense) what actions who is performing and figure what is the nature and scope of what harm. From that point, it is possible to think through alternative possibilities to solving a problem. Without this step, we have little more than ideological warfare, precluding possibilities for creating shared meaning. The force of reality, of factual events, loudly suggests one or a number of effective courses of action. Through action we can loosen bonds of prior commitments and strengthen the bonds that we share.

Common sense, then, suggests the sense we form by shared action, rooted in hearing, touch, sight, taste, smell, and movement. These are the senses that come from persons interacting in roles within a public sphere and in life worlds. Talk divorced from action grows like Pinocchio's nose, farther and farther out into abstraction and incommensurability.

Another dimension of deciding based on common sense rooted in action is naming. People of oral traditions know the power of naming to bring being into the world. Neither abstractions nor arbitrary signs, names make things real. The Catholic practice of christening newborn children harkens back to ancient wisdom of knowing that babies and grandparents have a special bond because one has just come from the other world (nonordinary reality) and the other is about to go there, so they have much to tell each other. When a baby is born, he or she may find the pain of birth—the pain of separation from the other world—is too much, and turn back. To prevent that, Celts name the child, binding him or her into the world (ordinary reality). Without a name, one lacks place, and, lacking place, one has no way to act in relation to others in the world (see, e.g., Rees and Rees 242-43).

Let us consider the efficacy of naming within the context of publics. We name a person as chair of a group, giving that person certain authority and responsibility to perform leadership. The others remain as "group members," an amorphous term, with little encouragement to act other than from their beliefs and values that may preclude open-minded exploration of new possibilities. As people speak in groups, roles emerge, both those the people bring with them and those created within publics. In public, a person, for example, may show considerable experience with ways that truckers treat women in the women's roles as drivers and cashiers in truck stops and mechanics in repair shops.[3] Knowing, from oral tradition, that words *do* things, public participants might name that person "The Trucker," naming him or her into a place and presence, a public identity from which he or she can act, with authority. This is the kind of acting that Sennett claims has largely disappeared as public spheres have been eroded by focus on self-disclosure (107-09). This is the action of acting together as strangers with one another in public, acting from communally created roles that enable people to invent and create ideas together without threatening other commitments that may come from more privatized values and beliefs.

I do not believe that people are likely to set aside their beliefs and values when they enter a group. We can, however, forefront commitments to public action by engaging citizens in commonsense action, in deeply embodied civic engagement. Naming is one of those actions that bind people together as a people acting in public.

Having considered ways to work with difference, let us consider oral wisdom's focus on balancing difference with what endures. Accepting "diversity" as the way life "really is" privileges difference at the expense of common sense and shared tradition. Oral mind directs our attention to the interconnection among the myriad of life forms, including those with different values and beliefs. To act as strangers in publics without personalizing (Sennett 259-64), while sustaining integrity with our vernacular voices, and without our differences becoming the currency that divides, we must envision some degree of common values and beliefs with which to act.

Hauser discusses the power of narrative form to forge and tap cultural memory: "The preserved and shared past becomes a vernacular inscription of beliefs and values. It permits intelligible discussion of fundamental commitments and recognition of virtuosity. Without cultural memory social actors are denied the very terms on which they might understand their own reflexivity in creating their identity" (*Vernacular* 156). Given his dismissal of beliefs and values as what may also preclude agreement, Hauser marks an enduring tension of civic engagement. Myth offers a way of addressing it.

More than stories, myth is the nonmaterial, nonordinary dimension of being that enlightens, offering coherence, oneness, and generation in spirit. In myth, spirit is what is real—its authority, Goodall writes, "drawn primarily from direct, lived experience and social relations rather than from formal textual practices" (41). It is through spirit that we interact with trees and animals, commune with god/dess, get a "sense" or "feeling" of a matter, and become inspired. It is the spirit of talk that satisfies or distresses. "The Wasteland," Pennick explains, "comes when the spiritual is abandoned in [favor] of the material. Inner nature is rejected and eternal truths are forgotten" (179).

In the shift from inner to outer consciousness accompanying the onslaught of literacy and its ideological productions, humans learn to ignore voices of spirit. It is with literacy we have also learned to forget our many (nonhuman) fellow beings, excluding those from our realms of interaction. Many oral peoples form relationships with bear, sycamore, or raven, imbuing themselves with the nature of that being. Enacting bear spirit gives them place within and between groups, affording them commonality and personal power to act (e.g., with eagle spirit of the United States). It also offers wisdom for taking the rest of the world into account when advocating change. Shifting attention from difference, myth enables us to recognize our inspirited oneness within which the many creatures and points of view contribute.

Marking the centrality of myth, Joseph Campbell writes: "A society that does not have a myth to support and give it coherence goes into dissolution" (47). Stories are a central way of re-membering myth. We have many kinds of stories: sacred stories that re-mind us of spirit in all of being; stories we tell to share experiences, forge and maintain bonds, instruct, and entertain. Stories may have a more or less material or spiritual orientation, more or less particular or universal dimensionality. All form bonds. The ones Jung identifies as archetypal in nature—tapping into the universal, natural, eternal, and cyclical—are the stories and ritual enactments of the birth of children, passages into stages of life, changing of the seasons, cycles of life and death; of the caretaker, the food gatherer, the mother, the child, the North wind; of things falling apart. These are the themes and experiences of all peoples in the world, the archetypes of experience that create us as the beings we enact, powerful unifiers of sentiment and action. Even stories of 9/11 provide shared knowing, reminding us of our humanity, togetherness, vulnerability, and our will in the age-old story of attack and defense. Given the power of story, rooted and told in action, we might consider how it works to forge civic as well as vernacular bonds, bridges between the literate and the oral, the public and vernacular.

I am reminded of standing on the dock in Juneau, waiting for the *Naa Kahidi* theatre production of creation to begin. An elder leaned over to me, and with a twinkle in his droll Tlingit[4] voice, said, "Hey, you know what those lines to that freighter out there are for?" After I said I did not, he growled, "those are rat lines." Yes, those are rat lines and they put the plates on them so the rats cannot scramble up the lines and eat up the passengers. "Yes," he chuckled, "the rats would go onto those boats and eat everything in sight. We have hungry rats here." "Yes," I chuckled, "I know. When we were little we took rowboats far back underneath the piers and saw rats big enough to swallow our whole boat." We laughed as he told of how they used to go through the ships with long sticks trying to beat the rats out, and I told him about… strangers bound together by story.

Acting together in public, swapping tales, archetypal tales of man fighting off monsters, we shared meaning made common in action. Yet, we did not have to share a life of rat experiences in Juneau to come together. Examples of coming together are everywhere: Chinua Achebe might have been in a town meeting telling of how things fall apart when literate missionaries arrive, I of how a speech department falls apart when faculty "go administration," and John Doe of how a family falls apart when mother departs. Things falling apart is an archetype offering guidance for how to act together in public in a situation where, say, a downtown community is falling apart from the invasion of a giant shopping mall. We can share in the spirit of the matter and in actions to find ways to revitalize the heart of the town.

The point is to include myth as a rhetorical resource, listening to spirit in talk, sharing stories for their unifying capabilities, naming into being, and always grounding in action. Without stories rooted in shared experience, I think there is little possibility of building common sense and practicing civic engagement. Remembering oral tradition of rhetoric facilitates discovering ways to act together in archetypal images and commonsense actions that breed vision and tolerance necessary to "gain assent among the interacting parties" (Hauser, *Vernacular* 275), because they speak to our very human nature.

NOTES

1. Walter Ong describes "the orality of a culture totally untouched by any knowledge of writing or print" as "'primary orality'" (11).
2. This is like, in Arendt's words, "the playing of the mind with itself, which comes to pass when the mind is shut off from all reality and 'senses' only itself" (284), resulting in "truths" that have no necessary connection to the world perceived through our senses.
3. This is nearly always with courtesy and respect.
4. Tlingits are a Southeast Alaska tribe.

WORKS CITED

Achebe, Chinua. *Things Fall Apart*. New York: Fawcett Crest, 1959.

Arendt, Hannah. *The Human Condition*. Chicago: U of Chicago P, 1958.

Campbell, Joseph. *Transformation of Myth Through Time*. New York: Harper, 1975.

Goodall, Jr., H. L. "Mysteries of the Future Told: Communication as the Material Manifestation of Spirituality." *World Communication* 22 (1993): 40-49.

Habermas, Jürgen. *Legitimation Crisis*. Boston: Beacon, 1973.

Hauser, Gerard A. E-mail to the author. 21 Aug. 2002.

---. *Vernacular Voices: The Rhetoric of Publics and Public Spheres*. Columbia: South Carolina UP, 1999.

Havelock, Eric A. *The Muse Learns to Write: Reflections on Orality and Literacy from Antiquity to the Present*. New Haven, CT: Yale UP, 1986.

Jung, Carl. 1957. *The Undiscovered Self*. Trans. R. F. C. Hull. Princeton, NJ: Princeton UP, 1990.

Lord, Albert B. *The Singer of Tales*. 1960. 2nd ed. Cambridge, MA: Harvard UP, 2000.

Mouffe, Chantal. "Democratic Politics and the Question of Identity." *The Identity in Question*. Ed. John Rajchman. New York: Routledge, 1995. 33-46.

Ong, Walter J. *Orality and Literacy: The Technologizing of the Word*. New York: Routledge, 1982.

Pennick, Nigel. *Celtic Sacred Landscapes*. New York: Thames and Hudson, 1996.

Rees, Alwyn, and Brinley Rees. 1961. *Celtic Heritage*. London: Thames & Hudson, 1989.

Sennett, Richard. *The Fall of Public Man*. New York: Norton, 1976.

"Vernacular." *Oxford English Dictionary*. 2nd ed. 1989. 549.

38

Fanaticism, Civil Society, and the Arts of Representation in Sixteenth-Century Mexico

Susan Romano
University of New Mexico–Albuquerque

In *Civil Society and Fanaticism: Conjoined Histories,* Dominique Colas argues that the usual oppositions by which civil society is defined in Western intellectual thought—domestic versus public, nature versus society, civil society versus the state—obscure a fundamental and illuminating relationship between civil society and fanaticism, a dualism that gained presence in the discourses of sixteenth-century Europe. Locating the conceptual foundations of civil society in Aristotle's coinage *koinonia politikē* and its subsequent translation to the Latin *societas civilis,* Colas cites usage by the medieval theologian Giles of Rome but attributes the firming up of this lexical choice to Florentine humanist Leonardo Bruni and Protestant reformer Philipp Melanchthon. Melanchthon's commentary on the *Politics,* with the assistance of the printing press, shepherded the term *civil society* into the vernacular languages. Melanchthon defines fanatics as those who "do not accept the legitimacy of the 'interval' between the City of God and civil society" (Colas xviii).

Colas tracks this "interval" and the modes of protecting it or eradicating its permutations from the Reformation through Marx, noting that the various pressures working to extinguish the civic-friendly interval are consistently dubbed "fanatic." Culling commonalities from among historically situated fanaticisms and abstracting from their rhetorics and actions an underlying principle, Colas proposes a thesis of high interest to scholars and students of rhetoric and to those teachers of the arts of representation that mediate, so we believe, the discourses of civil society. Colas posits that *fanaticism* is a hatred, fear, and outright rejection of all forms of mediation—the political and symbolic alike.

AN AMERICAN TOPOGRAPHY

I won't elaborate on the examples by which Colas strengthens his case that fear of representation is handmaiden to fanaticism and hence enemy of civil society. Instead, in this chapter I probe and complicate Colas's thesis by examining the relationship between the arts of representation and fanaticism within an American historical topography. In the early sixteenth century, at the very time of the Melanchthon/Luther/Dürer defense of the civic interval in Europe, Spain was engaged in the spiritual, cultural, and material conquest of what is now Mexico, Peru, parts of Central America, and the Philippines. This conquest was carried out under a political philosophy intolerant of the newly articulated interval corresponding to civil society. Indeed, the conquest was advanced in no small part by acts of iconoclasm—the destruction of native representations from codices and entire libraries to small artifacts of the home. Yet, for this particular historical event, the will to destroy was paired with the impulse to educate. Pope and Crown charged the Catholic mendicant orders not with the eradication of native peoples (although genocide was certainly an effect of their efforts), but instead with their conversion to European Catholicism via education.

The insertion of education, of classroom, of teachers and pupils speaking, writing, and creating images into a theory of civil society can only enrich all proposed discussion of fear and representation, because it is in the classroom, broadly conceived, that these arts of speaking, writing, and image making are parsed, assigned, facilitated, and finally contested by those both in and outside these classrooms. This we well understand by our own experiences as institutionally sponsored educators in the rhetorical arts. Something happened in the Franciscan/fanatic-sponsored schools, in those sites designated for what surely was a fuzzy concept for the Pope and Emperor—teaching writing and scripting sermons and designing visual pedagogical materials. And what happened at these sites of language activity magnifies the incongruous and misfitting relationships between fanatical and fearful stances toward native representations and an increasingly urgent need to deploy the rhetorical power of many forms of representation in order to achieve the desired conversion to Christianity.

The Franciscan mission was to convert the masses and to educate the elite native population, and they brought to this mission their university training (e.g., University of Salamanca, University of Paris) in theology and rhetoric, their printing presses and engraving apparatuses, and their truth-bearing sacred texts, ready for dissemination. Yet, what on the surface appeared to be a simple matter of substitution and overlay—that is, these educators would destroy native representations, insert Christian imagery and text into the ensuing vacuum, then teach and produce only European cultural forms—became complicated and eventually experimental. Manipulation of a multiplicity of representational forms became the very heart of Franciscan persuasion, of the Franciscans' very rhetoric-sensitive and rhetoric-acute conversion pedagogies. In sum, the contest between Latinate languages (Spanish and Latin) and native languages (e.g., Nahuatl, Otomí, Chiapanecan) eventually resolved in the publication of over one hundred bi- and trilingual catechisms in multiple native vernaculars. The two opposing sets of sacred scriptures—native codices and the Catholic doctrinal tracts—were conjoined under Franciscan scholarship, when the eradication of native codices gave rise to their reinscription and recovery in visual and verbal trilingual forms. Both vernacular catechisms and new histories of *mexica* culture were eventually recalled and suppressed by a church/state fearing the circulation of native representations in all forms and guises. Understanding just how treasons to singular, truth-bearing representational forms came to be sponsored by committed fanatics entails a look at the specifics of the cross-cultural encounters they sponsored and experienced.

THE EXAMPLES: CROSS-CULTURAL ENCOUNTERS IN PUBLIC AND IN SCHOOL

Those twenty-five Franciscan educators arriving in New Spain during the 1520s in three separate contingencies recognized immediately the importance of their own language learning to the evangelization project. Yet, they did not postpone action until this learning had taken place. The earliest recorded encounters between friars and their target pupils are public rhetorical gambits in cultural indoctrination that precede linguistic competency and schooling initiatives. As if affirming Colas's thesis regarding the fear of dualism and rejection of the civic "interval," the friars chose precisely the issue of interval as topically appropriate for first encounters. Thus in denying the legitimacy of the interval, they assigned themselves one characteristic of fanaticism even as they launched the other: waves of iconoclastic, fear-driven attacks on native forms of representation.

Gesture and the City of God

The first incident took place in the *tianguis* or market place of Tlaxcala, a town southeast of what is now Mexico City and home of those who collaborated with Cortés to defeat the Moctezuma regime. Diego Muñoz Camargo, a *mestizo*-Tlaxcaltecan chronicler writing in the latter half of the sixteenth century, relays the following anecdote: The Spanish holy men, knowing not a word of the native languages, commenced their evangelical activities with gesture. In the markets and other large gathering places, these vernacular-ignorant friars argued the desirability of replacing the earthly city with the heavenly city by gesturing toward the ground and expressing disgust with its nastiness (fire, toads, and snakes), then raising their eyes and pointing to the amenable heavens. That these gestures went misunderstood is of course to understate the case. Muñoz Camargo reports that the town authorities recommended the Tlaxcaltecan citizenry feed and then politely avoid these strangers who were obviously suffering hunger, illness, and/or mental malady, and who would surely either recover or die. In any case, these "poor miserable men" were not to be harmed because clearly they were out of their heads (Muñoz Camargo 172-73).

Dialogue, Rationality, and the City of God

That the friars would choose as first lesson in their evangelization effort the illegitimacy of dualist political theory is possibly no accident, for in another early rhetorical encounter, a more formal one to be sure, they raised the same issue, and this time gained a strong counter-response from the native leaders. Cortés himself had arranged a meeting between the twelve—the second wave of Franciscans arriving in Vera Cruz in 1524—and the *principales* or leaders of a number of native nations. This meeting took the form of a series of talks or *coloquios* mediated by translators. During the dialogue, the Franciscans presented their case for the replacement of native gods with the European god and his vicar in Rome and, of course, the vicar's representatives in Mexico. Early in this *coloquio,* the friars argued directly for the merging of the earthly and godly cities, that is, for the illegitimacy of the civic interval:

> Este universal Dios y Señor, redemptor y criador Jesucristo tiene un reyno acá en el mundo, que se llama reyno de los cielos, y por otro nombre yglesia cathólica y llámase reyno de los cielos, porque ninguno yrá al cielo a reynar sino se subjetare a este reyno acá en el mundo. (Sahagún, Colloquios 85)
>
> This universal God and Lord, redeemer and creator Jesus Christ, has a kingdom here in the world, which is called the kingdom of heaven, and by another name the Catholic Church, and is called the kingdom of the heavens, because no one will go to heaven to reign unless subject to this kingdom here on earth. (my translation)

The native leaders responded to this proposal for theocracy by telling the friars that as representatives of the earthly city, *they* could not formulate a response but had to defer to the religious authorities, representatives of the other order. Thus dramatically asserting a counterposition by refusing to extend their military and administrative authority to those issues pertaining to the city of the gods, the native leaders honored the celebrated interval and in addition proclaimed their willingness to themselves be represented by others (Sahagún, *Colloquios* 86-87). In so doing, they legitimated the coexistence in their non-European social organization of both religious and secular orders, that is, the presence of the very dualism so feared by fanatics. When the native religious leaders arrived to replace the secular leaders at the dialogue table, they argued before the Franciscans that even were they, as religious leaders, to embrace the Spaniards' god and his vicar in Rome, the people of all the native nations would rise up against them, as the people would not wish to give up communal practices handed down from generation to generation (Sahagún, *Colloquios* 88-89). This practical argument redoubled the legitimacy of community or earthly practices, associated here with peace and order and tied to a certain autonomy of family and place. There would seem to have been room in indigenous social organization for some form of popular expression developed familially, in the home, and locally, by region. More was at stake here than god swapping.

The Writing: Process and Politics

One of the bilingual manuscripts documenting this dialogue (a popular European form of the day) between the native leaders and the Franciscans was composed in 1564 and attributed to the Franciscan Bernardino de Sahagún, who was not present at this purportedly historical event, having arrived six years later in 1529. Sahagún reports in a note to "the prudent reader" first his collaboration with four native students and four native elders in sorting the papers and composing the dialogue. Only then does he personally authorize the work by way of European testimony: he knows, he says, of this dialogue by way of his contacts with the "twelve" friars of 1524 who were the very interlocutors. Thus, the *Colloquios* were composed primarily on the authority of the Nahuas themselves—first elders and then a cadre of Franciscan-educated, trilingual *latinos* or "Latinists," native youth who had taken their formal studies in Latin and Nahuatl grammar at the Franciscan College of Santa Cruz de Tlaltelolco, established in 1536. The 1564 *Colloquios* manuscript was suppressed by the Crown in 1570 and recalled to Spain to prevent its circulation in Mexico, prompting the Franciscan superior to secret away a copy in the convent archives where it was likely destroyed during the post-independence anticlerical movement. Another copy survived untouched for four hundred years, until the 1920s, in the Vatican archives (Duverger 38-45).

The history of composition, truncated publication, suppression, and delayed circulation of this document marks clearly the tensions between writing practices and fanatic ideologies of representation, exposing significant ruptures in the Franciscans' official and fanatical stance toward representation even as they adhered to an aggressive conversion agenda.

Schooling: Latin Grammar and Tri-Lingualism for Native Pupils

The very early conversion gambits—two of what surely were many—must have impressed on the Franciscans the necessity of learning the native vernaculars and learning them well. Indeed, by about mid-century, the mendicant orders had sponsored publication of vocabularies (dictionaries) and grammars for several native vernaculars. By the end of the century, over one hundred bi- or trilingual catechisms and numerous collections of sermons had been published to serve—possibly—a reading public of converts who were not Spanish speaking and a European and *criollo* clergy in need of indoctrination materials in the vernaculars. The schools sponsored by the Franciscans turned out trilingual native scholars who were given large roles—perhaps larger than could be publicly admitted—in reconstructing doctrinal materials and, more significantly perhaps, in producing pre-Hispanic sacred and profane histories. These university-sponsored activities triggered the disarticulation of correspondences between fanatical fear of representation and actual writing practices. Arguably, the positioning of the Franciscan educators in relation to the composing tools and methods of two cultures called into question their received assumptions about how language works. It was their positioning as teachers of the arts of representation that placed them at the forefront of this re-examination.

Although few contested the appropriateness of functional literacy education for indigenous peoples, the teaching of Latin grammar at the college generated significant criticism. In 1536, the Franciscans culled the best of their students from area primary schools to form the first student body at the first European institution of higher education in the Americas, Santa Cruz de Tlaltelolco, whose curricular offerings included Latin grammar and the grammars of the native vernaculars, rhetoric, philosophy, organ performance, and native medicine. To be sure, the literature of schooling during this period is rife with social anxieties about the wisdom of teaching the native pupils anything but doctrine, reading, and writing. Objections ranged from the class-based, glass-ceiling argument "but they can't be priests so why teach them Latin" to more disingenuous protests asserting that the native pupils would surpass their teachers in scholarship and would acquire knowledge of the flaws in the Spanish character (Domingo de Betanzos and Diego de la Cruz, and Jerónimo López, cited in Gómez Canedo 184-88, 335-36). Resistance was not limited to European critics: Some native families whose sons were tapped for educational privilege resisted by substituting the sons of their servants and enemies for their own (Gonzalbo Aizpuru 36), and when Archbishop Zumárraga inaugurated a set of schools for girls, parents hid their daughters in refusal of this dubious privilege (Zumárraga 122, 127).

Criticism notwithstanding, the Franciscans continued to advance a conversion agenda that required them to subvert European ideologies of fanaticism via their practices in representation. An even more significant ideological departure is found in the ethno-historical work of Sahagún, compiler of the *Colloquios*. Working in three locations in the valley of Mexico across fifty years to recover the history of native idolatry so as to better suppress it, Sahagún first persuaded native artists to reproduce some of the codex images destroyed by the Spaniards or hidden by the native population. He then asked a group of elders to "sing" (tell or read) these pictures in the pre-Hispanic style of *calmecac* education, and he and his pupils recorded these singings and tellings in Nahuatl and Spanish (Sahagún, *Historia* 73-75). That the will to textualize truth drove Sahagún's fifty-year project every bit as much as it drove the vernacular translations of Christian doctrine from the Latin is clear beyond shadow of doubt, yet whereas the production of vernacular catechisms relied solely on European technologies of production—the printing press, the engraving machinery—Sahagún's project adopted and adapted the native methods of composing and interpreting, where the visual preceded the verbal, interpretation meant "singing" the pictures, and where, quite possibly, room for revisionism may have been available, or not. Sahagún sought certainty in meaning, checking and cross checking the collected stories against those of new crops of informants and with newly educated *latino* collaborators. No conscious rupture with fanatical ideologies of representation, no rebellion against the teleologies of Order and Church, Sahagún's is a practical infidelity of the sort that occurs when people work together over text and in the course of this work make available opportunities to circulate new expressions and to compose in hybrid media using hybrid arts and methods.

To say that all schooling in the arts of representation gives rise to expressive diversity would be an exaggeration—idealistic, hopeful, and resistant to refutation, but certainly subject to careful historicizing. My sense is that in the case of conquest and conversion in sixteenth-century Mexico, it was the combination of certain competing exigencies that gave rise to new literacies, even as the Inquisition and the state/church authorities worked hard at their suppression. The competing exigencies were: first, the Franciscans' strong belief in a direct correspondence between text and truth that was not to be compromised, and second, the Franciscans' experience-based perception that effective conversion depended on knowledge and use of their audience's cultural forms. From these seeming incompatibilities arose new writing practices. This is neither to sanction nor to romanticize the Franciscan agenda, but rather to reassert that language and its learning does not consent readily to any agenda, liberal democratic or otherwise.

By faithfully fulfilling their mission, the Franciscans, unwittingly or not, subverted the system of beliefs about language to which they were professionally bound.

WHERE CIVIC SPACES RESIDE

At first blush, this particular topography—sixteenth-century Mexico—appears unpromising and unyielding as a period and place of significance in the history of rhetoric, given the narrowness of civic space, the impoverishment of those discursive activities we associate with the preservation of differences, and the want of expressive freedom and economic opportunity for the marginalized. Yet, a study of these first European educators in the Americas suggests that students of rhetoric may productively inquire into the practices of all persons facing challenges that lead them to develop new language activities. Such studies would delineate cultural assumptions about how language works, acknowledge subsequent disillusionments grounded in experience, and report on new gambits and their methods of deployment. In short, they would look to a series of crisis-generated successes and failures. These studies would be interested especially in the institutional positionings that complicate received wisdom and hence drive experimentation with language and the attendant commission of infidelities to tradition. What's troubling about the relentless search for civil society undertaken in the literature of radical democracy is a disposition blinded to cultural particularisms and expunged of the accidents of local histories.

WORKS CITED

Colas, Dominique. *Civil Society and Fanaticism: Conjoined Histories*. Trans. Amy Jacobs. Palo Alto, CA: Stanford UP, 1997.

Duverger, Christian. *La Conversión de los Indios de Nueva España con el Texto de* Los Coloquios de los Doce *de Bernardino de Sahagún*. 1564. México: Fonda de Cultura Económica, 1993.

Gómez Canedo, Lino. *La Educación de los Marginados durante la Epoca Colonial: Escuelas y Colegios para Indios y Mestizos en la Nueva España*. México: Editorial Porrúa, 1982.

Gonzalbo Aizpuru, Pilar. *Historia de la Educación en la Epoca Colonial: El Mundo Indígena*. México: El Colegio de México, 1990.

Muñoz Camargo, Diego. *Historia de Tlaxcala* (Ms. 210 de la Biblioteca Nacional de París). Tlaxcala, México: Universidad Autónoma de Tlaxcala, 1998.

Sahagún, Fr. Bernardino de. *Historia General de las Cosas de Nueva España*. Ed. Angel María Garibay K. México: Editorial Porrúa, 1999.

---. "Colloquios y Doctrina Christian[a]." *Coloquios y Doctrina Cristiana*. Ed. Miguel Léon-Portilla with Antonio Valeriano, Alonso Vegerano, Martín Jacobita, y Andrés Leonardo, y cuatro ancianos. México: Universidad Nacional Autónoma de México, 1986.

Zumárraga, Juan de. *Don Fray Juan de Zumárraga: Primer Obispo y Arzobispo de México*. Ed. Joaquín García Icazbalceta. Tomo IV. 2nd ed. México: Editorial Porrúa, 1988.

39

Service-Learning and Cultural Studies: Toward a Hybrid Pedagogy of Rhetorical Intervention

J. Blake Scott
University of Central Florida

Even as they have become more widespread, cultural studies approaches to composition have been critiqued for privileging semiotics over rhetoric, critical awareness over rhetorical agency. Some versions of service-learning, another recent approach to composition, have been critiqued on quite different grounds—for being hyperpragmatic at the expense of sustained critical analysis, especially of larger structural conditions. This chapter elaborates on these critiques and argues that these two types of approaches—cultural studies and service-learning—can usefully complement each other, each addressing the other's limitations. Although these approaches have arrived in rhetoric and composition from very different traditions, they can be combined in a more critically and rhetorically robust pedagogy of civic intervention. I end by showing how such a pedagogy might be enacted in a specific service-learning invention assignment.

In "(Teaching) Writing: Composition, Cultural Studies, Production," Julie Drew laments the cultural studies pattern of emphasizing "old-style, close readings of newer (read: popular culture) texts" in an effort to make students more savvy consumers (411).[1] My own survey of cultural studies-based writing pedagogies, including those described by Jim Berlin, the writers in the collection *Left Margins*, and others has led me to a similar observation. Although I wouldn't characterize the main activity of such pedagogies as "old-style readings," I do agree with Drew that these pedagogies tend to de-emphasize students' own rhetorical production of public discourse. In *Rhetorics, Poetics, and Cultures*, for example, Berlin describes a Codes and Critiques course in which students spend most of their time performing semiotic analyses and ideological critiques of popular media texts. This activity has an admirable goal: to help students better recognize the ways texts and their socio-ideological contexts serve power formations and shape subjects, including themselves—in short, to help students develop a critical literacy. In Berlin's pedagogy, however, the cultural production of signifying practices is an object of analysis rather than an experiential process; this pedagogy stops short of teaching students ways to intervene in cultural affairs with their own rhetoric. Furthermore, it problematically posits students as naive readers, unable without the teacher's guidance to see television programs and other texts as coded constructions (see Berlin 120).

In his article on critical writing about advertisements, Bruce McComiskey offers a cultural studies approach that begins to address Drew's critique and, in my view, holds more promise. In a set of short assignments, McComiskey has students critique and then attempt to intervene in the advertising for a new product. His heuristic for the critique, adapted from Richard Johnson's model of the cultural circuit, asks students questions about the ads' cultural production, contextual distribution (i.e., the magazine or other forum in which the ads appear), and critical consumption by readers of the forum. The questions embedded in this three-part heuristic prompt students to interrogate the ads' associations with other cultural entities, the competing sets of values they embody, and the effects they help create in readers. Under contextual distribution, for instance, one question asks students to comparatively critique the cultural values of the ad with those of the magazine in which it appears. The most promising part of McComiskey's approach is the final assignment, wherein students write critical letters to one of three public audiences involved in the ads' cultural circulation—the company that makes the product in the ads, the editors of the forum in which the ads occur, or the editors and readers of *Consumer Reports*. In this last assignment, then, students are invited to rhetorically intervene in the cultural process, challenging values that do not serve the audiences' interests. This shift to the students' own rhetoric occurs only at the end of the course, however; one gets the sense that critical inquiry is the course's *main* course and that the critical letter is something like an after-dinner mint. Although McComiskey's heuristic usefully guides students through an analysis of the cultural process, it does not guide them through the writing process.

Although she laments the lack of focus on student production, Drew does not argue for abandoning cultural studies approaches. Instead, she proposes reconfiguring them to help students ethically critique and negotiate their own writing contexts. More specifically, Drew calls for expanding students' writing processes to include the "practice of analyzing the cultural forces [such as institutional structures and social values] that are necessarily constitutive of the academic texts they will produce" (416). Although I support Drew's proposal, I wonder why she limits it to academic texts and the context of the classroom.[2] In highlighting the larger cultural conditions, circulation, and effects of discourse, cultural analysis can be just as useful for extra-academic, public writing assignments such as those found in a service-learning course. In addition, Drew's proposal unnecessarily limits students' cultural analysis to the production process, stopping short of tracking the ways their texts circulate and are transformed. On this point, McComiskey's approach better tracks the socio-discursive lives of texts (although not of the students) as they are placed in certain contexts and either accommodated, rejected, or negotiated by readers.

Partly in response to traditions of writing instruction that deprivilege students' rhetorical intervention, many instructors have incorporated service-learning assignments into their courses. According to the Commission of National and Community Service, service-learning involves students in experiential learning that enhances the academic curriculum, addresses a community need, and entails structured reflection about the experience (Deans 1). Primarily grounded in the pragmatic practice of real-world experience, service-learning has been described by Thomas Deans and others as the next logical step of the social turn in composition: It widens students' writing to nonacademic contexts, asks them to collaborate with community partners as well as peers, and enables them to combine social deliberation with civic action (Deans 9-10).

The stripe of service-learning in which students write *as* their service—what Deans calls writing *for* the community—seems to flow most directly from the pragmatist, social constructionist tradition. In this version of service-learning, students produce texts needed by a community organization, and this production constitutes their service. A student or group of students might produce a set of documents for a nonprofit agency's fundraiser, for example, or write and design a campus organization's newsletter or Web site. Such an assignment clearly puts the focus on student writing within a classroom and community context. A typical invention activity for this type of project is an analysis of the organization and its discursive practices, something like James Porter's forum analysis. Porter defines a forum as a site for discursive exchange by members of a discourse community. His forum analysis expands a traditional rhetorical analysis by having students examine the background and conventions of the discourse community for which they plan to write. Students producing a newsletter for an organization, for example, would study not only their immediate rhetorical situation but would also study past issues of the newsletter and characteristics of the organization it serves. Although a forum analysis is a good starting point, it doesn't adequately account for the cultural circulation of texts, and it remains locked in an explanatory rather than critical stance. "Knowledge of the background and discourse conventions of a discursive formation," McComiskey explains, "does not necessarily enable a critical understanding of how cultural meaning is [re]produced in particular texts, nor does it encourage participants in discursive formations to adopt critical subject positions in relation to particular discourses" (384).

By definition, service-learning should not only be pragmatic but also critical, combining real-world action and critical reflection. Yet such reflection is not integral to many service-learning classes, either overlooked or tacked on as personal writing in journals or logs that seldom takes up ideological critique or leads to ethical intervention. Chris Anson explains that "[j]ournal writing in many service courses may serve the purpose of creating a log or record of experience, but falls short of encouraging the critical examination of ideas, or the sort of consciousness-raising reflection, that is the mark of highly successful learning" (169). To illustrate, in describing a "dialogic journal" assignment for a service-learning project, Deans explains that this journal will be read only by the instructor, and he includes such expressivist prompts as "What are you noticing about your community agency?" and "Which events are most memorable to you?" Bruce Herzberg also discusses the inadequacy of personal reflection in service-learning courses, arguing that this type of reflection prevents students from recognizing the complexity of community problems and solutions, moving beyond uncritical empathy, and gaining critical self-consciousness (59). Even when service-learning courses do foreground more critical reflection, this reflection doesn't necessarily account for the institutional structures and other conditions that shape and reshape student writing as it circulates through culture.[3] Without such an examination, students are less prepared to negotiate and ethically intervene in cultural discourses.

Incorporating critical cultural analysis into a service-learning frame can address the limitations and draw on the strengths of both approaches. In this more robust, hybrid pedagogy, service-learning keeps the focus on students' own rhetorical production and intervention. In addition, by positioning students in complex real-world contexts that require collaboration with classmates, the teacher, agency workers, and possibly agency clients, service-learning can highlight power relations and their underlying, often competing ideologies. Depending on the time frame of the project, service-learning may also enable students to determine how and to what effects their texts are taken up as they circulate. At the same time, the infusion of cultural studies can enrich the reflection component of service-learning. If adapted to service-learning contexts, cultural studies heuristics such as McComiskey's can push students past purely practical and uncritically empathetic stances, help them account for the fuller circulation and effects of their texts, facilitate their critique of the cultural conditions and values impacting their texts, and enable them to more strategically intervene in problematic cultural practices.

Like McComiskey, I've found Johnson's model of the cultural circuit especially useful for writing pedagogy. In his landmark article "What Is Cultural Studies Anyway?" Johnson, former head of the Birmingham school, presents a model of cultural circulation that tracks the transformations of cultural forms—such as texts, technologies, and subject positions—along the trajectory of their production, textual representation, distribution, reception, and incorporation into people's lives, where they become part of new conditions for production. Although Johnson's circuit implies a stage-by-stage progression of these cultural processes, they can be interwoven. The interpretation and use of a text, for example, can reshape its form or alter its patterns of distribution. In addition, cultural forms are articulated out of material and ideological conditions throughout their circulation. A text's production, for instance, is partly conditioned by such forces as economic constraints, institutional pressures, and the social relations and value systems of the interlocutors. Like the rhetorical triangle, the cultural circuit should be conceptualized as embedded in a web of cultural conditions. Johnson also explains that cultural studies are primarily concerned with tracking subjective forms. This emphasis is even more apparent in the adaptation of the circuit by the authors of *Doing Cultural Studies*; this version adds social identities as a major component (du Gay, Hall, Janes, Mackay, and Negus 3).

Berlin and Drew also gesture to the cultural circuit in describing their approaches. Berlin explains that "the objects of cultural studies are the production, distribution, and reception of signifying practices within the myriad social formations that are shaping subjectivities ("Composition" 101). Yet Berlin's approach, even less than McComiskey's, focuses on discourse other than the students'. Drew addresses this limitation in arguing that a cultural studies approach to writing instruction should account for the production, circulation, consumption, and reproduction of *student* writing (415). Despite acknowledging the full circuit, however, Drew limits her discussion to the production process and academic writing.

To illustrate how I use Johnson's circuit and adapt the work of Porter, McComiskey, and others, I now turn to a specific heuristic used by my service-learning students. In addition to addressing questions about stylistic and other discursive conventions, as Porter does, this heuristic prompts students to critique the power relations in which their texts participate. This critique moves beyond personal reflection to social deliberation about the ethics of their texts, specifically about their texts' responsiveness to and effects on the targeted audiences and other stakeholders. In this vein, students answer such questions as "What knowledges and interpretations of this knowledge does the text enable and foreclose?"

My heuristic follows McComiskey's lead in organizing questions around the parts of the cultural circuit (rather than types of discursive conventions). As Drew suggests, however, I focus on the cultural processes of student texts rather than advertisements, television programs, or even the texts of a particular discourse community. Students critique the power relations, values, and effects of their writing as it is being collaboratively produced, after the sponsoring agency revises it and makes it available to their audiences, and, if possible, as their audiences begin to interpret and use it. In deliberating about their texts' delivery and distribution, for example, students answer such questions as "How are the text and its possible effects reshaped by the medium and forum of distribution?" "How are competing sets of values renegotiated in this distribution?" and "Whose values get privileged?" To ethically interrogate the uses of their texts, students deliberate about how their texts impinge on and are transformed by the material practices of their users, paying particular attention to possible harmful effects and ethical problems. To aid students' invention about intervention, I pose such questions as "How could the texts and their contexts of distribution more respectfully depict the audiences and their needs?" and "How could the text be more responsive to the audiences' and community's needs, values, and contexts?"

In my experience, such questions become more concrete and useful when applied to students' service-learning projects. As I mentioned earlier, these projects already highlight the multiple transformations that texts can undergo and the negotiation of different sets of values. In addition, students already play active roles in the power relations involved in the texts' production, and may be able to determine first-hand the texts' appropriations and effects. Finally, service-learning students may be better positioned for meaningful ethical intervention. A magazine is unlikely to change its practices based on a student's letter of complaint, as in McComiskey's scenario. I *have* seen agencies revise their discourse and practices based on input from service-learning students however; already situated as cowriters, these students had some access to the agency's means of production.

I've also revised McComiskey's heuristic by encouraging students to involve other stakeholders in ethical critique and intervention. In this revision, I have drawn on a model of intercultural inquiry developed by Linda Flower, Elenore Long, and Lorraine Higgins at Carnegie Mellon and Pittsburgh's Community Literacy Center. Their brand of service-learning teaches students to not only write *about* and *for* the community, but also to write *with* the community, creating a critical dialogue about civic exigencies and their rhetorical responses to them with such stakeholders as classmates, agency partners, members of the targeted audience, and members of the wider community. To this end I ask students, "In what ways and to what extent does the agency involve clients in the production and evaluation of its texts?" As Flower and her colleagues explain, an intercultural inquiry would seek out rival interpretations of writing exigencies; involve more accountable deliberation about constraints, options, and outcomes; and develop more responsive courses of action.

As the fuller list of questions in the Appendix to this chapter illustrate, we don't have to choose between critical consciousness and rhetorical participation in our writing classes. Cultural studies offers a rich array of approaches for developing the former, and service-learning offers a way to keep the focus on the latter. Integrating service-learning and cultural studies enables both approaches to better foster Cicero's ideal of the good person writing effectively *and* ethically about important civic issues.

NOTES

1. See also Susan Miller's critique of Berlin in which she underscores "Rhetoric is not [...] semiotics" (499).
2. In their essay on reframing service-learning through activism, Donna Bickford and Nedra Reynolds take the similar stance that students' ideological critiques should focus on their classrooms and institutions (236).
3. Bickford and Reynolds argue that for service-learning projects to be activist, students must examine how cultural practices and spaces configure and maintain boundaries and social differences.

WORKS CITED

Anson, Chris M. "On Reflection: The Role of Logs and Journals in Service-Learning Courses." *Writing the Community: Concepts and Models for Service-Learning in Composition*. Ed. Linda Adler-Kassler et al. Washington, DC: American Association for Higher Education, 1997. 167-80.

Berlin, James A. "Composition Studies and Cultural Studies: Collapsing Boundaries." *Into the Field: Sites of Composition Studies*. Ed. Anne Ruggles Gere. New York: MLA, 1993. 99-116.

---. *Rhetorics, Poetics, and Cultures*. Urbana, IL: National Council of Teachers of English, 1996.

Bickford, Donna M., and Nedra Reynolds. "Activism and Service-Learning: Reframing Volunteerism As Acts of Dissent." *Pedagogy* 2.2 (2002): 229-52.

Deans, Thomas. *Writing Partnerships: Service-Learning in Composition*. Urbana, IL: National Council of Teachers of English, 2000.

Drew, Julie. "(Teaching) Writing: Composition, Cultural Studies, Production." *JAC* 19.3 (1999): 411-29.

du Gay, Paul, Stuart Hall, Linda Janes, Hugh Mackay, and Keith Negus, eds. *Doing Cultural Studies: The Story of the Sony Walkman*. London: Sage, 1997.

Fitts, Karen, and Alan W. France, ed. *Left Margins: Cultural Studies and Composition Pedagogy*. Albany: State U of New York P, 1995.

Flower, Linda, Elenore Long, and Lorraine Higgins. *Learning to Rival: A Literate Practice for Intercultural Inquiry*. Mahwah, NJ: Erlbaum, 2000.

Herzberg, Bruce. "Community Service and Critical Teaching." *Writing the Community: Concepts and Models for Service-Learning in Composition*. Ed. Linda Adler-Kassler et al. Washington, DC: American Association for Higher Education, 1997. 57-69.

Johnson, Richard. "What Is Cultural Studies Anyway?" *Social Text* 6 (1987): 38-80.

McComiskey, Bruce. "Social-Process Rhetorical Inquiry: Cultural Studies Methodologies for Critical Writing about Advertisements." *JAC* 17.3 (1997): 381-400.

Miller, Susan. "Technologies of Self?-Formation." *JAC* 17.3 (1997): 497-500.

Porter, James E. "Intertextuality and the Discourse Community." *Rhetoric Review* 5 (1986): 34-47.

APPENDIX: CULTURAL STUDIES HEURISTIC FOR SERVICE-LEARNING

Production

- How would you map the roles and interpersonal dynamics of the agency personnel? The power relations between your group and your agency supervisors? The agency's relationship to its clients/audiences?
- What values does the agency want embedded in the text? How do these compare to your values and the values of the eventual audience? How will you negotiate contesting values?
- Who controls and who has access to the agency's means of production? In what ways and to what extent does the agency involve clients in the production and evaluation of its texts?
- What material, social, institutional, and political constraints shape your creation of the text?

Textual Representation

- How does the text portray its subjects, especially its targeted audiences. What are the implications of these depictions?
- How is the agency's ethos projected in the text? How does this ethos compare to the agency's actions toward their clients?
- What interpretive practices does the text enable and what does it foreclose?

Distribution

- What would a diagram of the text's life cycle look like?
- Through what avenues does the text reach and circulate among its users? Who regulates these avenues, and how?
- How are the text and its possible effects reshaped by the medium and forum of distribution? How are competing sets of values renegotiated in this distribution? Whose values get privileged?
- How has the agency revised the text?

Uses

- What cultural norms, patterns of behavior, and other conditions will affect the audience's interpretation of the text?
- How does the text impinge on the material practices of its users, and how is it in turn transformed by these practices?
- What are the positive and negative effects of the text on its audiences and wider community? What, if any, ethical problems do you see with the texts' uses?

Intervention

- How could the agency create more of an intercultural dialogue with its clients/audiences in the document production and distribution processes?
- How could the text and its context of distribution more respectfully depict the audiences and their needs? Better accommodate the audiences' and community's needs and values?
- How could the agency more responsively shape audiences' uses of its texts?
- What other documents could you and/or the agency have produced to address the same community-based problems or needs? What would you change about the agency's approach or specific responses?
- What are the underlying causes of the community's problems and needs? In what other forms of activism might you participate in response to them?

Author Index

A

B

C

D

E

F

G

H

J

K

L

M

N

O

P

R

S

T

W

Subject Index

A

B

C

D

O

P

Q

R

S

T

U

V

W

X